DAWN OF THE PLANET OF THE APES

DAWN OF THE PLANET OF THE APES, November 2015. Published by BOOM! Studios, a division of Boom Entertainment, Inc. Dawn of the Planet of the Apes is ™ & © 2015 Twentieth Century Fox Film Corporation. Originally published in single magazine form as DAWN OF THE PLANET OF THE APES No. 1-6. ™ & © 2014, 2015 Twentieth Century Fox Film Corporation. All Rights Reserved. BOOM! Studios™ and the BOOM! Studios logo are trademarks of Boom Entertainment, Inc., registered in various countries and categories. All characters, events, and institutions depicted herein are fictional. Any similarity between any of the names, characters, persons, events, and/or institutions in this publication to actual names, characters, and persons, whether living or dead, events, and/or institutions is unintended and purely coincidental. BOOM! Studios does not read or accept unsolicited submissions of ideas, stories, or artwork.

A catalog record of this book is available from OCLC and from the BOOM! Studios website, www.boom-studios.com, on the Librarians Page.

BOOM! Studios, 5670 Wilshire Boulevard, Suite 450, Los Angeles, CA 90036-5679. Printed in China. First Printing.

ISBN: 978-1-60886-766-0, eISBN: 978-1-61398-437-6

DAWN OF THE PLANET OF THE APES™

WRITTEN BY
Michael Moreci

ILLUSTRATED BY
Dan McDaid

INKS BY
Adam Gorham
CHAPTER 3 PAGES 7-16
CHAPTER 4 PAGES 1, 2, 9, 10 13

COLORS BY
Jason Wordie

LETTERS BY
Ed Dukeshire

COVER BY
Jay Shaw

DESIGNER
Kara Leopard

ASSISTANT EDITOR
Alex Galer

EDITOR
Dafna Pleban

Special Thanks to Mark Bomback, Dylan Clark and Josh Izzo.

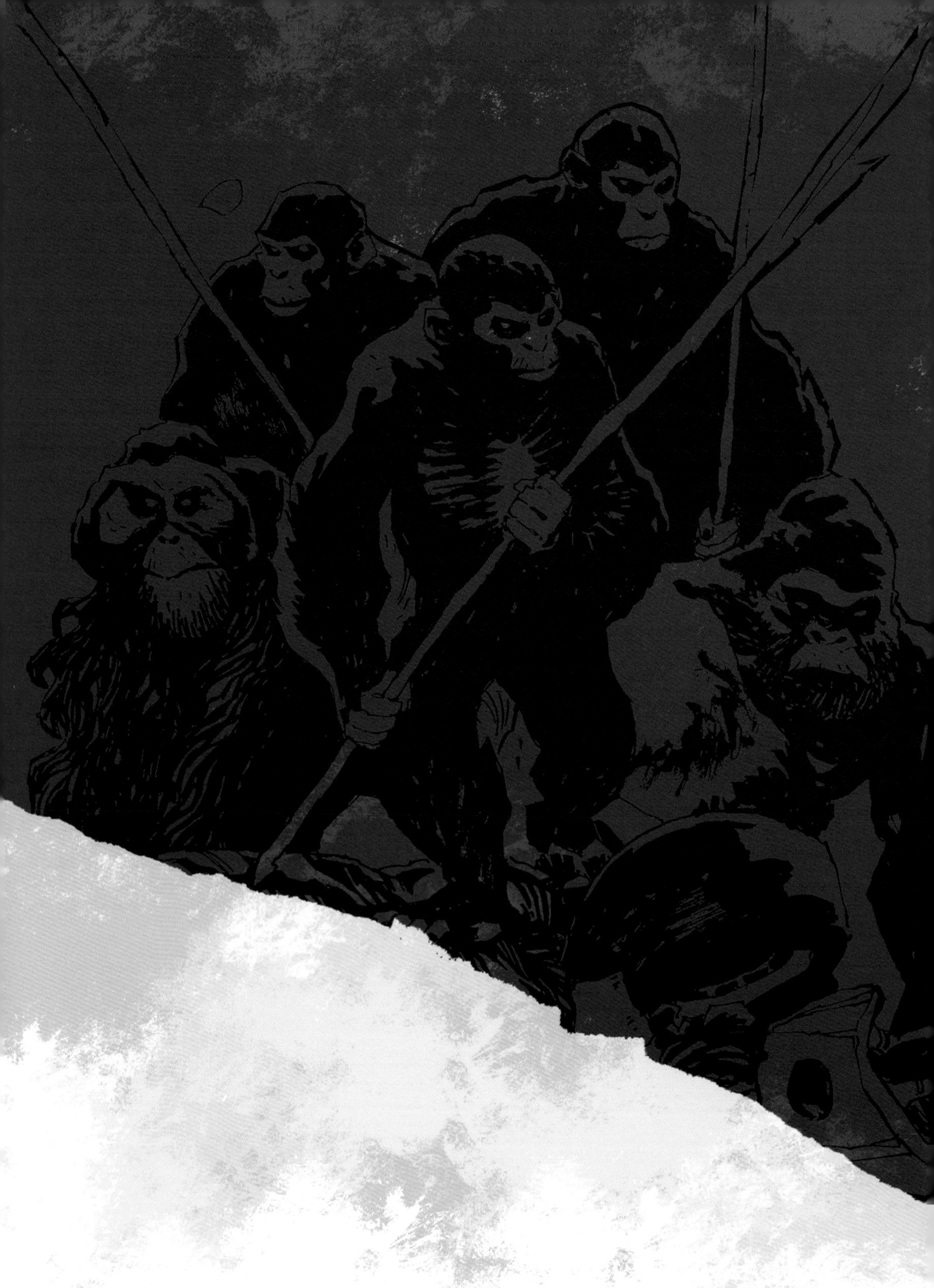

CHAPTER ONE

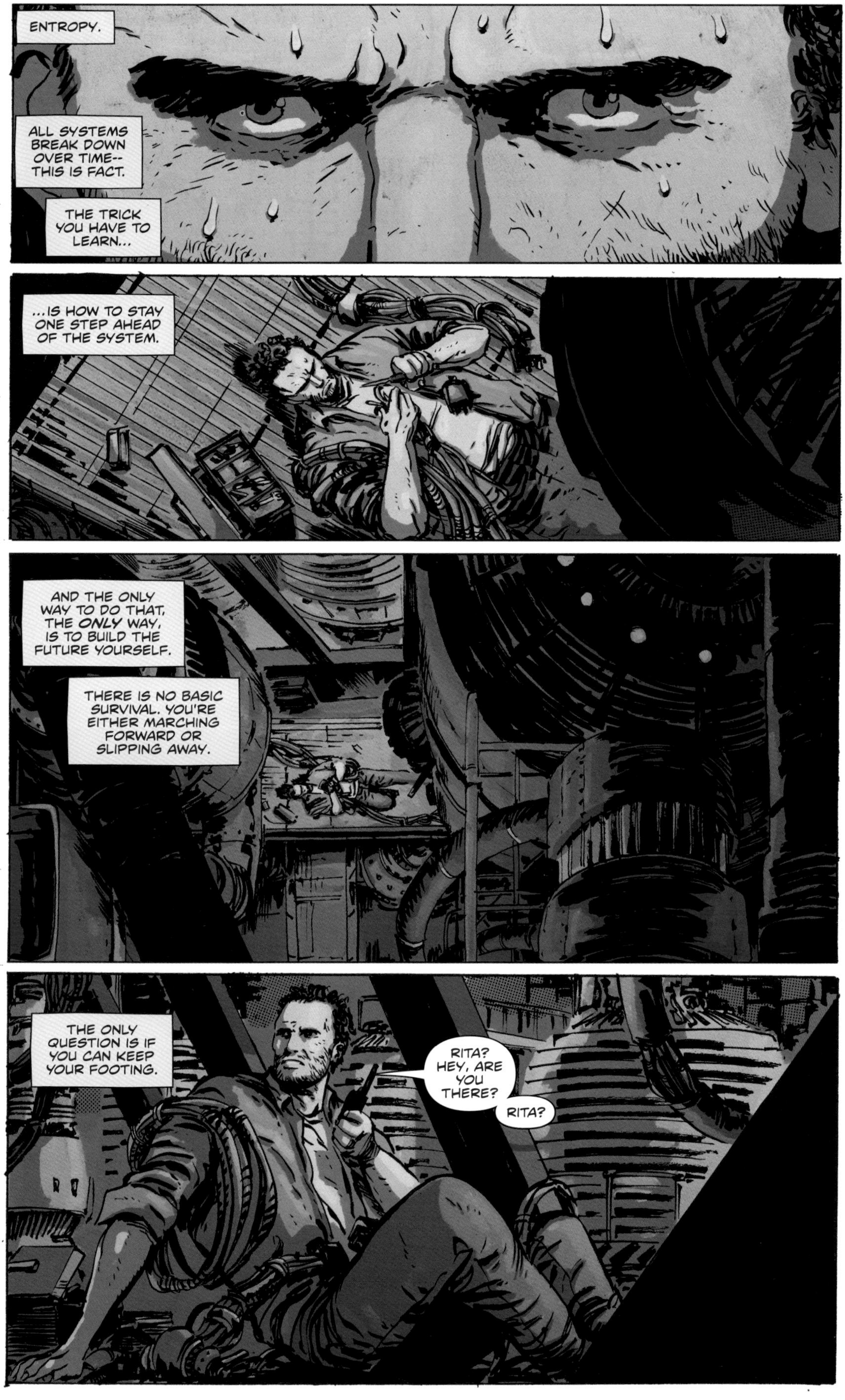
ENTROPY.
ALL SYSTEMS BREAK DOWN OVER TIME-- THIS IS FACT.
THE TRICK YOU HAVE TO LEARN...
...IS HOW TO STAY ONE STEP AHEAD OF THE SYSTEM.
AND THE ONLY WAY TO DO THAT, THE *ONLY* WAY, IS TO BUILD THE FUTURE YOURSELF.
THERE IS NO BASIC SURVIVAL. YOU'RE EITHER MARCHING FORWARD OR SLIPPING AWAY.
THE ONLY QUESTION IS IF YOU CAN KEEP YOUR FOOTING.
RITA? HEY, ARE YOU THERE?
RITA?

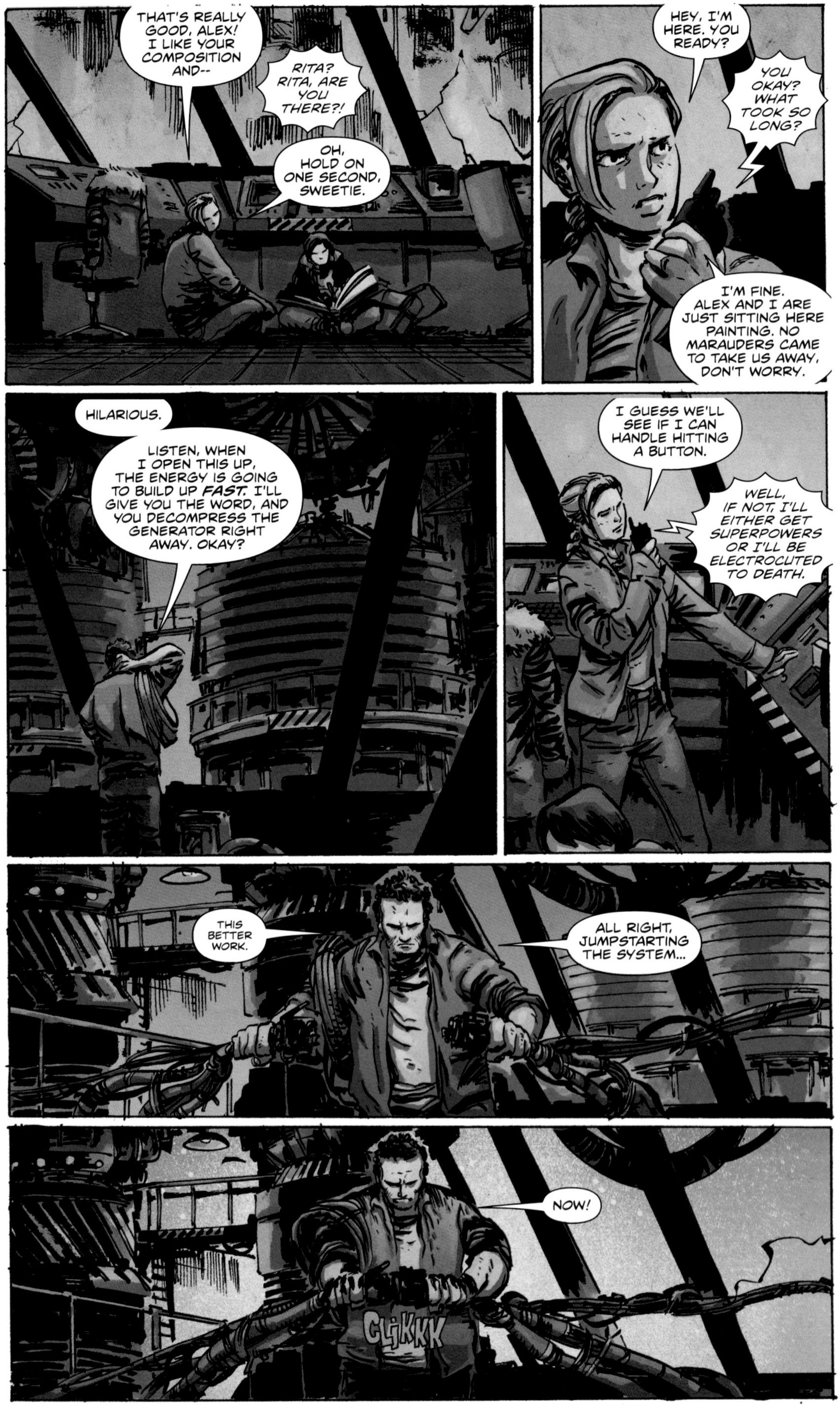
THAT'S REALLY GOOD, ALEX! I LIKE YOUR COMPOSITION AND--
RITA? RITA, ARE YOU THERE?!
OH, HOLD ON ONE SECOND, SWEETIE.
HEY, I'M HERE. YOU READY?
YOU OKAY? WHAT TOOK SO LONG?
I'M FINE. ALEX AND I ARE JUST SITTING HERE PAINTING. NO MARAUDERS CAME TO TAKE US AWAY, DON'T WORRY.
HILARIOUS.
LISTEN, WHEN I OPEN THIS UP, THE ENERGY IS GOING TO BUILD UP FAST. I'LL GIVE YOU THE WORD, AND YOU DECOMPRESS THE GENERATOR RIGHT AWAY. OKAY?
I GUESS WE'LL SEE IF I CAN HANDLE HITTING A BUTTON.
WELL, IF NOT, I'LL EITHER GET SUPERPOWERS OR I'LL BE ELECTROCUTED TO DEATH.
THIS BETTER WORK.
ALL RIGHT, JUMPSTARTING THE SYSTEM...
NOW!
CLIKKK

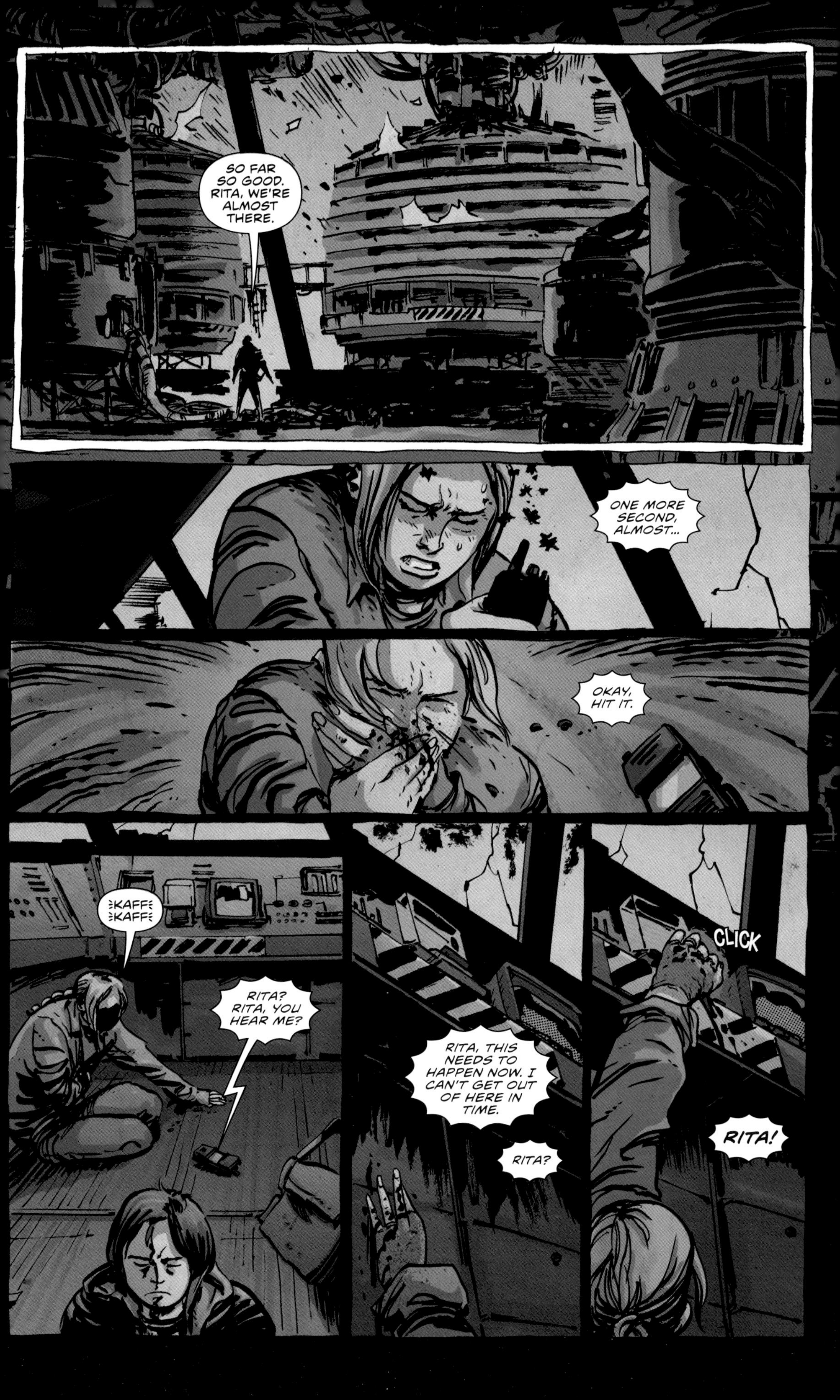
SO FAR SO GOOD. RITA, WE'RE ALMOST THERE.
ONE MORE SECOND, ALMOST...
OKAY, HIT IT.
KAFF KAFF
RITA? RITA, YOU HEAR ME?
RITA, THIS NEEDS TO HAPPEN NOW. I CAN'T GET OUT OF HERE IN TIME.
RITA?
CLICK
RITA!

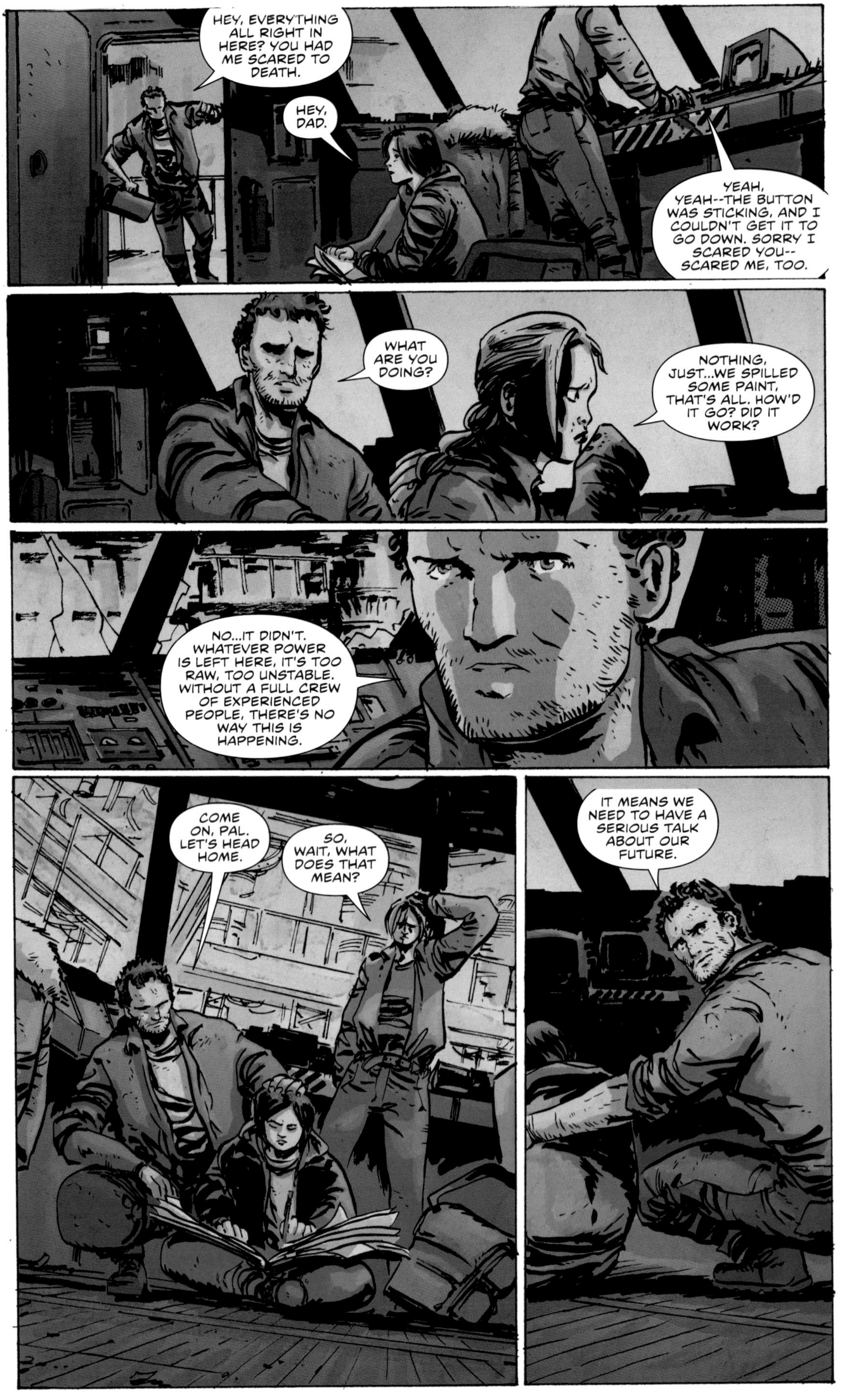
HEY, EVERYTHING ALL RIGHT IN HERE? YOU HAD ME SCARED TO DEATH.
HEY, DAD.
YEAH, YEAH--THE BUTTON WAS STICKING, AND I COULDN'T GET IT TO GO DOWN. SORRY I SCARED YOU-- SCARED ME, TOO.
WHAT ARE YOU DOING?
NOTHING, JUST...WE SPILLED SOME PAINT, THAT'S ALL. HOW'D IT GO? DID IT WORK?
NO...IT DIDN'T. WHATEVER POWER IS LEFT HERE, IT'S TOO RAW, TOO UNSTABLE. WITHOUT A FULL CREW OF EXPERIENCED PEOPLE, THERE'S NO WAY THIS IS HAPPENING.
COME ON, PAL. LET'S HEAD HOME.
SO, WAIT, WHAT DOES THAT MEAN?
IT MEANS WE NEED TO HAVE A SERIOUS TALK ABOUT OUR FUTURE.

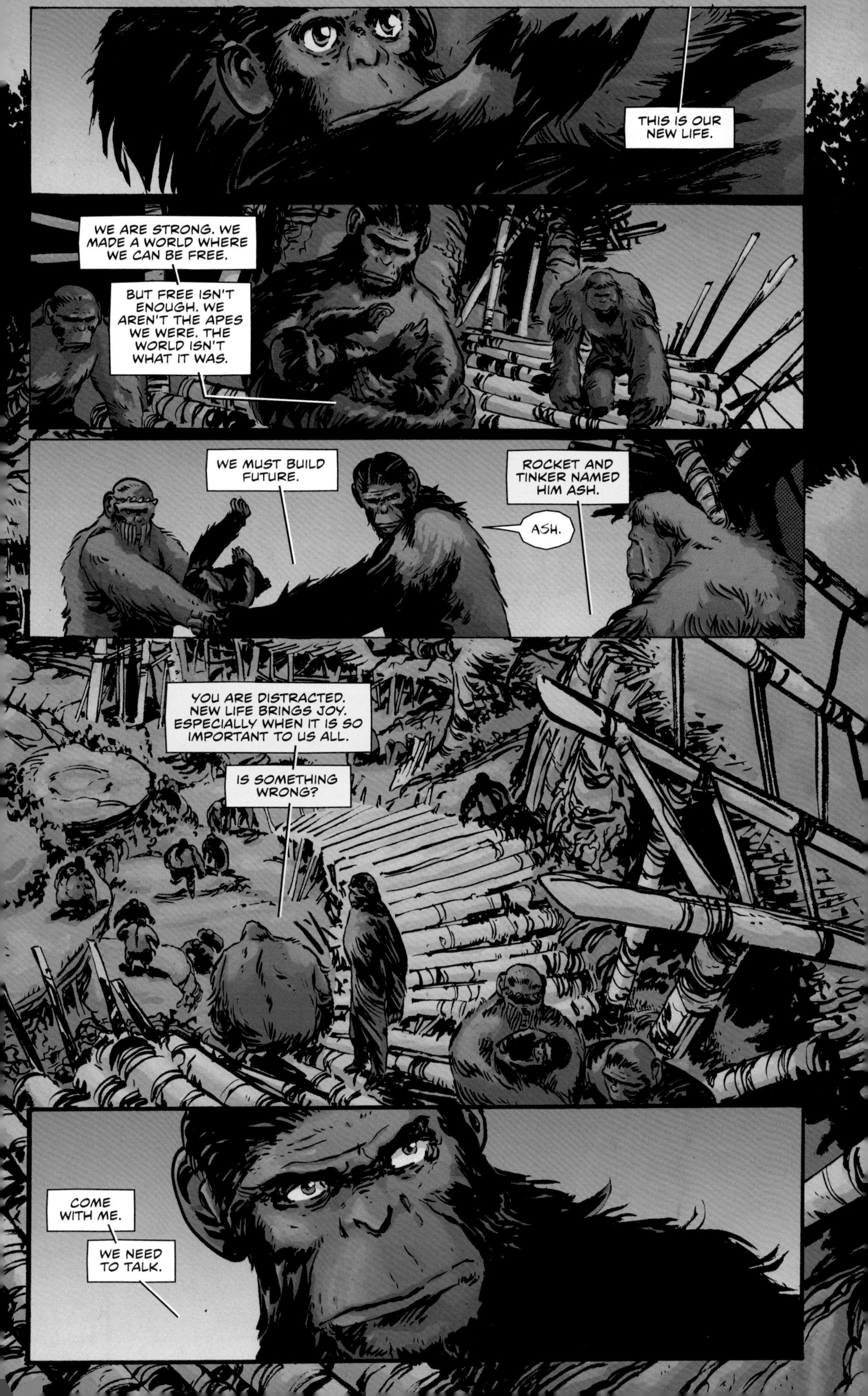
THIS IS OUR NEW LIFE.
WE ARE STRONG. WE MADE A WORLD WHERE WE CAN BE FREE.
BUT FREE ISN'T ENOUGH. WE AREN'T THE APES WE WERE. THE WORLD ISN'T WHAT IT WAS.
WE MUST BUILD FUTURE.
ASH.
ROCKET AND TINKER NAMED HIM ASH.
YOU ARE DISTRACTED. NEW LIFE BRINGS JOY. ESPECIALLY WHEN IT IS SO IMPORTANT TO US ALL.
IS SOMETHING WRONG?
COME WITH ME.
WE NEED TO TALK.

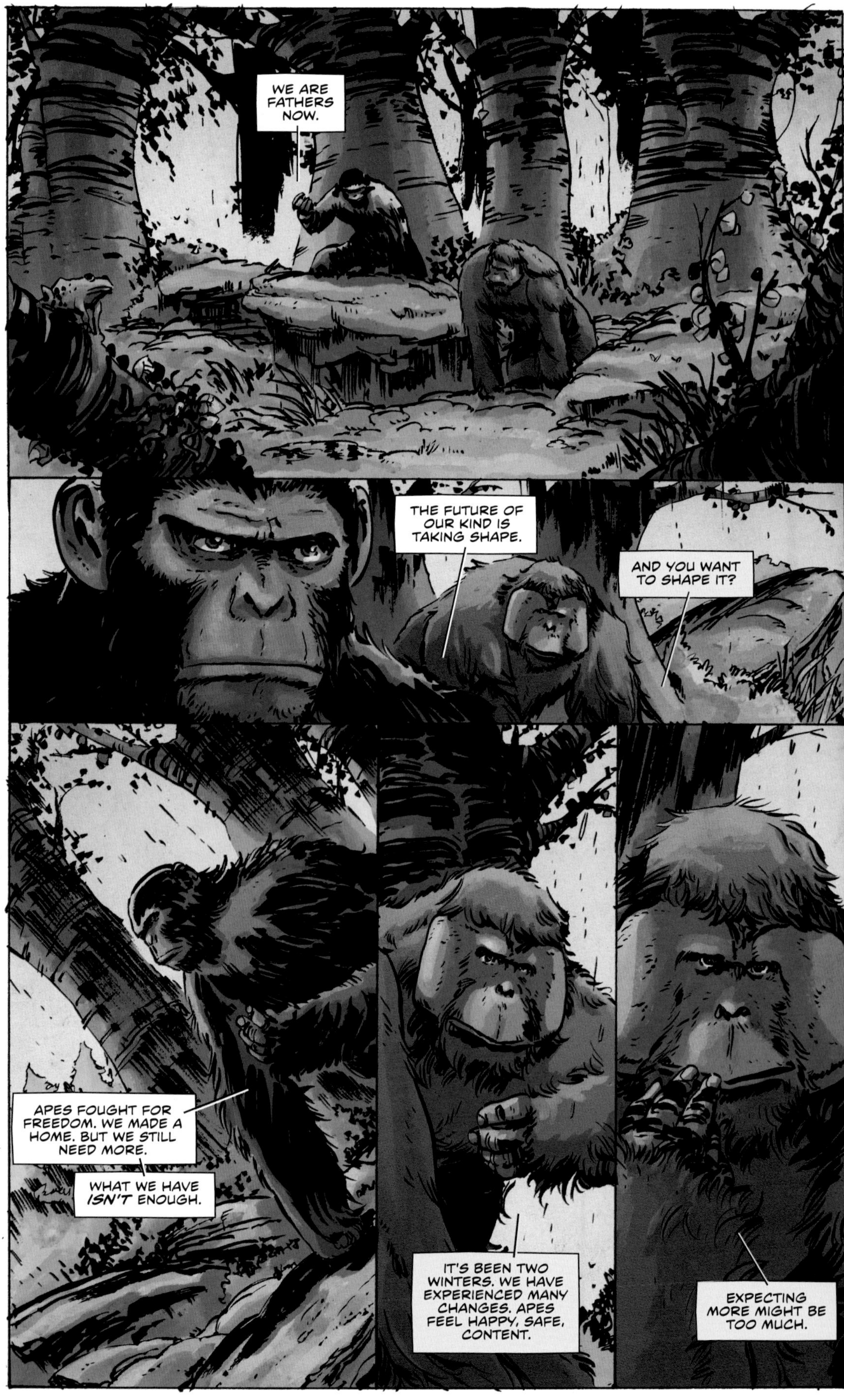
WE ARE FATHERS NOW.
THE FUTURE OF OUR KIND IS TAKING SHAPE.
AND YOU WANT TO SHAPE IT?
APES FOUGHT FOR FREEDOM. WE MADE A HOME. BUT WE STILL NEED MORE.
WHAT WE HAVE *ISN'T* ENOUGH.
IT'S BEEN TWO WINTERS. WE HAVE EXPERIENCED MANY CHANGES. APES FEEL HAPPY, SAFE, CONTENT.
EXPECTING MORE MIGHT BE TOO MUCH.

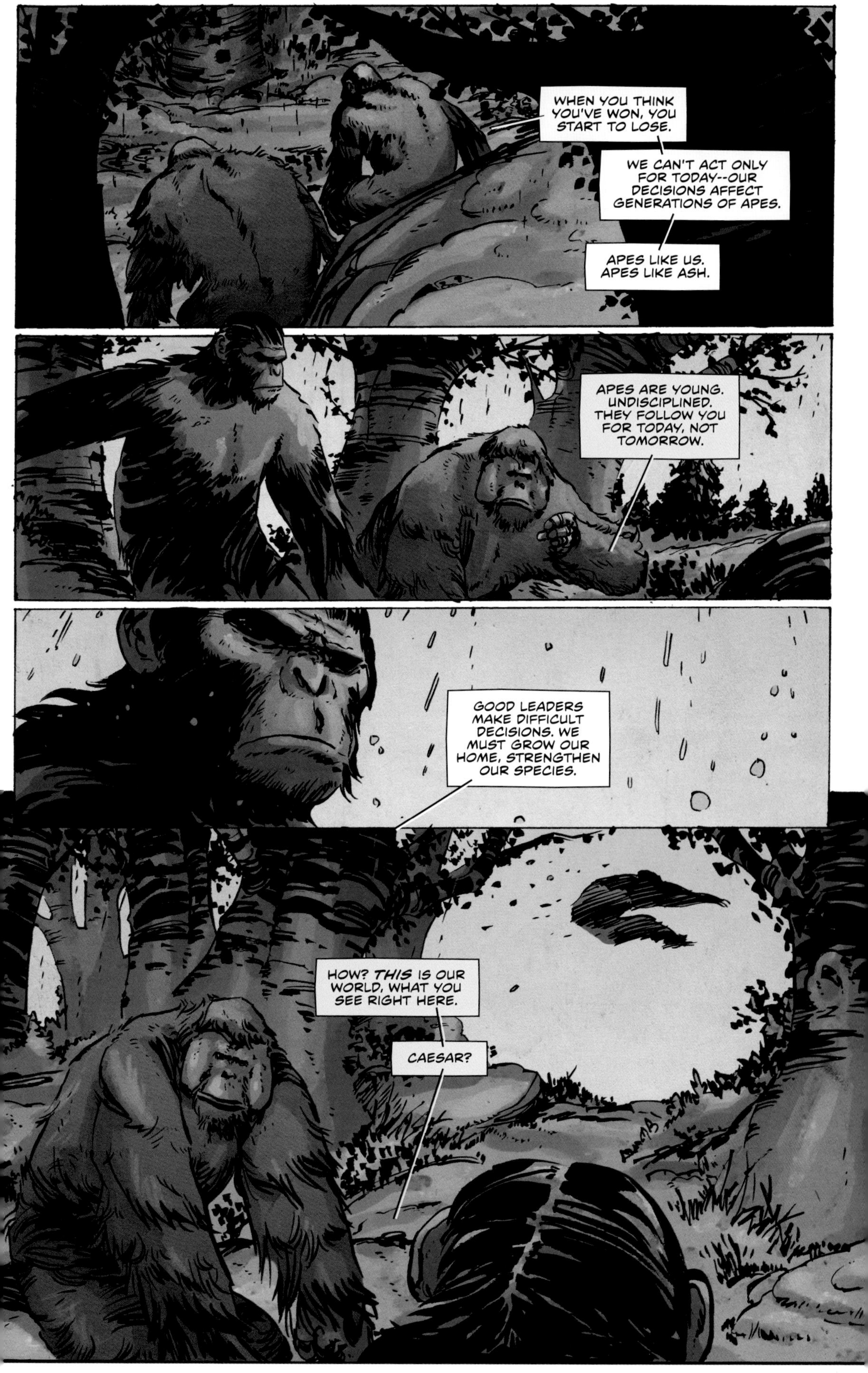
WHEN YOU THINK YOU'VE WON, YOU START TO LOSE.
WE CAN'T ACT ONLY FOR TODAY--OUR DECISIONS AFFECT GENERATIONS OF APES.
APES LIKE US. APES LIKE ASH.
APES ARE YOUNG. UNDISCIPLINED. THEY FOLLOW YOU FOR TODAY, NOT TOMORROW.
GOOD LEADERS MAKE DIFFICULT DECISIONS. WE MUST GROW OUR HOME, STRENGTHEN OUR SPECIES.
HOW? *THIS* IS OUR WORLD, WHAT YOU SEE RIGHT HERE.
CAESAR?

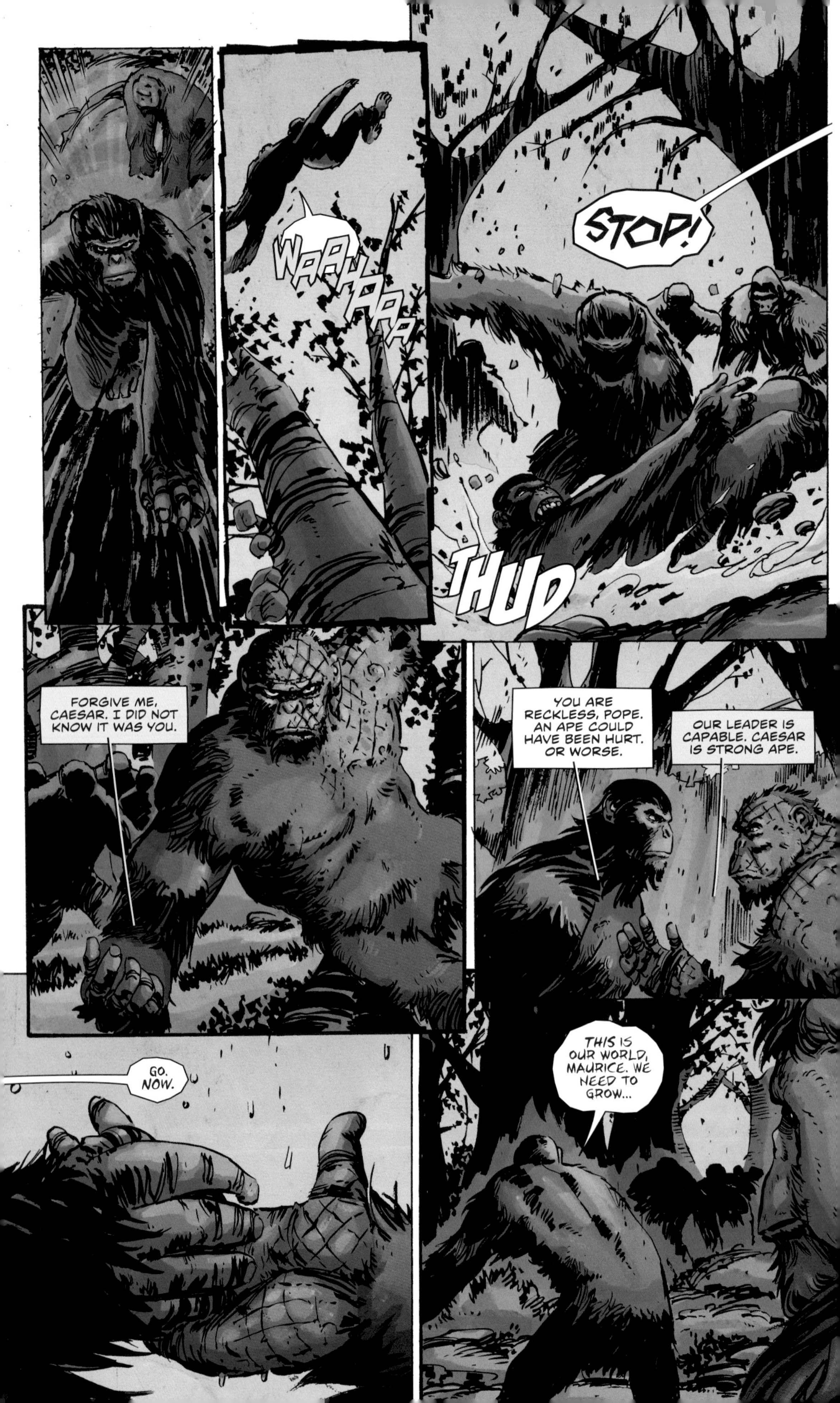
WAAAHAAA
STOP!
THUD
FORGIVE ME, CAESAR. I DID NOT KNOW IT WAS YOU.
YOU ARE RECKLESS, POPE. AN APE COULD HAVE BEEN HURT. OR WORSE.
OUR LEADER IS CAPABLE. CAESAR IS STRONG APE.
GO. NOW.
THIS IS OUR WORLD, MAURICE. WE NEED TO GROW...

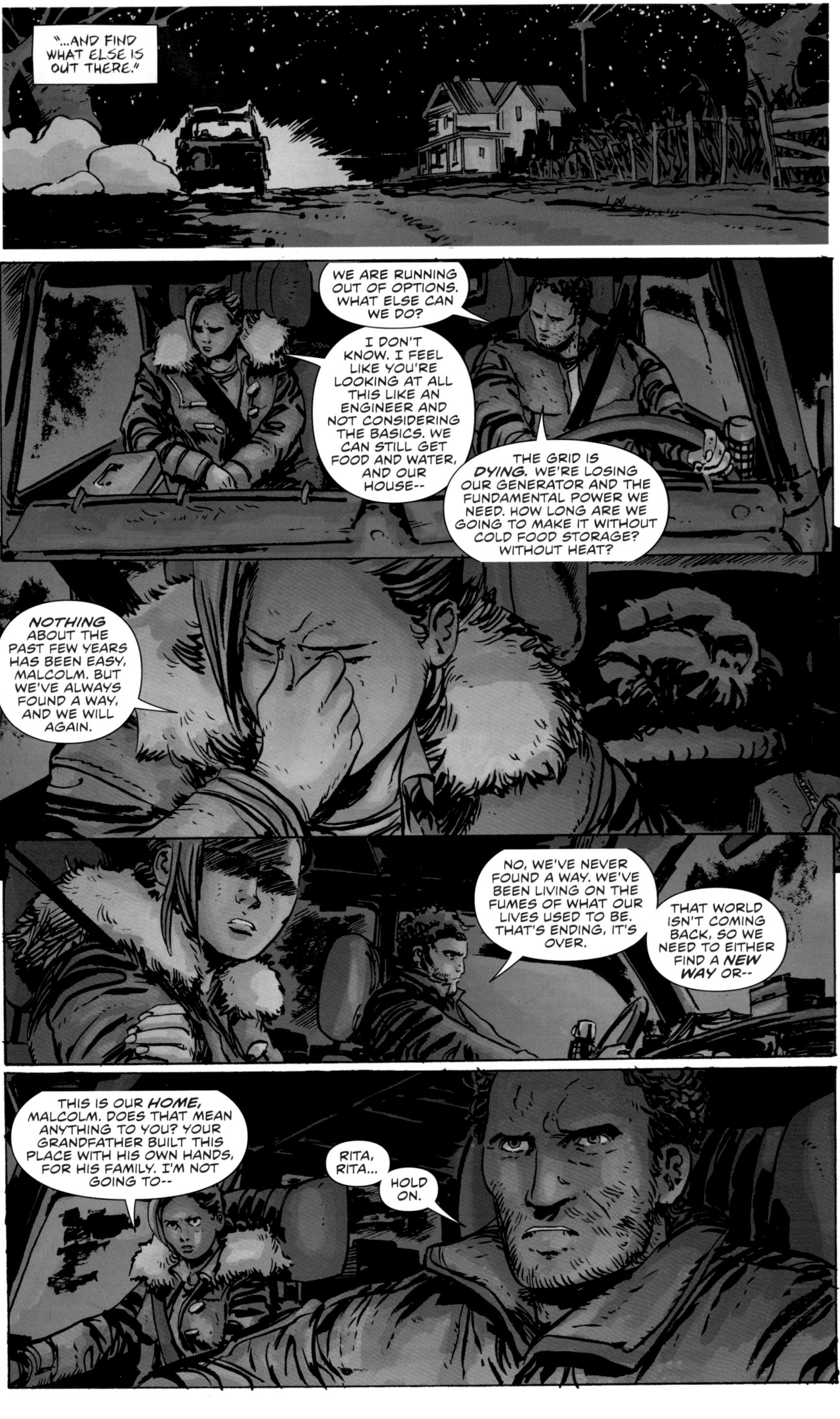
"...AND FIND WHAT ELSE IS OUT THERE."
WE ARE RUNNING OUT OF OPTIONS. WHAT ELSE CAN WE DO?
I DON'T KNOW. I FEEL LIKE YOU'RE LOOKING AT ALL THIS LIKE AN ENGINEER AND NOT CONSIDERING THE BASICS. WE CAN STILL GET FOOD AND WATER, AND OUR HOUSE--
THE GRID IS DYING. WE'RE LOSING OUR GENERATOR AND THE FUNDAMENTAL POWER WE NEED. HOW LONG ARE WE GOING TO MAKE IT WITHOUT COLD FOOD STORAGE? WITHOUT HEAT?
NOTHING ABOUT THE PAST FEW YEARS HAS BEEN EASY, MALCOLM. BUT WE'VE ALWAYS FOUND A WAY, AND WE WILL AGAIN.
NO, WE'VE NEVER FOUND A WAY. WE'VE BEEN LIVING ON THE FUMES OF WHAT OUR LIVES USED TO BE. THAT'S ENDING, IT'S OVER.
THAT WORLD ISN'T COMING BACK, SO WE NEED TO EITHER FIND A NEW WAY OR--
THIS IS OUR HOME, MALCOLM. DOES THAT MEAN ANYTHING TO YOU? YOUR GRANDFATHER BUILT THIS PLACE WITH HIS OWN HANDS, FOR HIS FAMILY. I'M NOT GOING TO--
RITA, RITA...
HOLD ON.

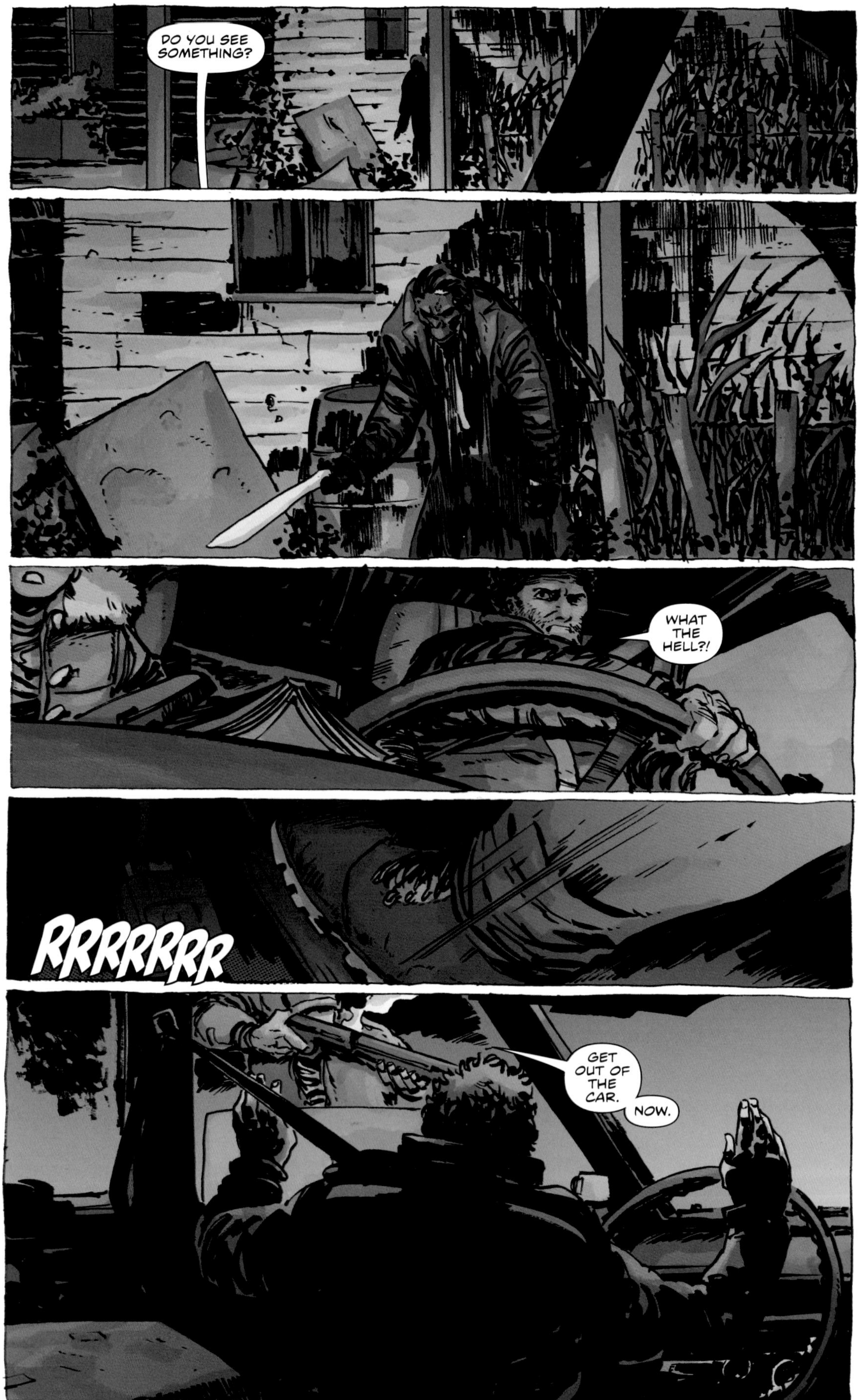
DO YOU SEE SOMETHING?
WHAT THE HELL?!
RRRRRRR
GET OUT OF THE CAR.
NOW.

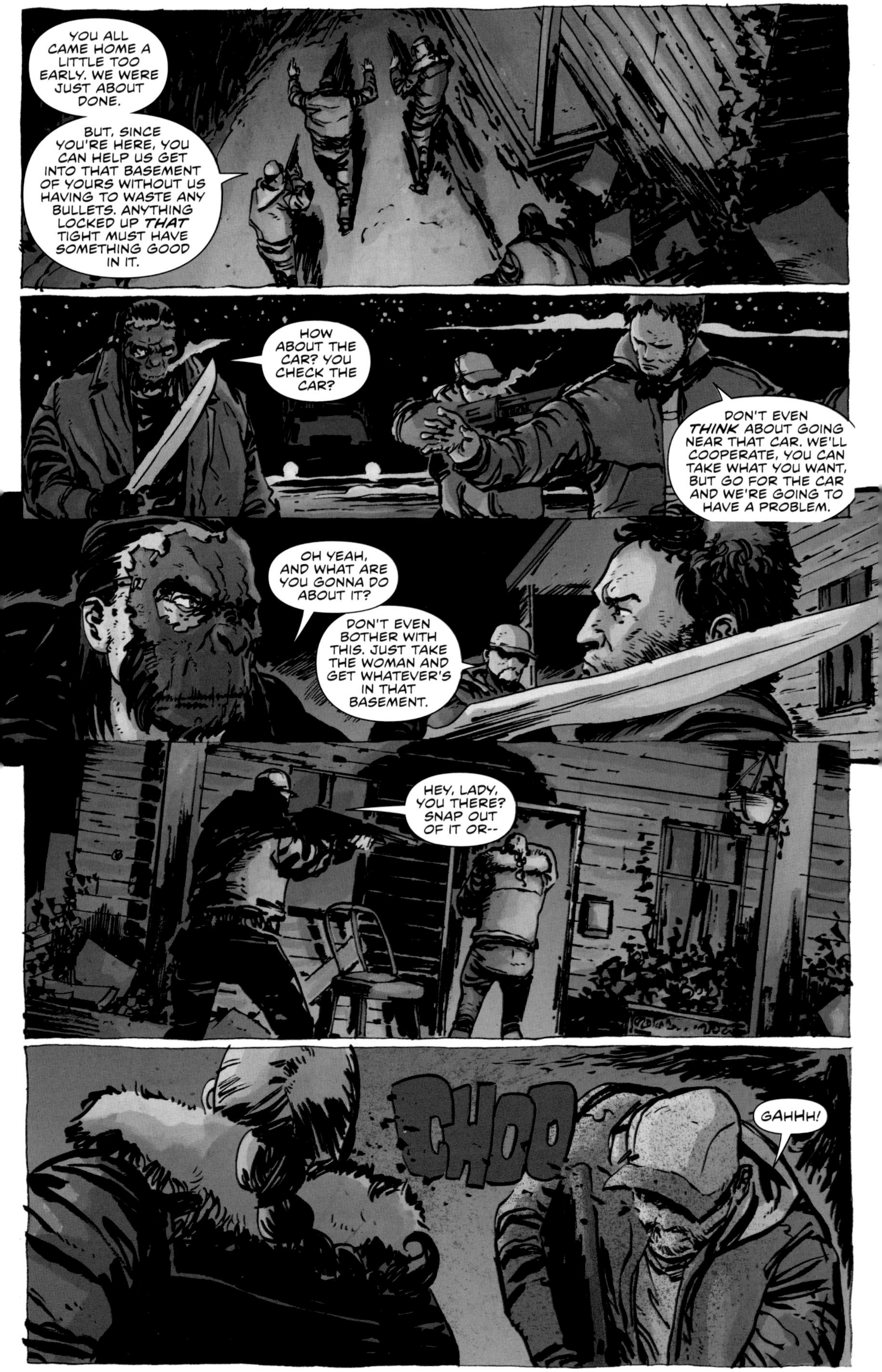

YOU ALL CAME HOME A LITTLE TOO EARLY. WE WERE JUST ABOUT DONE.
BUT, SINCE YOU'RE HERE, YOU CAN HELP US GET INTO THAT BASEMENT OF YOURS WITHOUT US HAVING TO WASTE ANY BULLETS. ANYTHING LOCKED UP THAT TIGHT MUST HAVE SOMETHING GOOD IN IT.
HOW ABOUT THE CAR? YOU CHECK THE CAR?
DON'T EVEN THINK ABOUT GOING NEAR THAT CAR. WE'LL COOPERATE, YOU CAN TAKE WHAT YOU WANT, BUT GO FOR THE CAR AND WE'RE GOING TO HAVE A PROBLEM.
OH YEAH, AND WHAT ARE YOU GONNA DO ABOUT IT?
DON'T EVEN BOTHER WITH THIS. JUST TAKE THE WOMAN AND GET WHATEVER'S IN THAT BASEMENT.
HEY, LADY, YOU THERE? SNAP OUT OF IT OR--
CHOO
GAHHH!

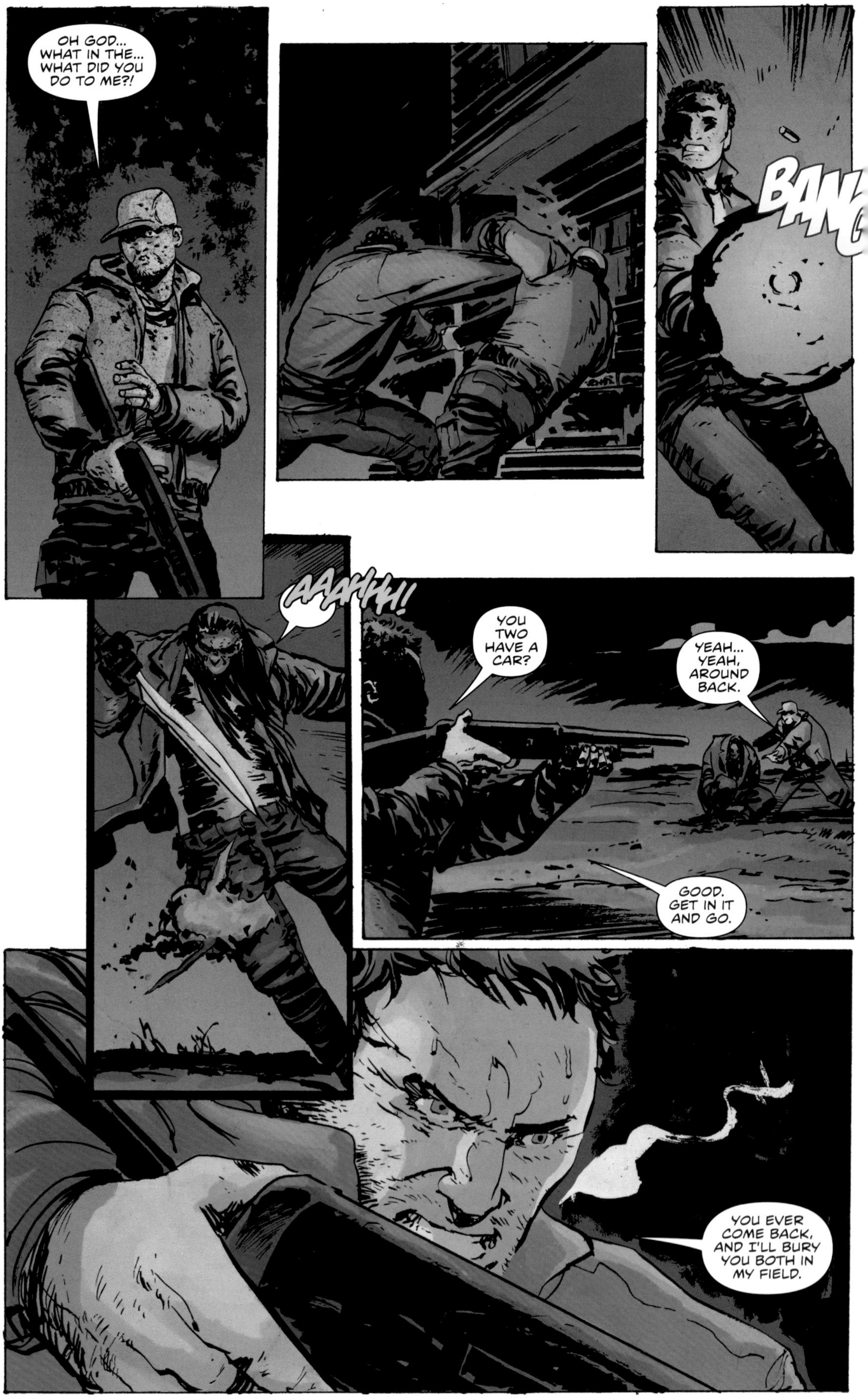
OH GOD... WHAT IN THE... WHAT DID YOU DO TO ME?!
BANG
AAAHHH!
YOU TWO HAVE A CAR?
YEAH... YEAH, AROUND BACK.
GOOD. GET IN IT AND GO.
YOU EVER COME BACK, AND I'LL BURY YOU BOTH IN MY FIELD.

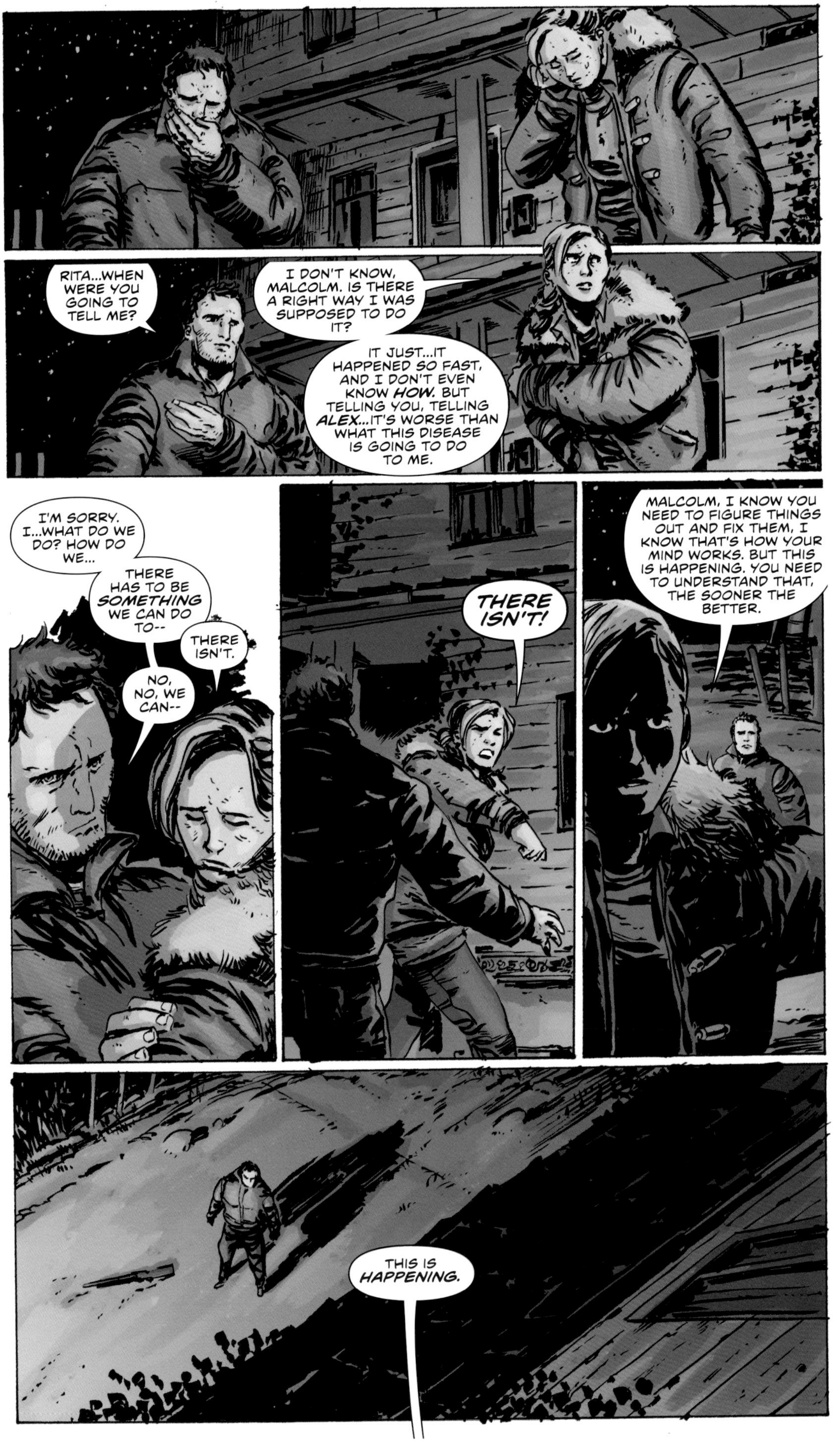
RITA...WHEN WERE YOU GOING TO TELL ME?
I DON'T KNOW, MALCOLM. IS THERE A RIGHT WAY I WAS SUPPOSED TO DO IT?
IT JUST...IT HAPPENED SO FAST, AND I DON'T EVEN KNOW HOW. BUT TELLING YOU, TELLING ALEX...IT'S WORSE THAN WHAT THIS DISEASE IS GOING TO DO TO ME.
I'M SORRY. I...WHAT DO WE DO? HOW DO WE...
THERE HAS TO BE SOMETHING WE CAN DO TO--
THERE ISN'T.
NO, NO, WE CAN--
THERE ISN'T!
MALCOLM, I KNOW YOU NEED TO FIGURE THINGS OUT AND FIX THEM, I KNOW THAT'S HOW YOUR MIND WORKS. BUT THIS IS HAPPENING. YOU NEED TO UNDERSTAND THAT, THE SOONER THE BETTER.
THIS IS HAPPENING.

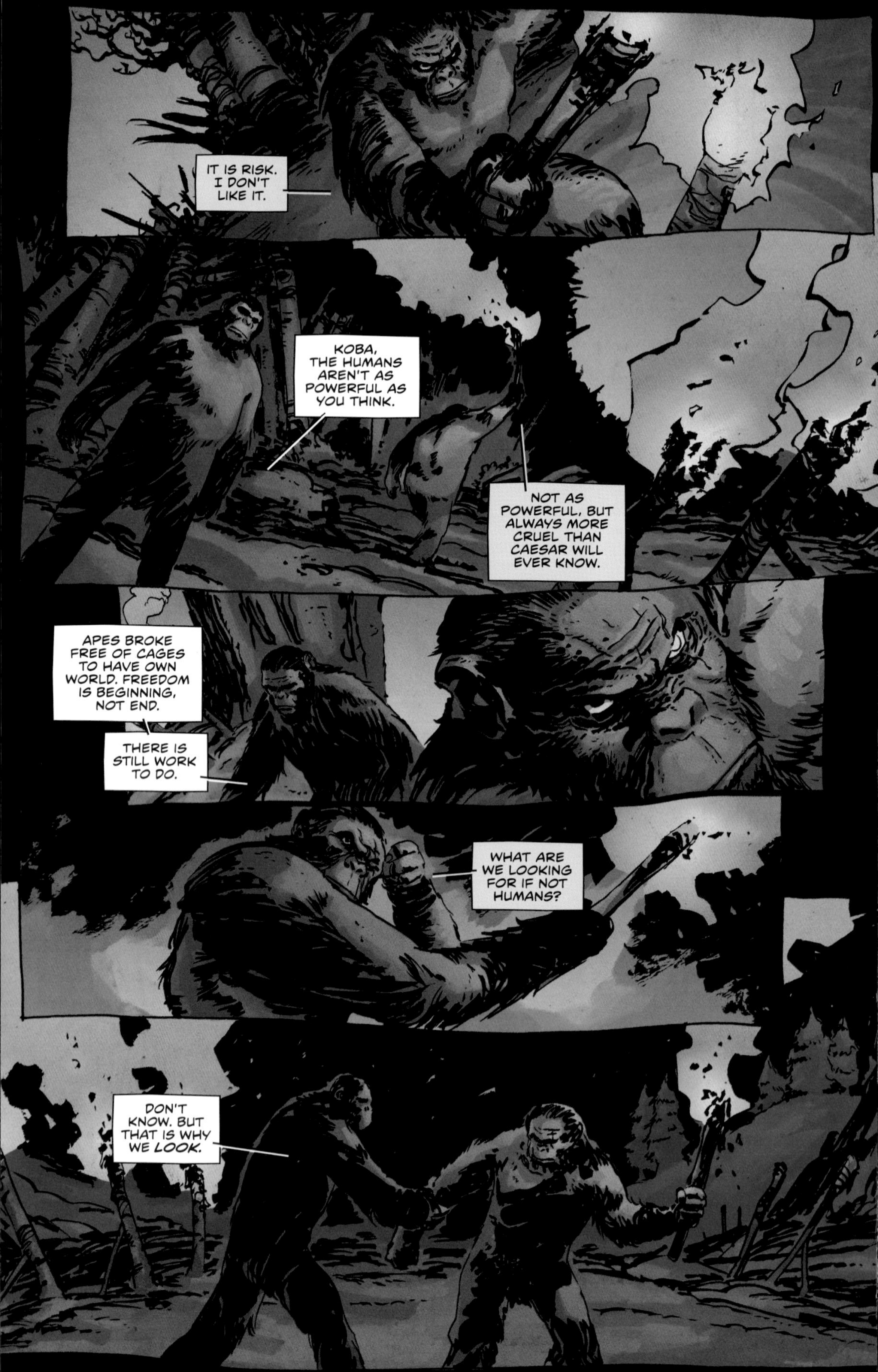
IT IS RISK. I DON'T LIKE IT.
KOBA, THE HUMANS AREN'T AS POWERFUL AS YOU THINK.
NOT AS POWERFUL, BUT ALWAYS MORE CRUEL THAN CAESAR WILL EVER KNOW.
APES BROKE FREE OF CAGES TO HAVE OWN WORLD. FREEDOM IS BEGINNING, NOT END.
THERE IS STILL WORK TO DO.
WHAT ARE WE LOOKING FOR IF NOT HUMANS?
DON'T KNOW. BUT THAT IS WHY WE *LOOK.*

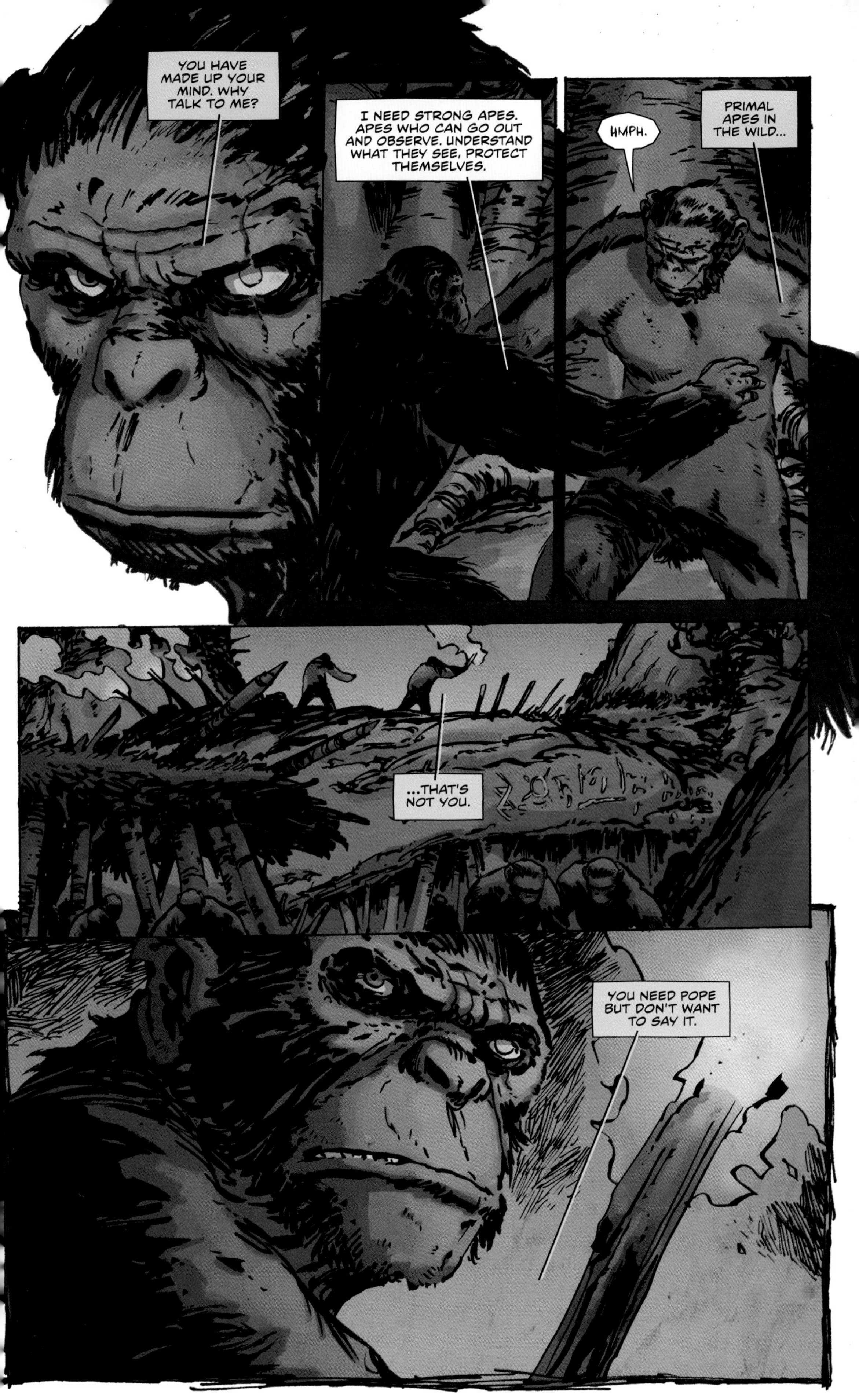
YOU HAVE MADE UP YOUR MIND. WHY TALK TO ME?
I NEED STRONG APES. APES WHO CAN GO OUT AND OBSERVE. UNDERSTAND WHAT THEY SEE, PROTECT THEMSELVES.
HMPH.
PRIMAL APES IN THE WILD...
...THAT'S NOT YOU.
YOU NEED POPE BUT DON'T WANT TO SAY IT.

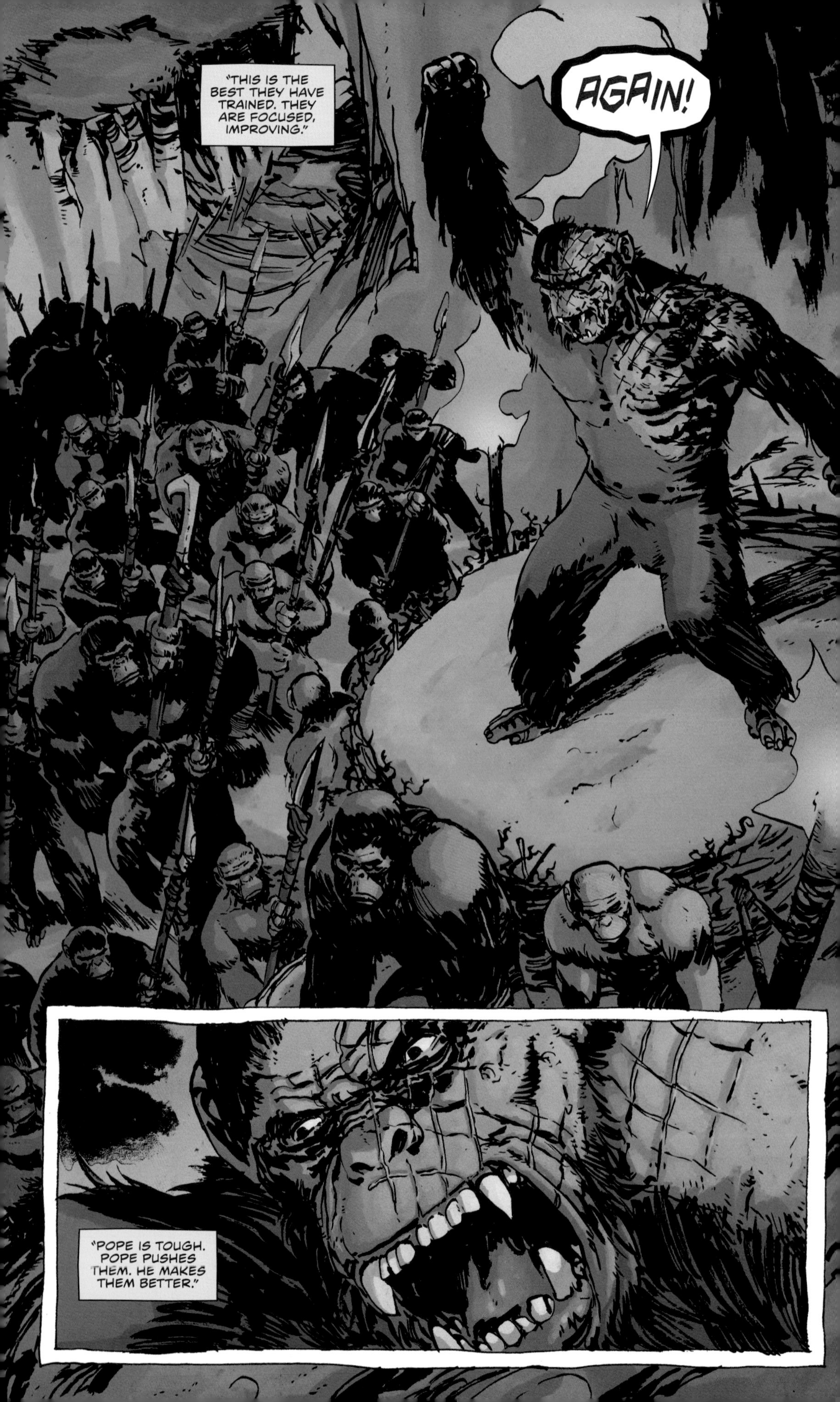
"THIS IS THE BEST THEY HAVE TRAINED. THEY ARE FOCUSED, IMPROVING."
AGAIN!
"POPE IS TOUGH. POPE PUSHES THEM. HE MAKES THEM BETTER."

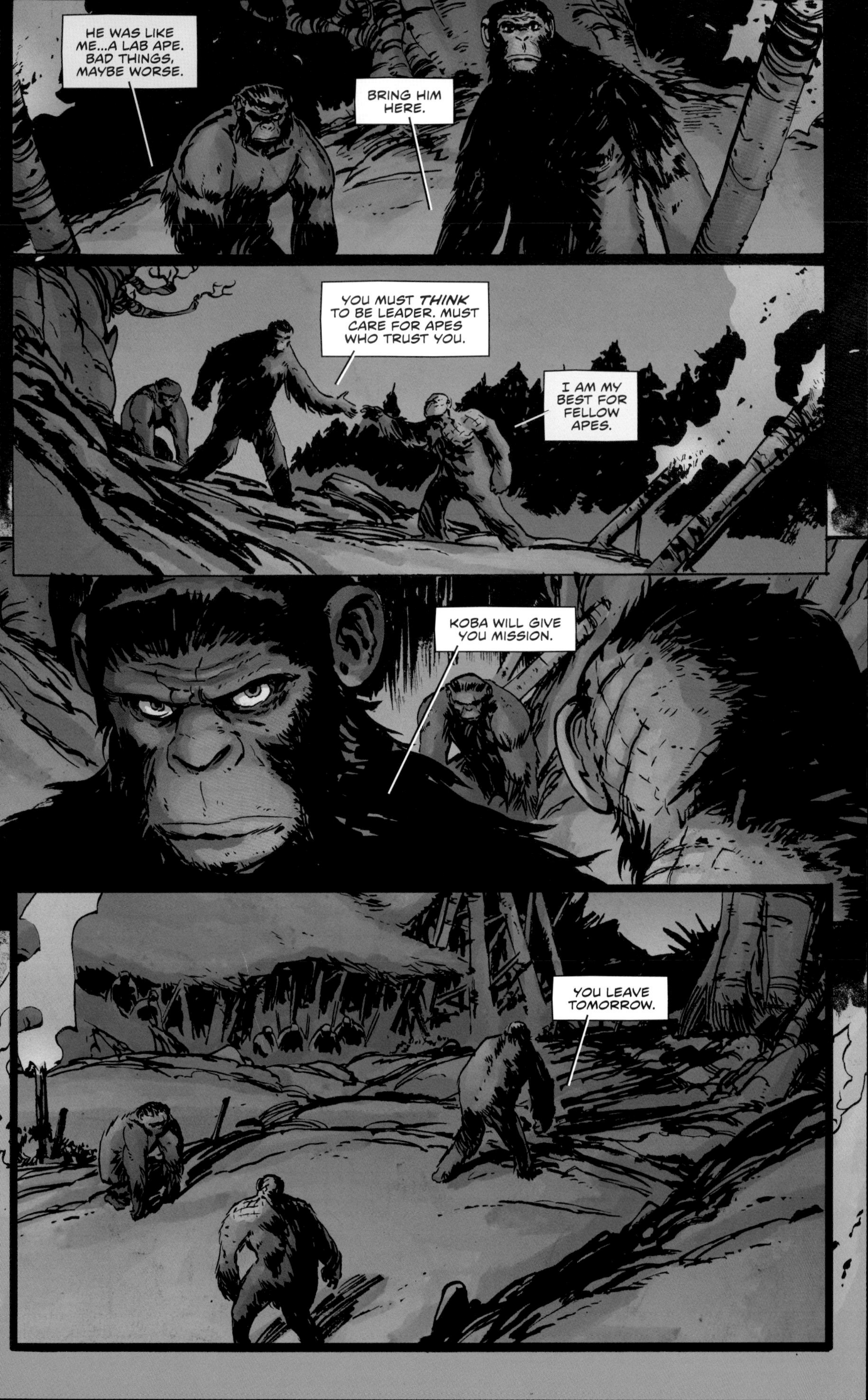
HE WAS LIKE ME...A LAB APE. BAD THINGS, MAYBE WORSE.
BRING HIM HERE.
YOU MUST *THINK* TO BE LEADER. MUST CARE FOR APES WHO TRUST YOU.
I AM MY BEST FOR FELLOW APES.
KOBA WILL GIVE YOU MISSION.
YOU LEAVE TOMORROW.

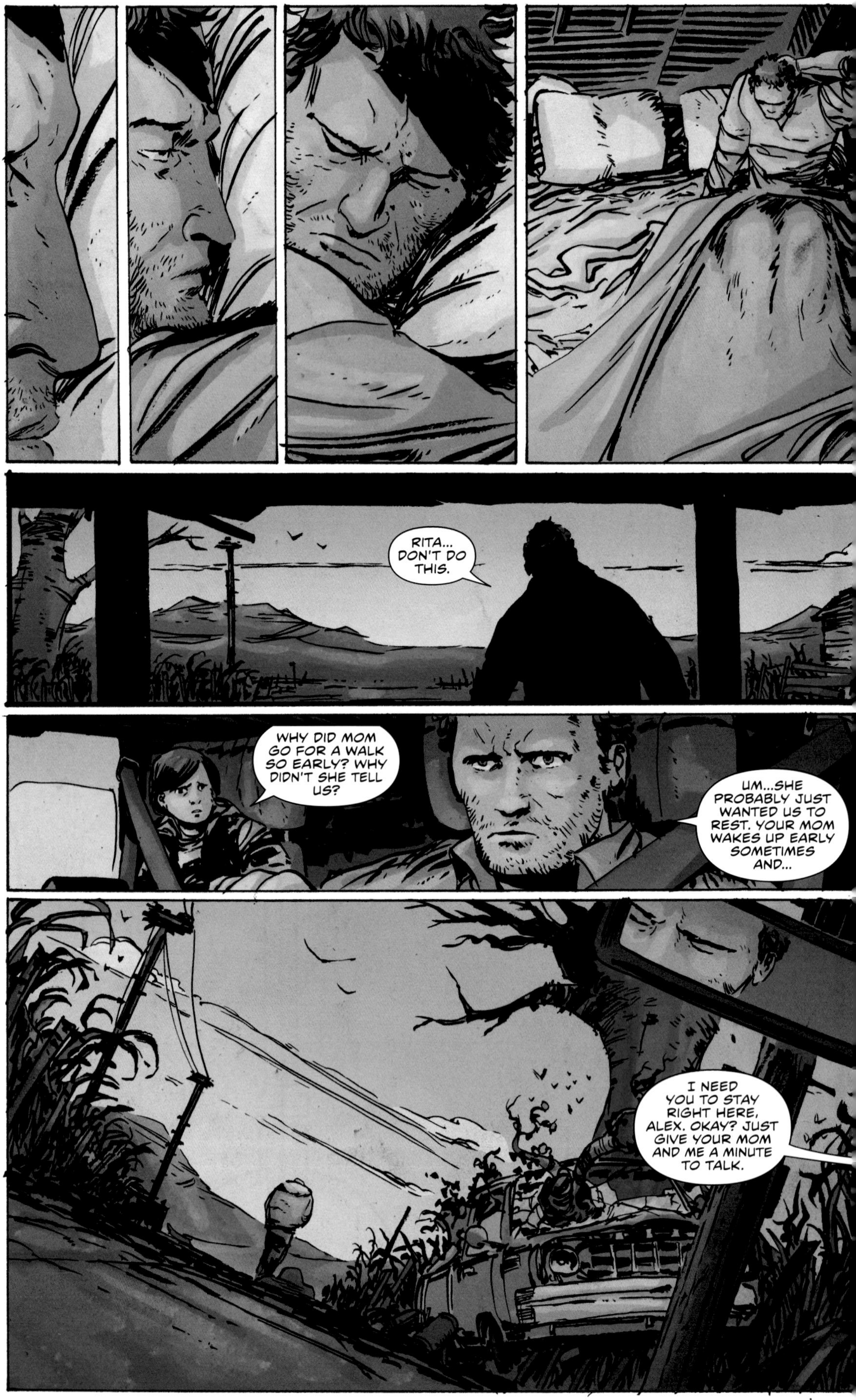
RITA... DON'T DO THIS.
WHY DID MOM GO FOR A WALK SO EARLY? WHY DIDN'T SHE TELL US?
UM...SHE PROBABLY JUST WANTED US TO REST. YOUR MOM WAKES UP EARLY SOMETIMES AND...
I NEED YOU TO STAY RIGHT HERE, ALEX. OKAY? JUST GIVE YOUR MOM AND ME A MINUTE TO TALK.

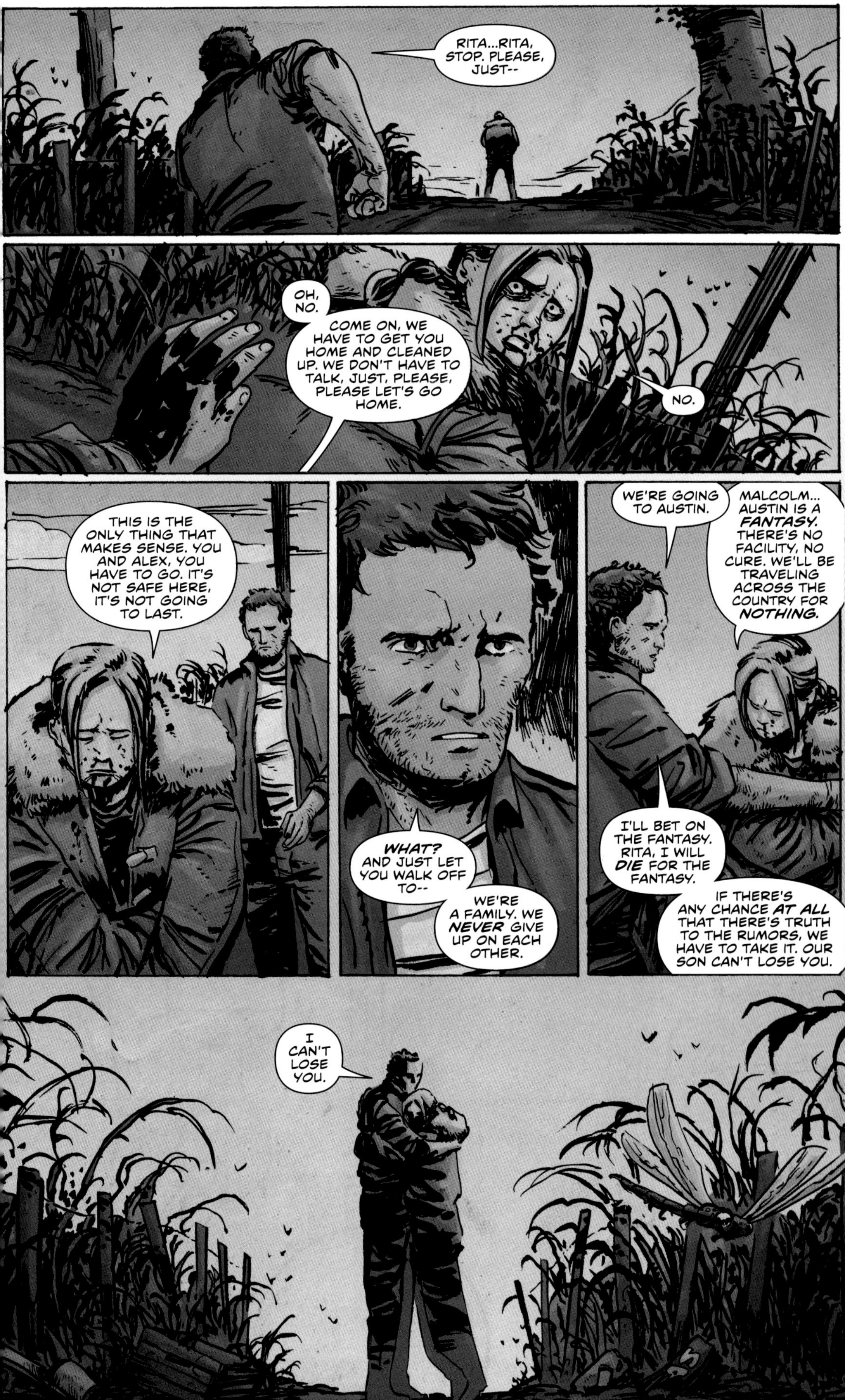
RITA...RITA, STOP. PLEASE, JUST--
OH, NO.
COME ON, WE HAVE TO GET YOU HOME AND CLEANED UP. WE DON'T HAVE TO TALK, JUST, PLEASE, PLEASE LET'S GO HOME.
NO.
THIS IS THE ONLY THING THAT MAKES SENSE. YOU AND ALEX, YOU HAVE TO GO. IT'S NOT SAFE HERE, IT'S NOT GOING TO LAST.
WHAT? AND JUST LET YOU WALK OFF TO--
WE'RE A FAMILY. WE NEVER GIVE UP ON EACH OTHER.
WE'RE GOING TO AUSTIN.
MALCOLM... AUSTIN IS A FANTASY. THERE'S NO FACILITY, NO CURE. WE'LL BE TRAVELING ACROSS THE COUNTRY FOR NOTHING.
I'LL BET ON THE FANTASY. RITA, I WILL DIE FOR THE FANTASY.
IF THERE'S ANY CHANCE AT ALL THAT THERE'S TRUTH TO THE RUMORS, WE HAVE TO TAKE IT. OUR SON CAN'T LOSE YOU.
I CAN'T LOSE YOU.

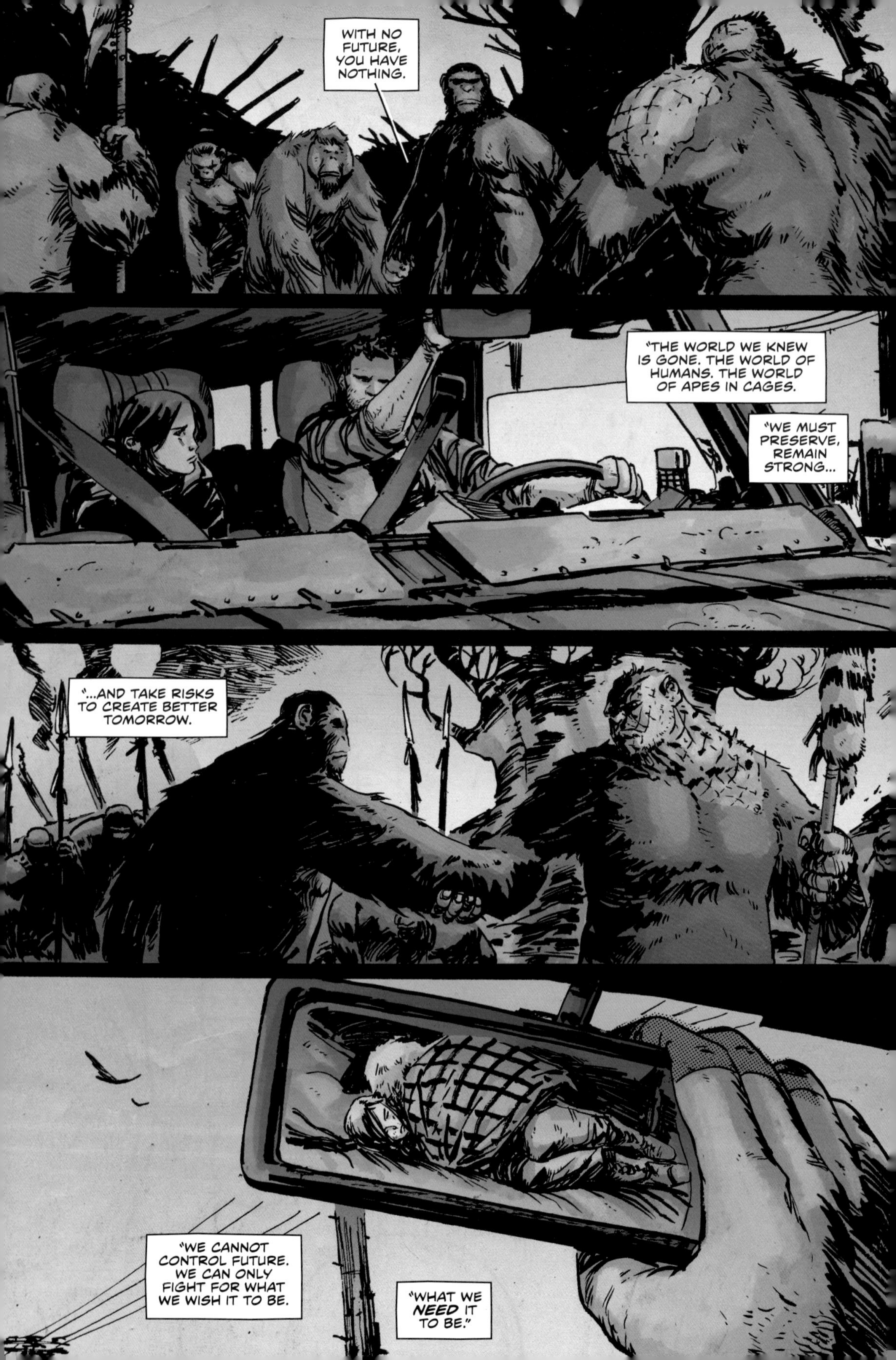
WITH NO FUTURE, YOU HAVE NOTHING.
"THE WORLD WE KNEW IS GONE. THE WORLD OF HUMANS. THE WORLD OF APES IN CAGES.
"WE MUST PRESERVE, REMAIN STRONG...
"...AND TAKE RISKS TO CREATE BETTER TOMORROW.
"WE CANNOT CONTROL FUTURE. WE CAN ONLY FIGHT FOR WHAT WE WISH IT TO BE.
"WHAT WE *NEED* IT TO BE."

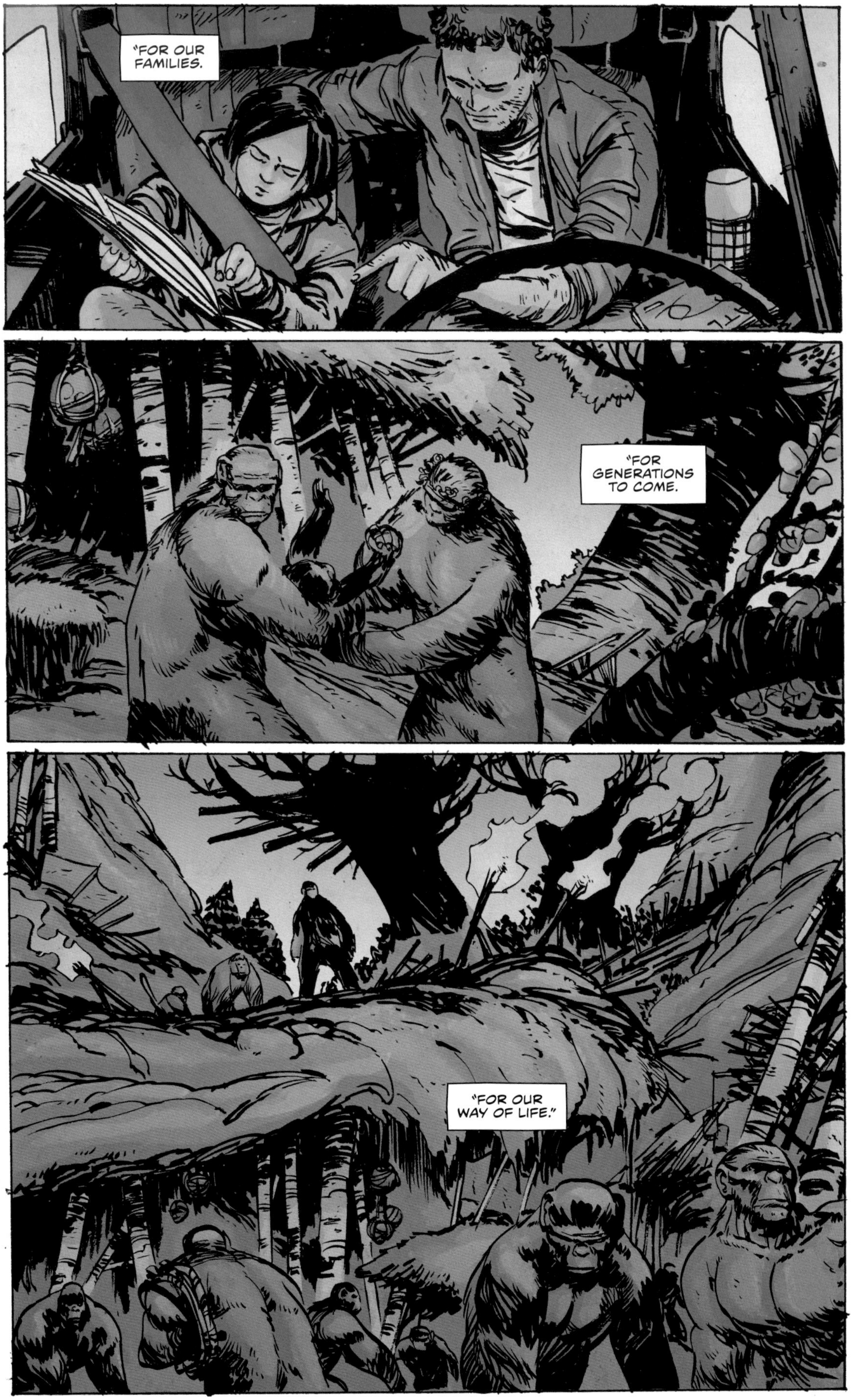

"FOR OUR FAMILIES.
"FOR GENERATIONS TO COME.
"FOR OUR WAY OF LIFE."

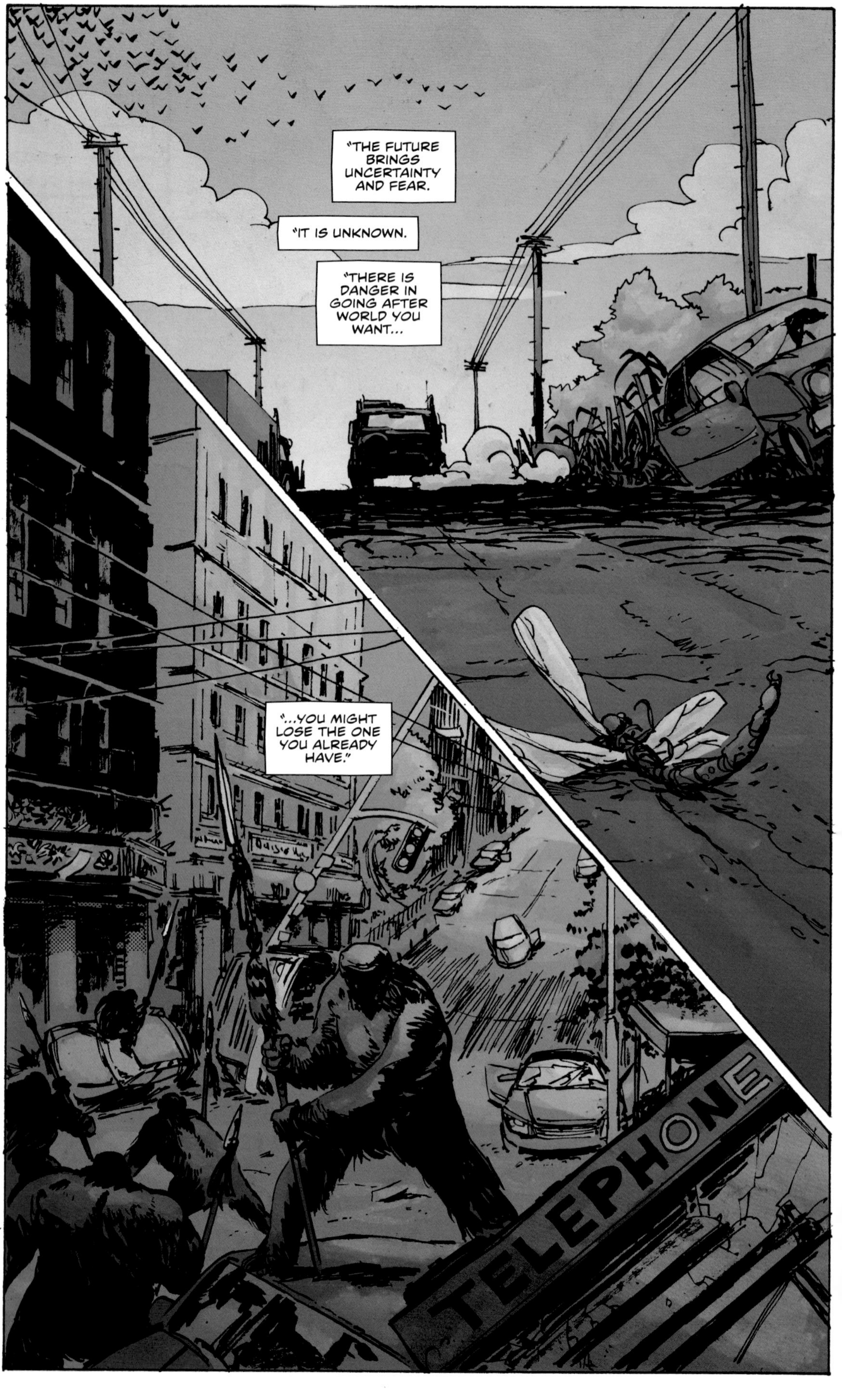
"THE FUTURE BRINGS UNCERTAINTY AND FEAR.
"IT IS UNKNOWN.
"THERE IS DANGER IN GOING AFTER WORLD YOU WANT...
"...YOU MIGHT LOSE THE ONE YOU ALREADY HAVE."
TELEPHONE

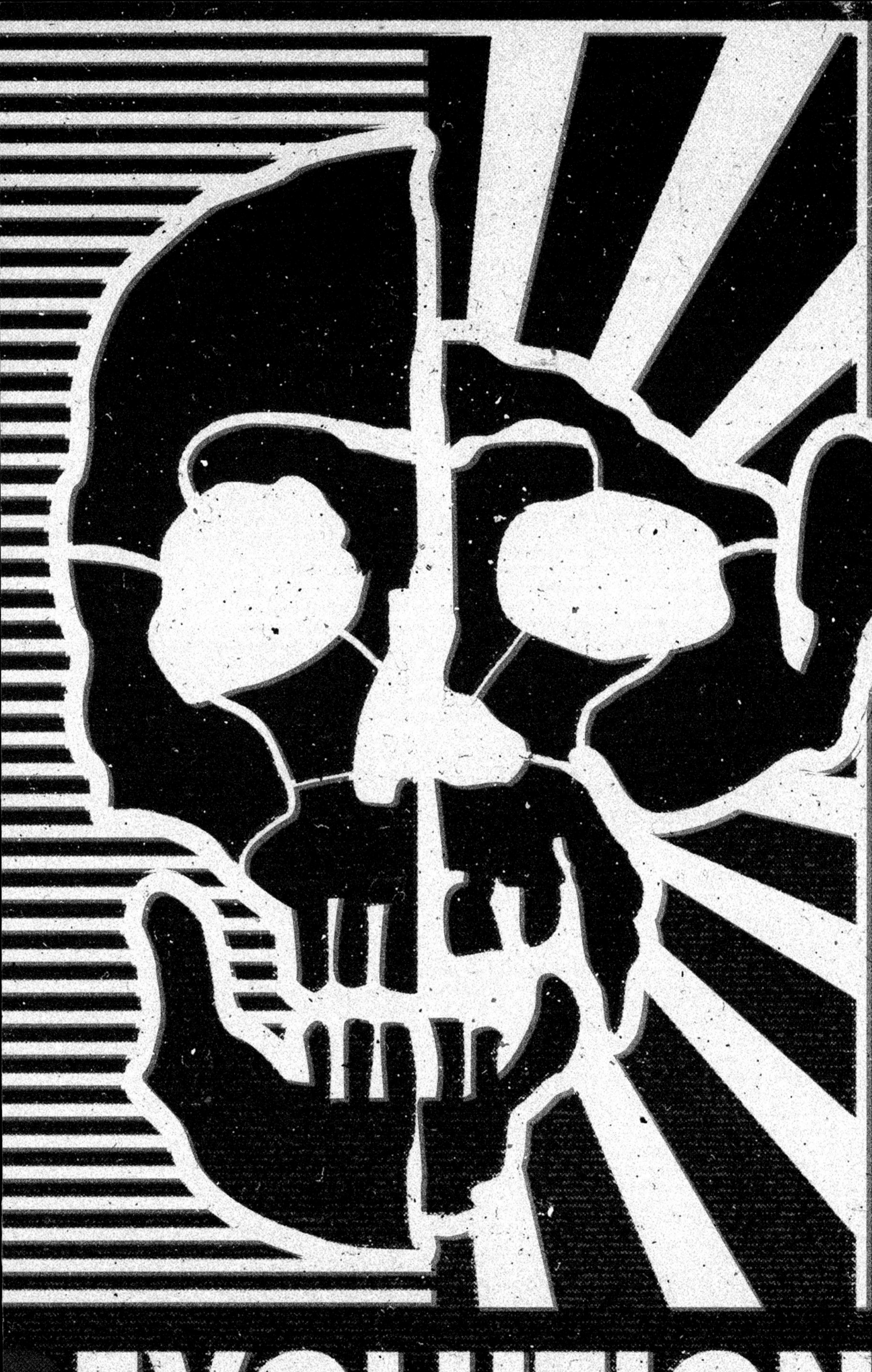

EVOLUTION

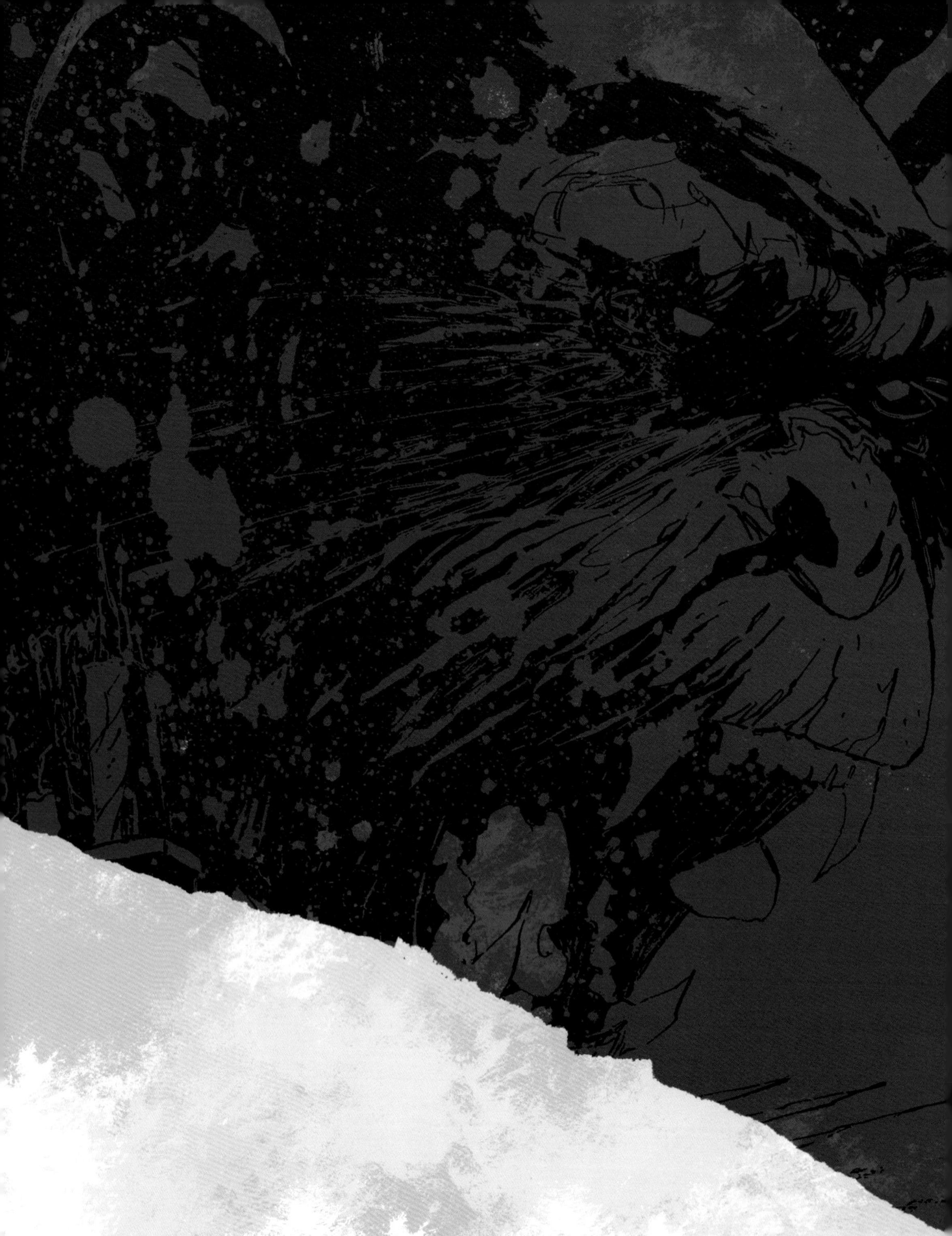

CHAPTER**TWO**

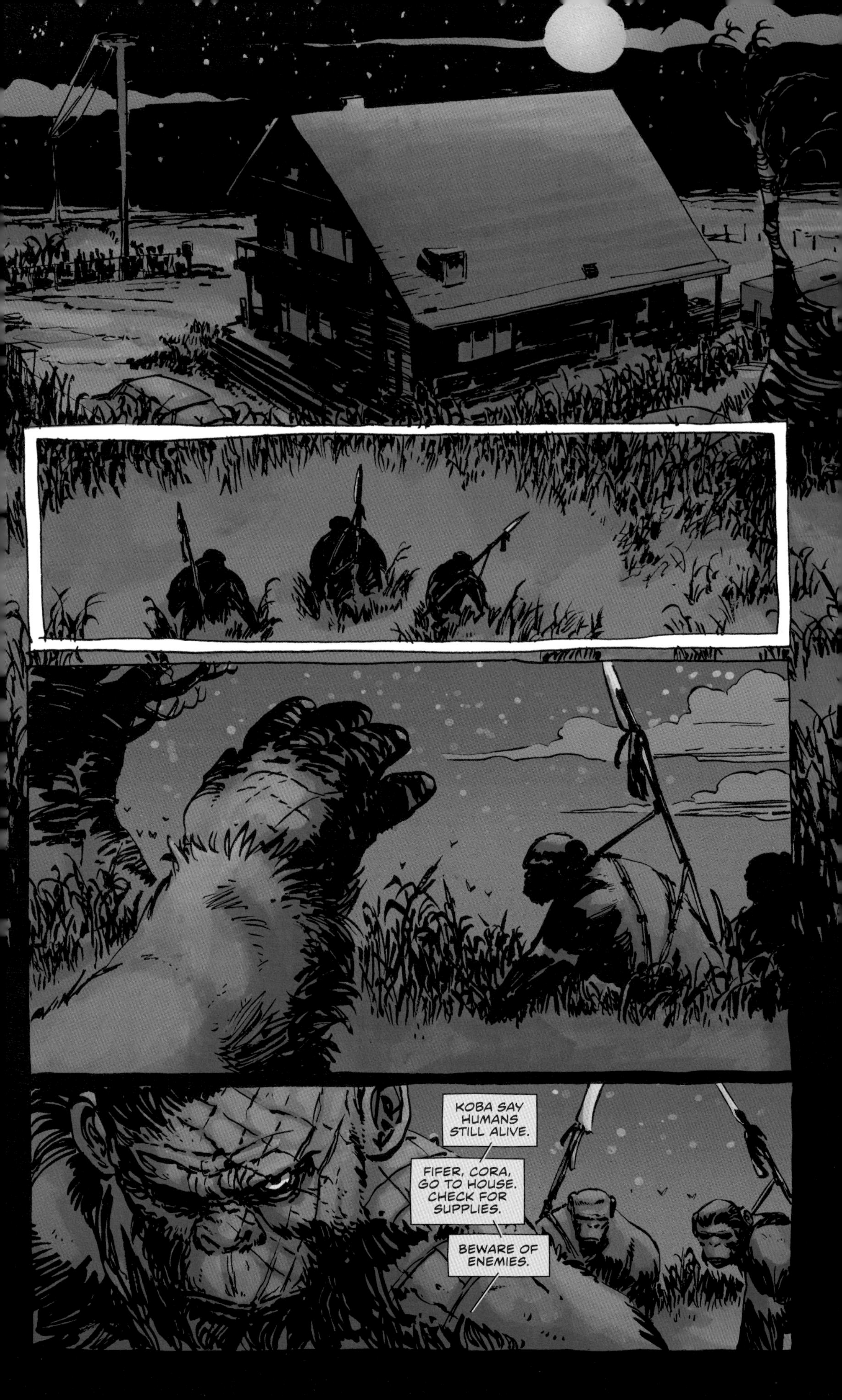
KOBA SAY HUMANS STILL ALIVE.
FIFER, CORA, GO TO HOUSE. CHECK FOR SUPPLIES.
BEWARE OF ENEMIES.

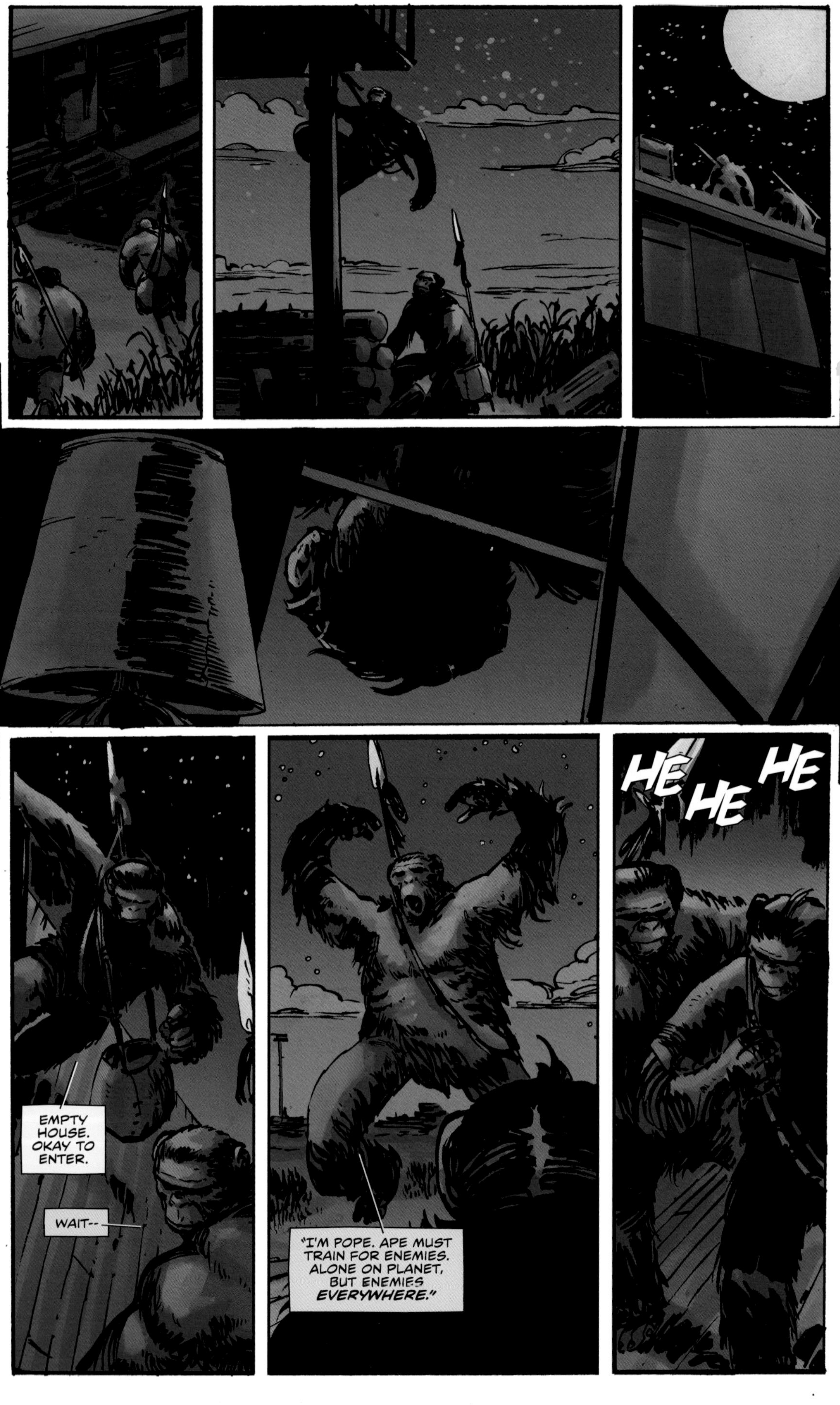
EMPTY HOUSE. OKAY TO ENTER.
WAIT--
"I'M POPE. APE MUST TRAIN FOR ENEMIES. ALONE ON PLANET, BUT ENEMIES *EVERYWHERE.*"
HE HE HE

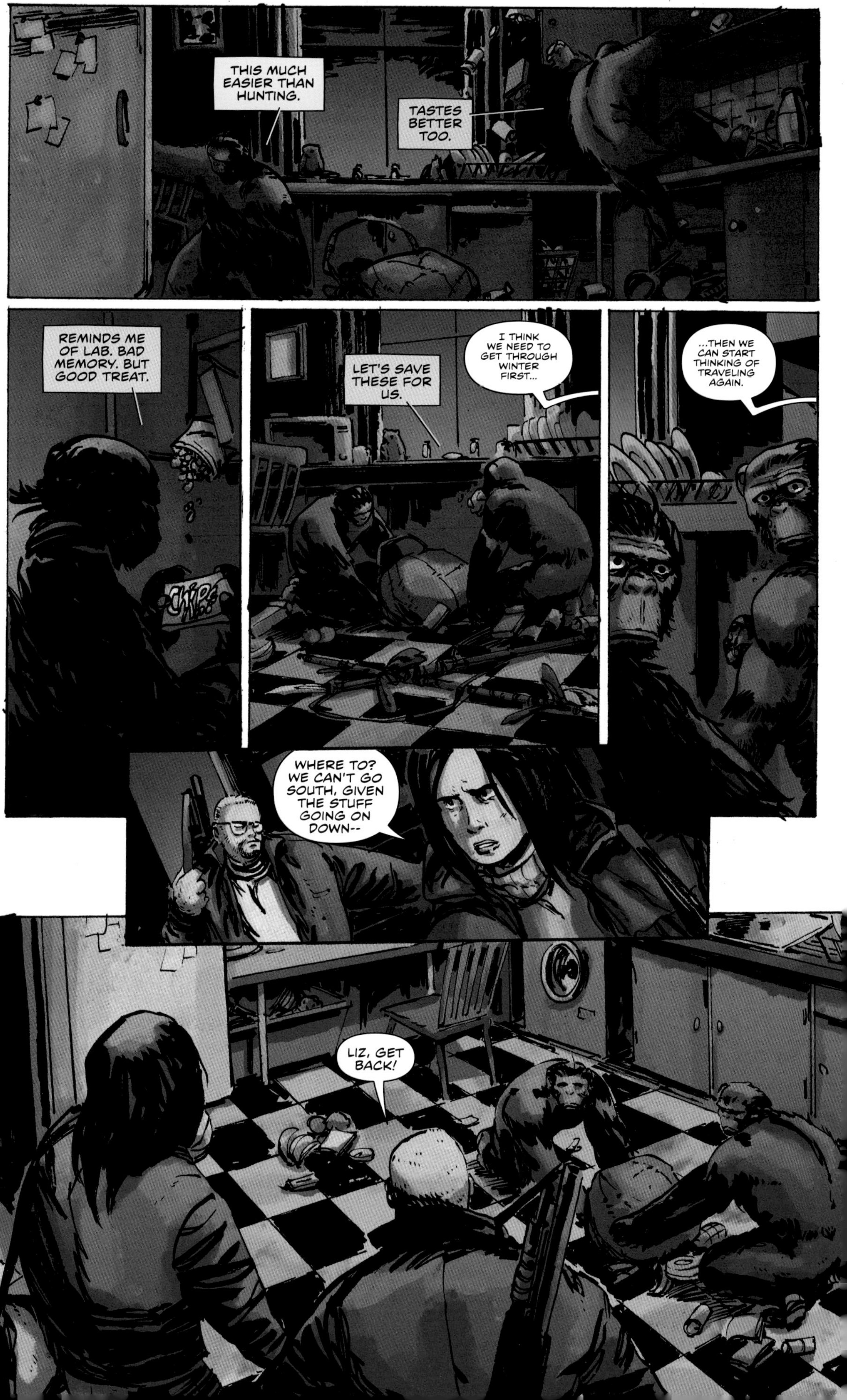
THIS MUCH EASIER THAN HUNTING.
TASTES BETTER TOO.
REMINDS ME OF LAB. BAD MEMORY. BUT GOOD TREAT.
LET'S SAVE THESE FOR US.
I THINK WE NEED TO GET THROUGH WINTER FIRST...
...THEN WE CAN START THINKING OF TRAVELING AGAIN.
WHERE TO? WE CAN'T GO SOUTH, GIVEN THE STUFF GOING ON DOWN--
LIZ, GET BACK!

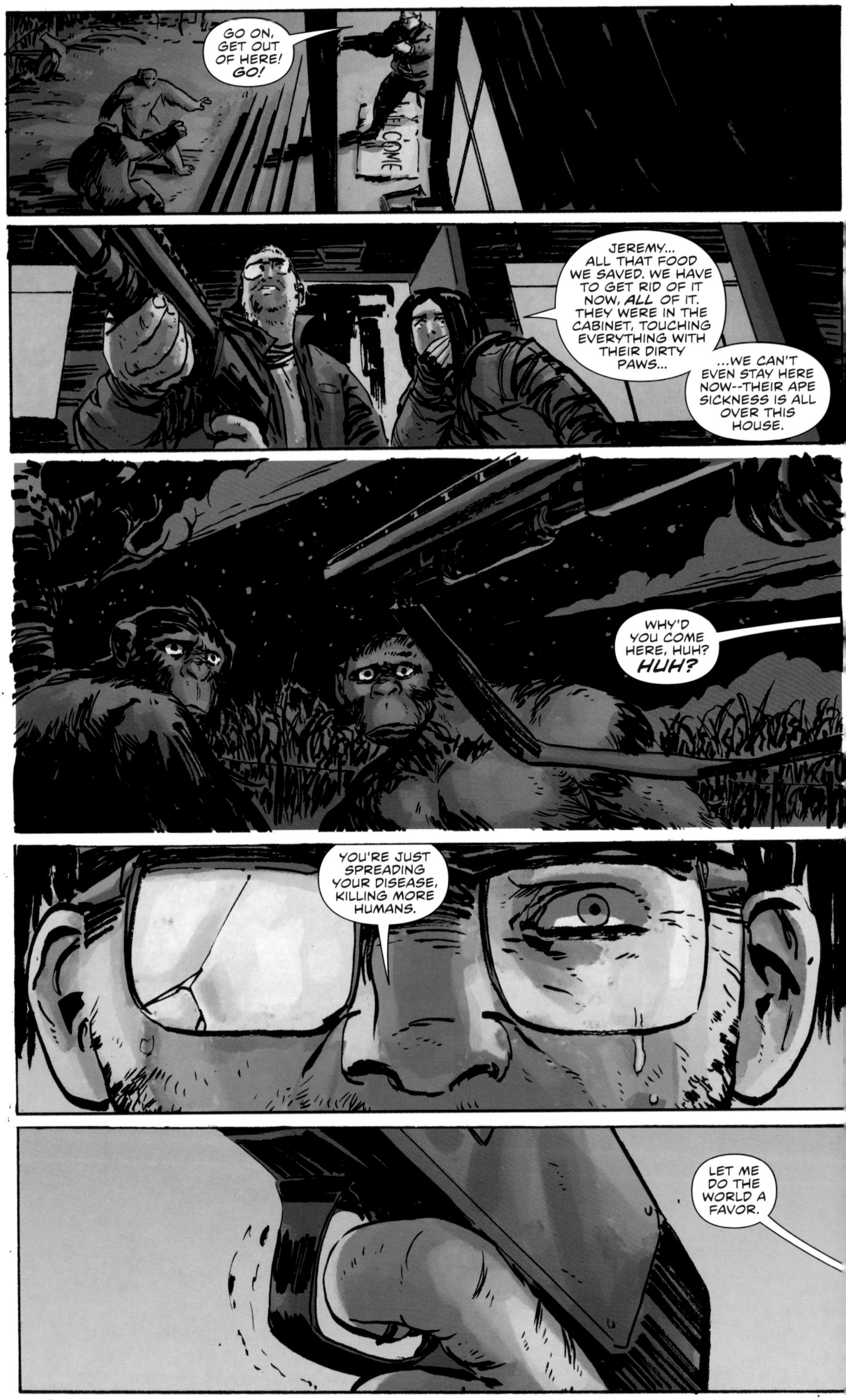
GO ON, GET OUT OF HERE! GO!
JEREMY... ALL THAT FOOD WE SAVED. WE HAVE TO GET RID OF IT NOW, ALL OF IT. THEY WERE IN THE CABINET, TOUCHING EVERYTHING WITH THEIR DIRTY PAWS...
...WE CAN'T EVEN STAY HERE NOW--THEIR APE SICKNESS IS ALL OVER THIS HOUSE.
WHY'D YOU COME HERE, HUH? HUH?
YOU'RE JUST SPREADING YOUR DISEASE, KILLING MORE HUMANS.
LET ME DO THE WORLD A FAVOR.

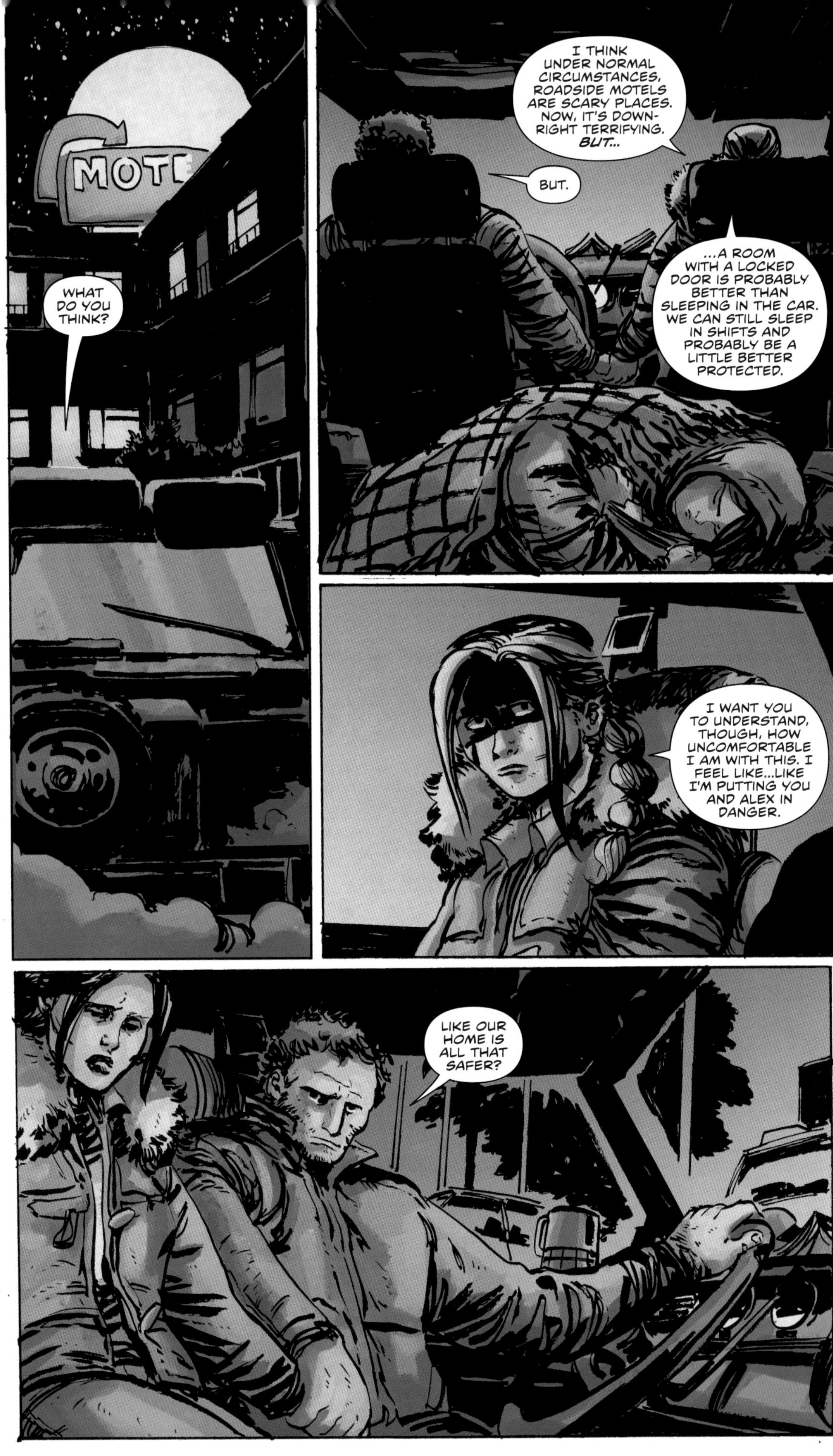
MOTE
WHAT DO YOU THINK?
I THINK UNDER NORMAL CIRCUMSTANCES, ROADSIDE MOTELS ARE SCARY PLACES. NOW, IT'S DOWN-RIGHT TERRIFYING. *BUT...*
BUT.
...A ROOM WITH A LOCKED DOOR IS PROBABLY BETTER THAN SLEEPING IN THE CAR. WE CAN STILL SLEEP IN SHIFTS AND PROBABLY BE A LITTLE BETTER PROTECTED.
I WANT YOU TO UNDERSTAND, THOUGH, HOW UNCOMFORTABLE I AM WITH THIS. I FEEL LIKE...LIKE I'M PUTTING YOU AND ALEX IN DANGER.
LIKE OUR HOME IS ALL THAT SAFER?

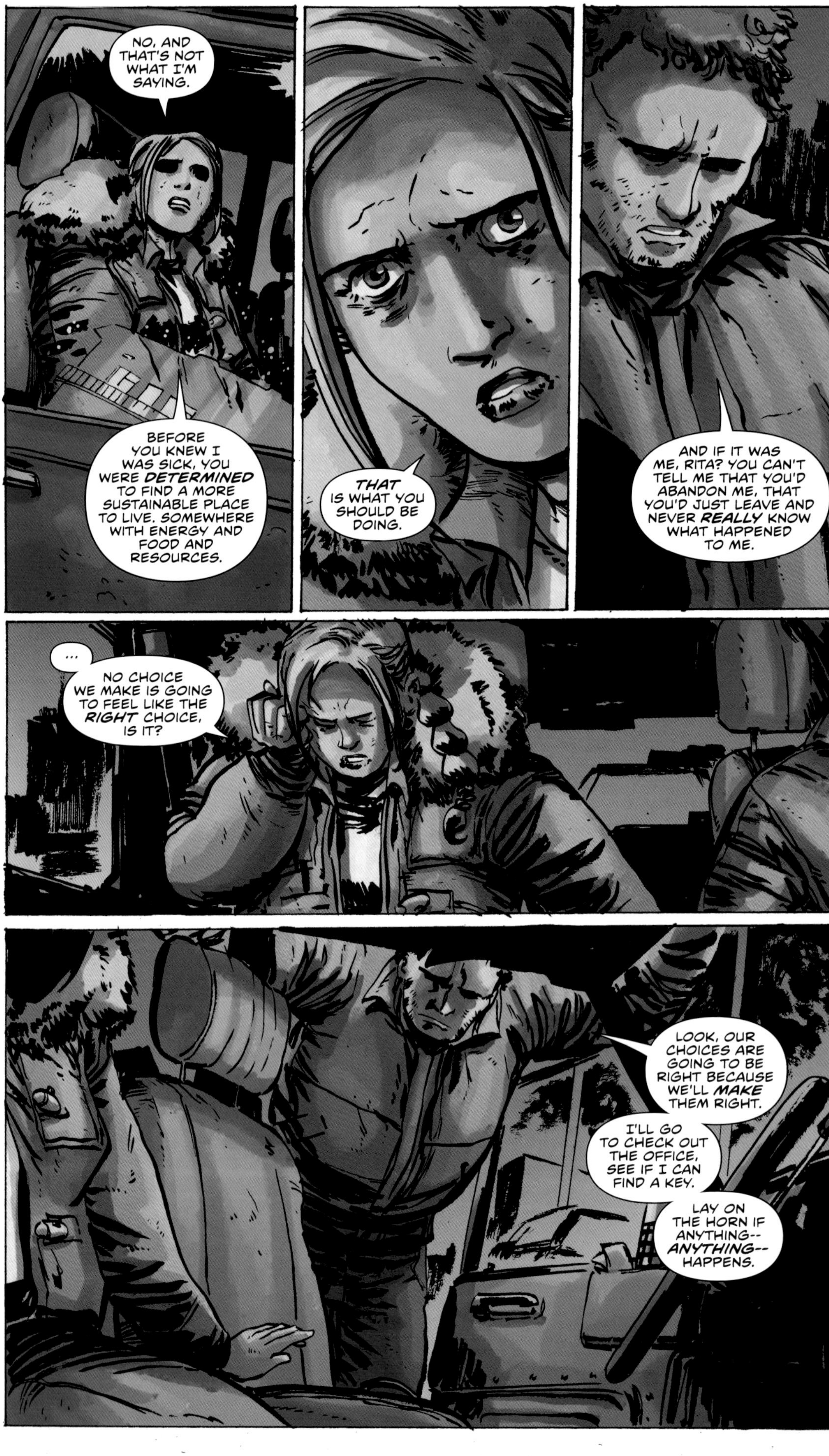
NO, AND THAT'S NOT WHAT I'M SAYING.
BEFORE YOU KNEW I WAS SICK, YOU WERE DETERMINED TO FIND A MORE SUSTAINABLE PLACE TO LIVE. SOMEWHERE WITH ENERGY AND FOOD AND RESOURCES.
THAT IS WHAT YOU SHOULD BE DOING.
AND IF IT WAS ME, RITA? YOU CAN'T TELL ME THAT YOU'D ABANDON ME, THAT YOU'D JUST LEAVE AND NEVER REALLY KNOW WHAT HAPPENED TO ME.
...
NO CHOICE WE MAKE IS GOING TO FEEL LIKE THE RIGHT CHOICE, IS IT?
LOOK, OUR CHOICES ARE GOING TO BE RIGHT BECAUSE WE'LL MAKE THEM RIGHT.
I'LL GO TO CHECK OUT THE OFFICE, SEE IF I CAN FIND A KEY.
LAY ON THE HORN IF ANYTHING-- ANYTHING-- HAPPENS.

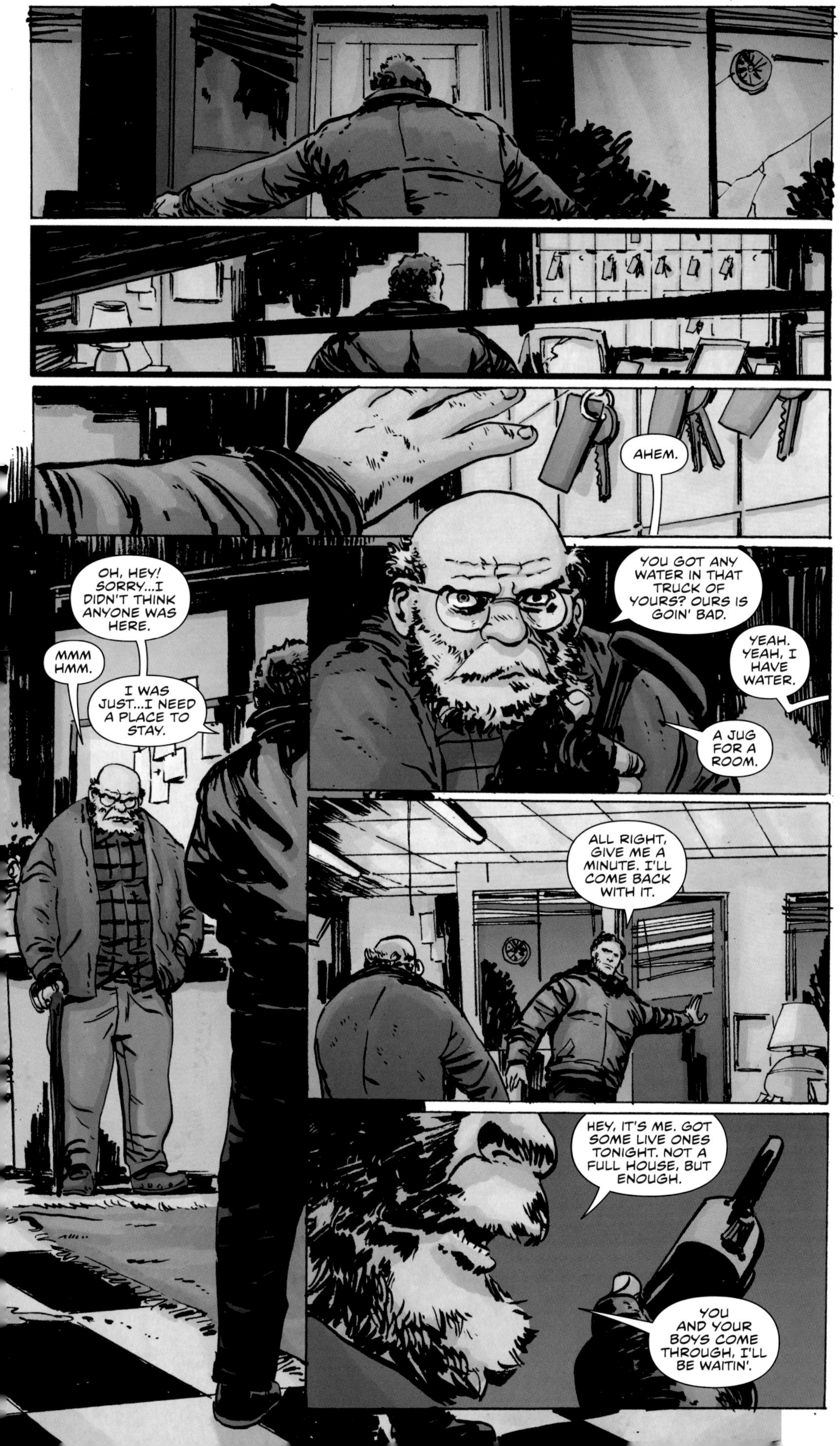
AHEM.
OH, HEY! SORRY...I DIDN'T THINK ANYONE WAS HERE.
MMM HMM.
I WAS JUST...I NEED A PLACE TO STAY.
YOU GOT ANY WATER IN THAT TRUCK OF YOURS? OURS IS GOIN' BAD.
YEAH. YEAH, I HAVE WATER.
A JUG FOR A ROOM.
ALL RIGHT, GIVE ME A MINUTE. I'LL COME BACK WITH IT.
HEY, IT'S ME. GOT SOME LIVE ONES TONIGHT. NOT A FULL HOUSE, BUT ENOUGH.
YOU AND YOUR BOYS COME THROUGH, I'LL BE WAITIN'.

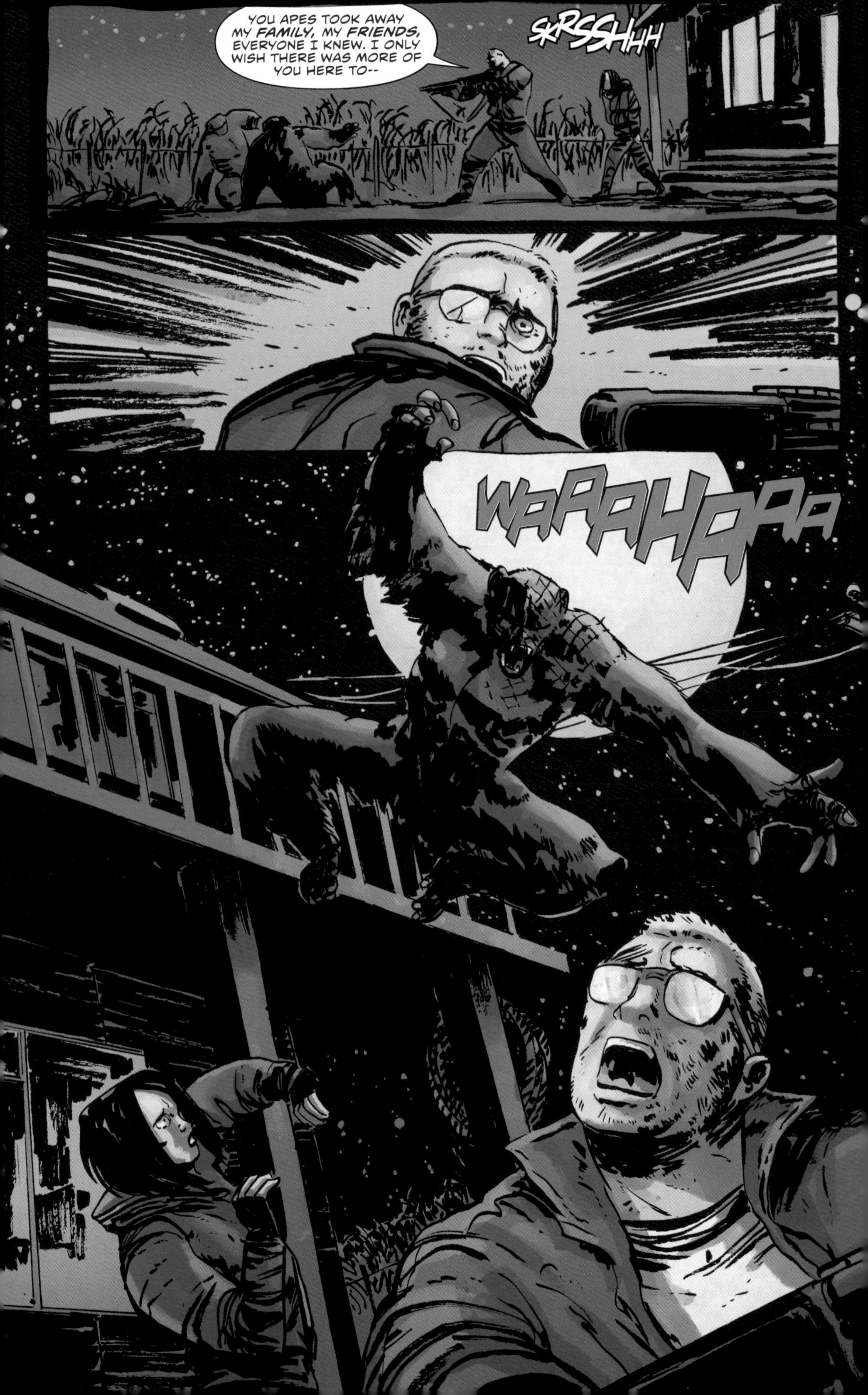
YOU APES TOOK AWAY MY *FAMILY*, MY *FRIENDS*, EVERYONE I KNEW. I ONLY WISH THERE WAS MORE OF YOU HERE TO--
SKRSSHHH
WAAAHAAA

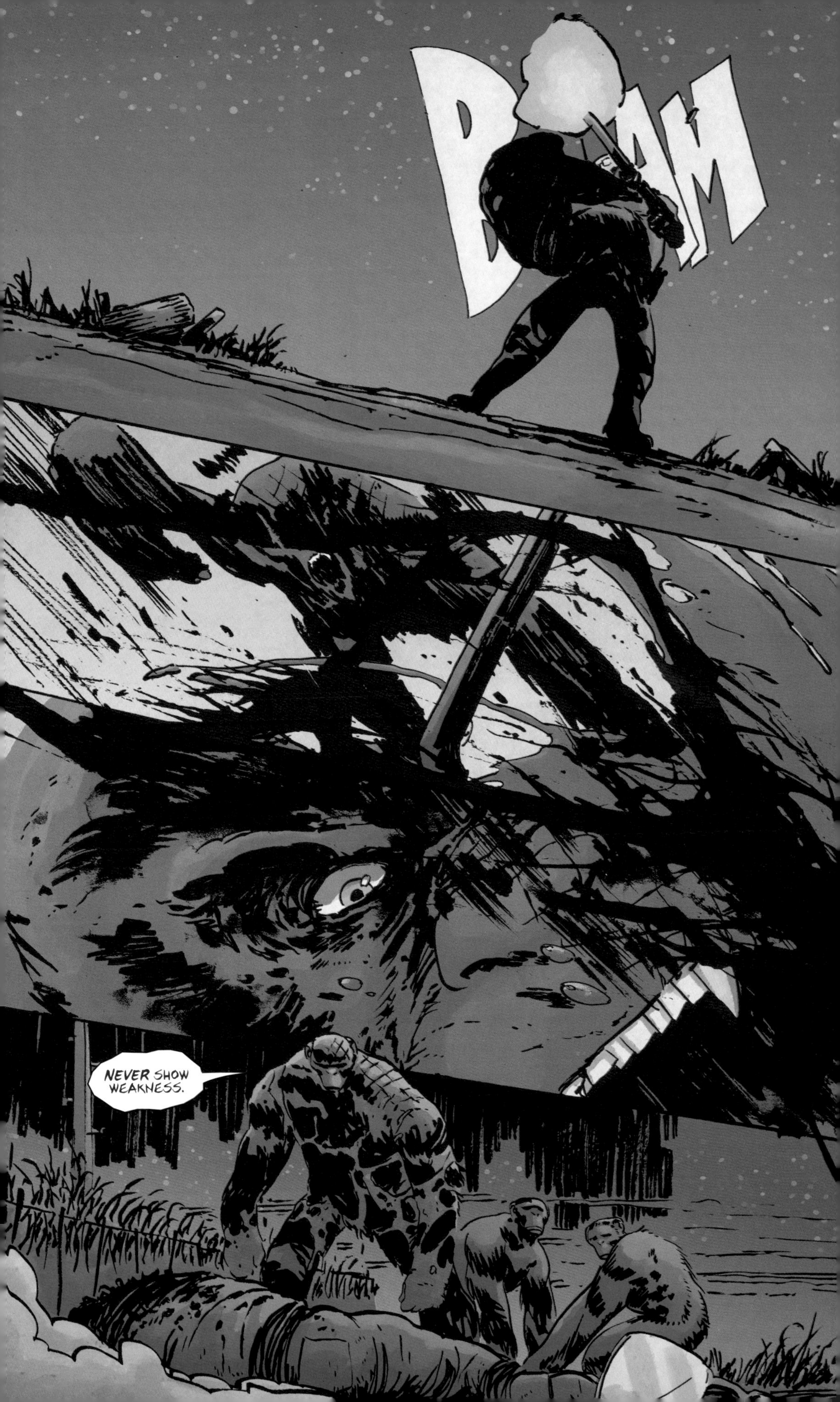
NEVER SHOW WEAKNESS.

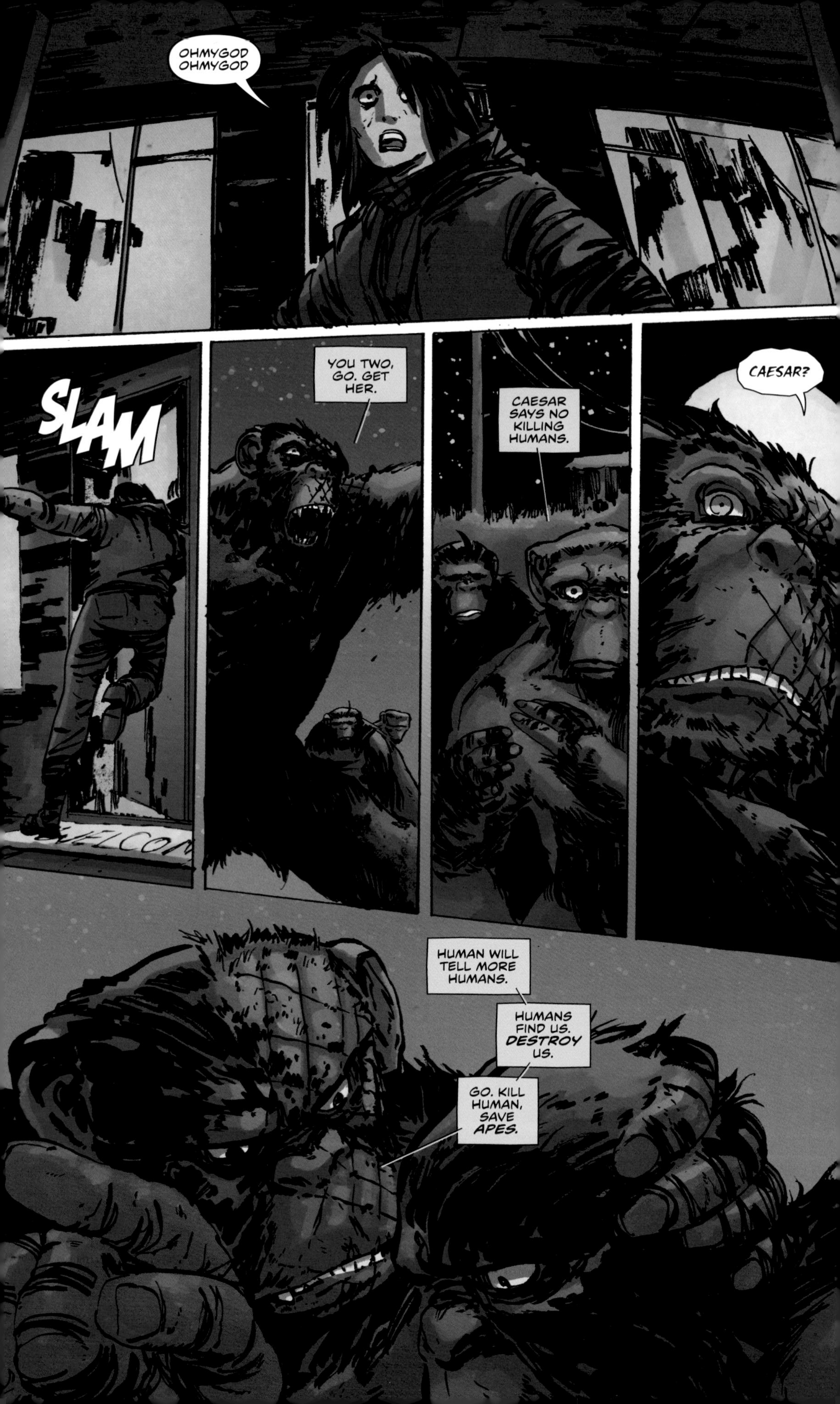
OHMYGOD OHMYGOD
SLAM
YOU TWO, GO. GET HER.
CAESAR SAYS NO KILLING HUMANS.
CAESAR?
HUMAN WILL TELL MORE HUMANS.
HUMANS FIND US. *DESTROY* US.
GO. KILL HUMAN, SAVE *APES*.

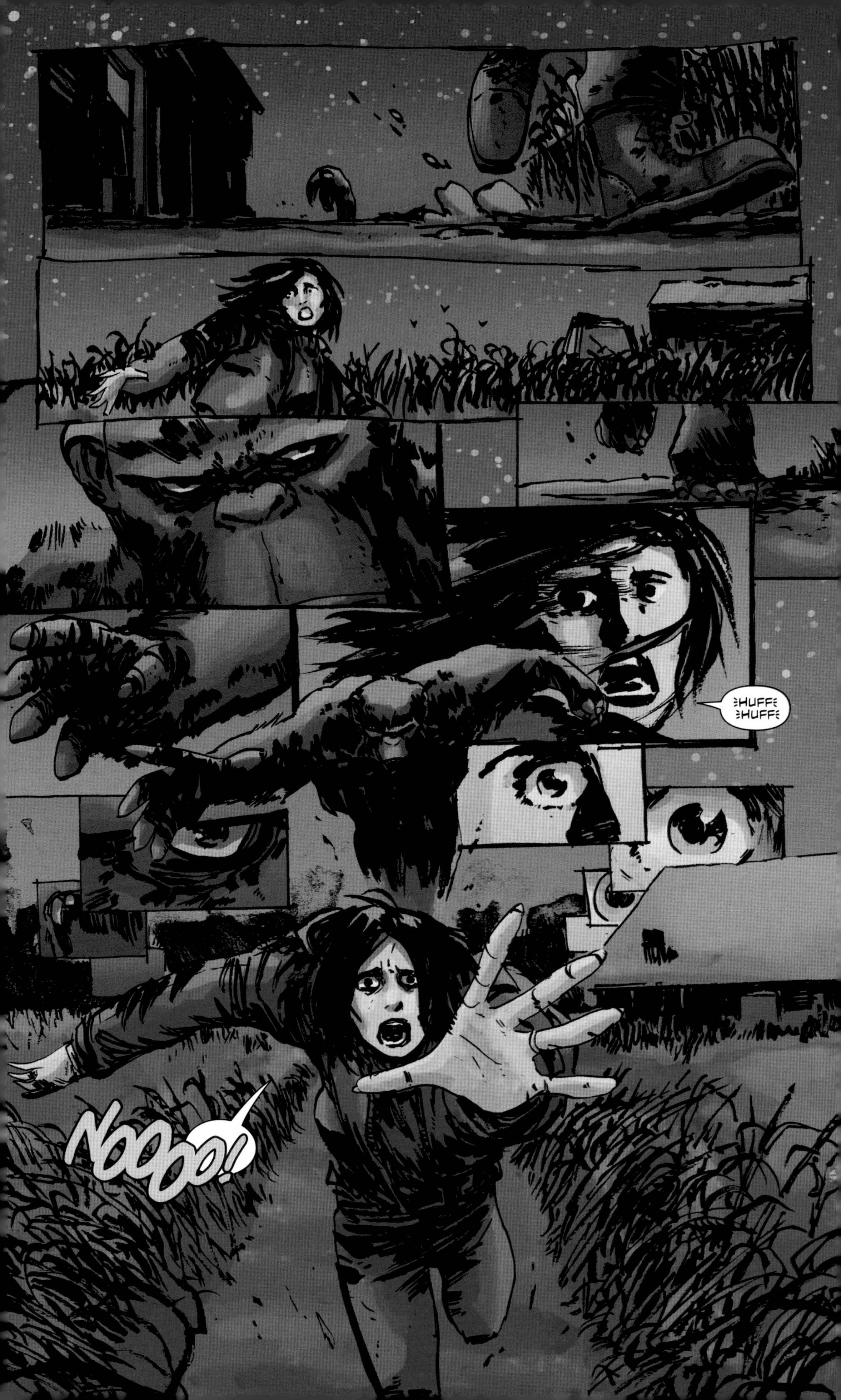
HUFF HUFF
NOOOO!

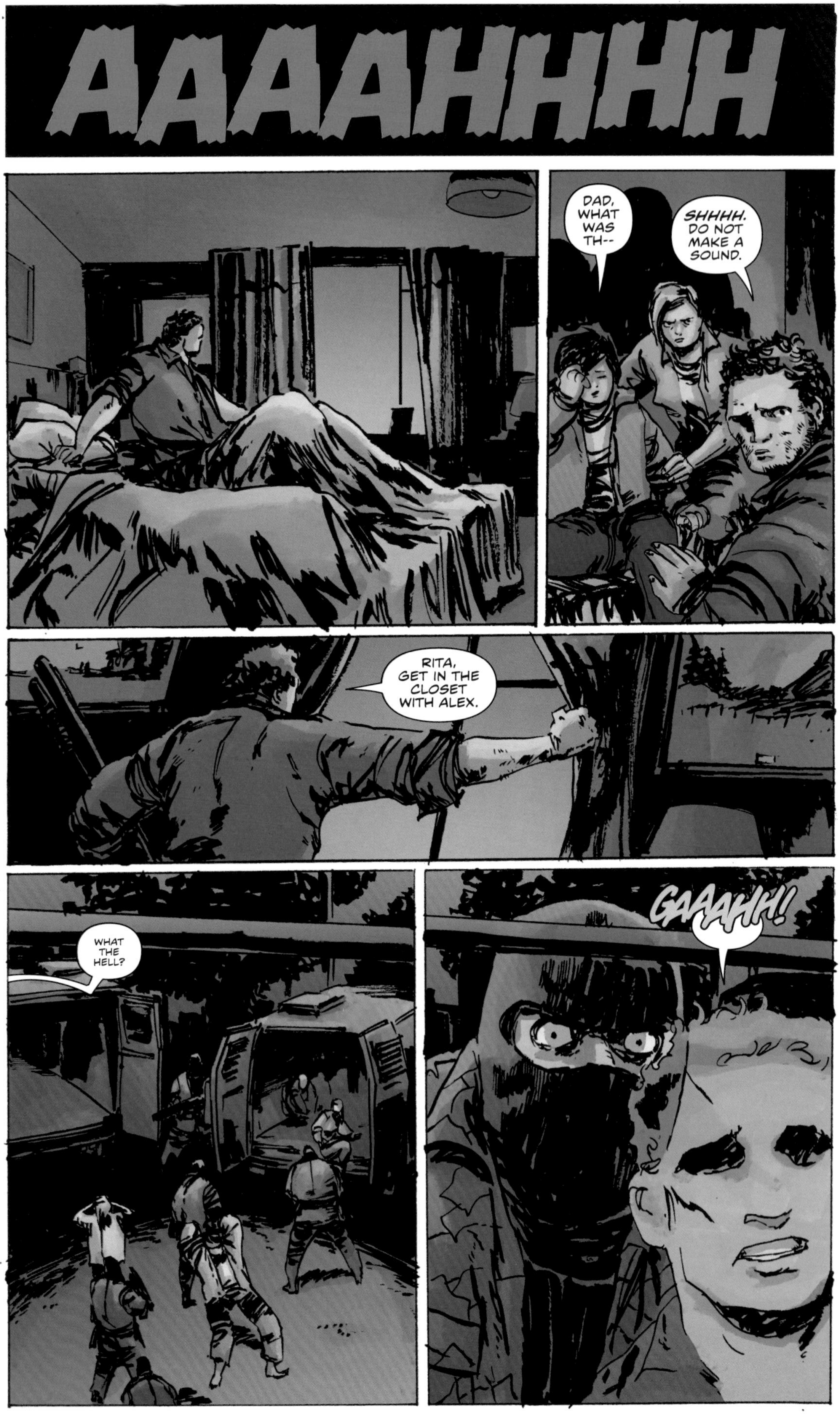
AAAAHHHH
DAD, WHAT WAS TH--
SHHHH. DO NOT MAKE A SOUND.
RITA, GET IN THE CLOSET WITH ALEX.
WHAT THE HELL?
GAAAHH!

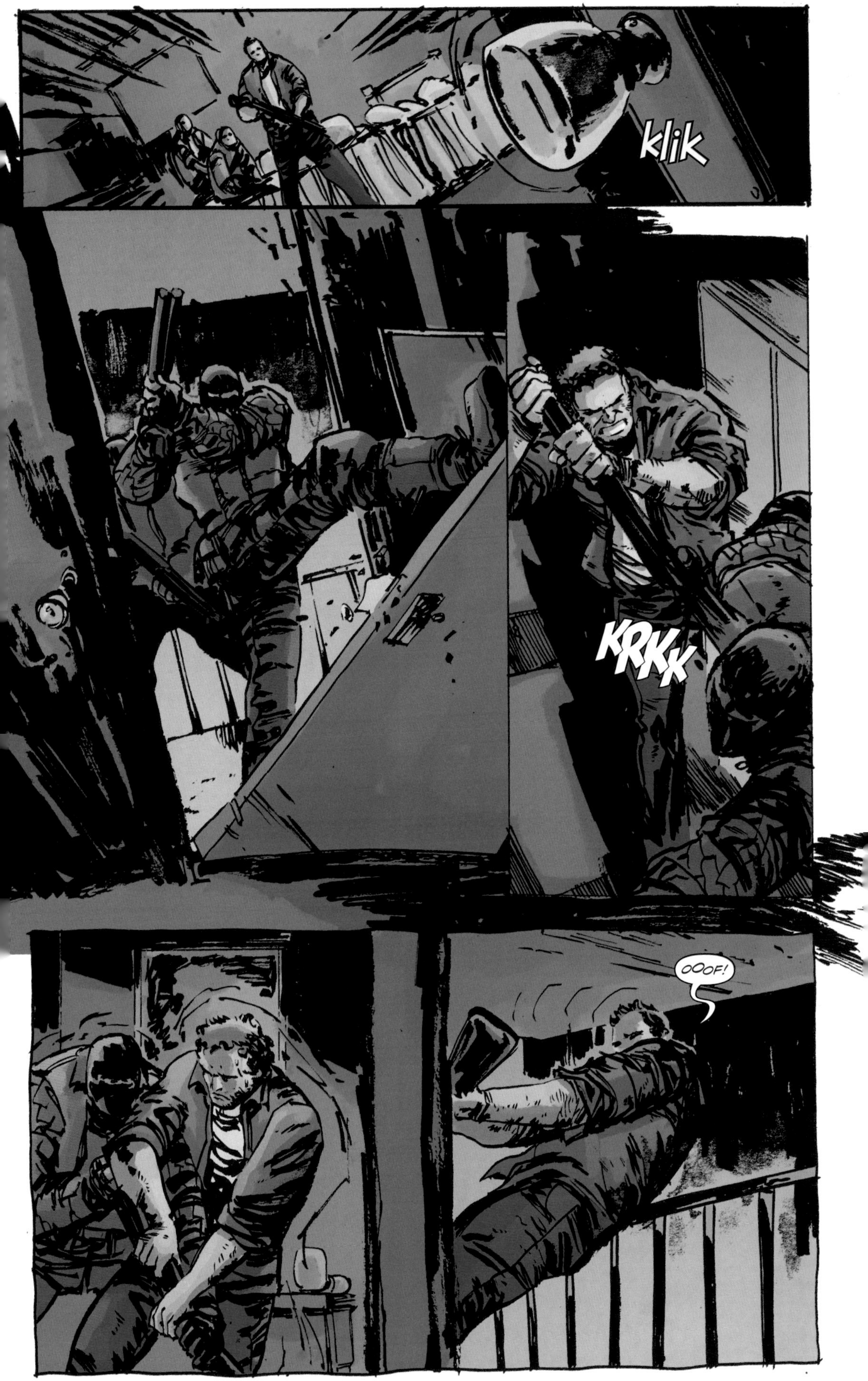
klik
KRKK
OOOF!

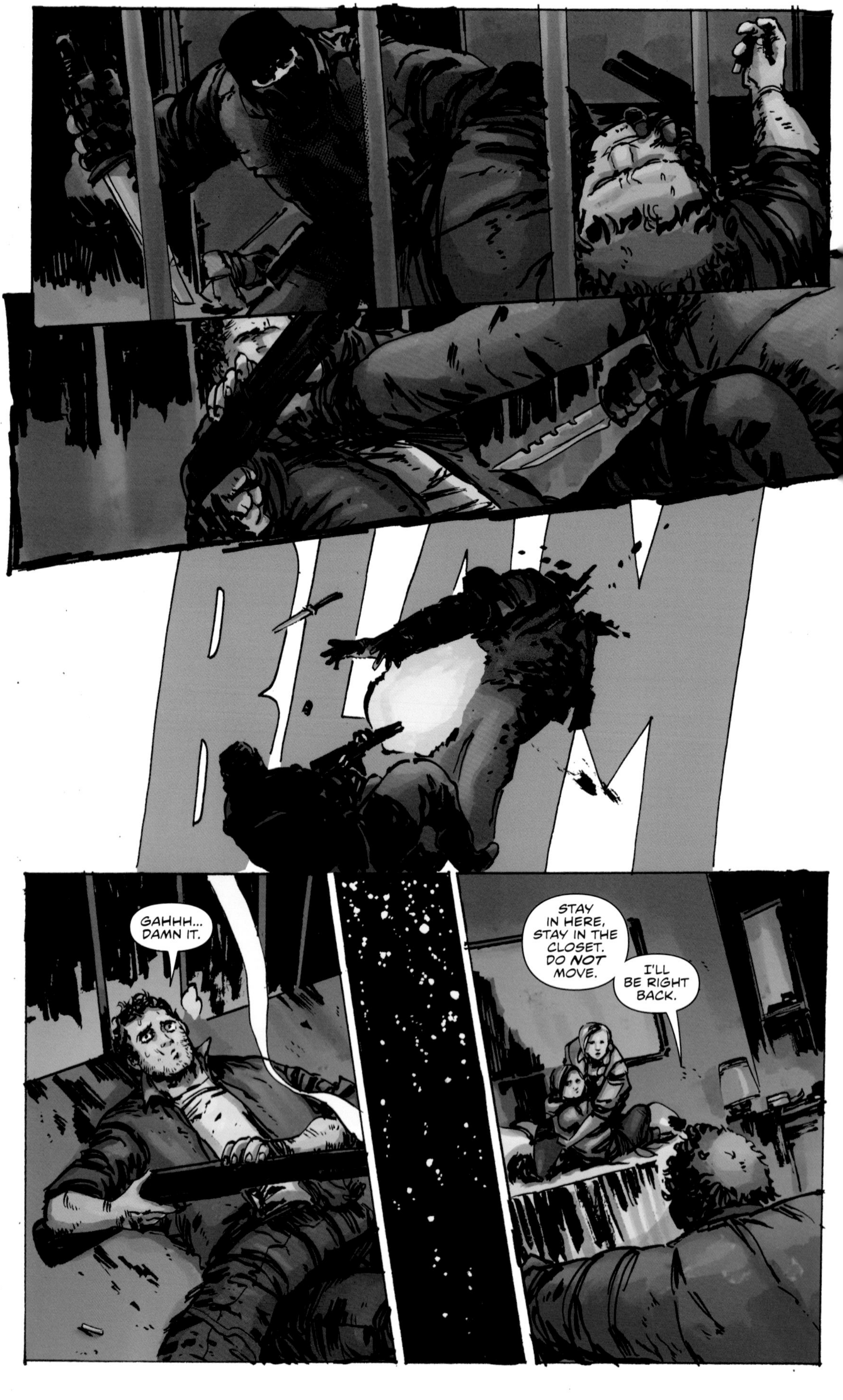
GAHHH... DAMN IT.
STAY IN HERE, STAY IN THE CLOSET. DO *NOT* MOVE.
I'LL BE RIGHT BACK.

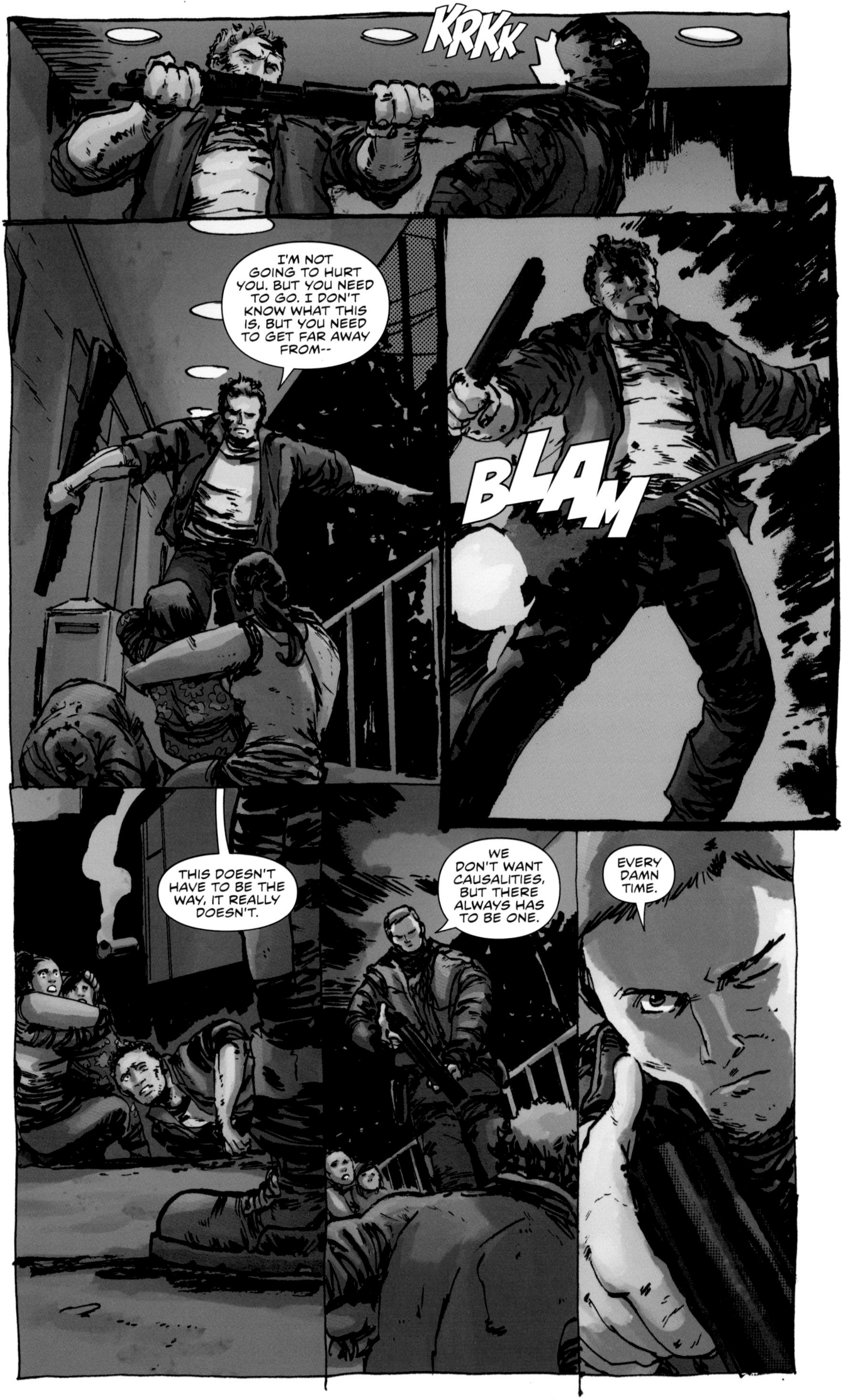
KRKK
I'M NOT GOING TO HURT YOU. BUT YOU NEED TO GO. I DON'T KNOW WHAT THIS IS, BUT YOU NEED TO GET FAR AWAY FROM--
BLAM
THIS DOESN'T HAVE TO BE THE WAY, IT REALLY DOESN'T.
WE DON'T WANT CAUSALITIES, BUT THERE ALWAYS HAS TO BE ONE.
EVERY DAMN TIME.

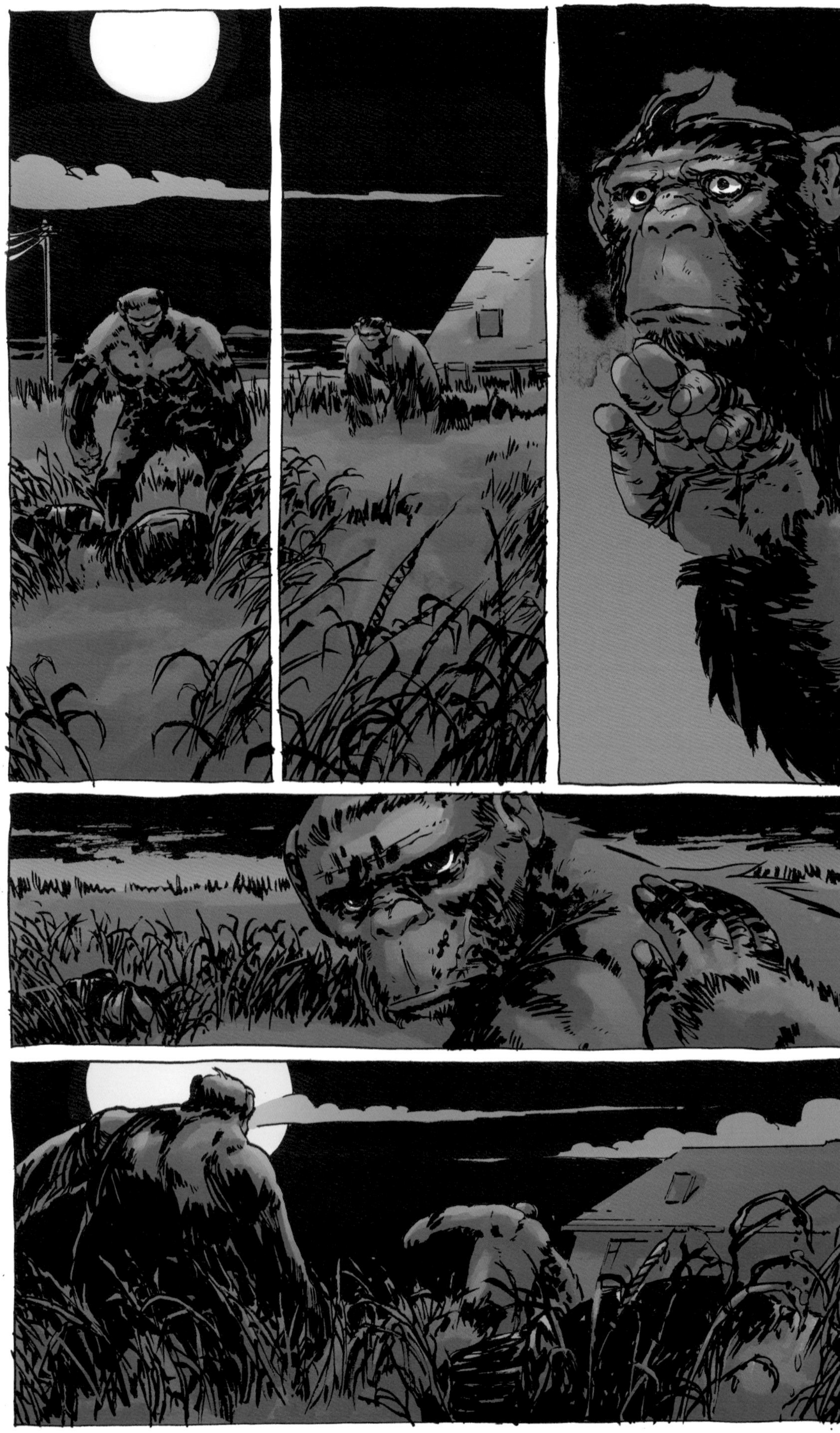

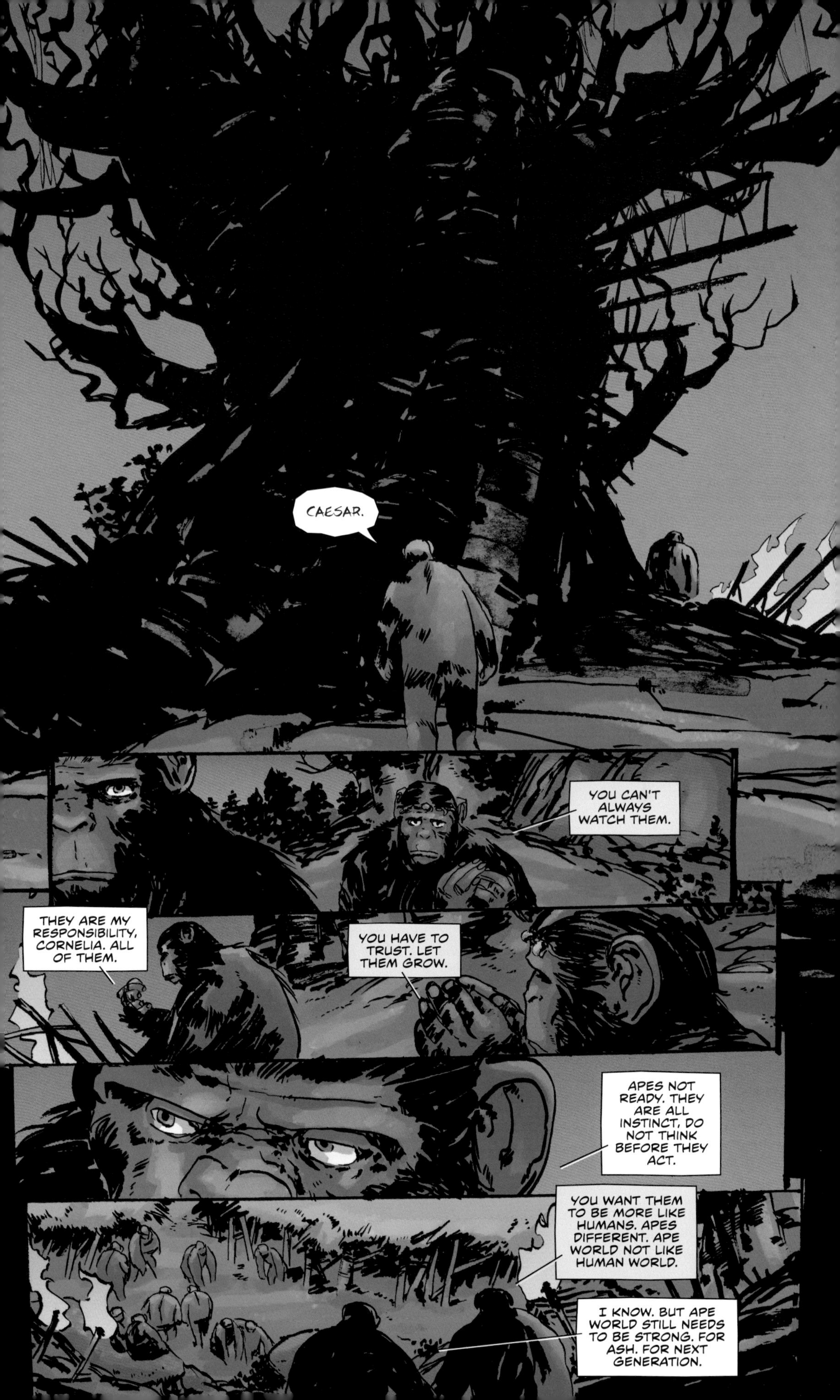
CAESAR.
YOU CAN'T ALWAYS WATCH THEM.
THEY ARE MY RESPONSIBILITY, CORNELIA. ALL OF THEM.
YOU HAVE TO TRUST. LET THEM GROW.
APES NOT READY. THEY ARE ALL INSTINCT, DO NOT THINK BEFORE THEY ACT.
YOU WANT THEM TO BE MORE LIKE HUMANS. APES DIFFERENT. APE WORLD NOT LIKE HUMAN WORLD.
I KNOW. BUT APE WORLD STILL NEEDS TO BE STRONG. FOR ASH. FOR NEXT GENERATION.

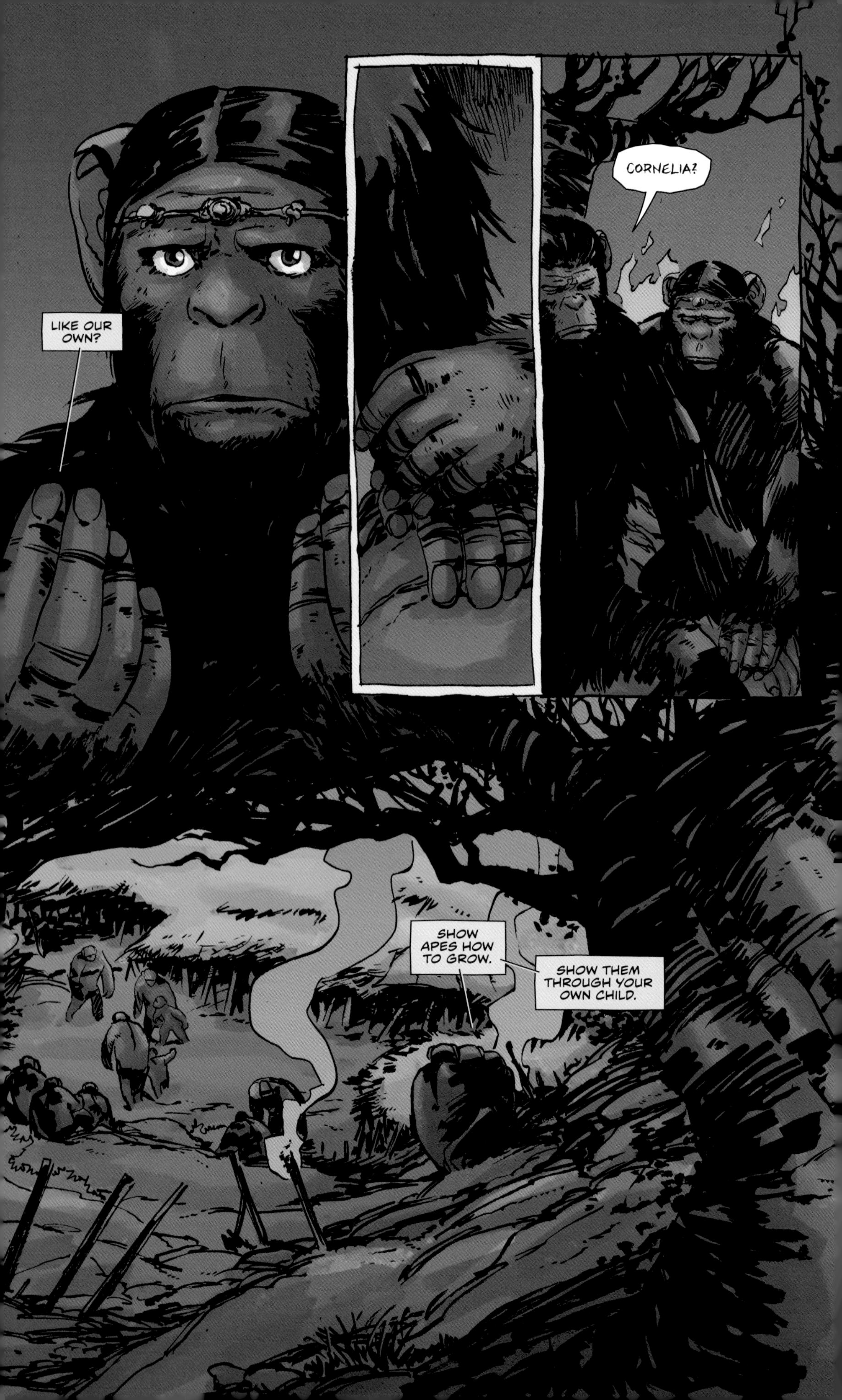
LIKE OUR OWN?
CORNELIA?
SHOW APES HOW TO GROW.
SHOW THEM THROUGH YOUR OWN CHILD.

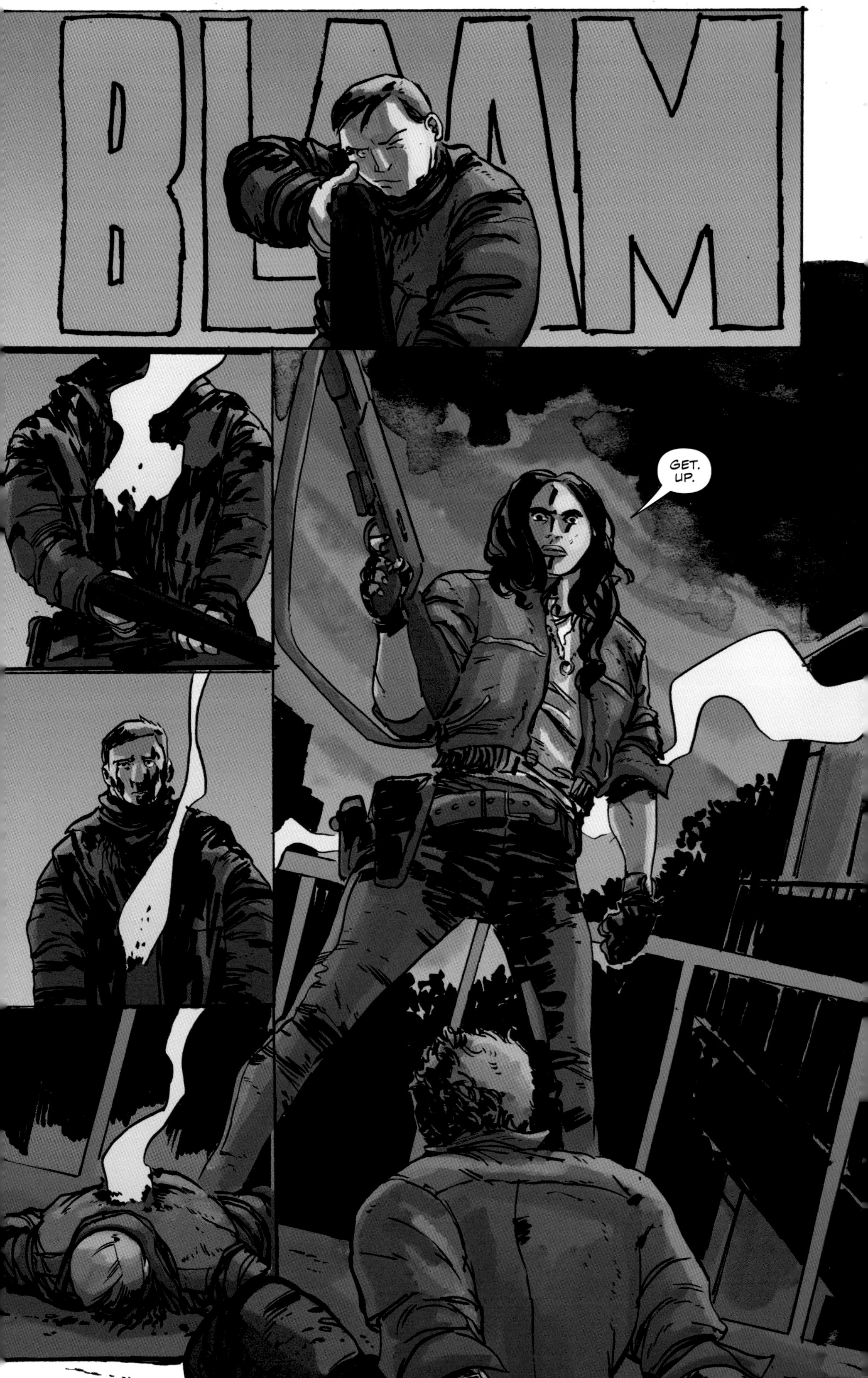
BLAAM
GET. UP.

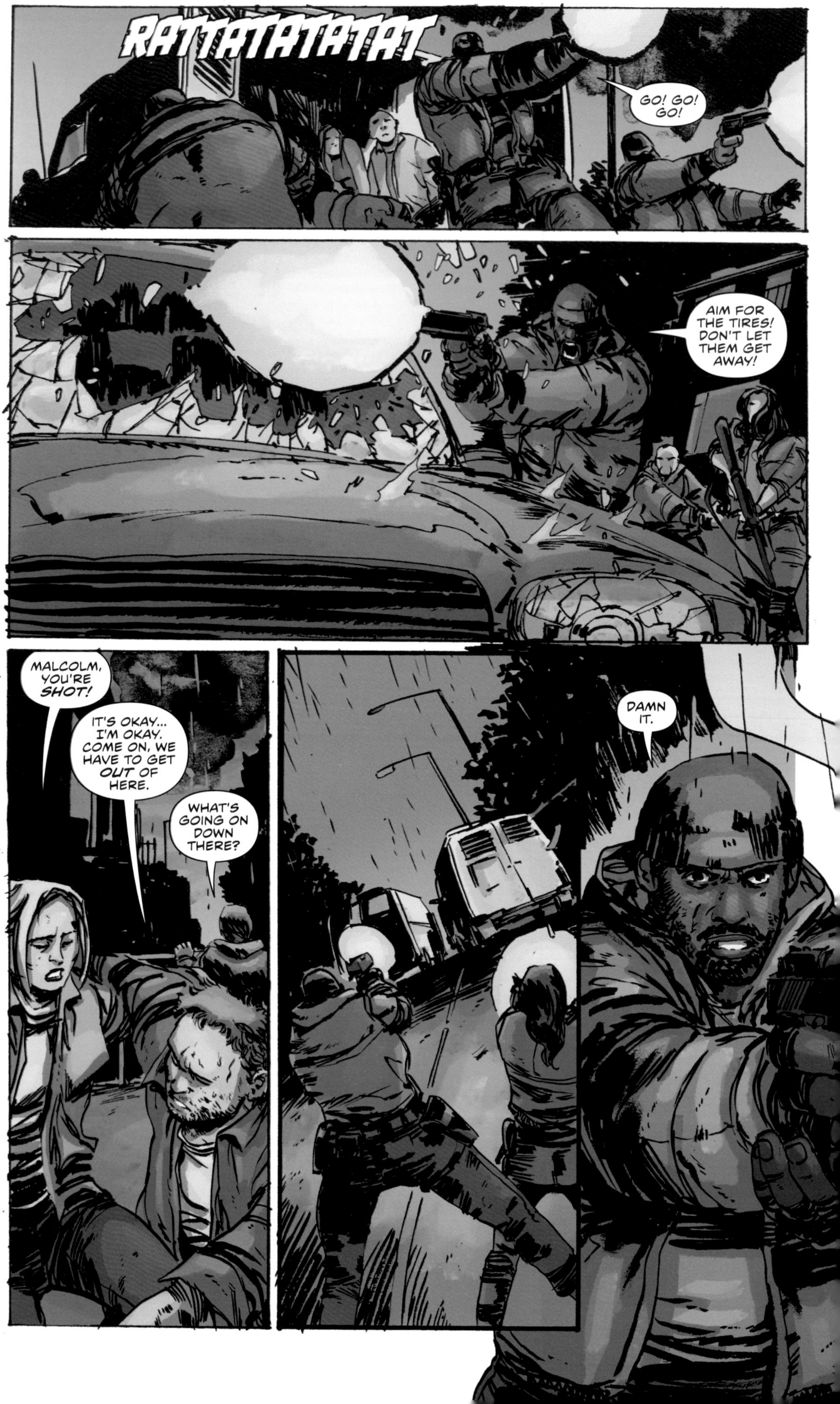
RATTATATATAT
GO! GO! GO!
AIM FOR THE TIRES! DON'T LET THEM GET AWAY!
MALCOLM, YOU'RE SHOT!
IT'S OKAY... I'M OKAY. COME ON, WE HAVE TO GET OUT OF HERE.
WHAT'S GOING ON DOWN THERE?
DAMN IT.

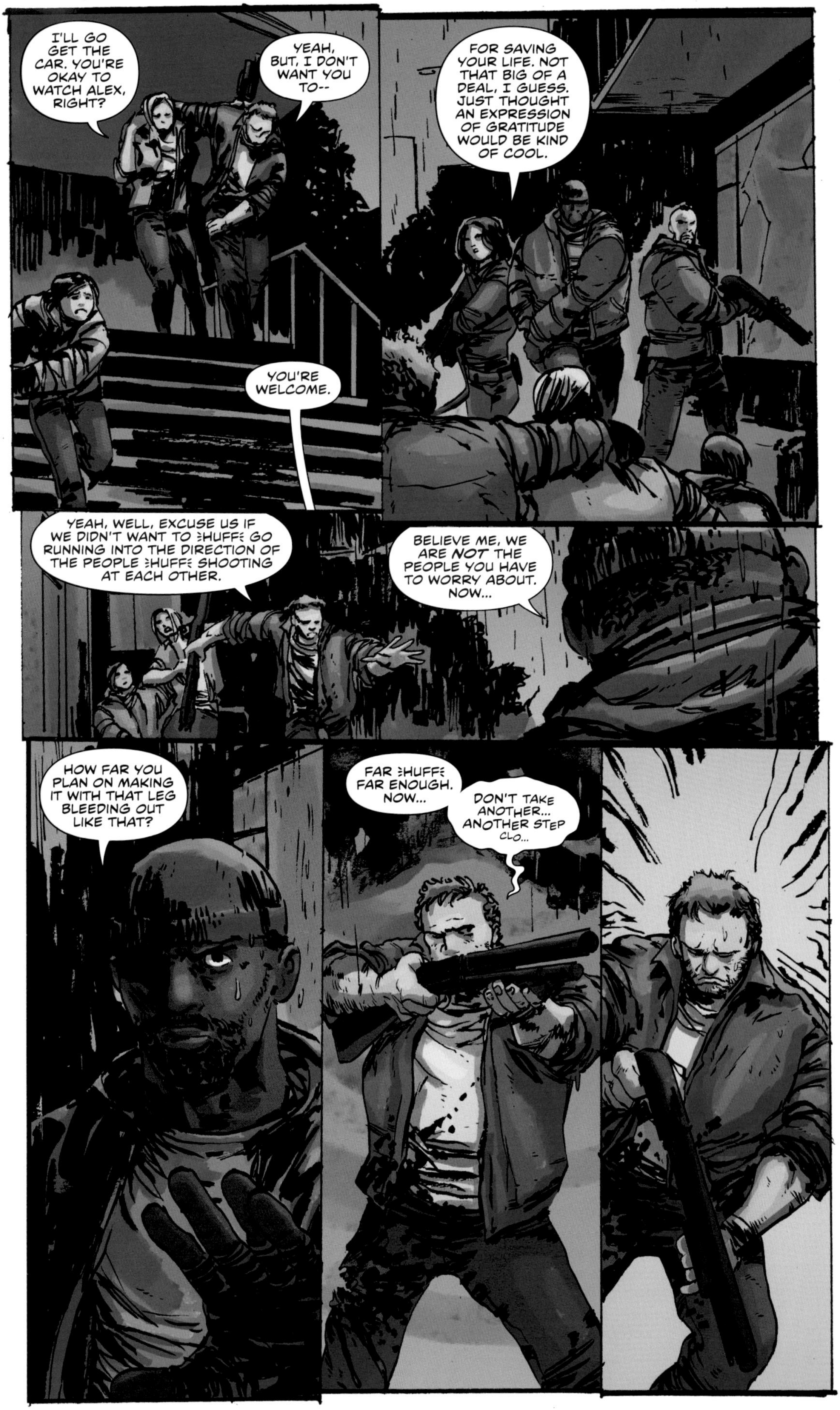
I'LL GO GET THE CAR. YOU'RE OKAY TO WATCH ALEX, RIGHT?
YEAH, BUT, I DON'T WANT YOU TO--
FOR SAVING YOUR LIFE. NOT THAT BIG OF A DEAL, I GUESS. JUST THOUGHT AN EXPRESSION OF GRATITUDE WOULD BE KIND OF COOL.
YOU'RE WELCOME.
YEAH, WELL, EXCUSE US IF WE DIDN'T WANT TO HUFF GO RUNNING INTO THE DIRECTION OF THE PEOPLE HUFF SHOOTING AT EACH OTHER.
BELIEVE ME, WE ARE *NOT* THE PEOPLE YOU HAVE TO WORRY ABOUT. NOW...
HOW FAR YOU PLAN ON MAKING IT WITH THAT LEG BLEEDING OUT LIKE THAT?
FAR HUFF FAR ENOUGH. NOW...
DON'T TAKE ANOTHER... ANOTHER STEP CLO...

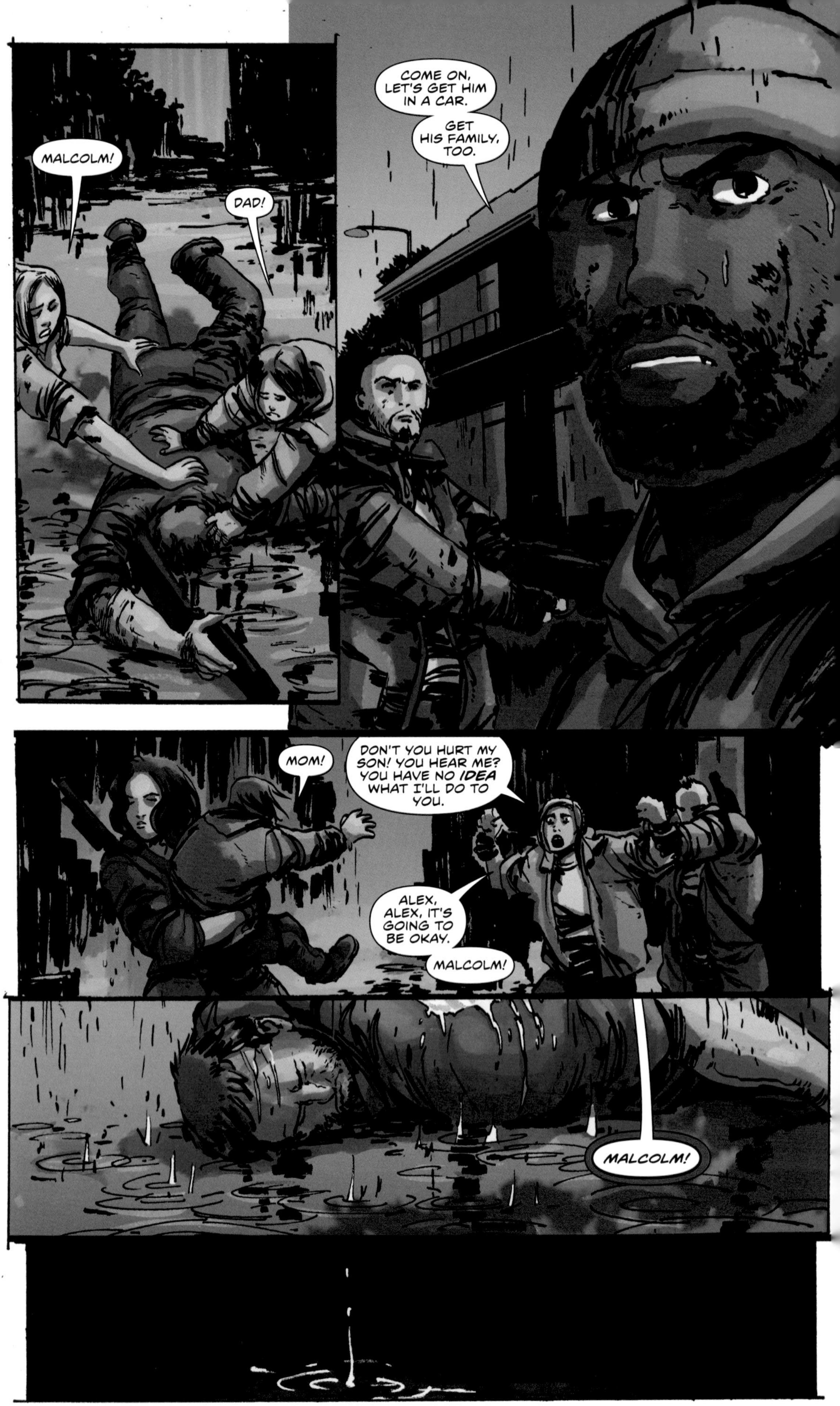
MALCOLM!
DAD!
COME ON, LET'S GET HIM IN A CAR.
GET HIS FAMILY, TOO.
MOM!
DON'T YOU HURT MY SON! YOU HEAR ME? YOU HAVE NO *IDEA* WHAT I'LL DO TO YOU.
ALEX, ALEX, IT'S GOING TO BE OKAY.
MALCOLM!
MALCOLM!

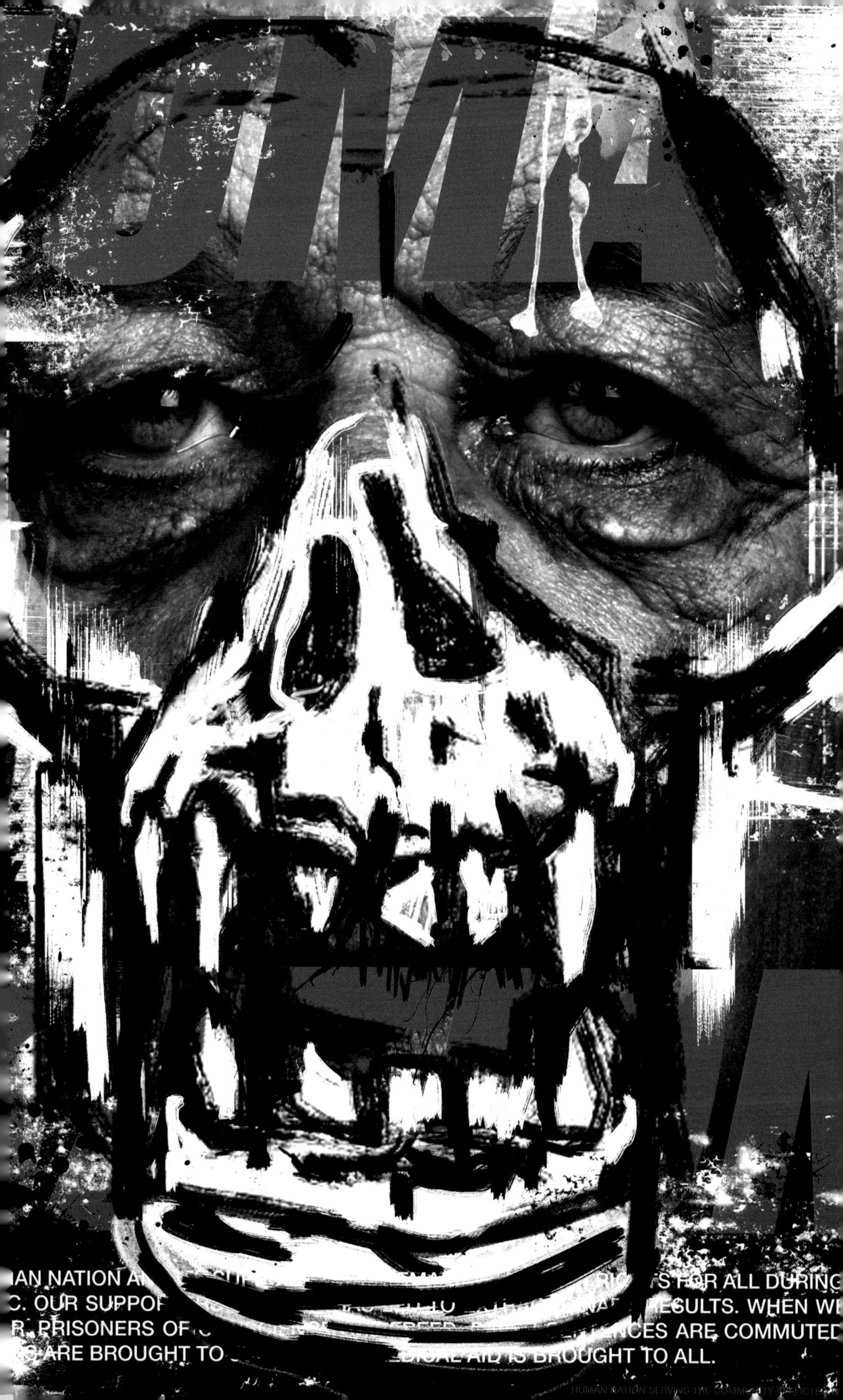

AN NATION A
S FOR ALL DURING
C. OUR SUPPO
ESULTS. WHEN W
R. PRISONERS OF
NCES ARE COMMUTED
ARE BROUGHT TO
DICAL AID IS BROUGHT TO ALL.
HUMAN NATION SERVING THE COMMUNITY

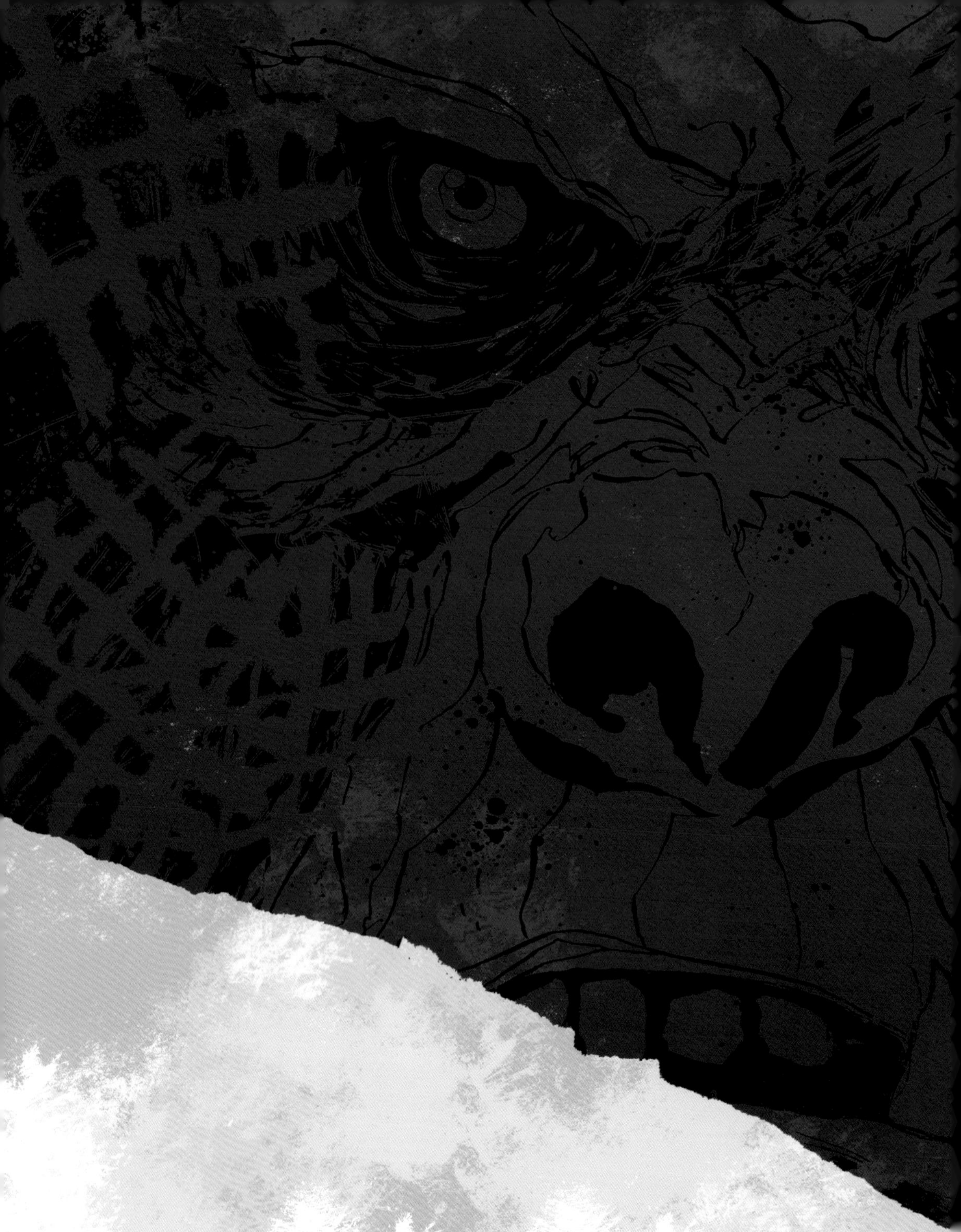

CHAPTER**THREE**

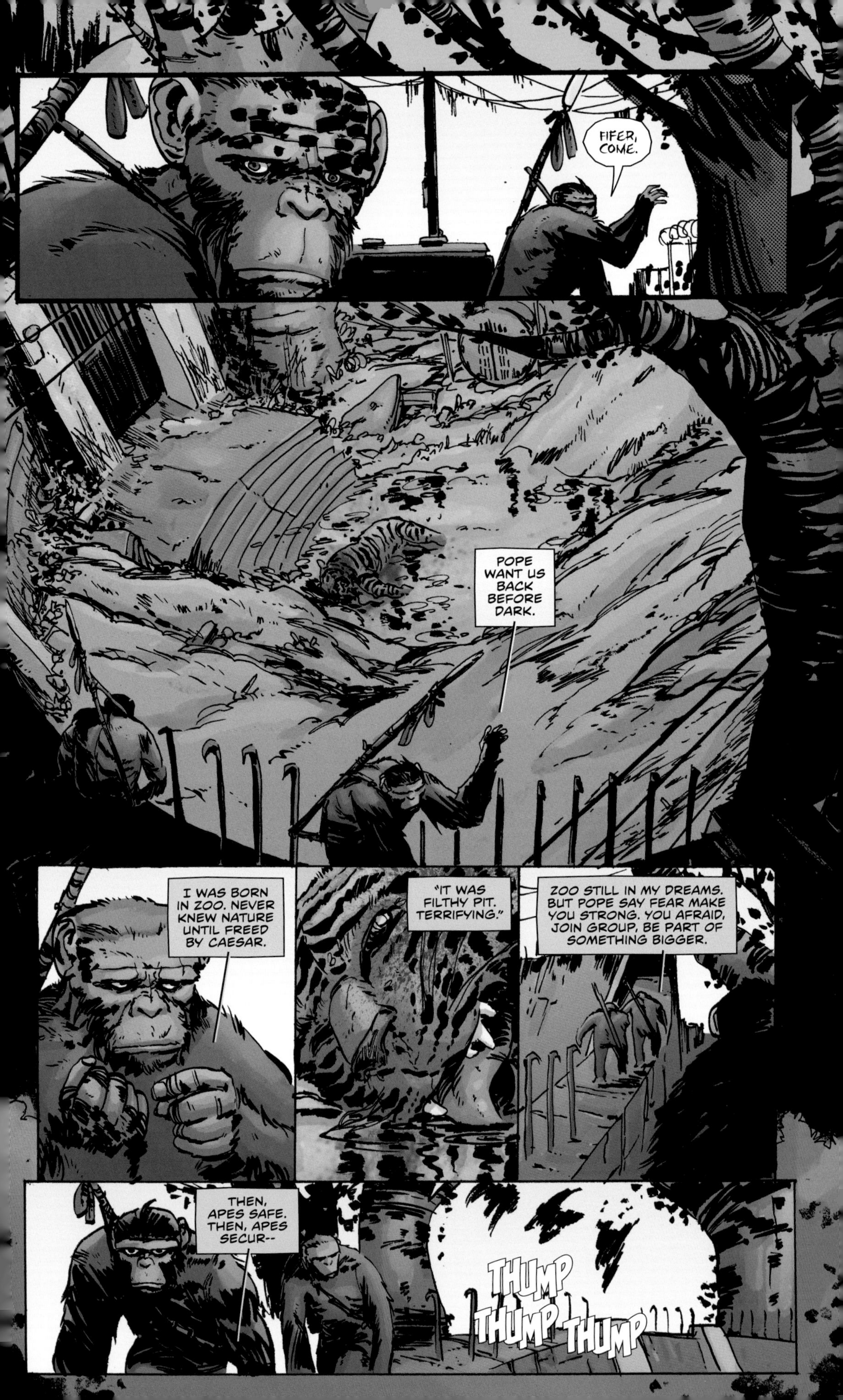
FIFER, COME.
POPE WANT US BACK BEFORE DARK.
I WAS BORN IN ZOO. NEVER KNEW NATURE UNTIL FREED BY CAESAR.
"IT WAS FILTHY PIT. TERRIFYING."
ZOO STILL IN MY DREAMS. BUT POPE SAY FEAR MAKE YOU STRONG. YOU AFRAID, JOIN GROUP, BE PART OF SOMETHING BIGGER.
THEN, APES SAFE. THEN, APES SECUR--
THUMP THUMP THUMP

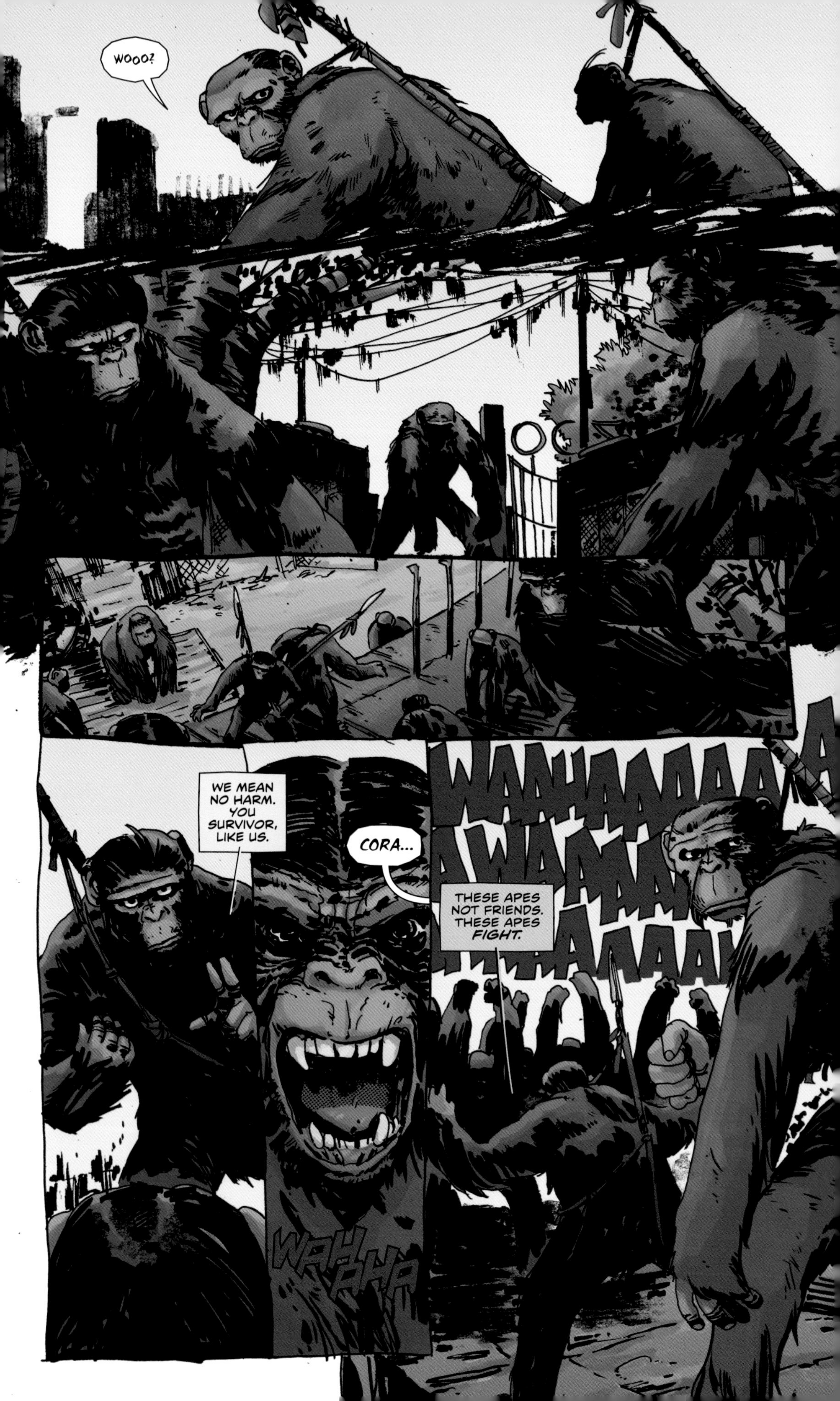
WOOO?
WE MEAN NO HARM. YOU SURVIVOR, LIKE US.
CORA...
WAHAAAAAA
AWAAAAAA
AAAAAAA
THESE APES NOT FRIENDS. THESE APES FIGHT.
WAH AHA

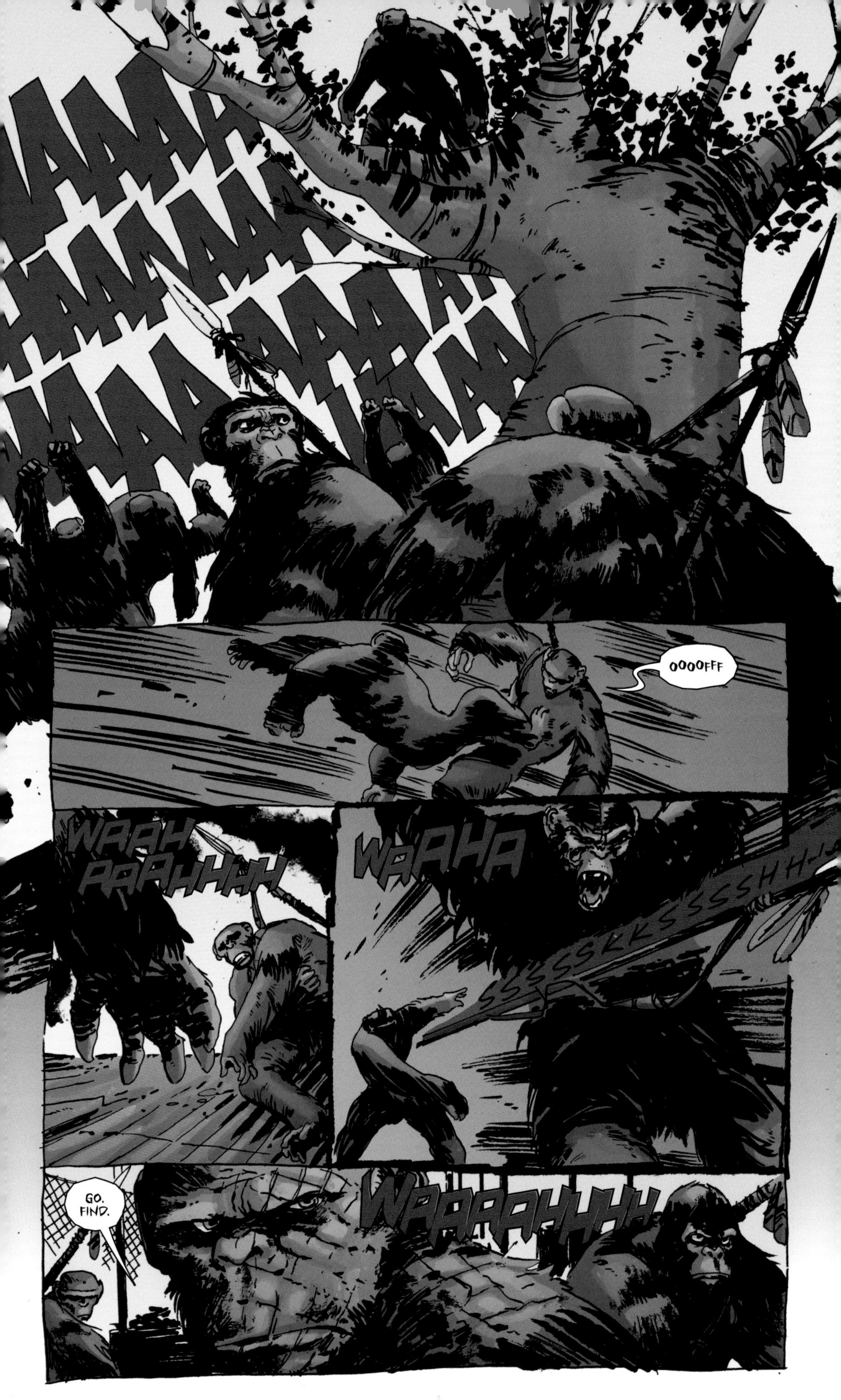
OOOOFFF
WAAHA
GO. FIND.

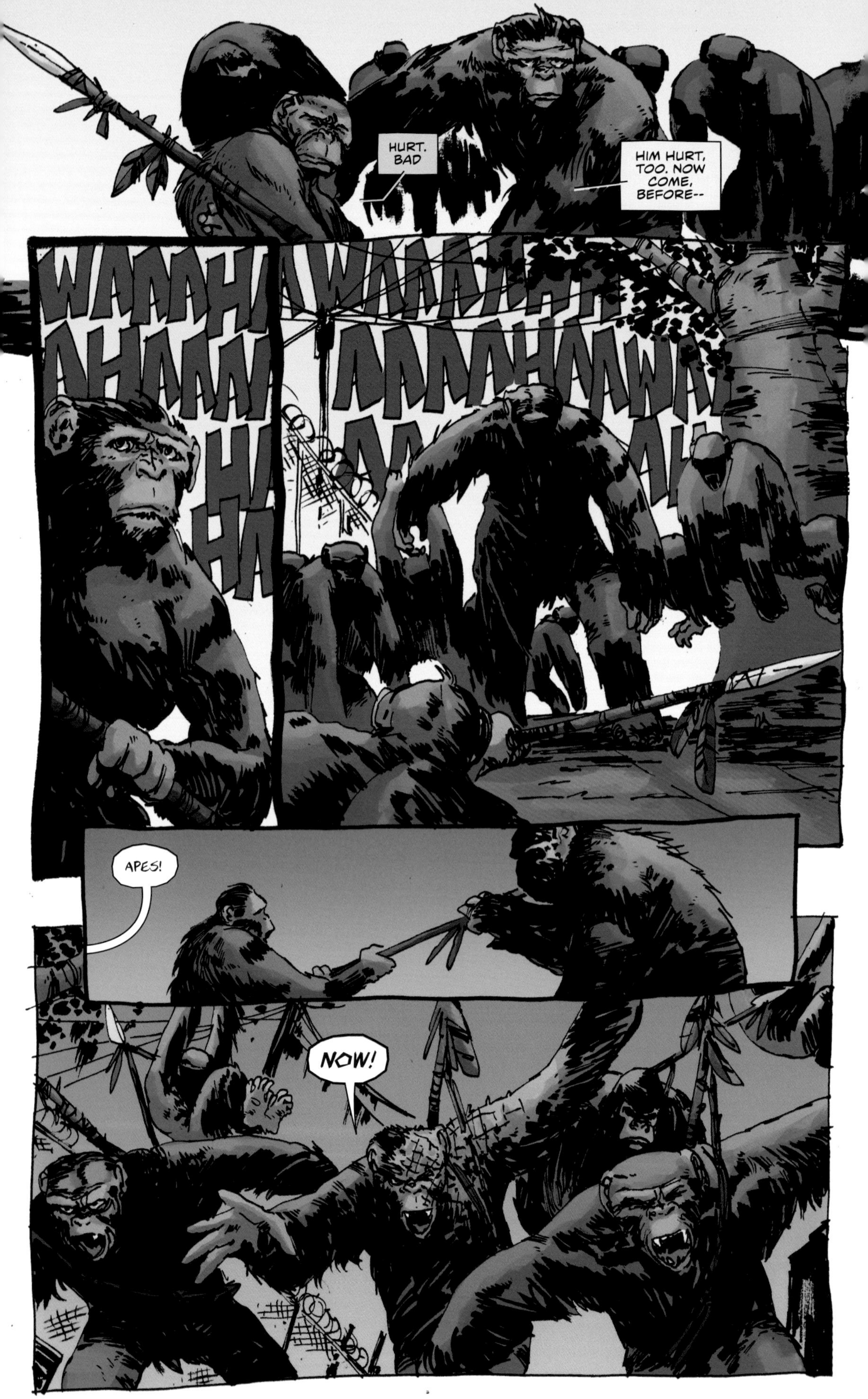
HURT. BAD
HIM HURT, TOO. NOW COME, BEFORE--
WAAAHAAHAAAAHAHA
WAAAAAAAAHAAAAAHAAWAAAAAH
APES!
NOW!

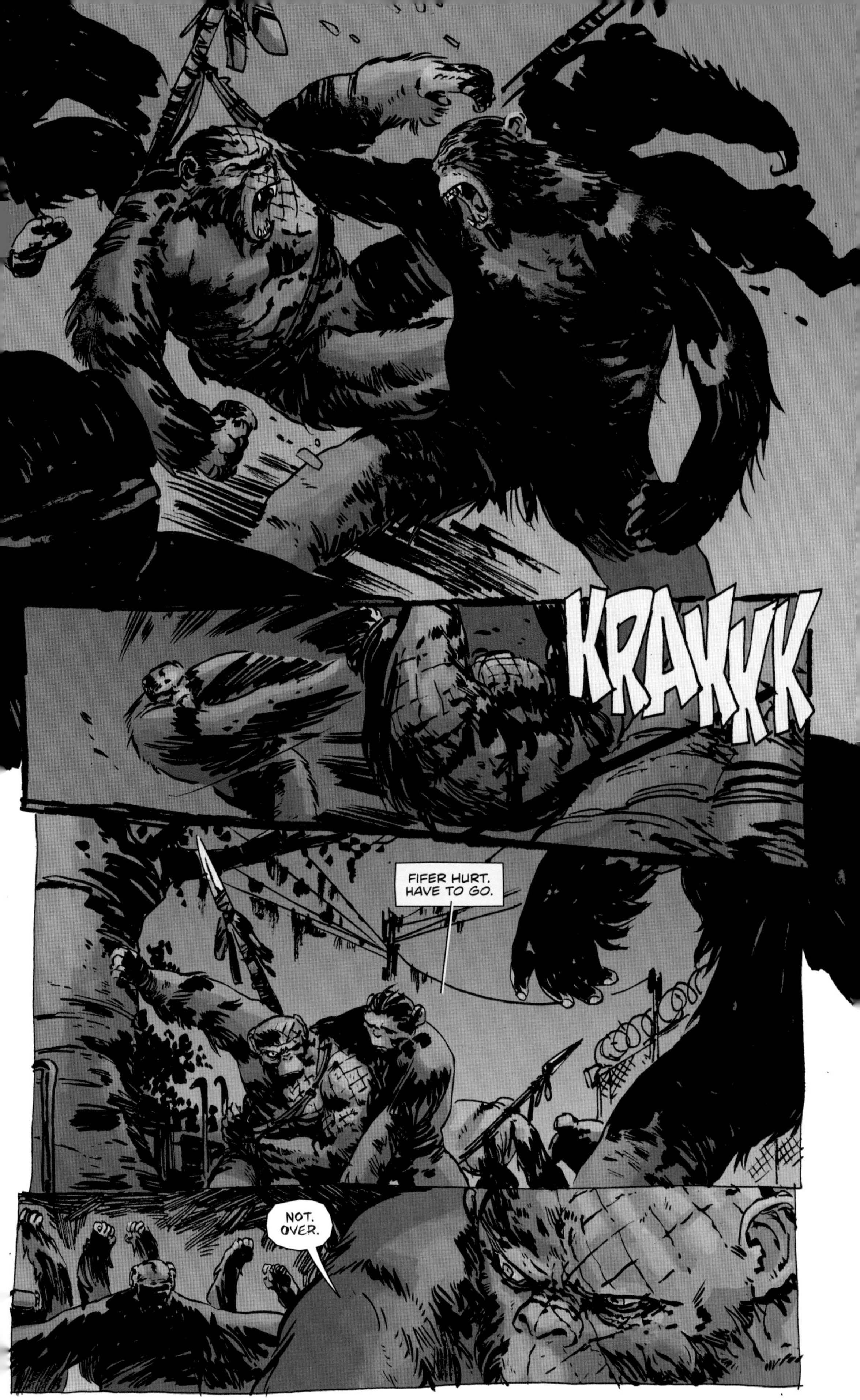
KRAKKK
FIFER HURT. HAVE TO GO.
NOT. OVER.

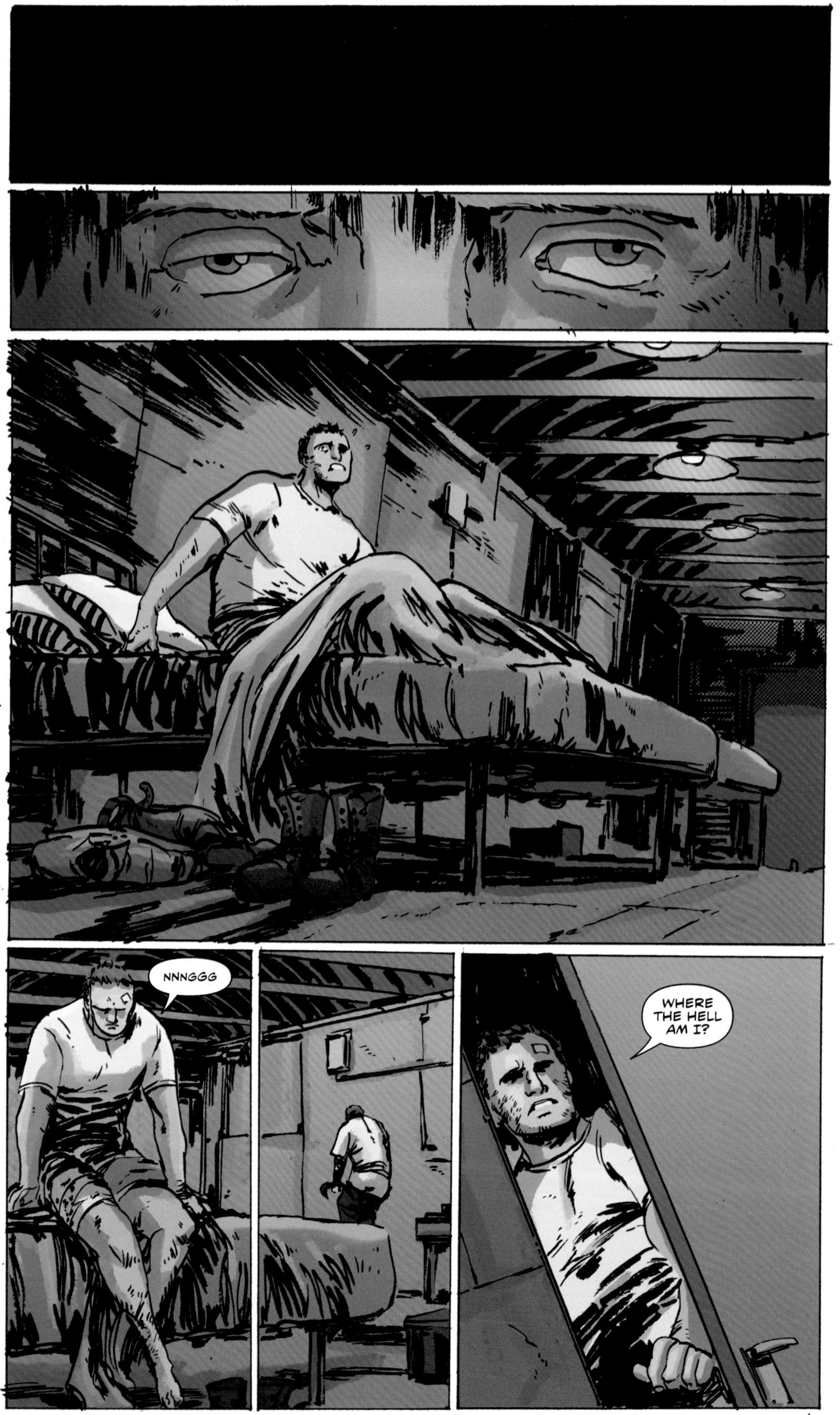
NNNGGG
WHERE THE HELL AM I?

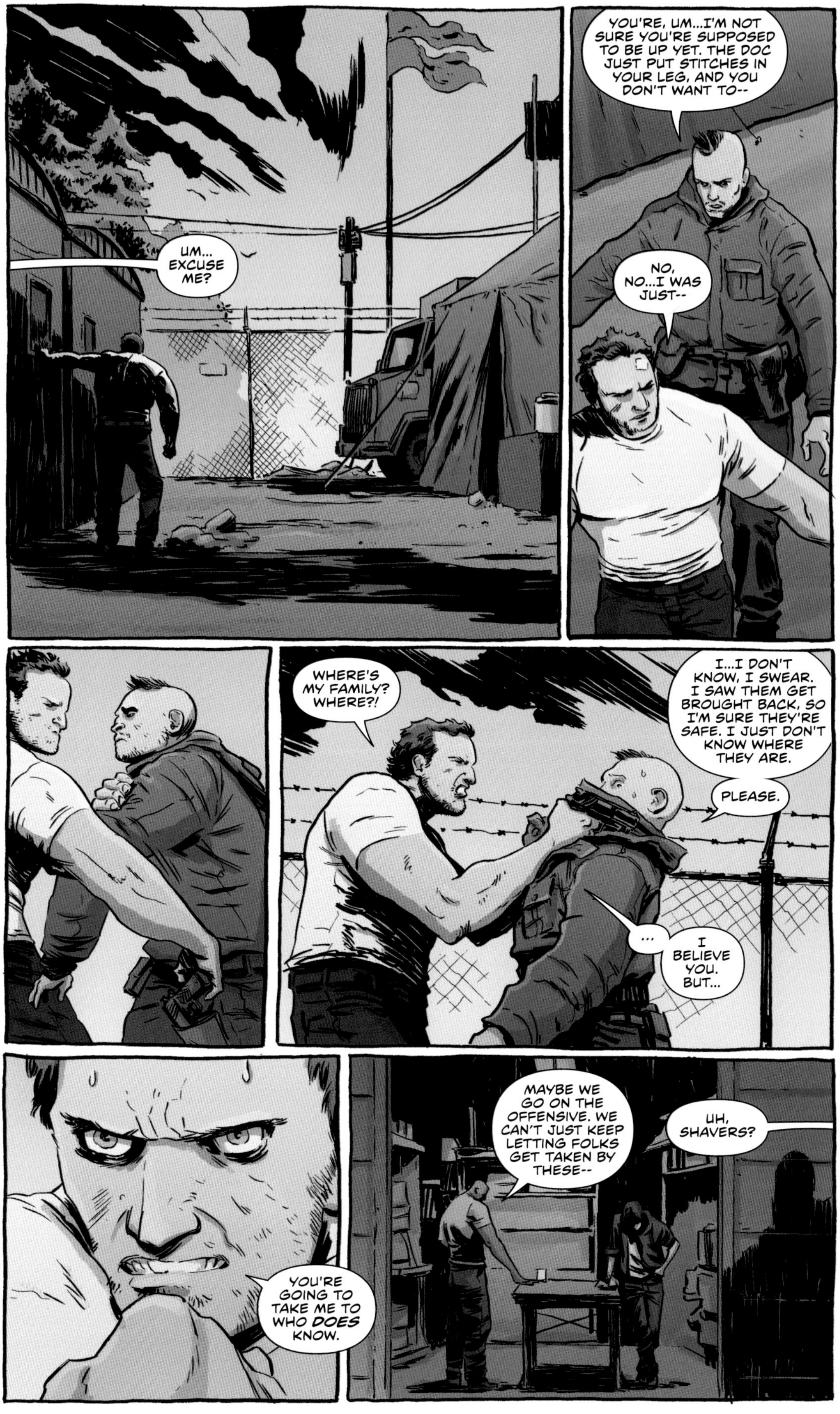
UM... EXCUSE ME?
YOU'RE, UM...I'M NOT SURE YOU'RE SUPPOSED TO BE UP YET. THE DOC JUST PUT STITCHES IN YOUR LEG, AND YOU DON'T WANT TO--
NO, NO...I WAS JUST--
WHERE'S MY FAMILY? WHERE?!
I...I DON'T KNOW, I SWEAR. I SAW THEM GET BROUGHT BACK, SO I'M SURE THEY'RE SAFE. I JUST DON'T KNOW WHERE THEY ARE.
PLEASE.
...
I BELIEVE YOU. BUT...
YOU'RE GOING TO TAKE ME TO WHO DOES KNOW.
MAYBE WE GO ON THE OFFENSIVE. WE CAN'T JUST KEEP LETTING FOLKS GET TAKEN BY THESE--
UH, SHAVERS?

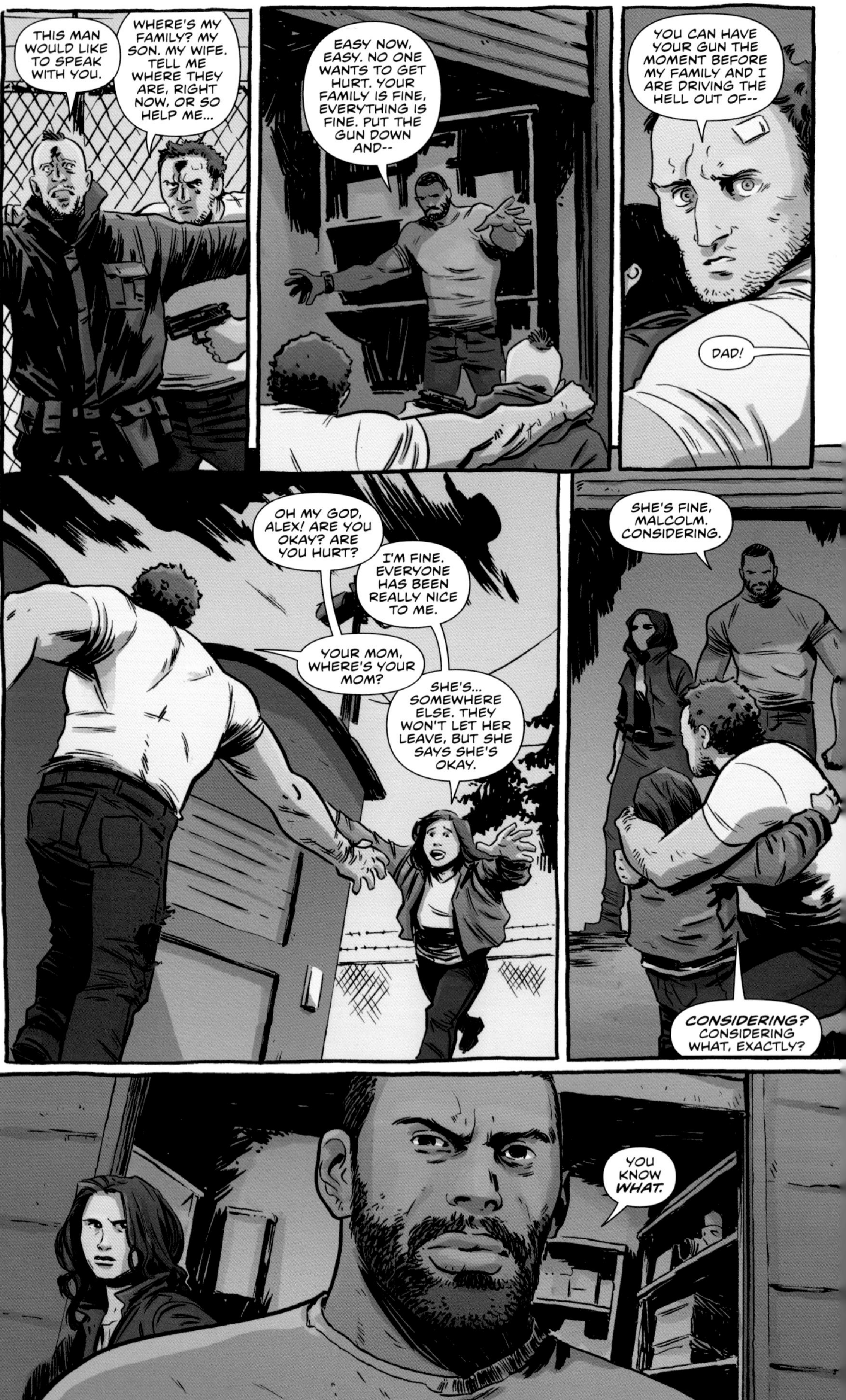
THIS MAN WOULD LIKE TO SPEAK WITH YOU.
WHERE'S MY FAMILY? MY SON. MY WIFE. TELL ME WHERE THEY ARE, RIGHT NOW, OR SO HELP ME...
EASY NOW, EASY. NO ONE WANTS TO GET HURT. YOUR FAMILY IS FINE, EVERYTHING IS FINE. PUT THE GUN DOWN AND--
YOU CAN HAVE YOUR GUN THE MOMENT BEFORE MY FAMILY AND I ARE DRIVING THE HELL OUT OF--
DAD!
OH MY GOD, ALEX! ARE YOU OKAY? ARE YOU HURT?
I'M FINE. EVERYONE HAS BEEN REALLY NICE TO ME.
YOUR MOM, WHERE'S YOUR MOM?
SHE'S... SOMEWHERE ELSE. THEY WON'T LET HER LEAVE, BUT SHE SAYS SHE'S OKAY.
SHE'S FINE, MALCOLM. CONSIDERING.
CONSIDERING? CONSIDERING WHAT, EXACTLY?
YOU KNOW WHAT.

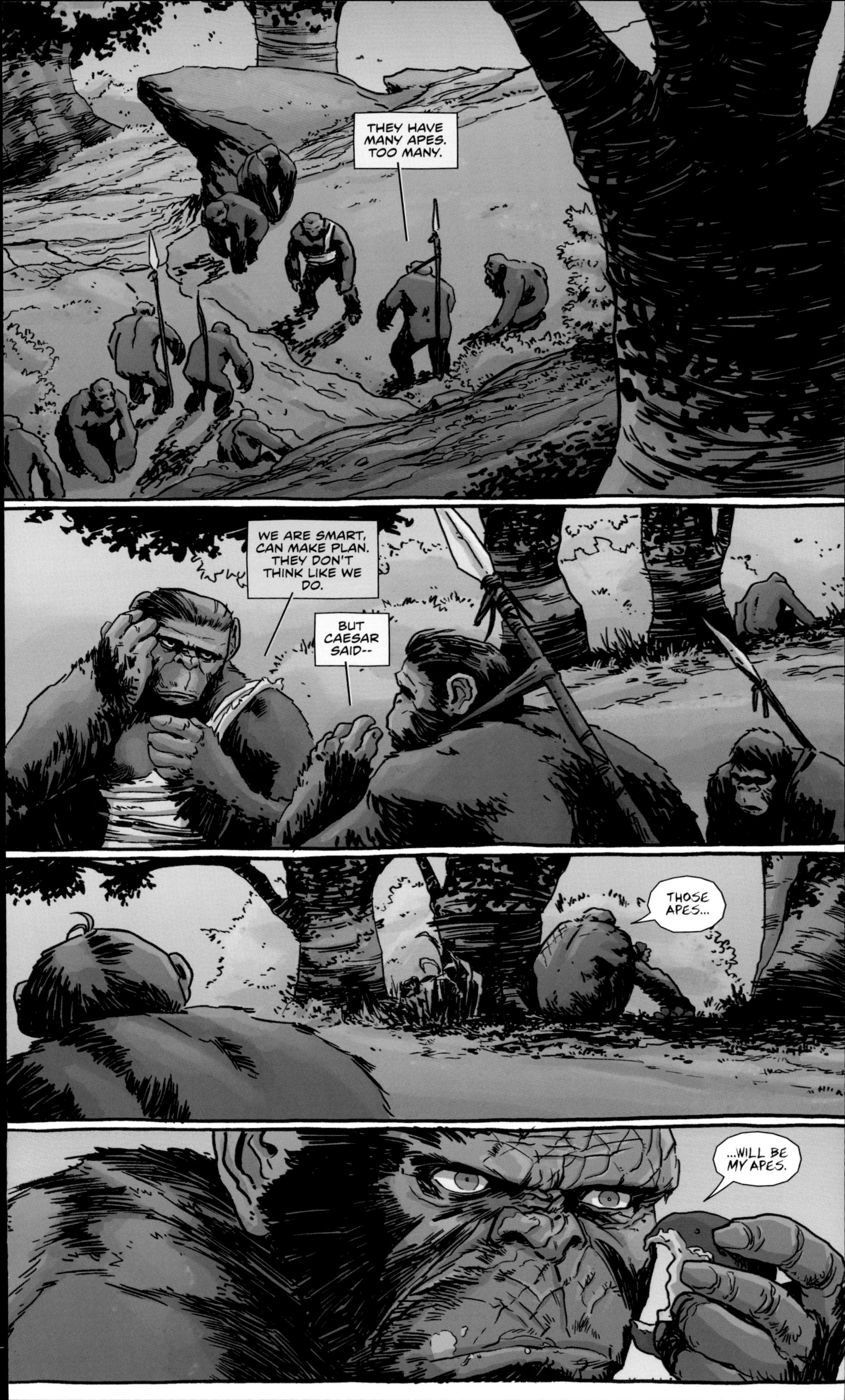
THEY HAVE MANY APES. TOO MANY.
WE ARE SMART, CAN MAKE PLAN. THEY DON'T THINK LIKE WE DO.
BUT CAESAR SAID--
THOSE APES...
...WILL BE MY APES.

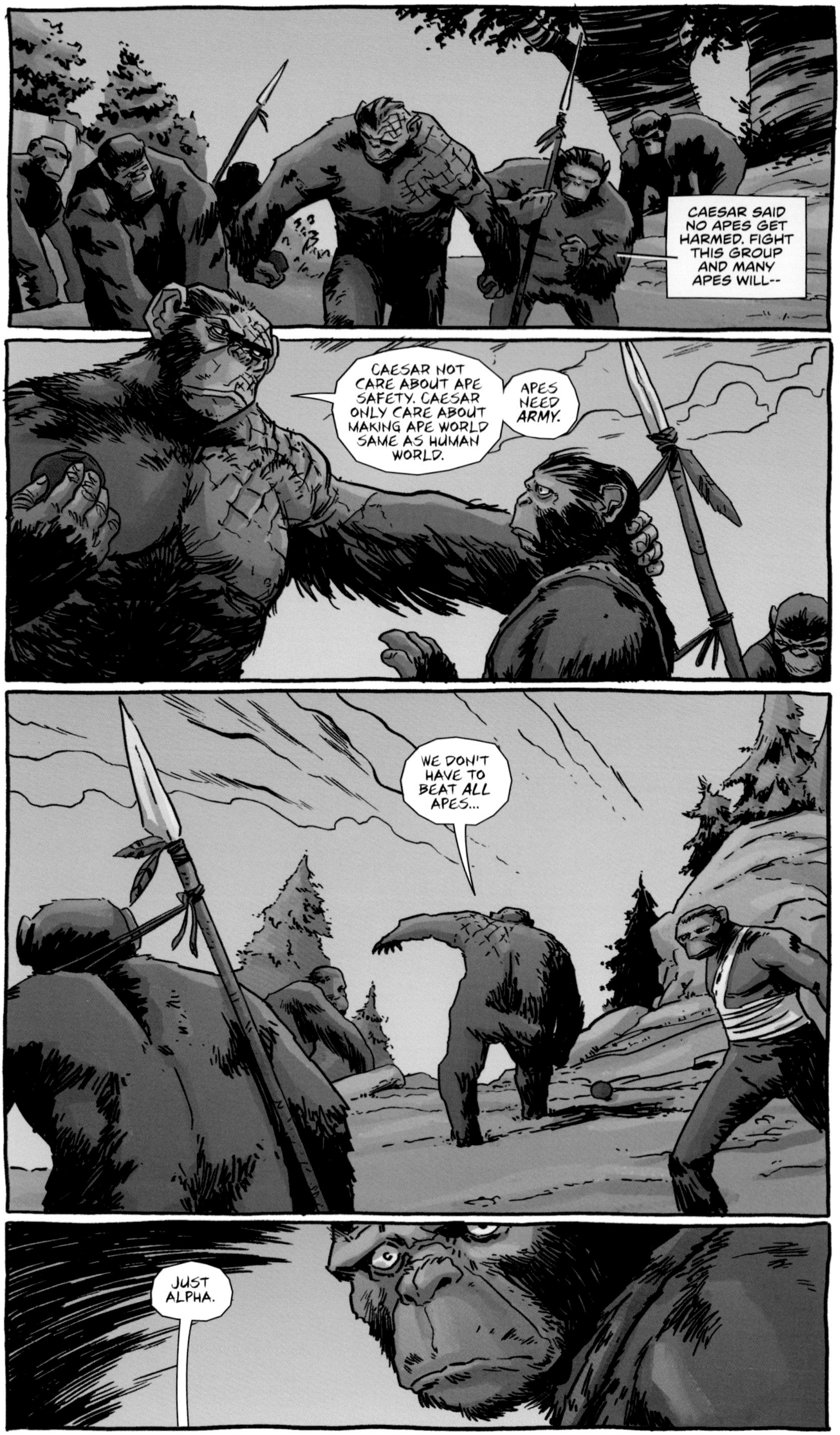
CAESAR SAID NO APES GET HARMED. FIGHT THIS GROUP AND MANY APES WILL--
CAESAR NOT CARE ABOUT APE SAFETY. CAESAR ONLY CARE ABOUT MAKING APE WORLD SAME AS HUMAN WORLD.
APES NEED *ARMY.*
WE DON'T HAVE TO BEAT *ALL* APES...
JUST ALPHA.

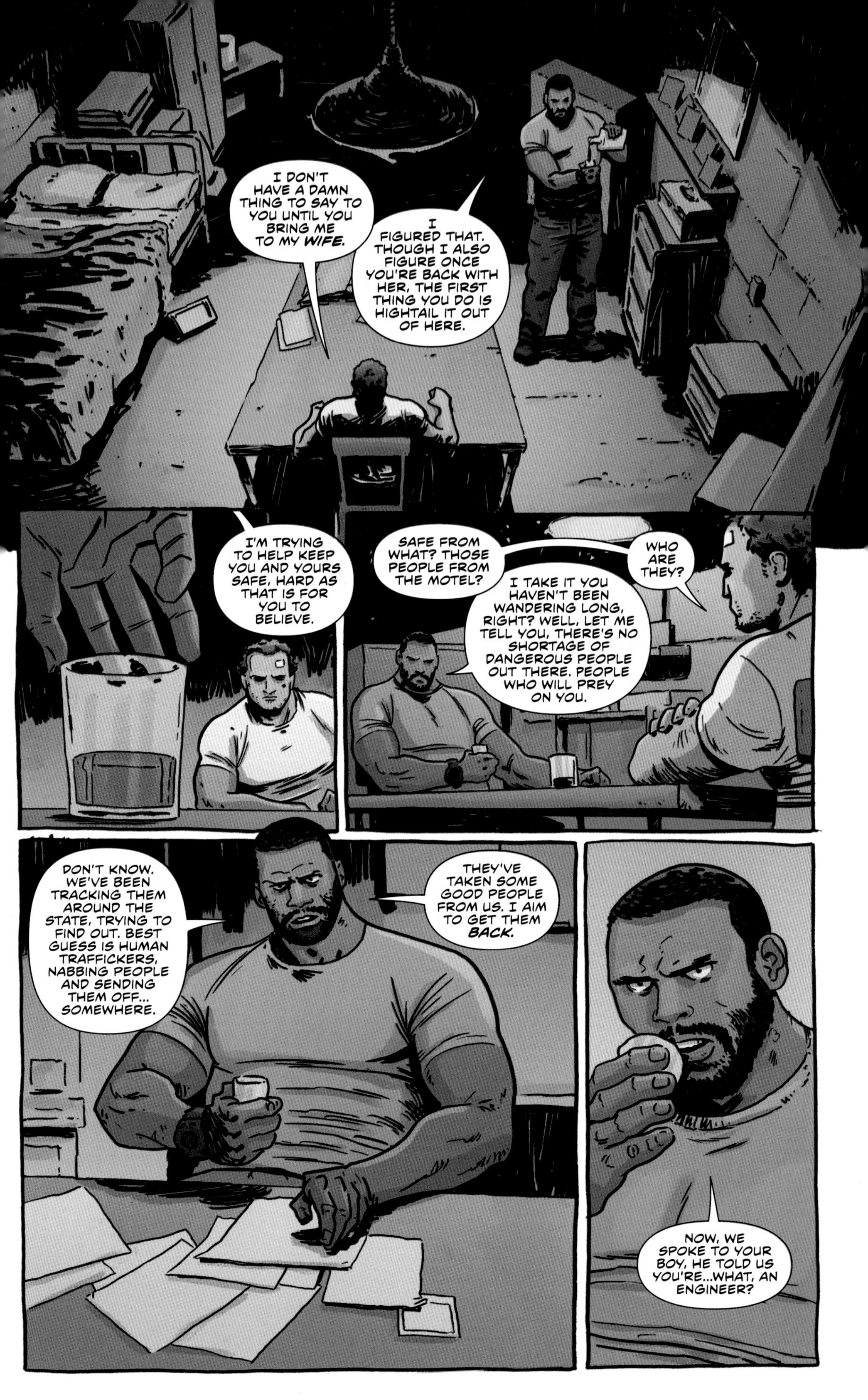
I DON'T HAVE A DAMN THING TO SAY TO YOU UNTIL YOU BRING ME TO MY *WIFE*.
I FIGURED THAT. THOUGH I ALSO FIGURE ONCE YOU'RE BACK WITH HER, THE FIRST THING YOU DO IS HIGHTAIL IT OUT OF HERE.
I'M TRYING TO HELP KEEP YOU AND YOURS SAFE, HARD AS THAT IS FOR YOU TO BELIEVE.
SAFE FROM WHAT? THOSE PEOPLE FROM THE MOTEL?
I TAKE IT YOU HAVEN'T BEEN WANDERING LONG, RIGHT? WELL, LET ME TELL YOU, THERE'S NO SHORTAGE OF DANGEROUS PEOPLE OUT THERE. PEOPLE WHO WILL PREY ON YOU.
WHO ARE THEY?
DON'T KNOW. WE'VE BEEN TRACKING THEM AROUND THE STATE, TRYING TO FIND OUT. BEST GUESS IS HUMAN TRAFFICKERS, NABBING PEOPLE AND SENDING THEM OFF... SOMEWHERE.
THEY'VE TAKEN SOME GOOD PEOPLE FROM US. I AIM TO GET THEM *BACK*.
NOW, WE SPOKE TO YOUR BOY, HE TOLD US YOU'RE...WHAT, AN ENGINEER?

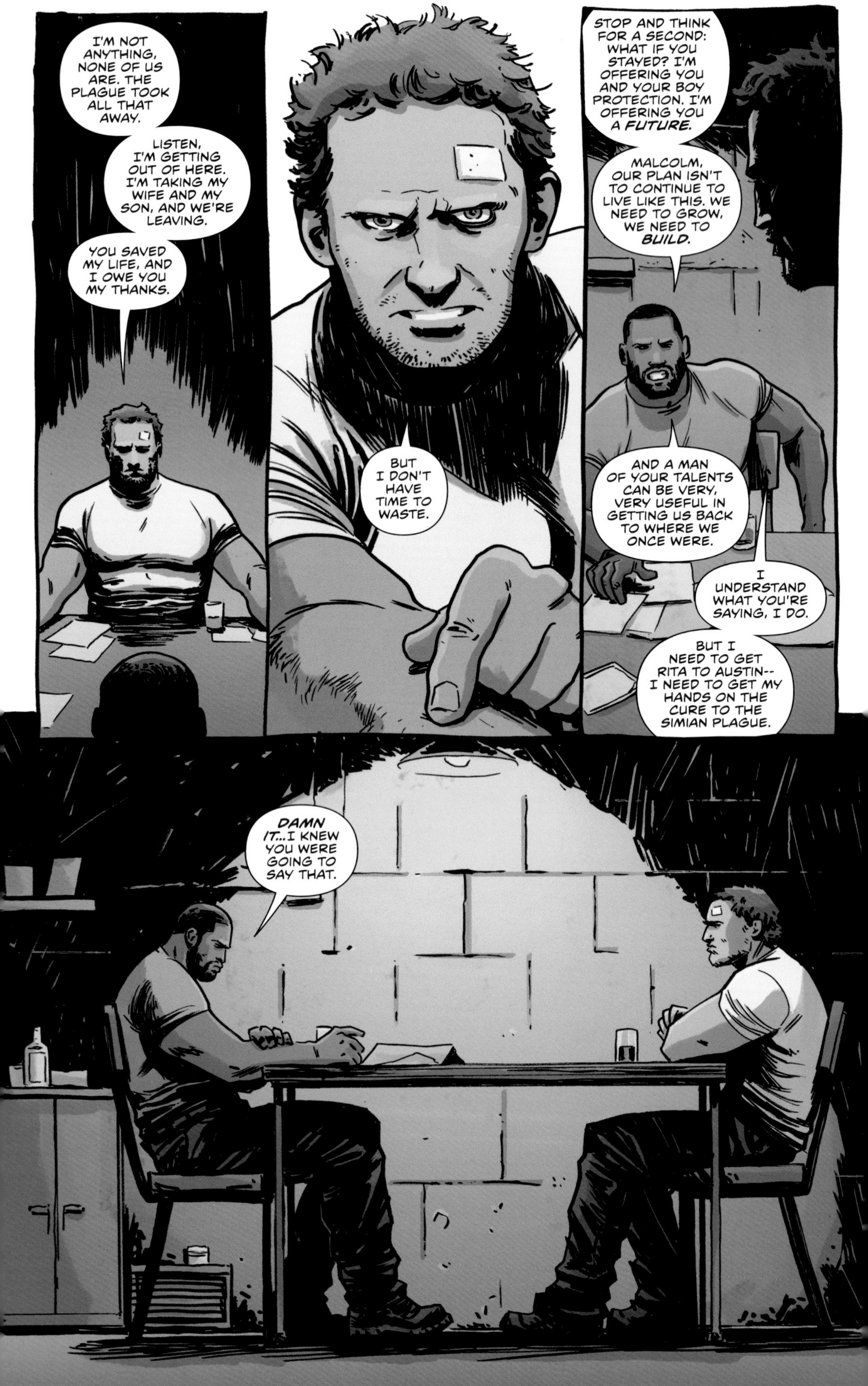
I'M NOT ANYTHING, NONE OF US ARE. THE PLAGUE TOOK ALL THAT AWAY.
LISTEN, I'M GETTING OUT OF HERE. I'M TAKING MY WIFE AND MY SON, AND WE'RE LEAVING.
YOU SAVED MY LIFE, AND I OWE YOU MY THANKS.
BUT I DON'T HAVE TIME TO WASTE.
STOP AND THINK FOR A SECOND: WHAT IF YOU STAYED? I'M OFFERING YOU AND YOUR BOY PROTECTION. I'M OFFERING YOU A *FUTURE.*
MALCOLM, OUR PLAN ISN'T TO CONTINUE TO LIVE LIKE THIS. WE NEED TO GROW, WE NEED TO *BUILD.*
AND A MAN OF YOUR TALENTS CAN BE VERY, VERY USEFUL IN GETTING US BACK TO WHERE WE ONCE WERE.
I UNDERSTAND WHAT YOU'RE SAYING, I DO.
BUT I NEED TO GET RITA TO AUSTIN-- I NEED TO GET MY HANDS ON THE CURE TO THE SIMIAN PLAGUE.
DAMN IT...I KNEW YOU WERE GOING TO SAY THAT.

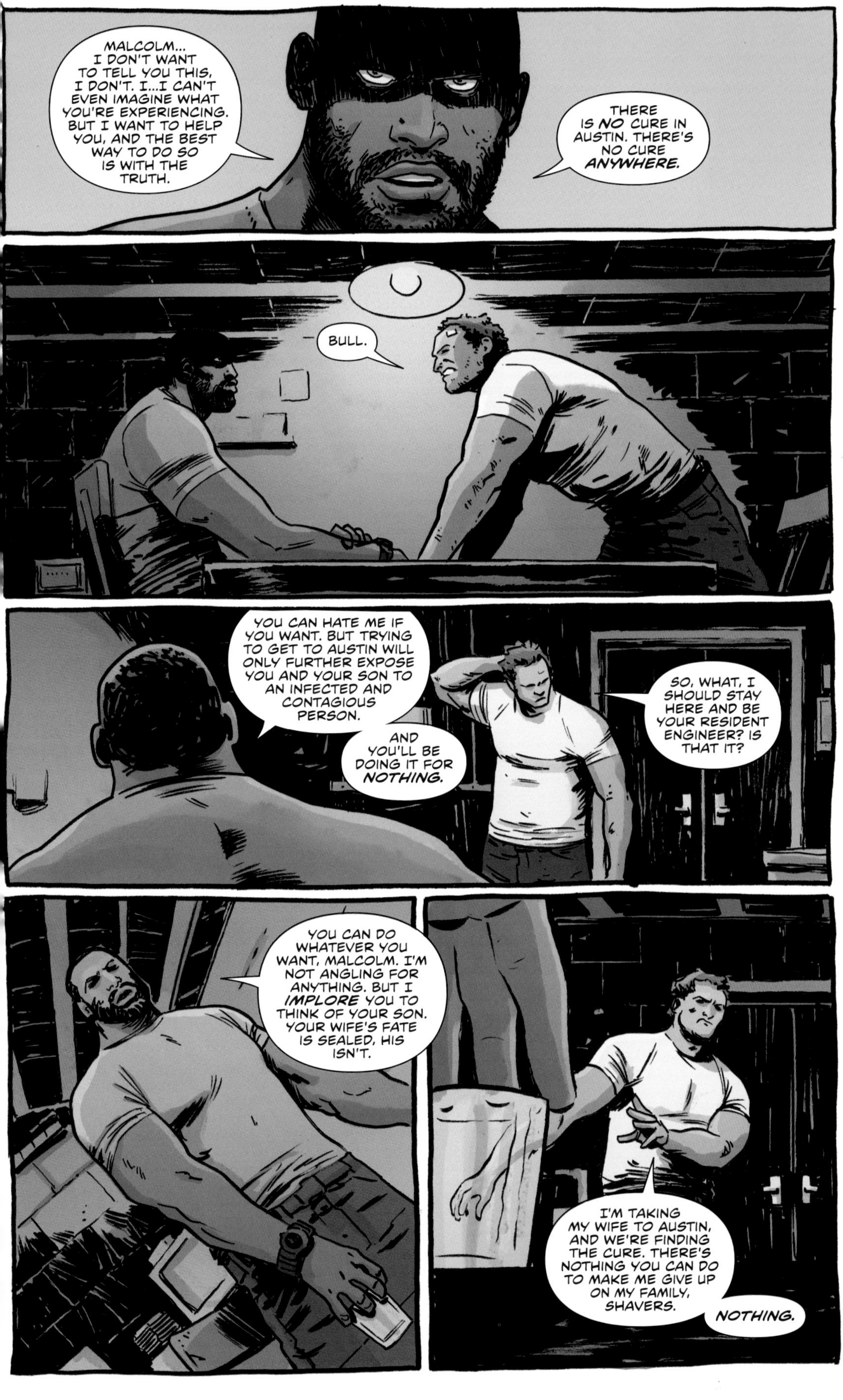
MALCOLM... I DON'T WANT TO TELL YOU THIS, I DON'T. I...I CAN'T EVEN IMAGINE WHAT YOU'RE EXPERIENCING. BUT I WANT TO HELP YOU, AND THE BEST WAY TO DO SO IS WITH THE TRUTH.
THERE IS NO CURE IN AUSTIN. THERE'S NO CURE ANYWHERE.
BULL.
YOU CAN HATE ME IF YOU WANT. BUT TRYING TO GET TO AUSTIN WILL ONLY FURTHER EXPOSE YOU AND YOUR SON TO AN INFECTED AND CONTAGIOUS PERSON.
AND YOU'LL BE DOING IT FOR NOTHING.
SO, WHAT, I SHOULD STAY HERE AND BE YOUR RESIDENT ENGINEER? IS THAT IT?
YOU CAN DO WHATEVER YOU WANT, MALCOLM. I'M NOT ANGLING FOR ANYTHING. BUT I IMPLORE YOU TO THINK OF YOUR SON. YOUR WIFE'S FATE IS SEALED, HIS ISN'T.
I'M TAKING MY WIFE TO AUSTIN, AND WE'RE FINDING THE CURE. THERE'S NOTHING YOU CAN DO TO MAKE ME GIVE UP ON MY FAMILY, SHAVERS.
NOTHING.

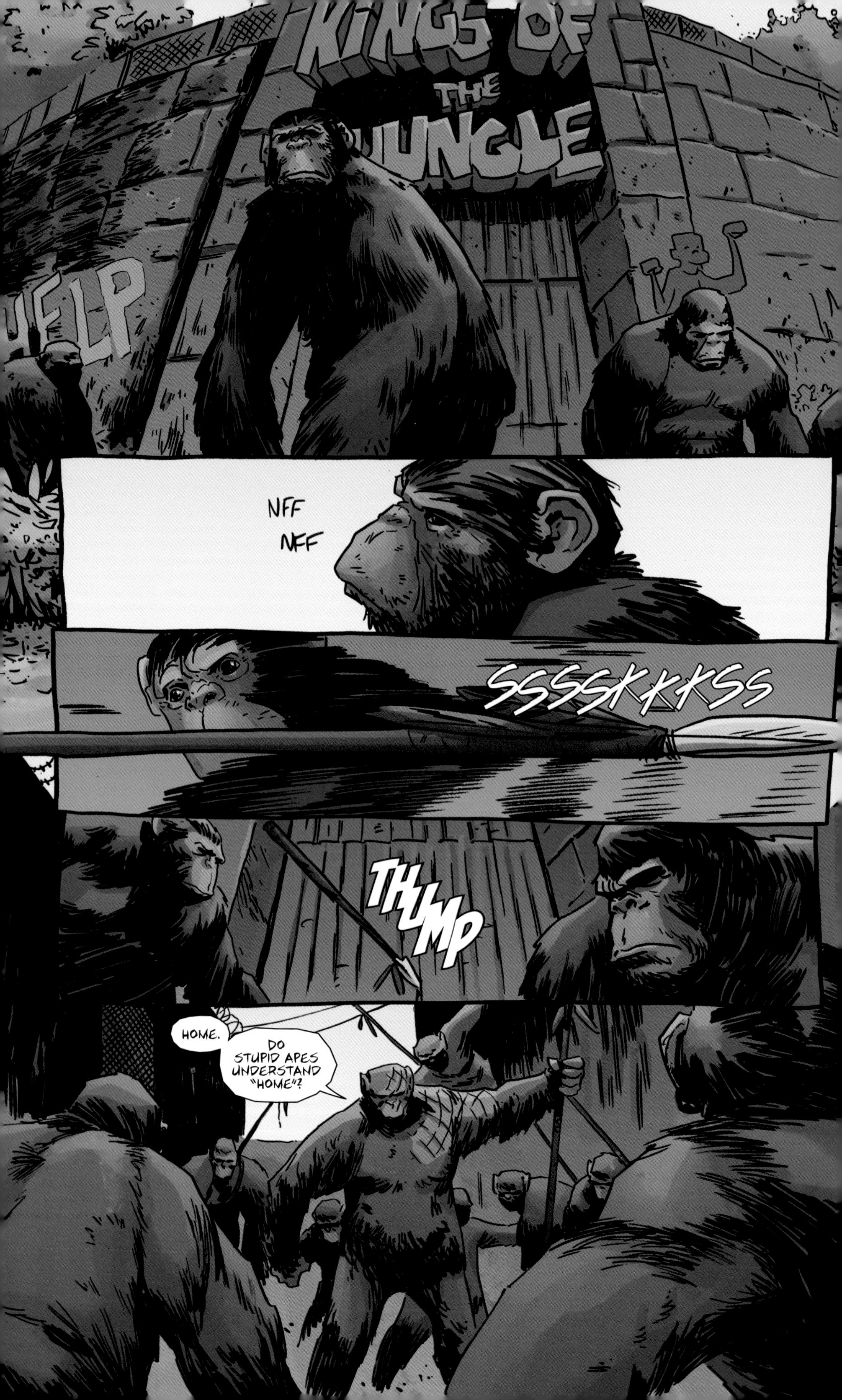

KINGS OF THE JUNGLE
HELP
NFF
NFF
SSSSKKKSS
THUMP
HOME.
DO STUPID APES UNDERSTAND "HOME"?

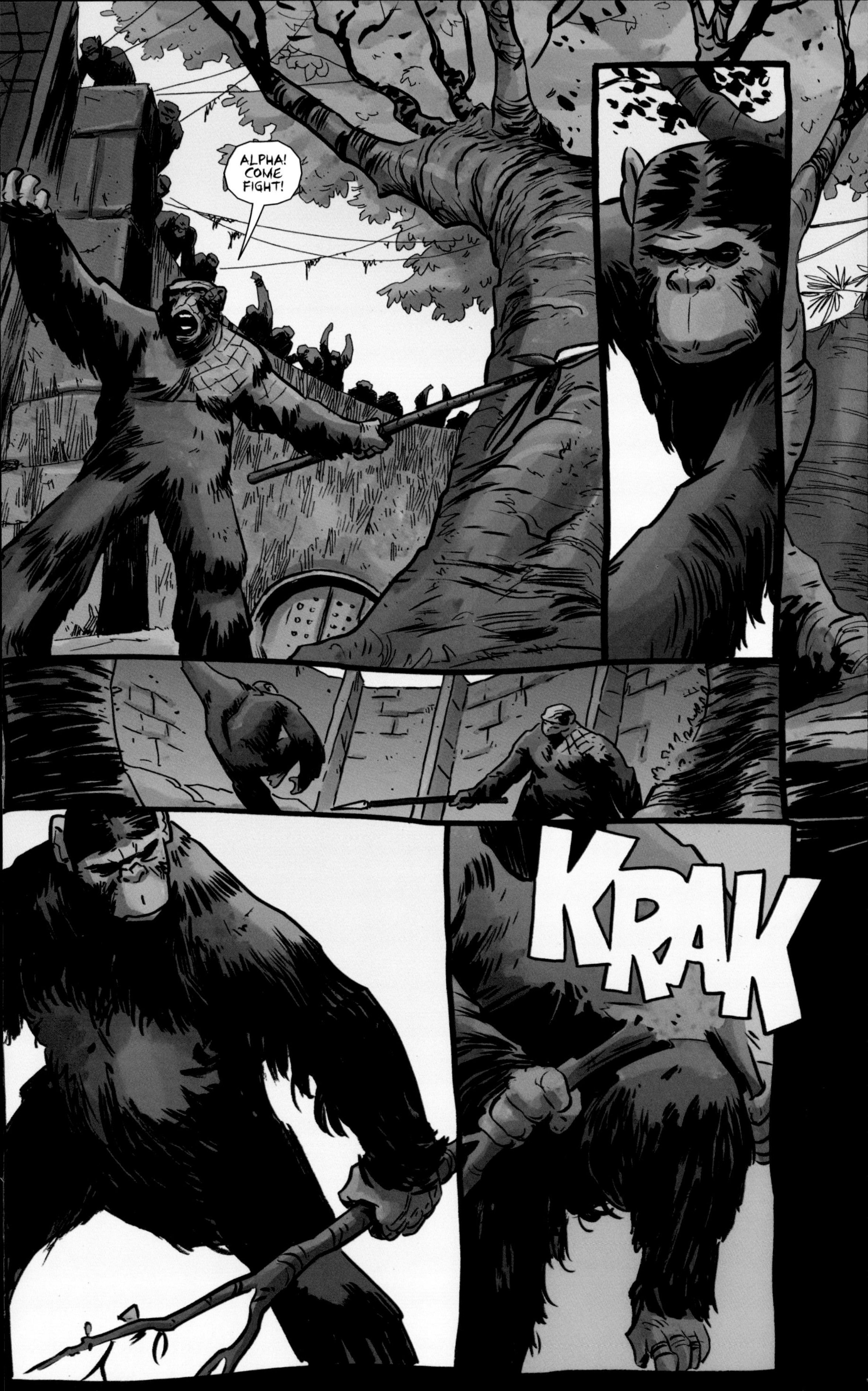
ALPHA! COME FIGHT!
KRAK

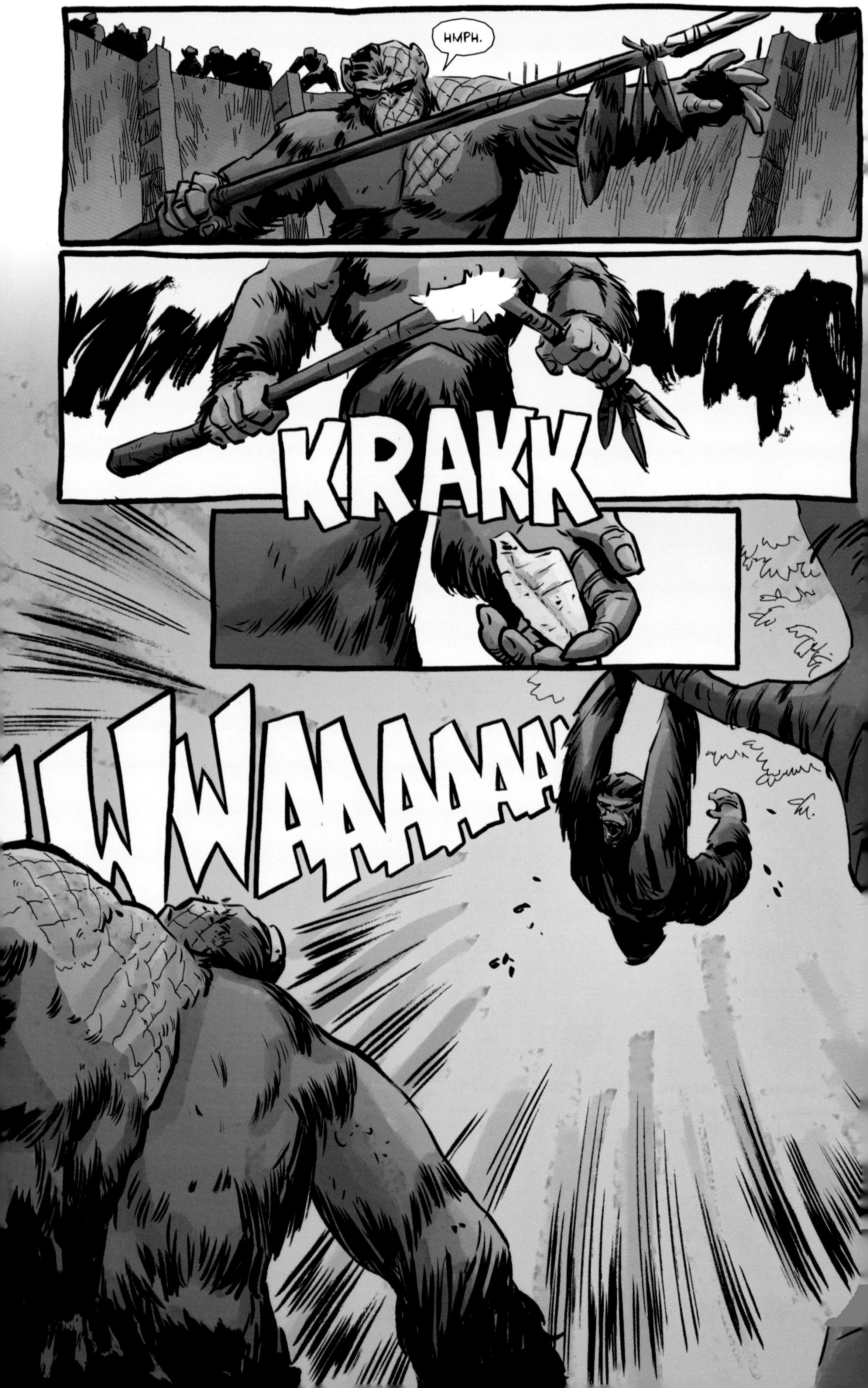
HMPH.
KRAKK
WAAAAAA

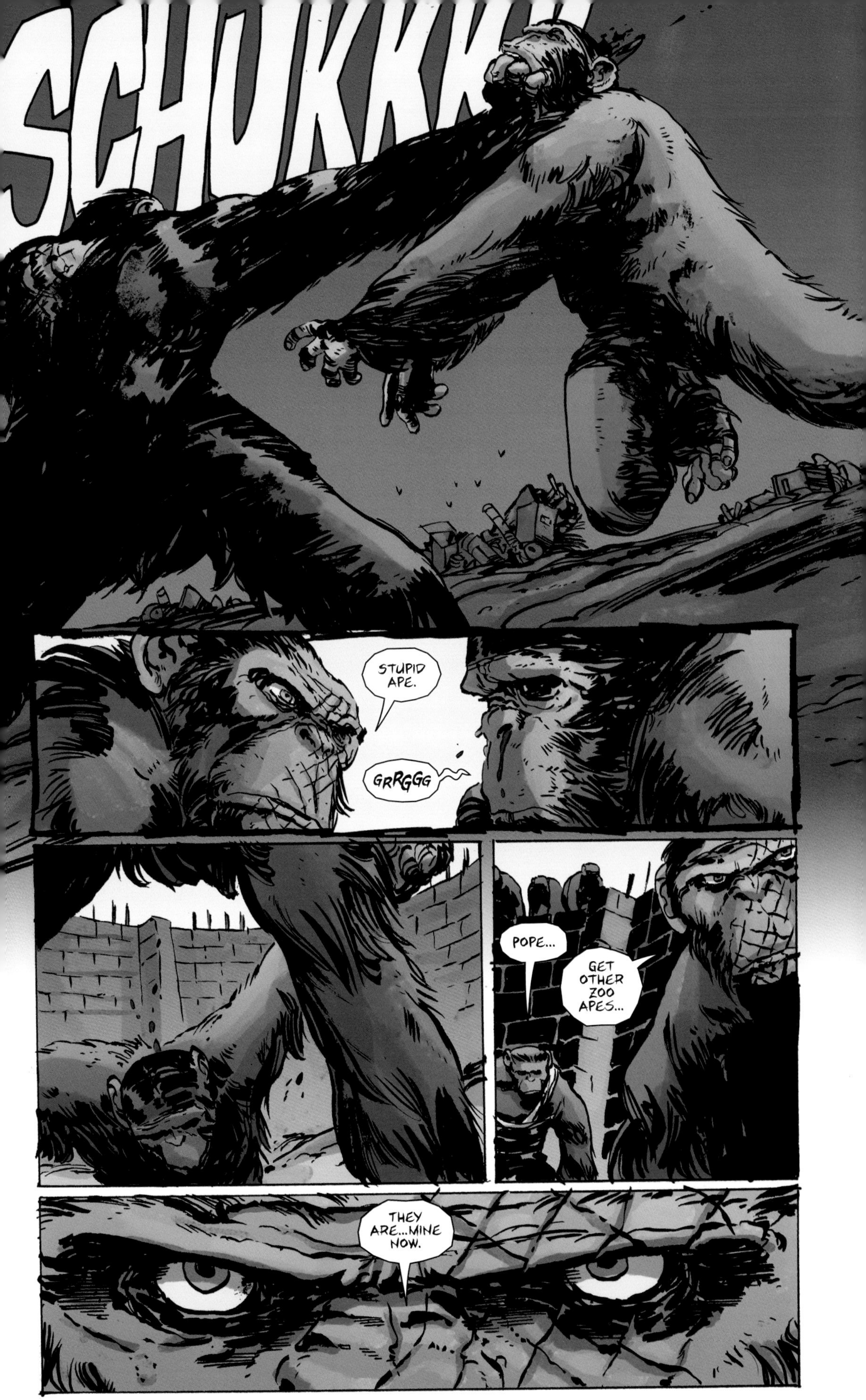
SCHUKKK
STUPID APE.
GRRGGG
POPE...
GET OTHER ZOO APES...
THEY ARE...MINE NOW.

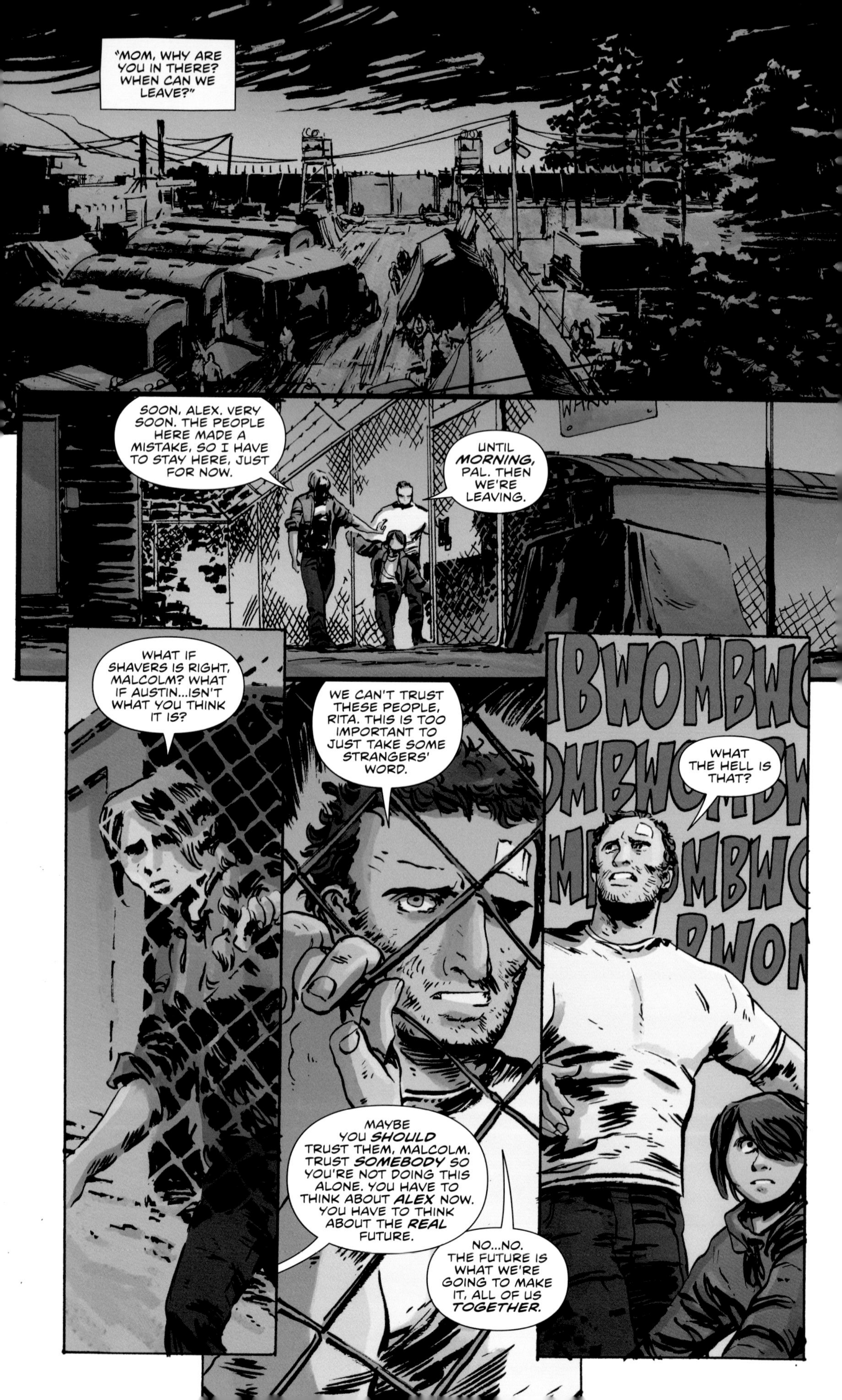
"MOM, WHY ARE YOU IN THERE? WHEN CAN WE LEAVE?"
SOON, ALEX. VERY SOON. THE PEOPLE HERE MADE A MISTAKE, SO I HAVE TO STAY HERE, JUST FOR NOW.
UNTIL *MORNING*, PAL. THEN WE'RE LEAVING.
WHAT IF SHAVERS IS RIGHT, MALCOLM? WHAT IF AUSTIN...ISN'T WHAT YOU THINK IT IS?
WE CAN'T TRUST THESE PEOPLE, RITA. THIS IS TOO IMPORTANT TO JUST TAKE SOME STRANGERS' WORD.
MAYBE YOU *SHOULD* TRUST THEM, MALCOLM. TRUST *SOMEBODY* SO YOU'RE NOT DOING THIS ALONE. YOU HAVE TO THINK ABOUT *ALEX* NOW. YOU HAVE TO THINK ABOUT THE *REAL* FUTURE.
NO...NO. THE FUTURE IS WHAT WE'RE GOING TO MAKE IT, ALL OF US *TOGETHER*.
BWOMBWO
WHAT THE HELL IS THAT?

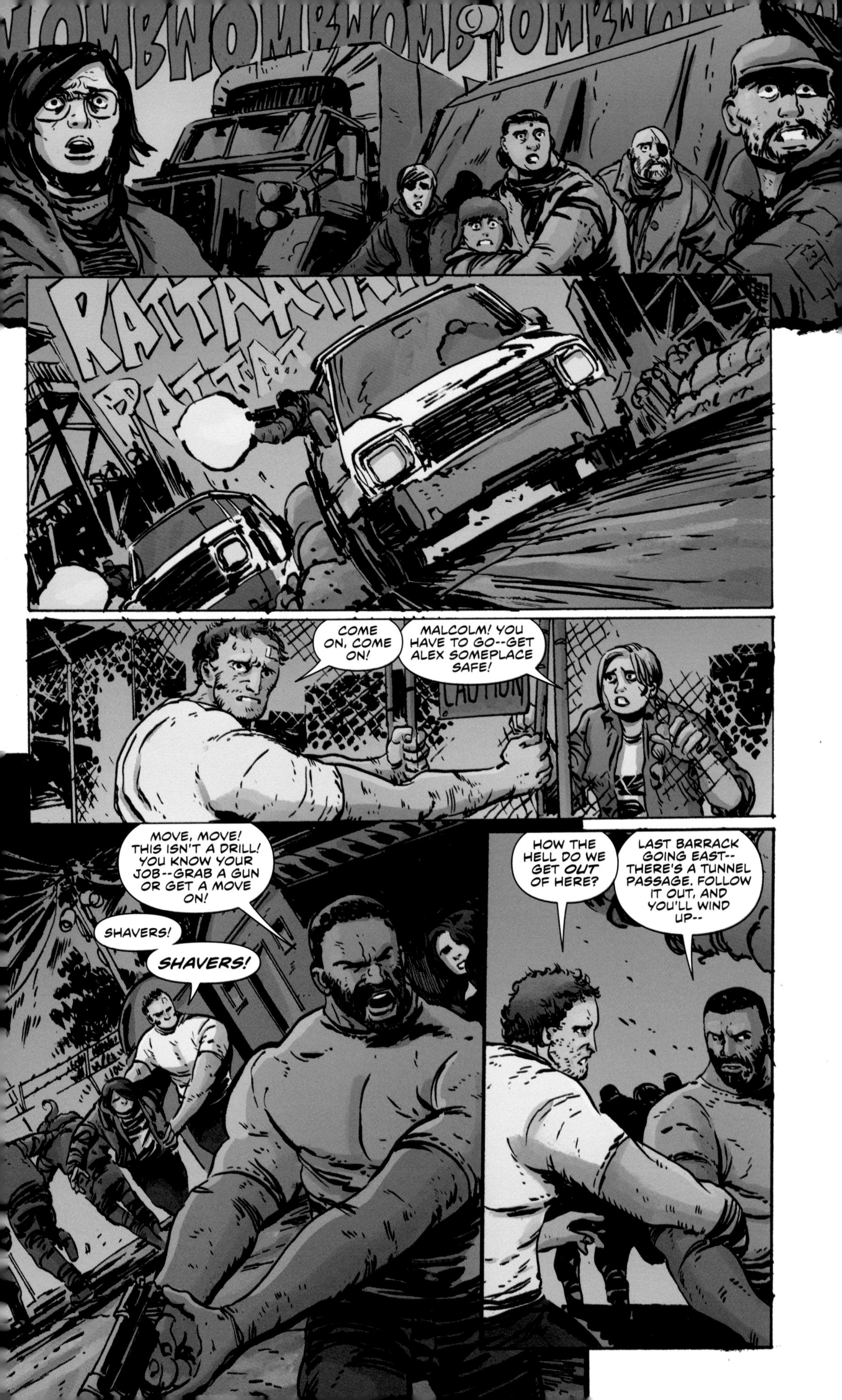
COME ON, COME ON!
MALCOLM! YOU HAVE TO GO--GET ALEX SOMEPLACE SAFE!
MOVE, MOVE! THIS ISN'T A DRILL! YOU KNOW YOUR JOB--GRAB A GUN OR GET A MOVE ON!
SHAVERS!
SHAVERS!
HOW THE HELL DO WE GET *OUT* OF HERE?
LAST BARRACK GOING EAST--THERE'S A TUNNEL PASSAGE. FOLLOW IT OUT, AND YOU'LL WIND UP--

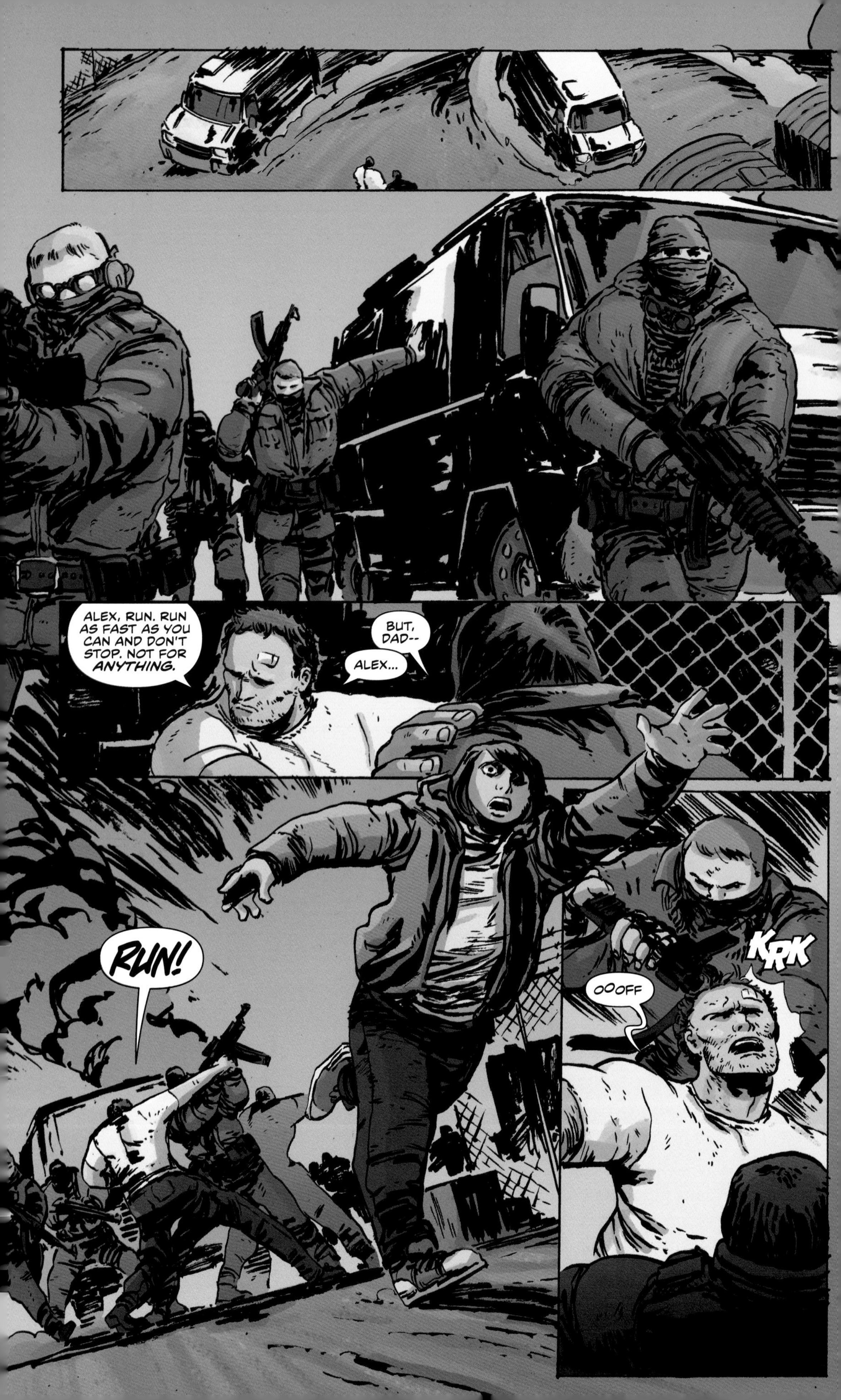
ALEX, RUN. RUN AS FAST AS YOU CAN AND DON'T STOP. NOT FOR ANYTHING.
BUT, DAD--
ALEX...
RUN!
KRK
OOOFF

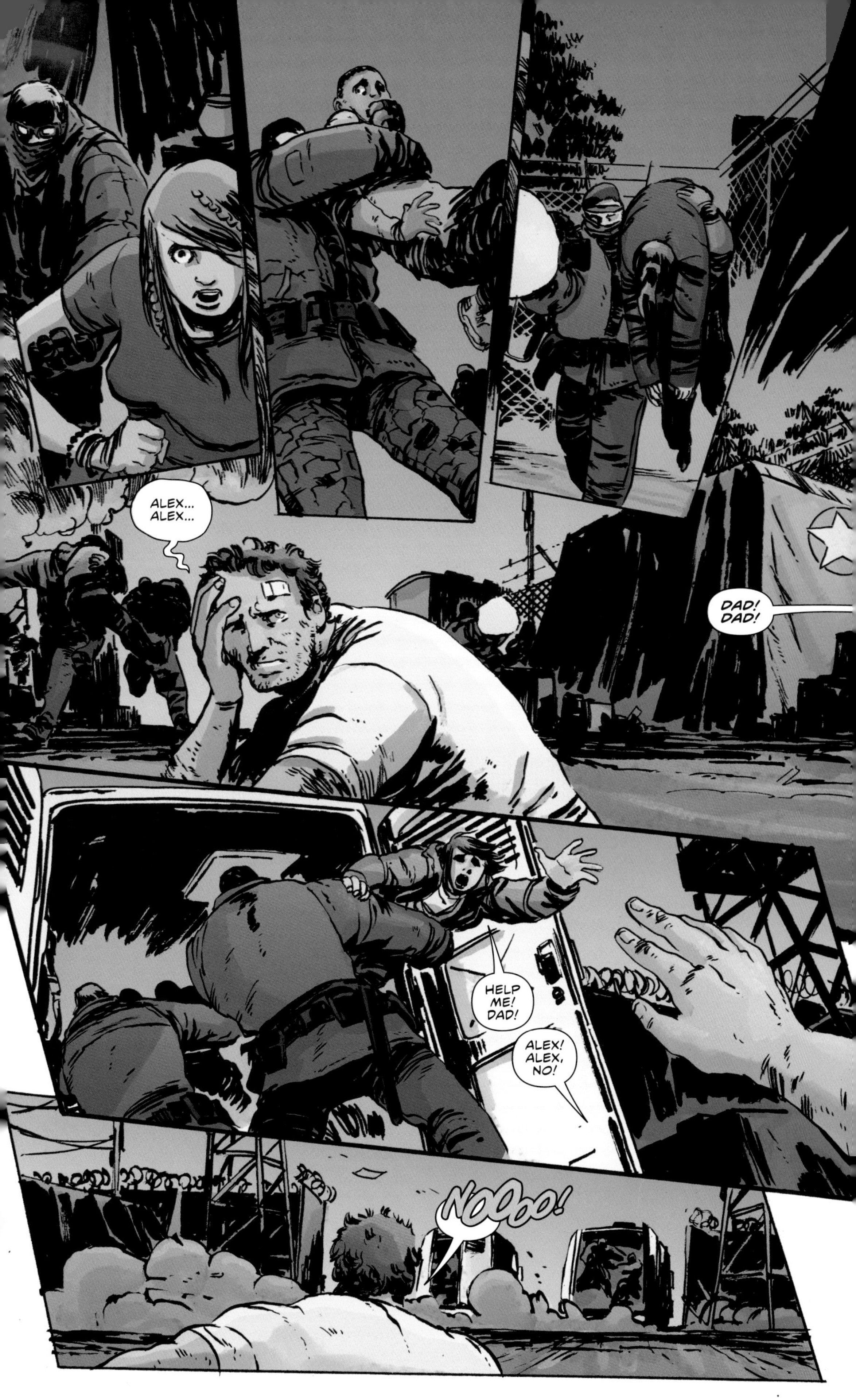
ALEX... ALEX...
DAD! DAD!
HELP ME! DAD!
ALEX! ALEX, NO!
NOOOOO!

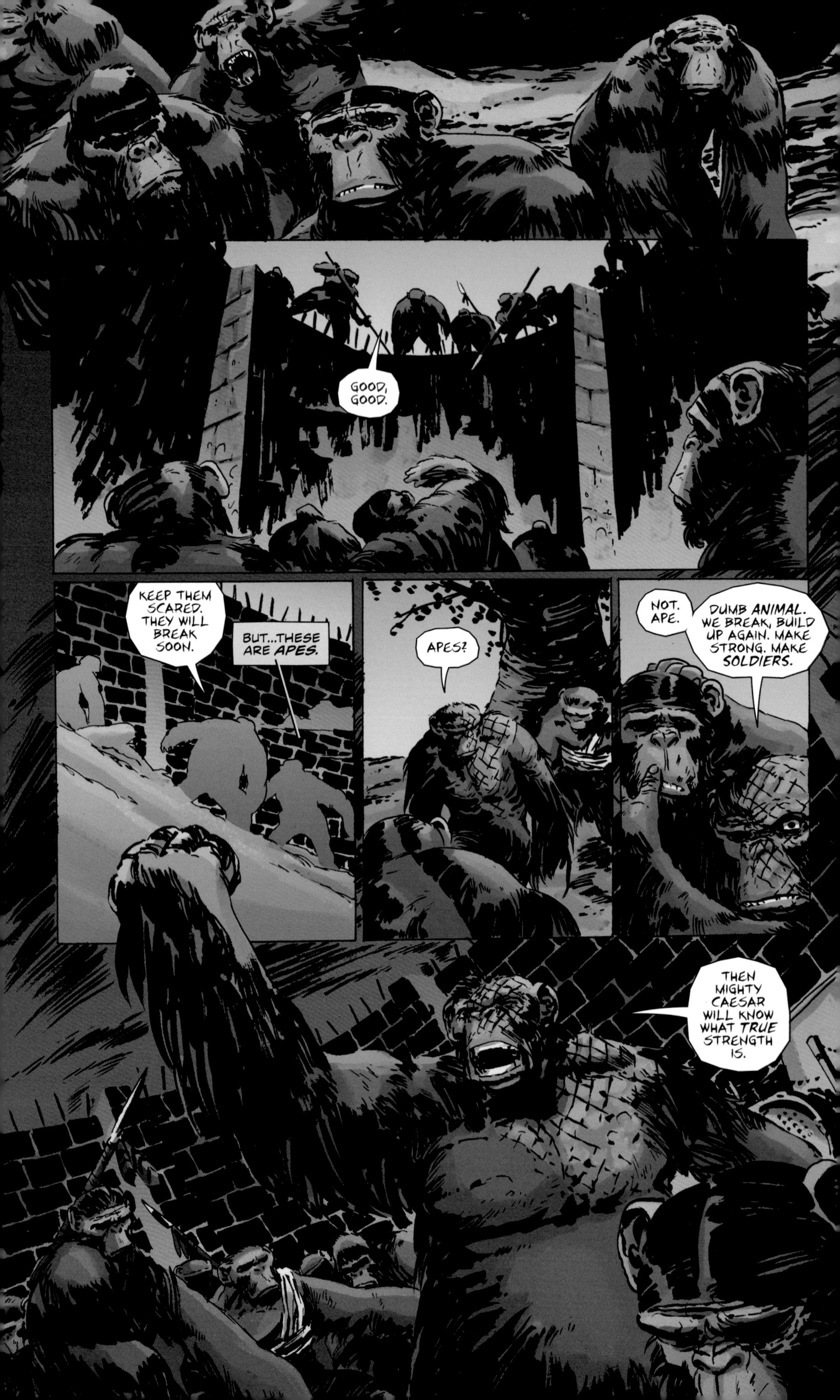
GOOD, GOOD.
KEEP THEM SCARED. THEY WILL BREAK SOON.
BUT...THESE ARE APES.
APES?
NOT. APE.
DUMB ANIMAL. WE BREAK, BUILD UP AGAIN. MAKE STRONG. MAKE SOLDIERS.
THEN MIGHTY CAESAR WILL KNOW WHAT TRUE STRENGTH IS.

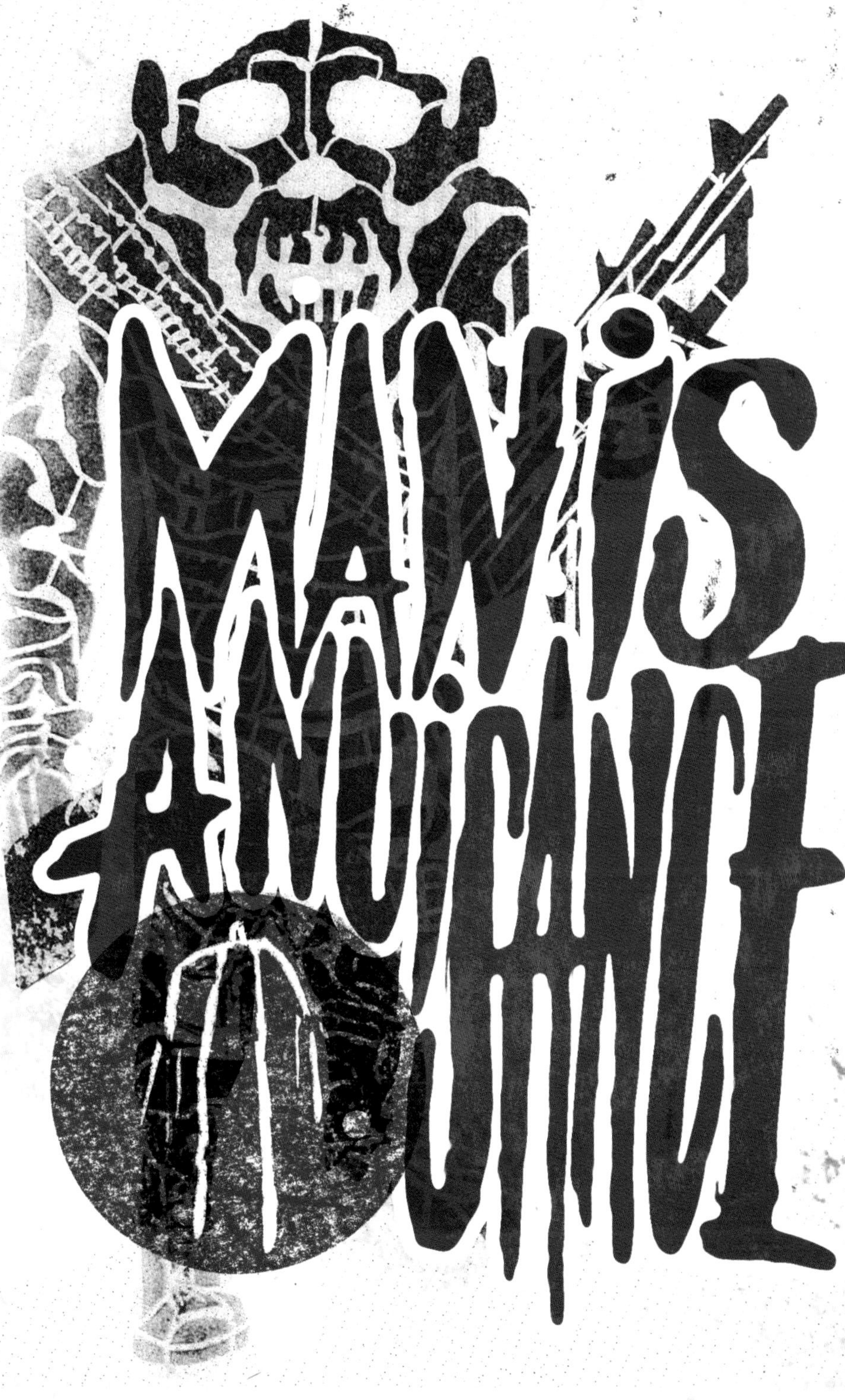

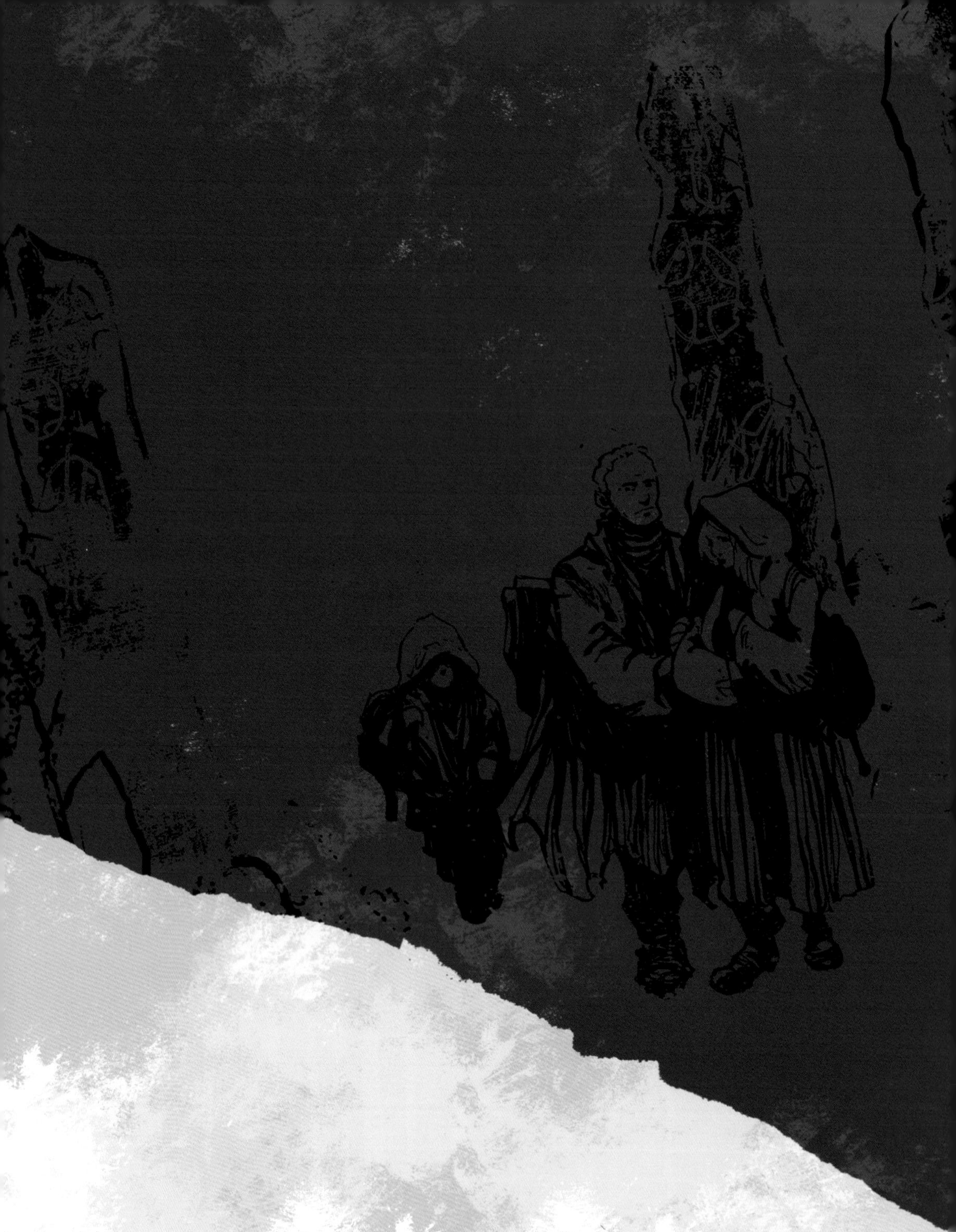

CHAPTER**FOUR**

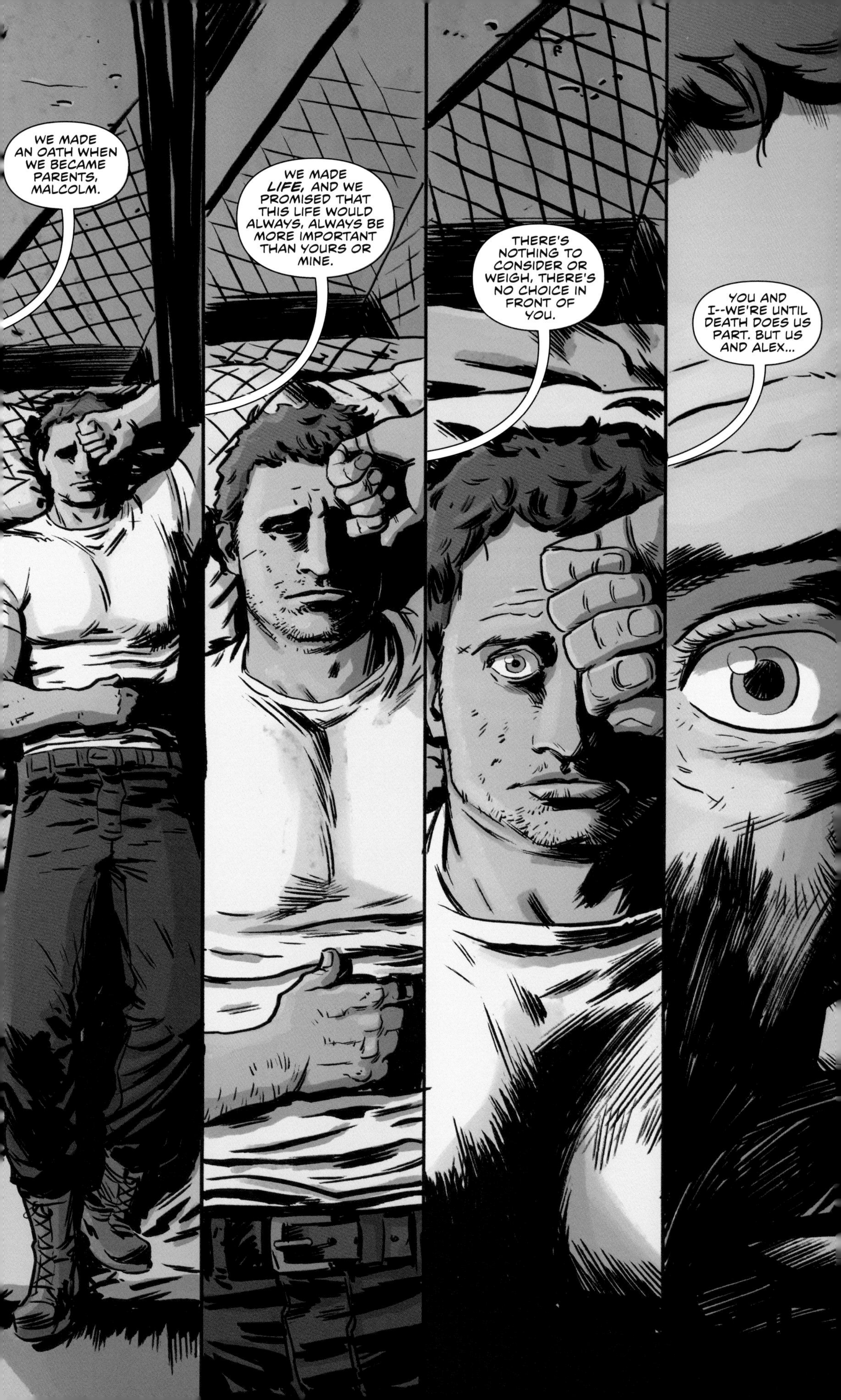
WE MADE AN OATH WHEN WE BECAME PARENTS, MALCOLM.
WE MADE *LIFE,* AND WE PROMISED THAT THIS LIFE WOULD ALWAYS, ALWAYS BE MORE IMPORTANT THAN YOURS OR MINE.
THERE'S NOTHING TO CONSIDER OR WEIGH, THERE'S NO CHOICE IN FRONT OF YOU.
YOU AND I--WE'RE UNTIL DEATH DOES US PART. BUT US AND ALEX...

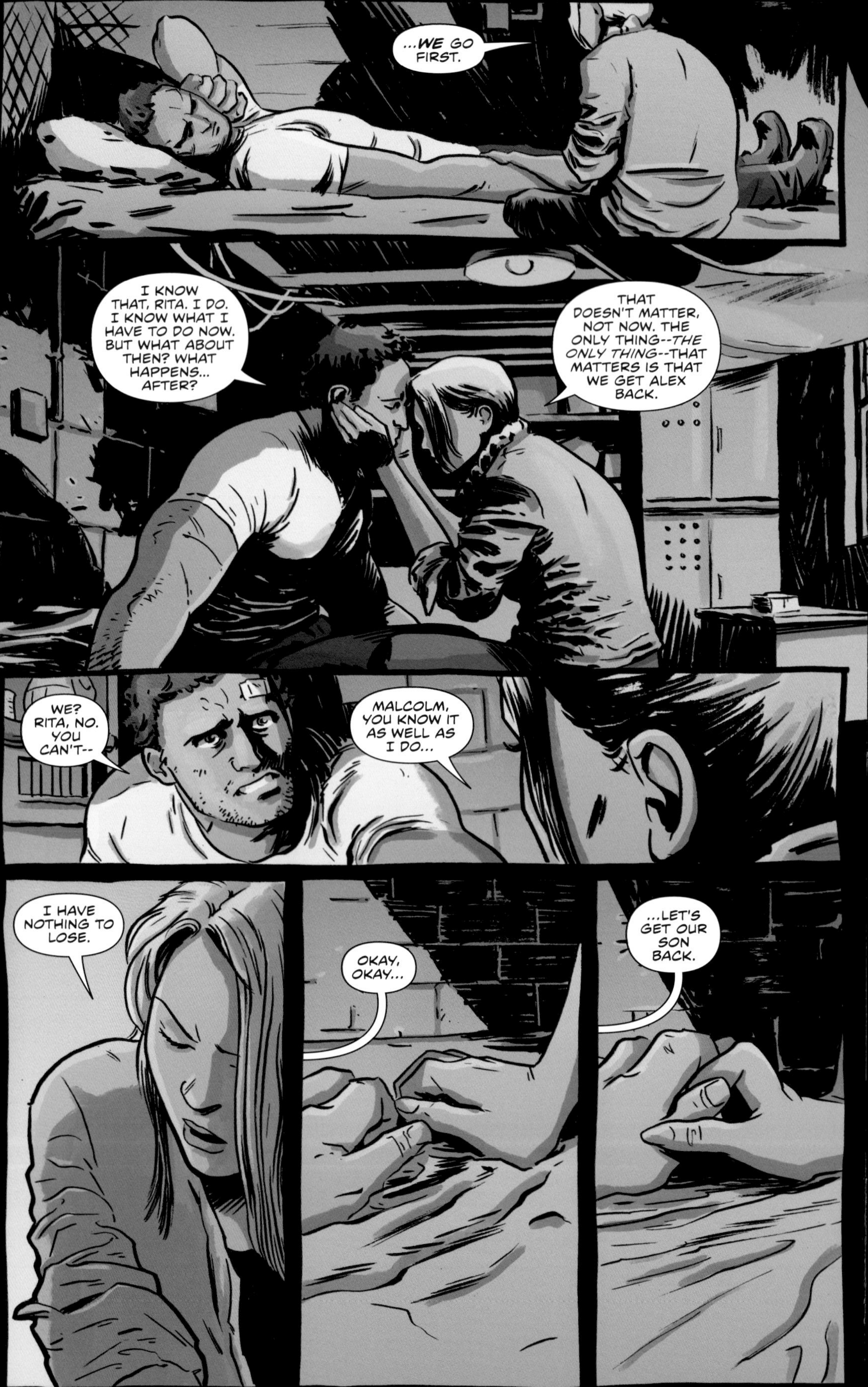
...WE GO FIRST.
I KNOW THAT, RITA. I DO. I KNOW WHAT I HAVE TO DO NOW. BUT WHAT ABOUT THEN? WHAT HAPPENS... AFTER?
THAT DOESN'T MATTER, NOT NOW. THE ONLY THING--THE ONLY THING--THAT MATTERS IS THAT WE GET ALEX BACK.
WE? RITA, NO. YOU CAN'T--
MALCOLM, YOU KNOW IT AS WELL AS I DO...
I HAVE NOTHING TO LOSE.
OKAY, OKAY...
...LET'S GET OUR SON BACK.

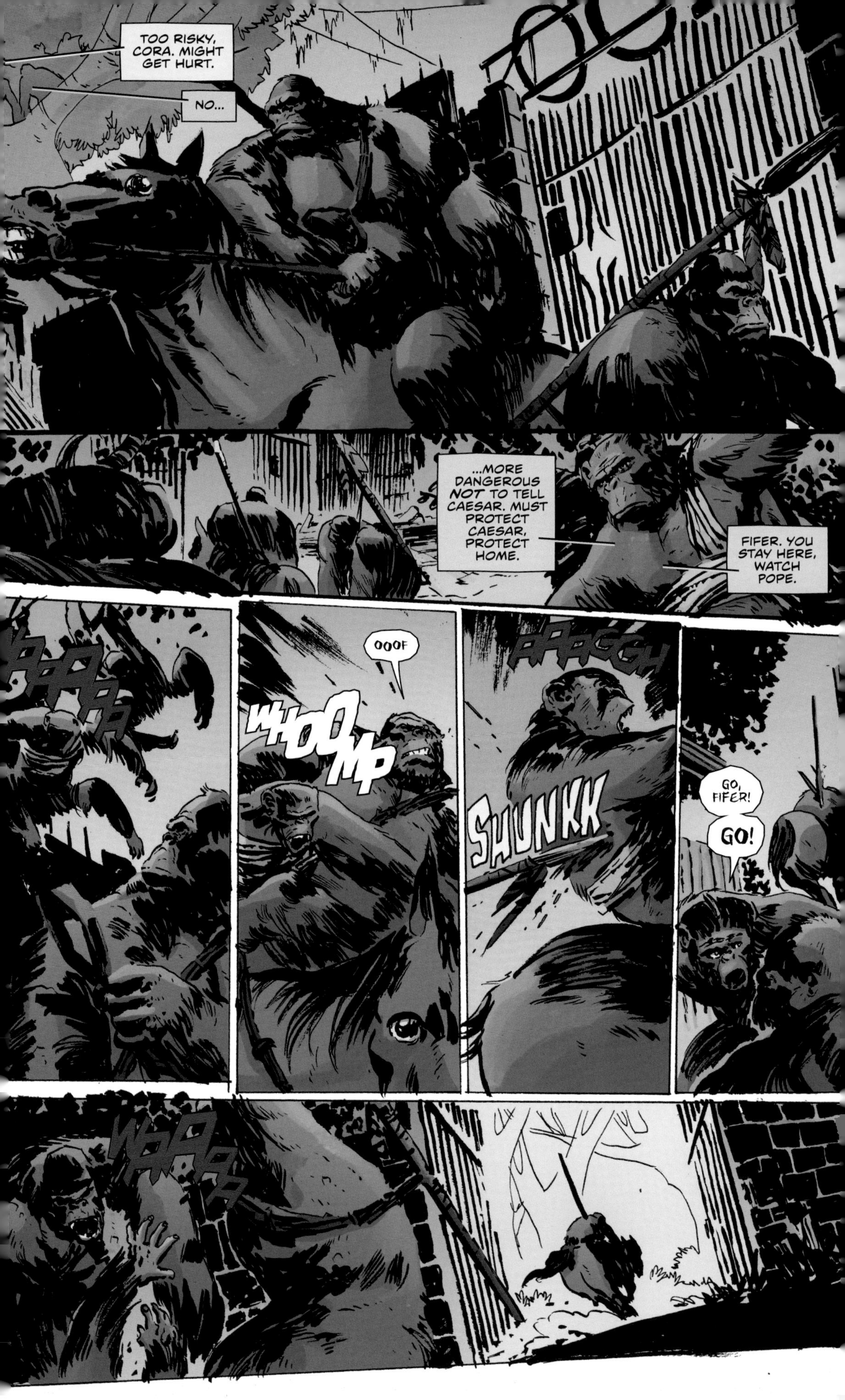

TOO RISKY, CORA. MIGHT GET HURT.
NO...
...MORE DANGEROUS NOT TO TELL CAESAR. MUST PROTECT CAESAR, PROTECT HOME.
FIFER. YOU STAY HERE, WATCH POPE.
OOOF
WHOOMP
ARRGGH
SHUNKK
GO, FIFER!
GO!

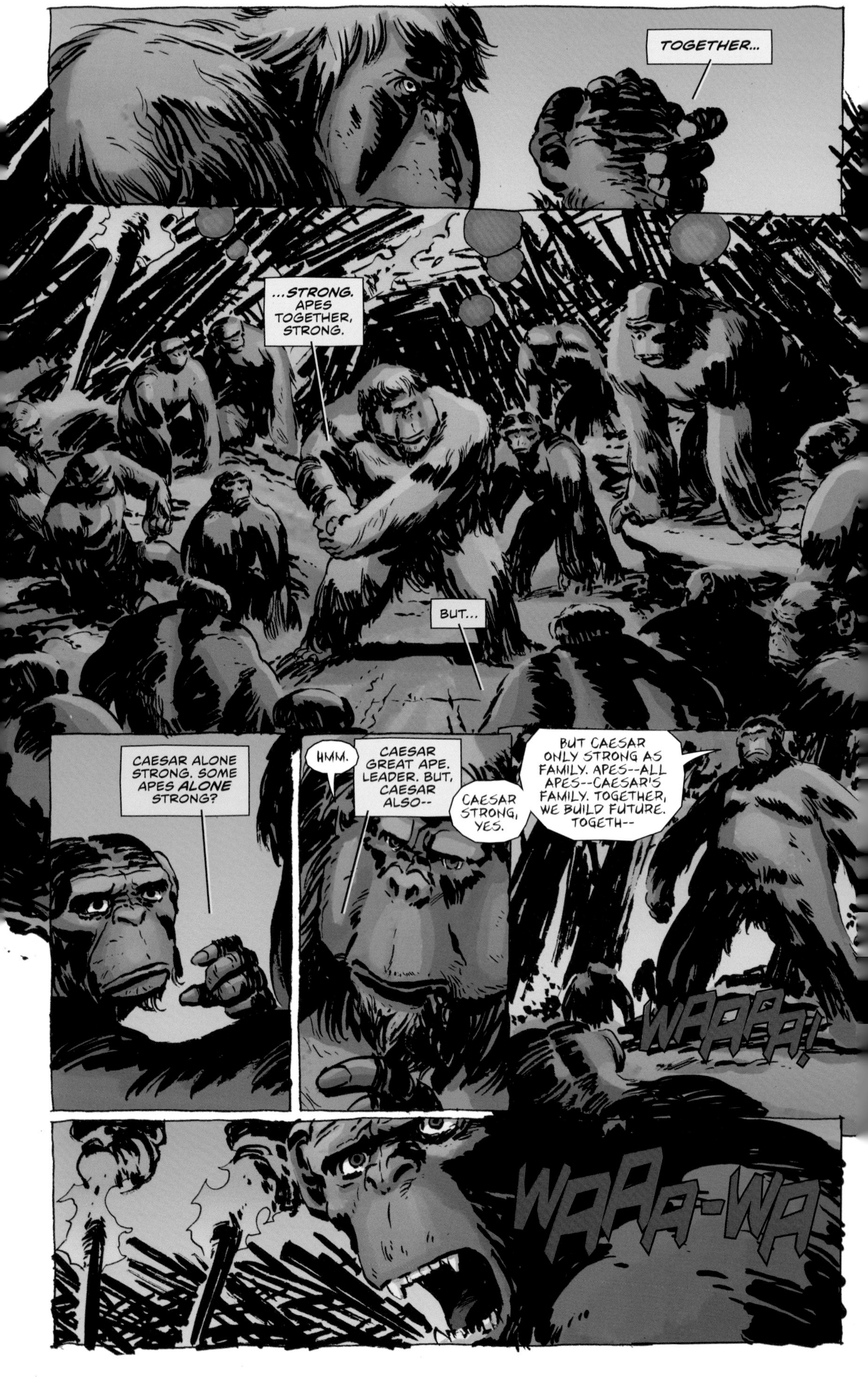
TOGETHER...
...STRONG. APES TOGETHER, STRONG.
BUT...
CAESAR ALONE STRONG. SOME APES ALONE STRONG?
HMM.
CAESAR GREAT APE. LEADER. BUT, CAESAR ALSO--
CAESAR STRONG, YES.
BUT CAESAR ONLY STRONG AS FAMILY. APES--ALL APES--CAESAR'S FAMILY. TOGETHER, WE BUILD FUTURE. TOGETH--
WAAAA!
WAAA-WA

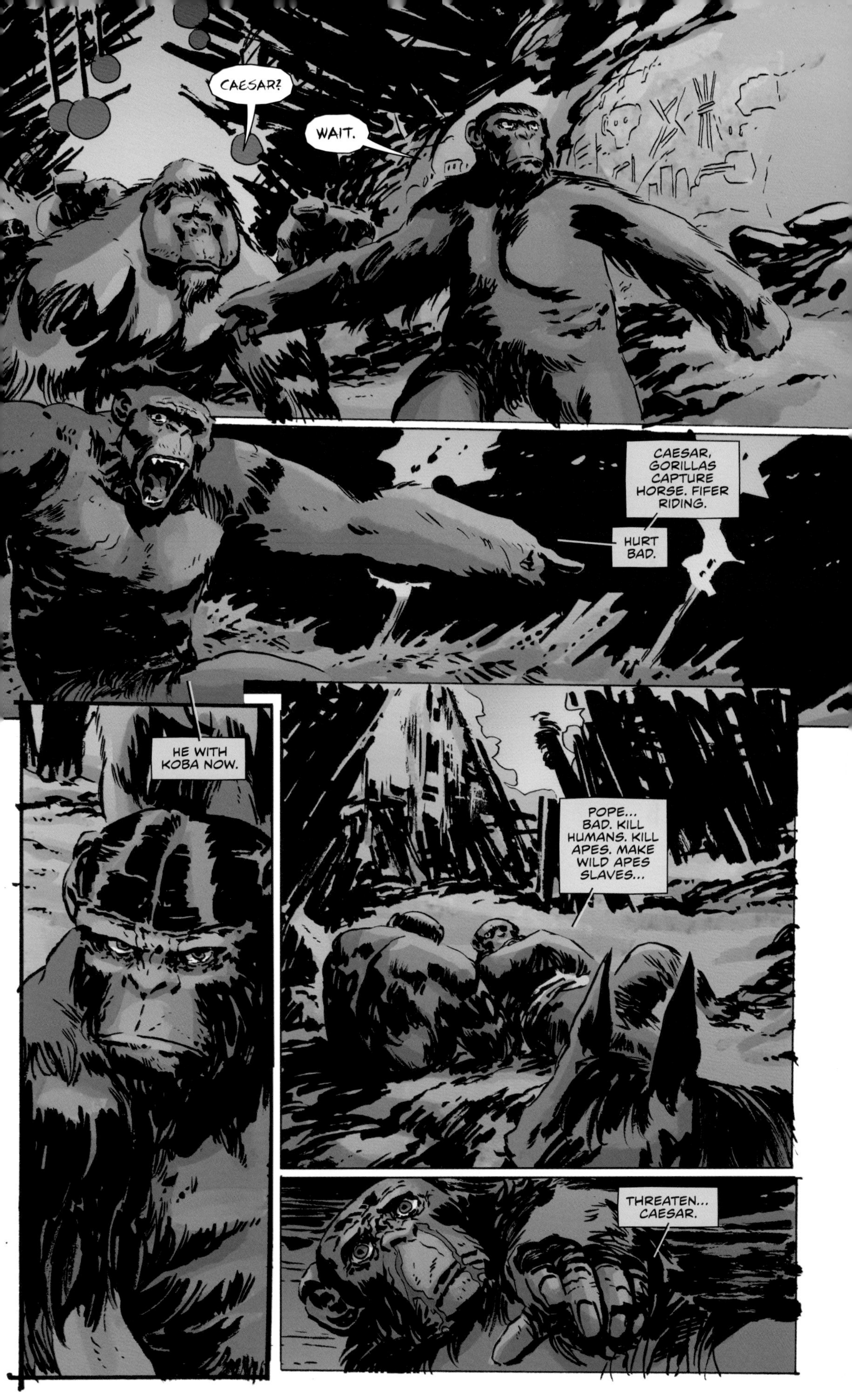
CAESAR?
WAIT.
CAESAR, GORILLAS CAPTURE HORSE. FIFER RIDING.
HURT BAD.
HE WITH KOBA NOW.
POPE... BAD. KILL HUMANS. KILL APES. MAKE WILD APES SLAVES...
THREATEN... CAESAR.

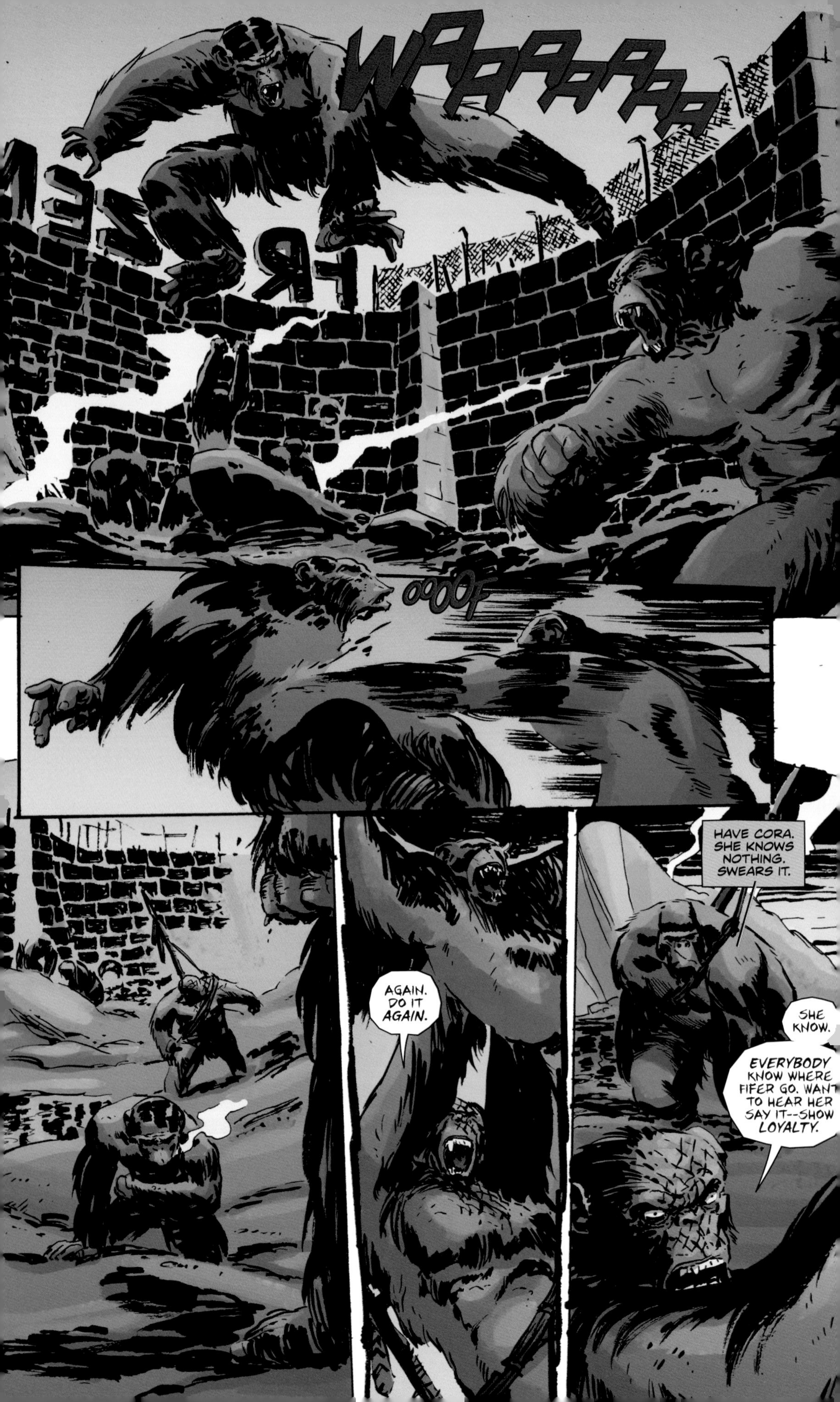
WAAAAAAA
OOOOF
AGAIN. DO IT AGAIN.
HAVE CORA. SHE KNOWS NOTHING. SWEARS IT.
SHE KNOW.
EVERYBODY KNOW WHERE FIFER GO. WANT TO HEAR HER SAY IT--SHOW LOYALTY.

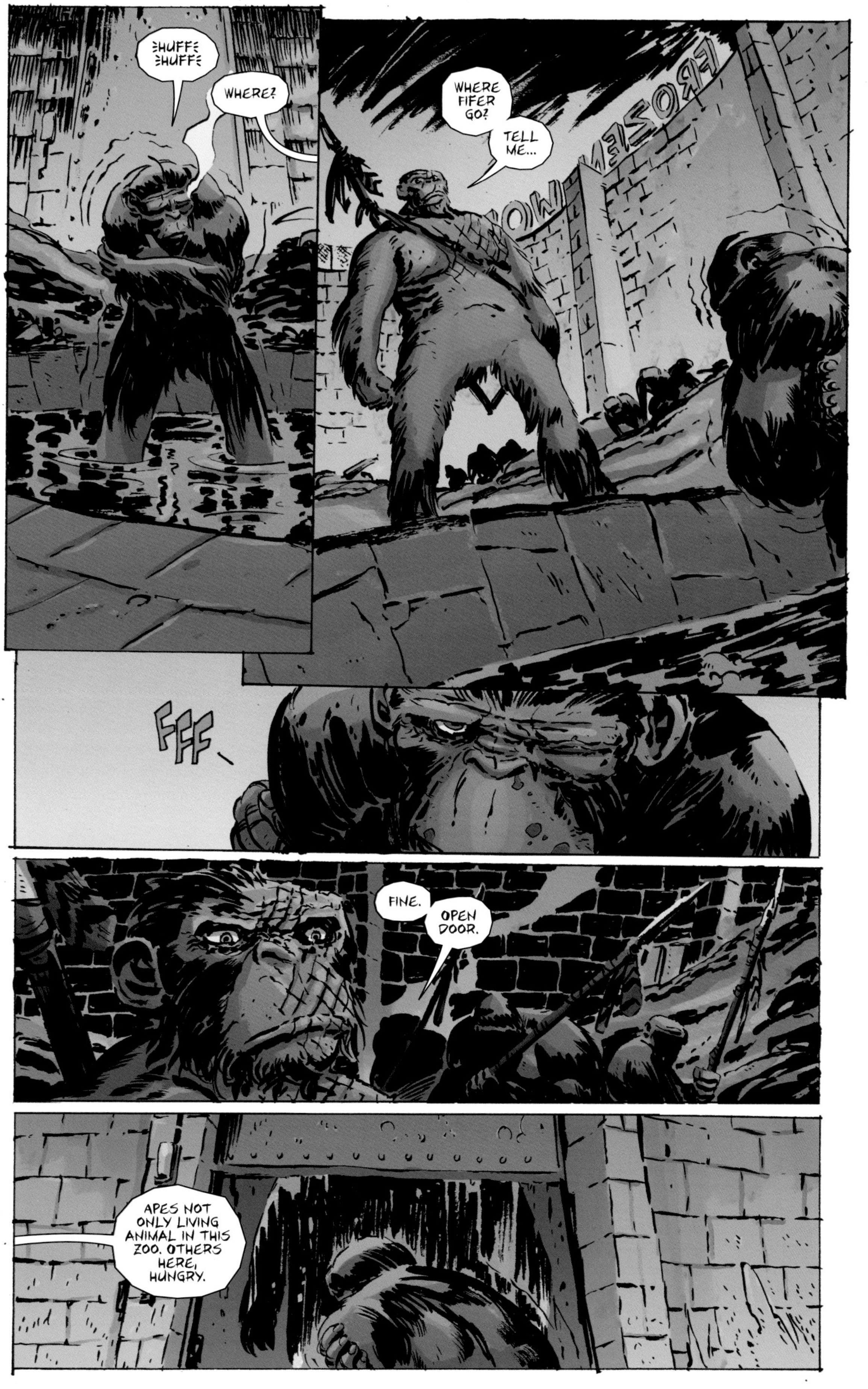
HUFF HUFF
WHERE?
WHERE FIFER GO?
TELL ME...
FROZEN WO
FFF
FINE.
OPEN DOOR.
APES NOT ONLY LIVING ANIMAL IN THIS ZOO. OTHERS HERE, HUNGRY.

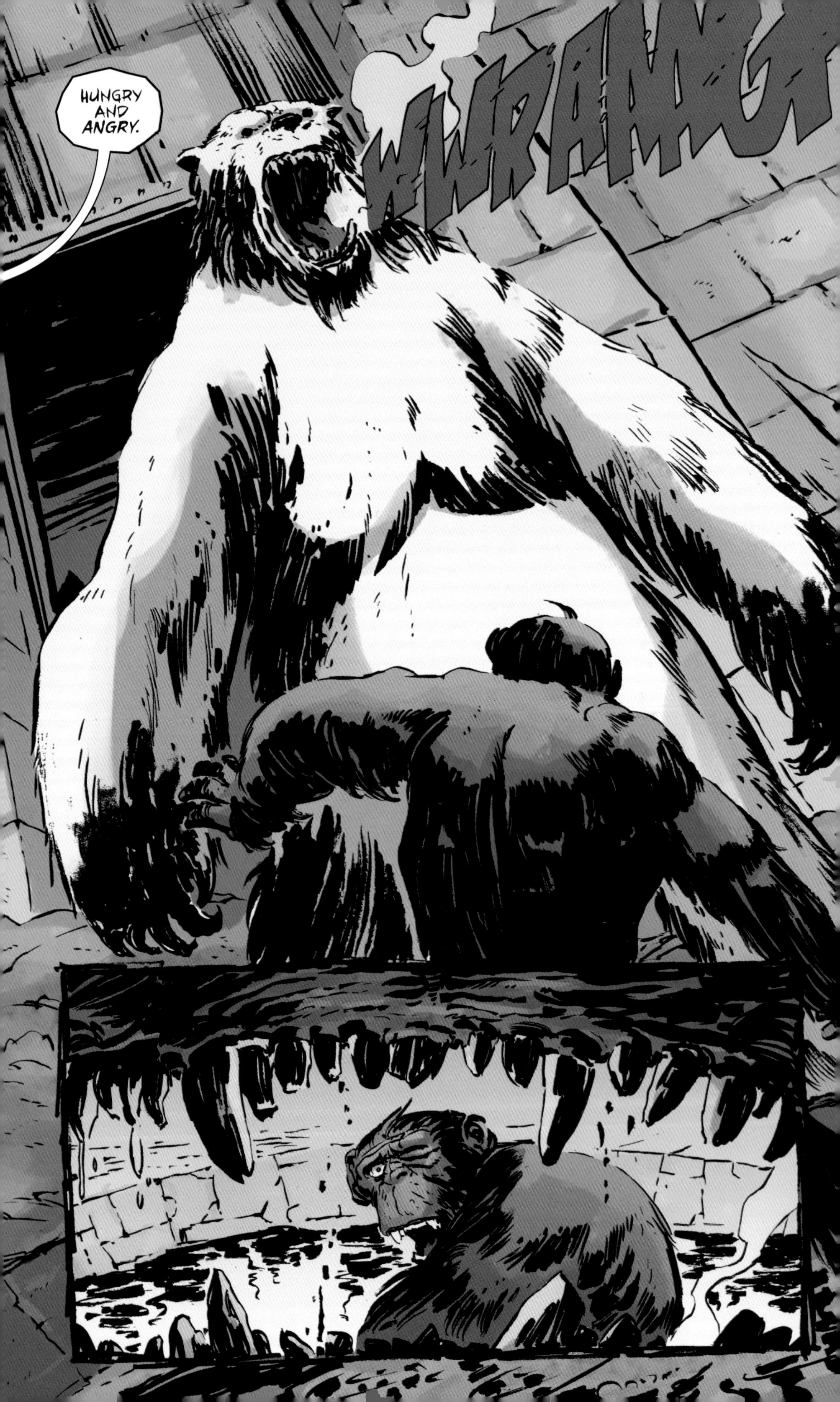
HUNGRY AND ANGRY.

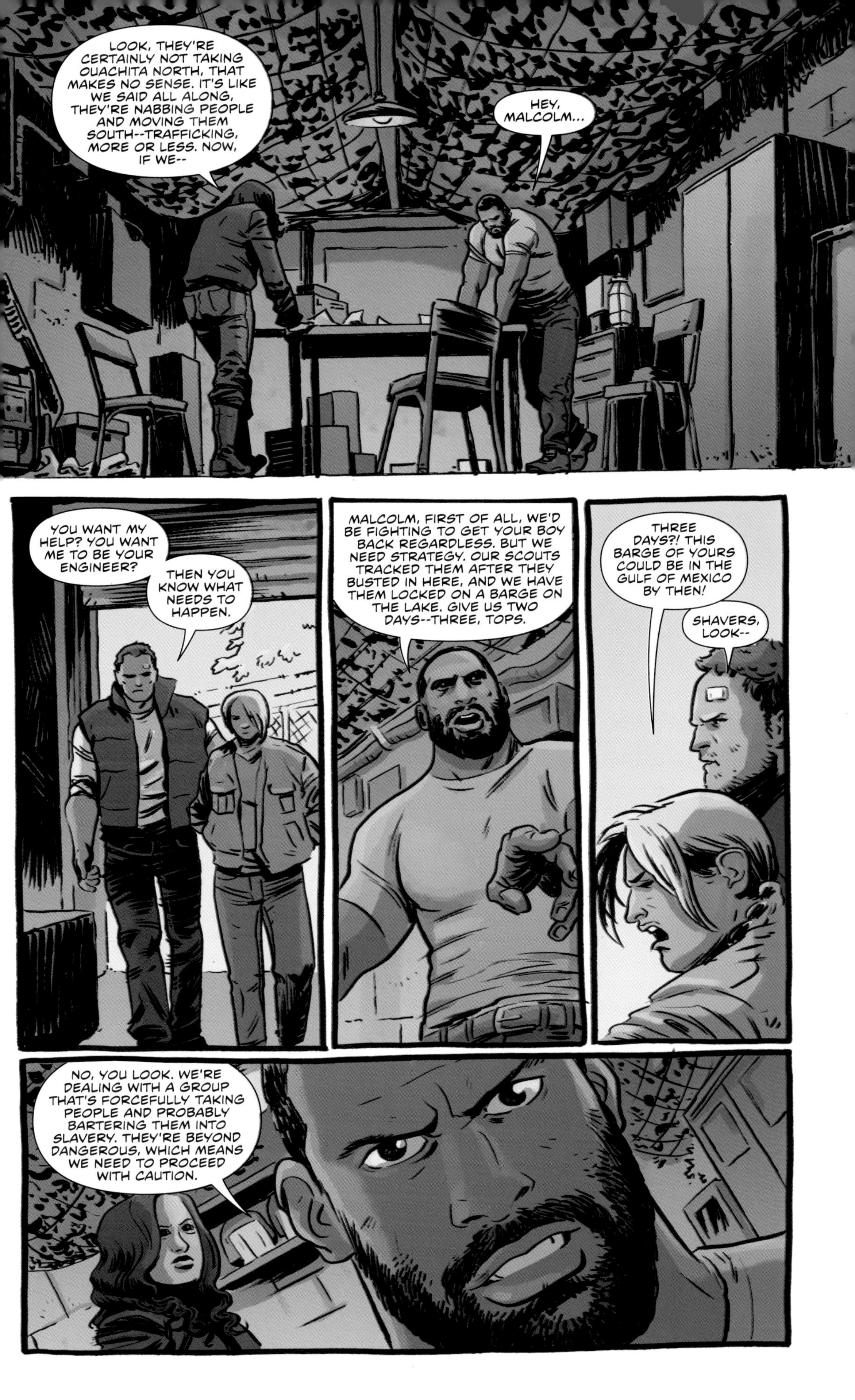
LOOK, THEY'RE CERTAINLY NOT TAKING OUACHITA NORTH, THAT MAKES NO SENSE. IT'S LIKE WE SAID ALL ALONG, THEY'RE NABBING PEOPLE AND MOVING THEM SOUTH--TRAFFICKING, MORE OR LESS. NOW, IF WE--
HEY, MALCOLM...
YOU WANT MY HELP? YOU WANT ME TO BE YOUR ENGINEER?
THEN YOU KNOW WHAT NEEDS TO HAPPEN.
MALCOLM, FIRST OF ALL, WE'D BE FIGHTING TO GET YOUR BOY BACK REGARDLESS. BUT WE NEED STRATEGY. OUR SCOUTS TRACKED THEM AFTER THEY BUSTED IN HERE, AND WE HAVE THEM LOCKED ON A BARGE ON THE LAKE. GIVE US TWO DAYS--THREE, TOPS.
THREE DAYS?! THIS BARGE OF YOURS COULD BE IN THE GULF OF MEXICO BY THEN!
SHAVERS, LOOK--
NO, YOU LOOK. WE'RE DEALING WITH A GROUP THAT'S FORCEFULLY TAKING PEOPLE AND PROBABLY BARTERING THEM INTO SLAVERY. THEY'RE BEYOND DANGEROUS, WHICH MEANS WE NEED TO PROCEED WITH CAUTION.

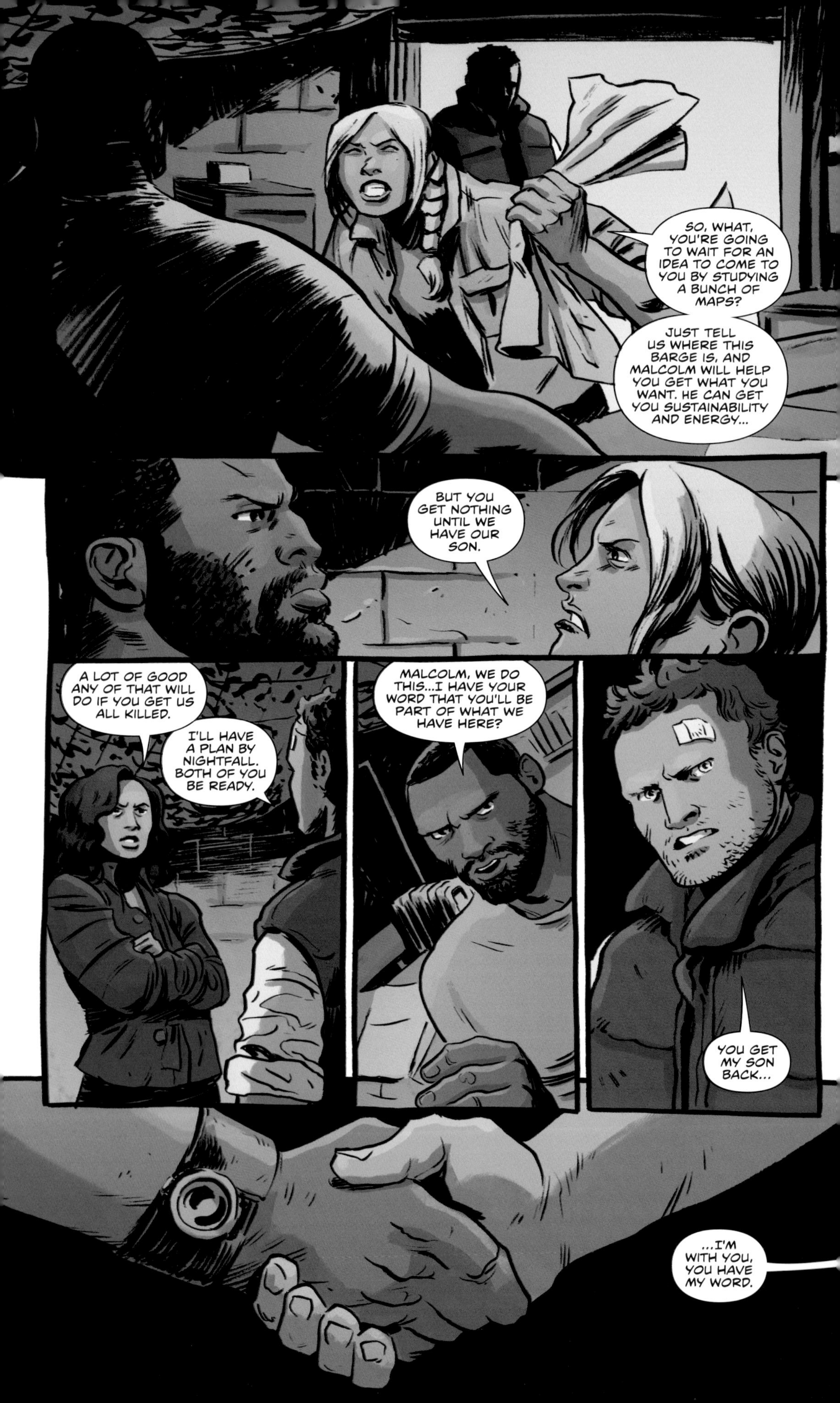
SO, WHAT, YOU'RE GOING TO WAIT FOR AN IDEA TO COME TO YOU BY STUDYING A BUNCH OF MAPS?
JUST TELL US WHERE THIS BARGE IS, AND MALCOLM WILL HELP YOU GET WHAT YOU WANT. HE CAN GET YOU SUSTAINABILITY AND ENERGY...
BUT YOU GET NOTHING UNTIL WE HAVE OUR SON.
A LOT OF GOOD ANY OF THAT WILL DO IF YOU GET US ALL KILLED.
I'LL HAVE A PLAN BY NIGHTFALL. BOTH OF YOU BE READY.
MALCOLM, WE DO THIS...I HAVE YOUR WORD THAT YOU'LL BE PART OF WHAT WE HAVE HERE?
YOU GET MY SON BACK...
...I'M WITH YOU, YOU HAVE MY WORD.

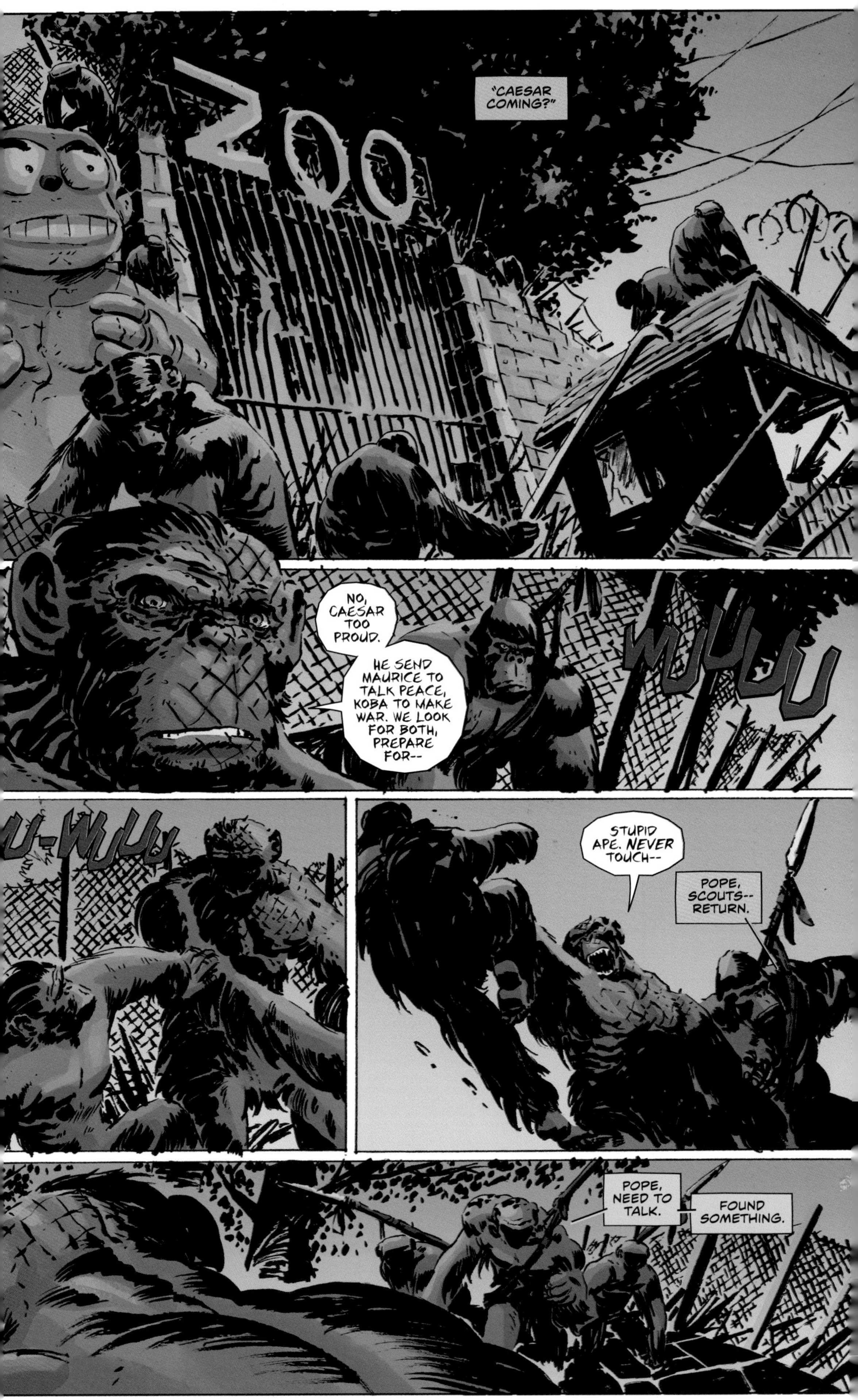
"CAESAR COMING?"
ZOO
NO, CAESAR TOO PROUD.
HE SEND MAURICE TO TALK PEACE, KOBA TO MAKE WAR. WE LOOK FOR BOTH, PREPARE FOR--
WUUUU
U-WUUU
STUPID APE. NEVER TOUCH--
POPE, SCOUTS-- RETURN.
POPE, NEED TO TALK.
FOUND SOMETHING.

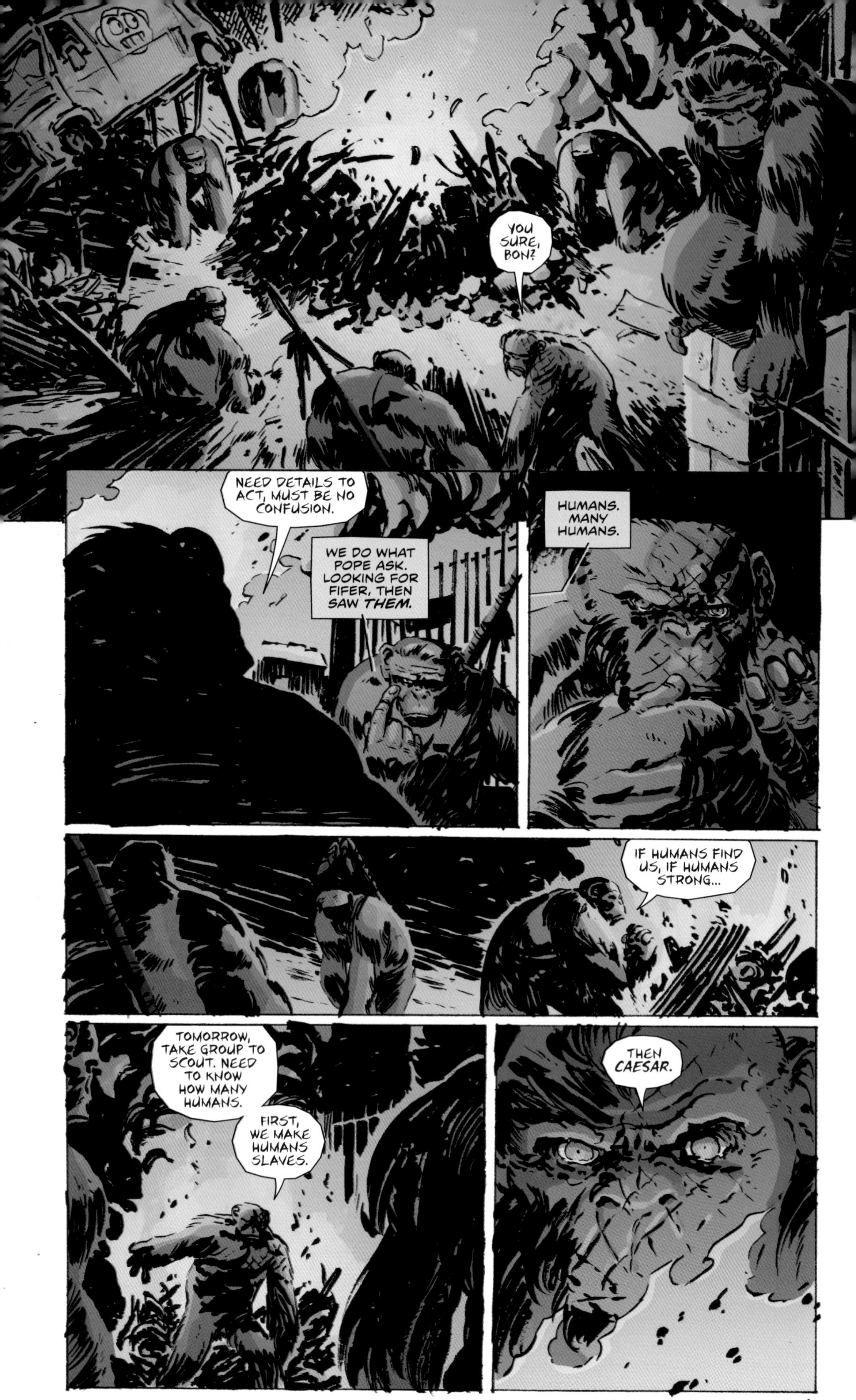
YOU SURE, BON?
NEED DETAILS TO ACT, MUST BE NO CONFUSION.
WE DO WHAT POPE ASK. LOOKING FOR FIFER, THEN SAW *THEM.*
HUMANS. MANY HUMANS.
IF HUMANS FIND US, IF HUMANS STRONG...
TOMORROW, TAKE GROUP TO SCOUT. NEED TO KNOW HOW MANY HUMANS.
FIRST, WE MAKE HUMANS SLAVES.
THEN *CAESAR.*

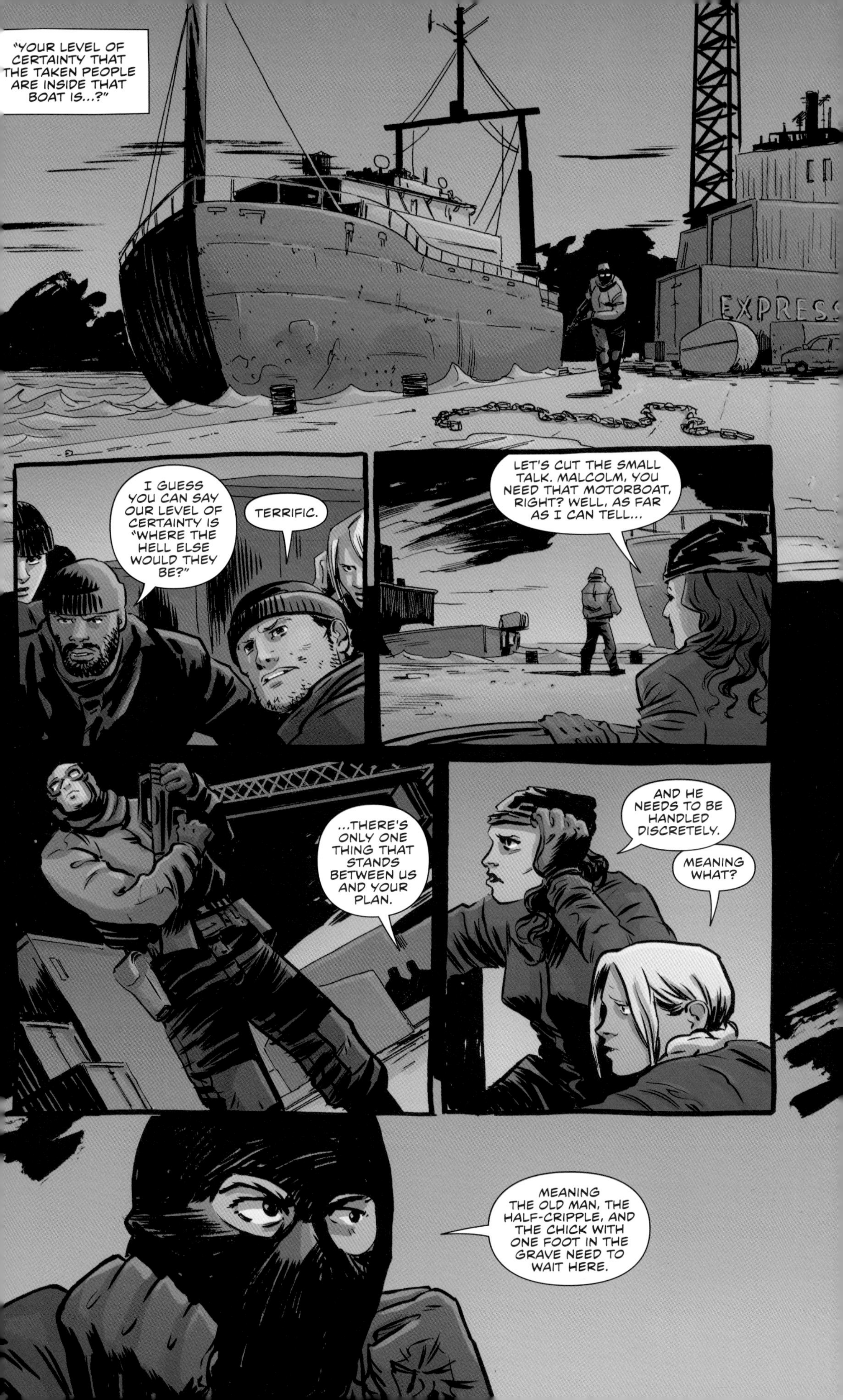
"YOUR LEVEL OF CERTAINTY THAT THE TAKEN PEOPLE ARE INSIDE THAT BOAT IS...?"
EXPRESS
I GUESS YOU CAN SAY OUR LEVEL OF CERTAINTY IS "WHERE THE HELL ELSE WOULD THEY BE?"
TERRIFIC.
LET'S CUT THE SMALL TALK. MALCOLM, YOU NEED THAT MOTORBOAT, RIGHT? WELL, AS FAR AS I CAN TELL...
...THERE'S ONLY ONE THING THAT STANDS BETWEEN US AND YOUR PLAN.
AND HE NEEDS TO BE HANDLED DISCRETELY.
MEANING WHAT?
MEANING THE OLD MAN, THE HALF-CRIPPLE, AND THE CHICK WITH ONE FOOT IN THE GRAVE NEED TO WAIT HERE.

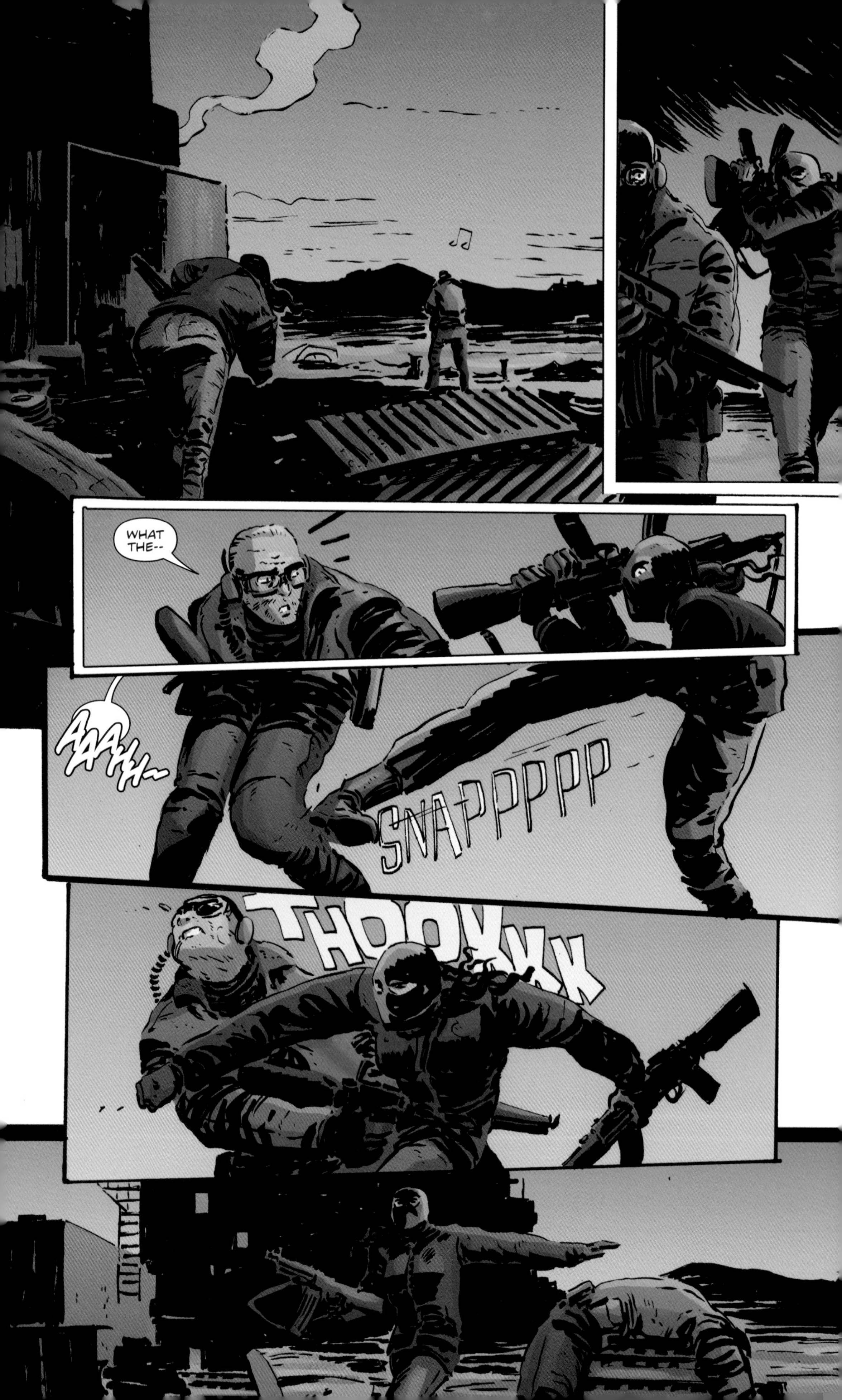
WHAT THE--
AAAHH--
SNAPPPPPP
THOOKK

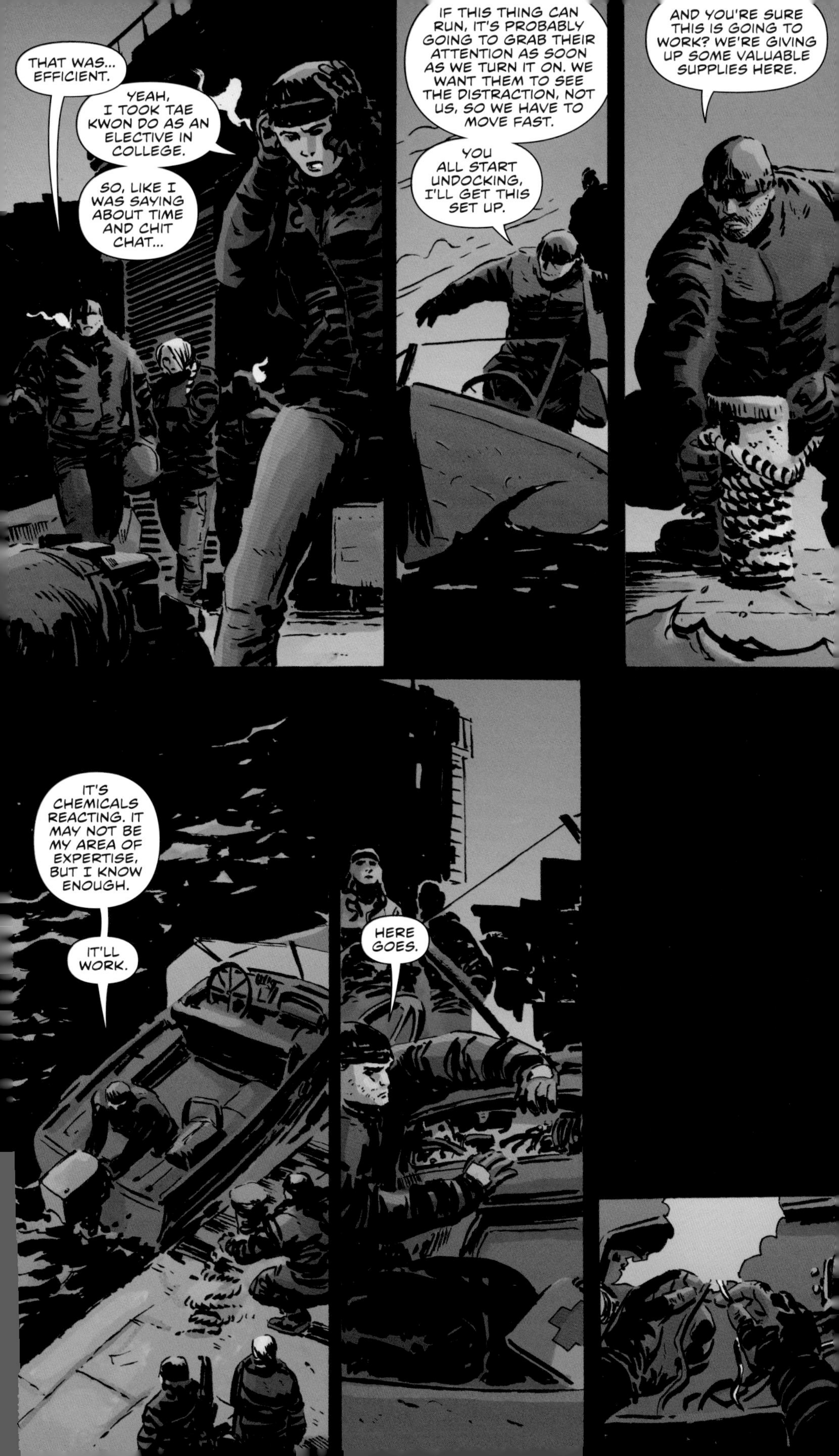

THAT WAS... EFFICIENT.
YEAH, I TOOK TAE KWON DO AS AN ELECTIVE IN COLLEGE.
SO, LIKE I WAS SAYING ABOUT TIME AND CHIT CHAT...
IF THIS THING CAN RUN, IT'S PROBABLY GOING TO GRAB THEIR ATTENTION AS SOON AS WE TURN IT ON. WE WANT THEM TO SEE THE DISTRACTION, NOT US, SO WE HAVE TO MOVE FAST.
YOU ALL START UNDOCKING, I'LL GET THIS SET UP.
AND YOU'RE SURE THIS IS GOING TO WORK? WE'RE GIVING UP SOME VALUABLE SUPPLIES HERE.
IT'S CHEMICALS REACTING. IT MAY NOT BE MY AREA OF EXPERTISE, BUT I KNOW ENOUGH.
IT'LL WORK.
HERE GOES.

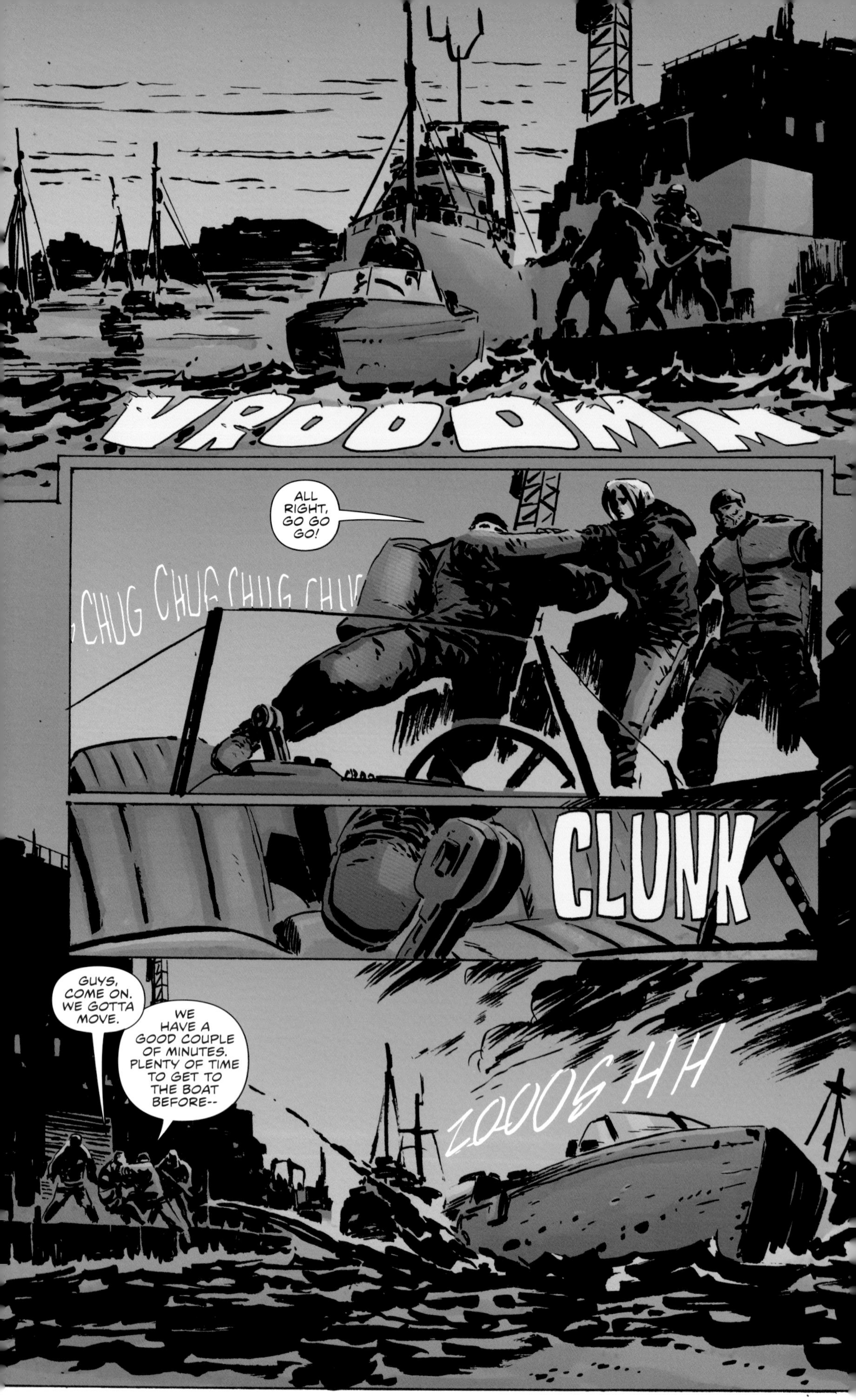
VROOOMMM
ALL RIGHT, GO GO GO!
CHUG CHUG CHUG CHUG
CLUNK
GUYS, COME ON. WE GOTTA MOVE.
WE HAVE A GOOD COUPLE OF MINUTES. PLENTY OF TIME TO GET TO THE BOAT BEFORE--
ZOOOSHH

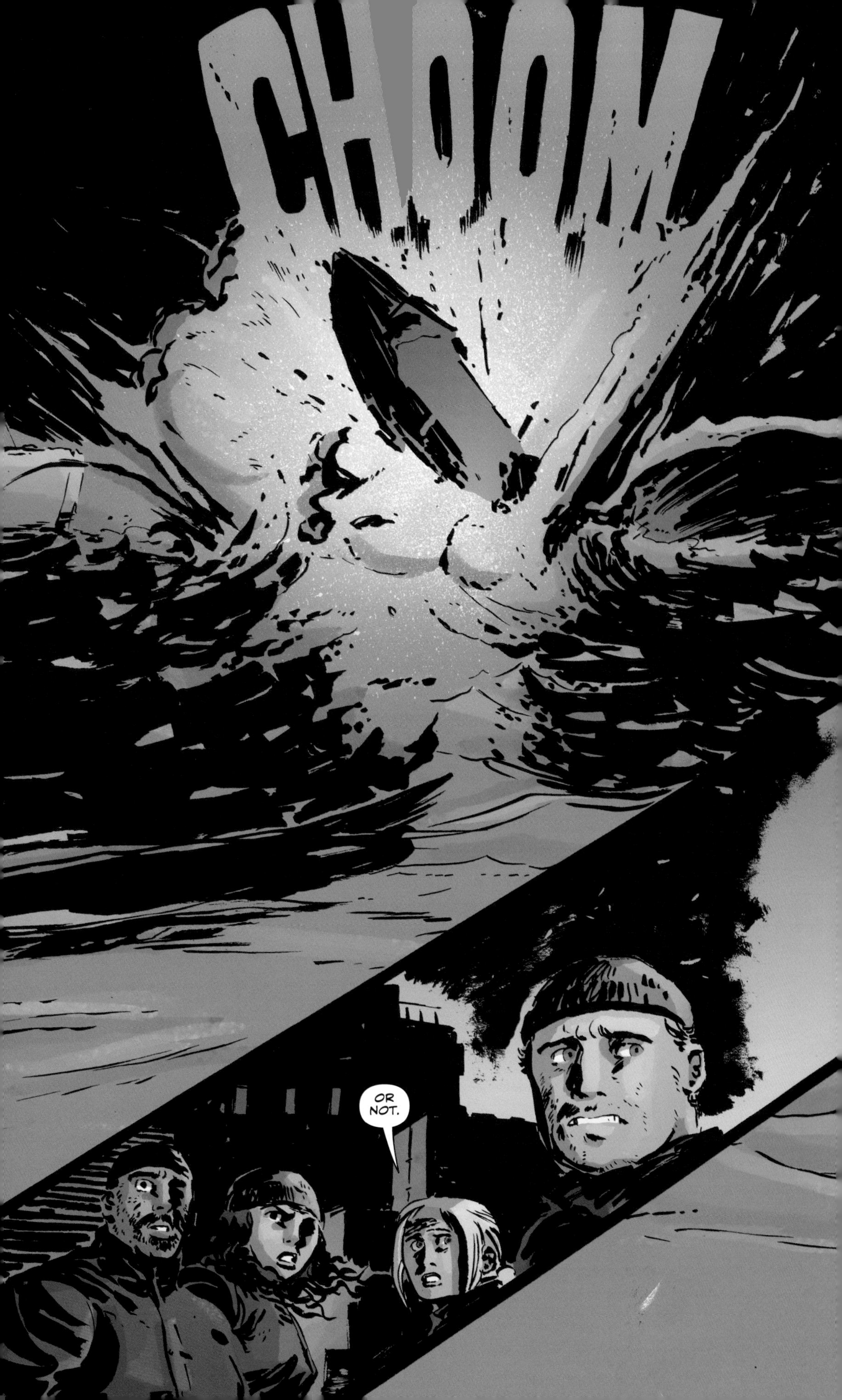
CHOOM
OR NOT.

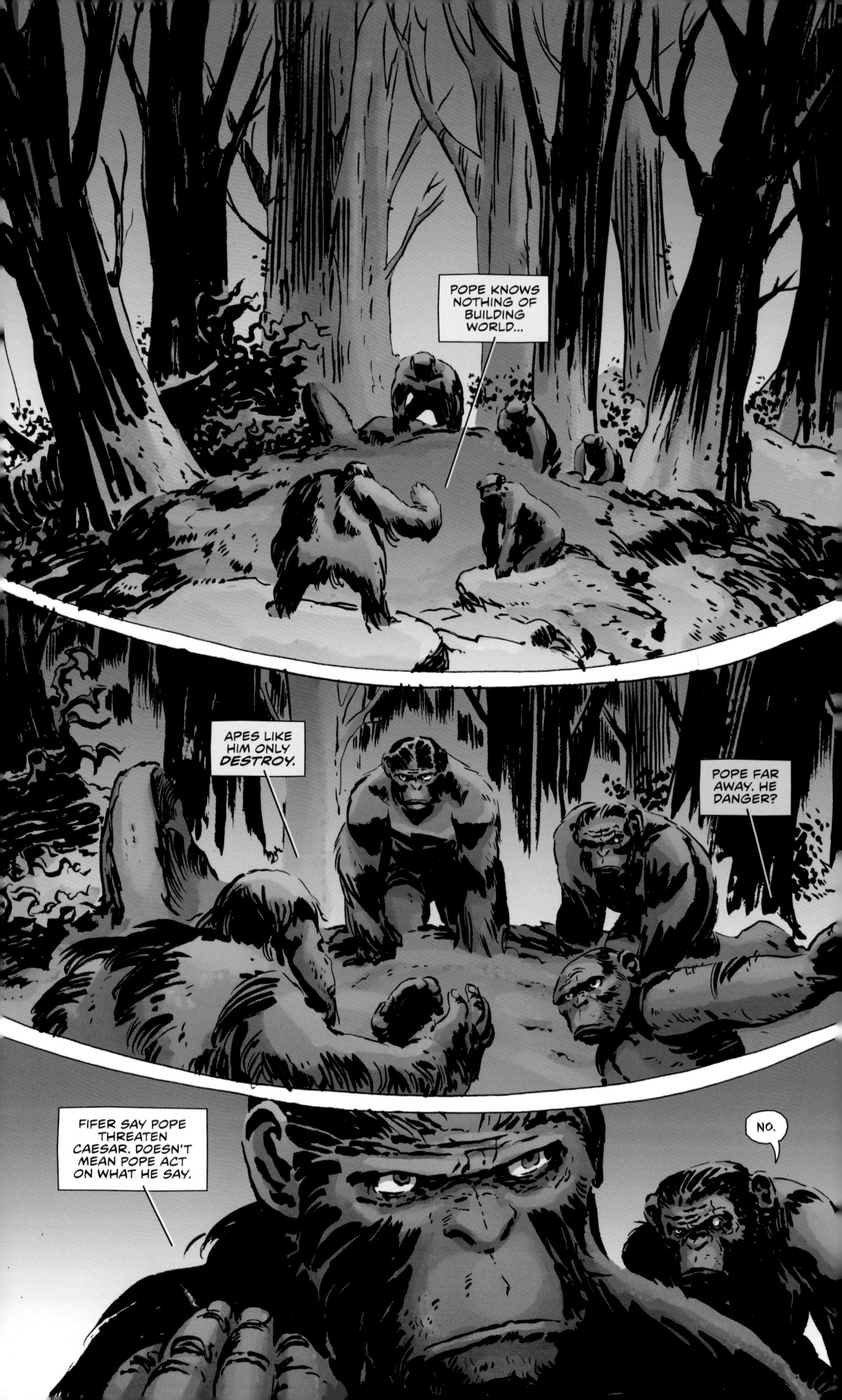
POPE KNOWS NOTHING OF BUILDING WORLD...
APES LIKE HIM ONLY DESTROY.
POPE FAR AWAY. HE DANGER?
FIFER SAY POPE THREATEN CAESAR. DOESN'T MEAN POPE ACT ON WHAT HE SAY.
NO.

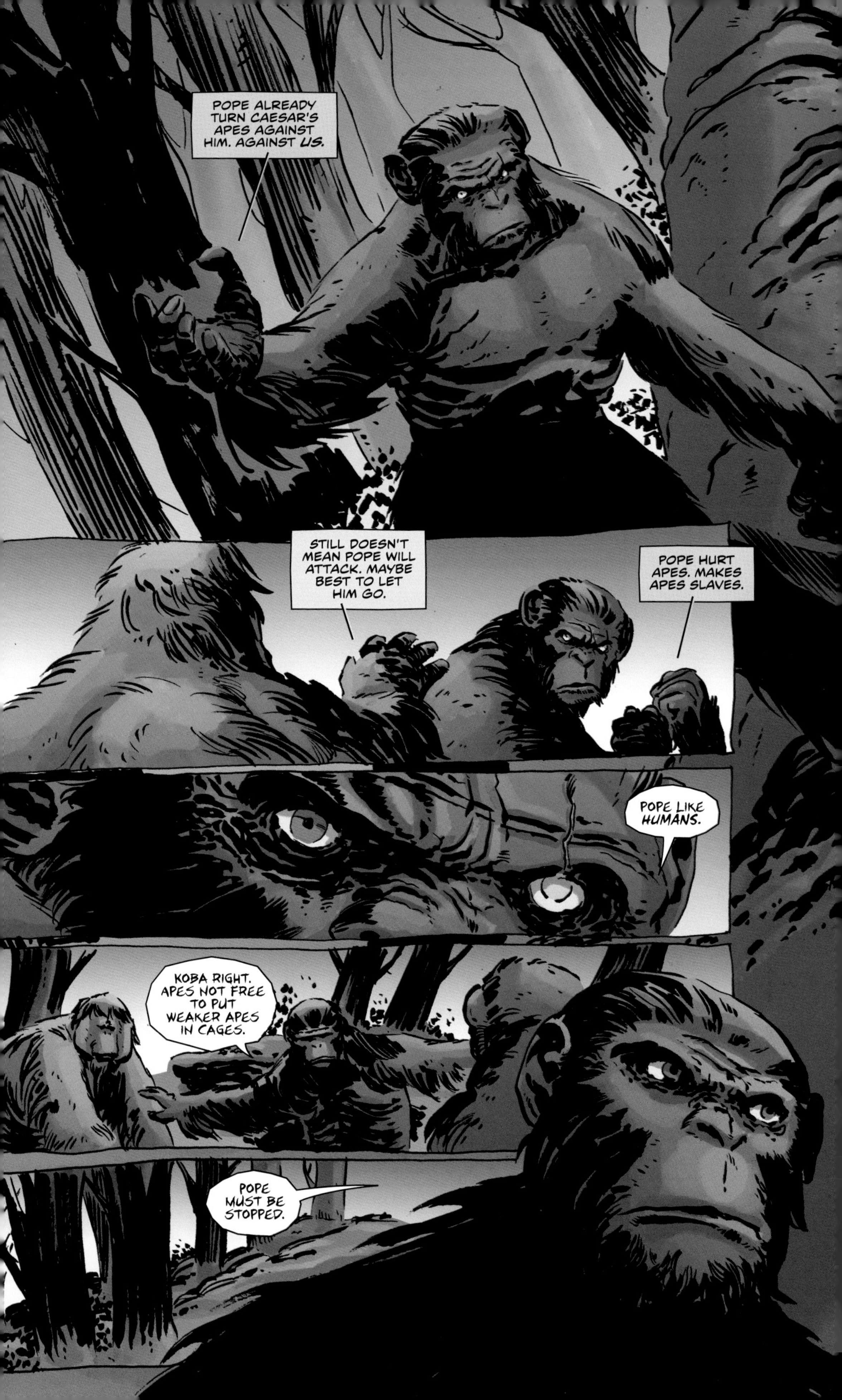
POPE ALREADY TURN CAESAR'S APES AGAINST HIM. AGAINST *US.*
STILL DOESN'T MEAN POPE WILL ATTACK. MAYBE BEST TO LET HIM GO.
POPE HURT APES. MAKES APES SLAVES.
POPE LIKE *HUMANS.*
KOBA RIGHT. APES NOT FREE TO PUT WEAKER APES IN CAGES.
POPE MUST BE STOPPED.

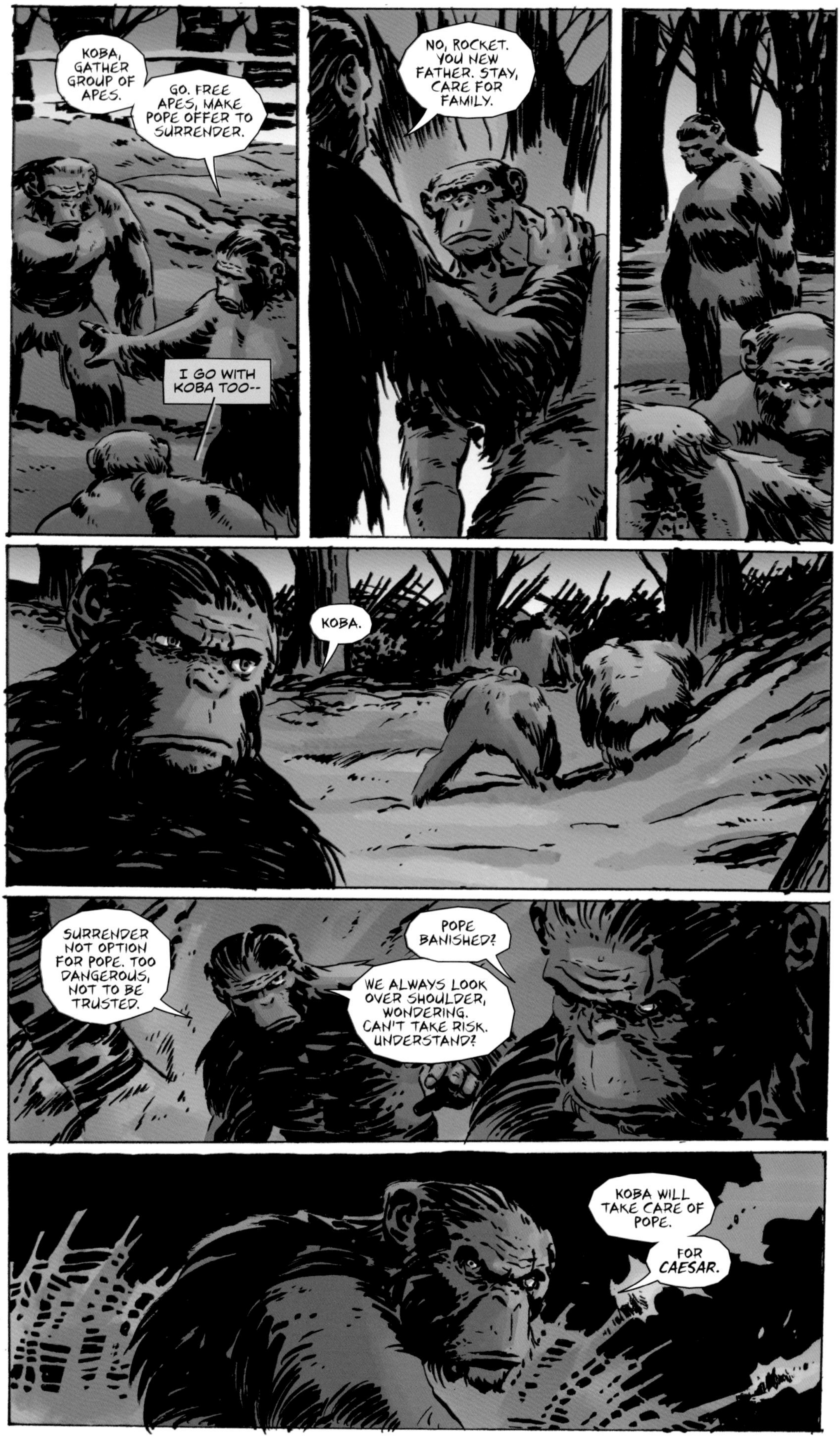
KOBA, GATHER GROUP OF APES.
GO. FREE APES, MAKE POPE OFFER TO SURRENDER.
I GO WITH KOBA TOO--
NO, ROCKET. YOU NEW FATHER. STAY, CARE FOR FAMILY.
KOBA.
SURRENDER NOT OPTION FOR POPE. TOO DANGEROUS, NOT TO BE TRUSTED.
POPE BANISHED?
WE ALWAYS LOOK OVER SHOULDER, WONDERING. CAN'T TAKE RISK. UNDERSTAND?
KOBA WILL TAKE CARE OF POPE.
FOR CAESAR.

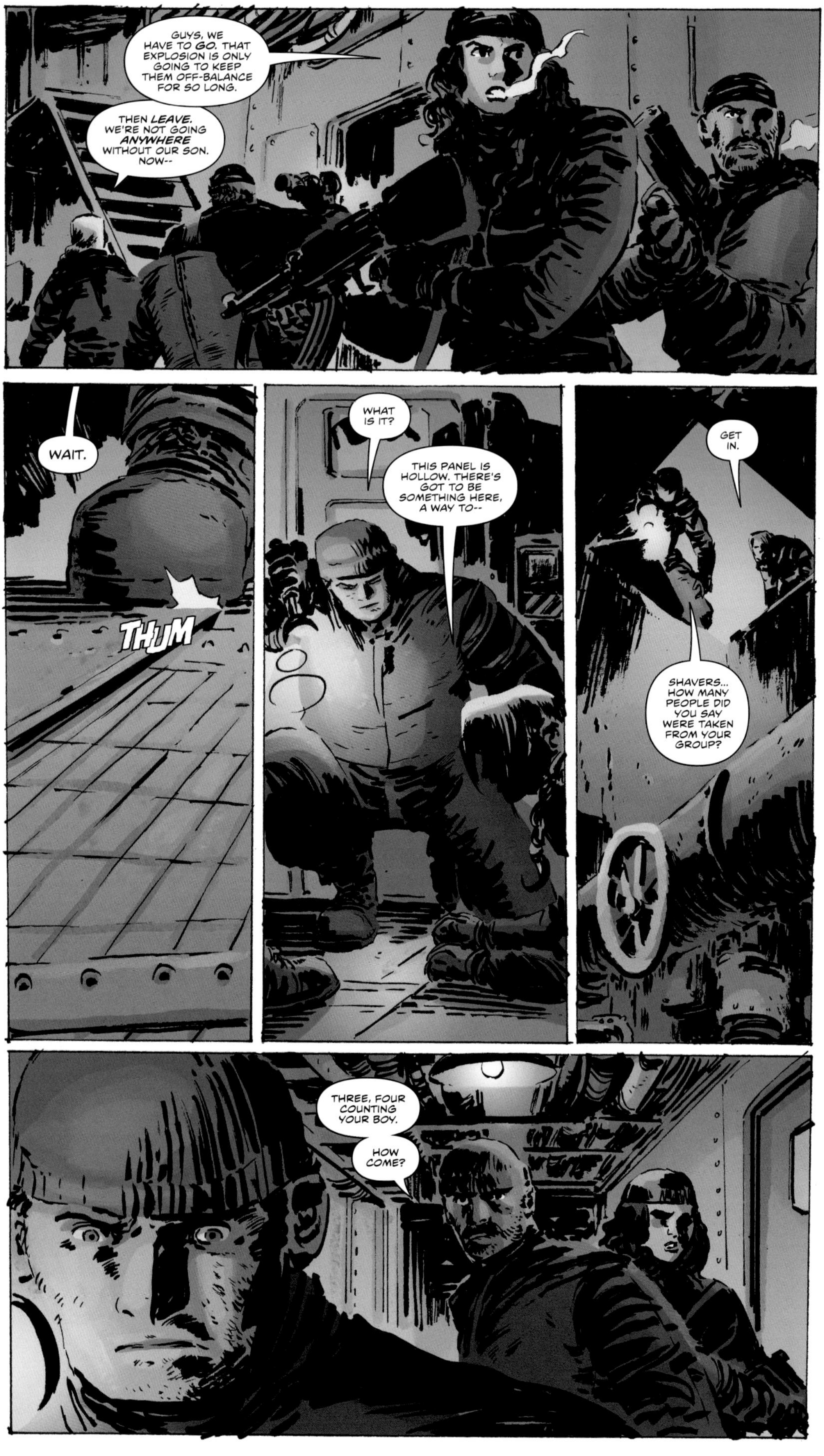

GUYS, WE HAVE TO GO. THAT EXPLOSION IS ONLY GOING TO KEEP THEM OFF-BALANCE FOR SO LONG.
THEN LEAVE. WE'RE NOT GOING ANYWHERE WITHOUT OUR SON. NOW--
WAIT.
THUM
WHAT IS IT?
THIS PANEL IS HOLLOW. THERE'S GOT TO BE SOMETHING HERE, A WAY TO--
GET IN.
SHAVERS... HOW MANY PEOPLE DID YOU SAY WERE TAKEN FROM YOUR GROUP?
THREE, FOUR COUNTING YOUR BOY.
HOW COME?

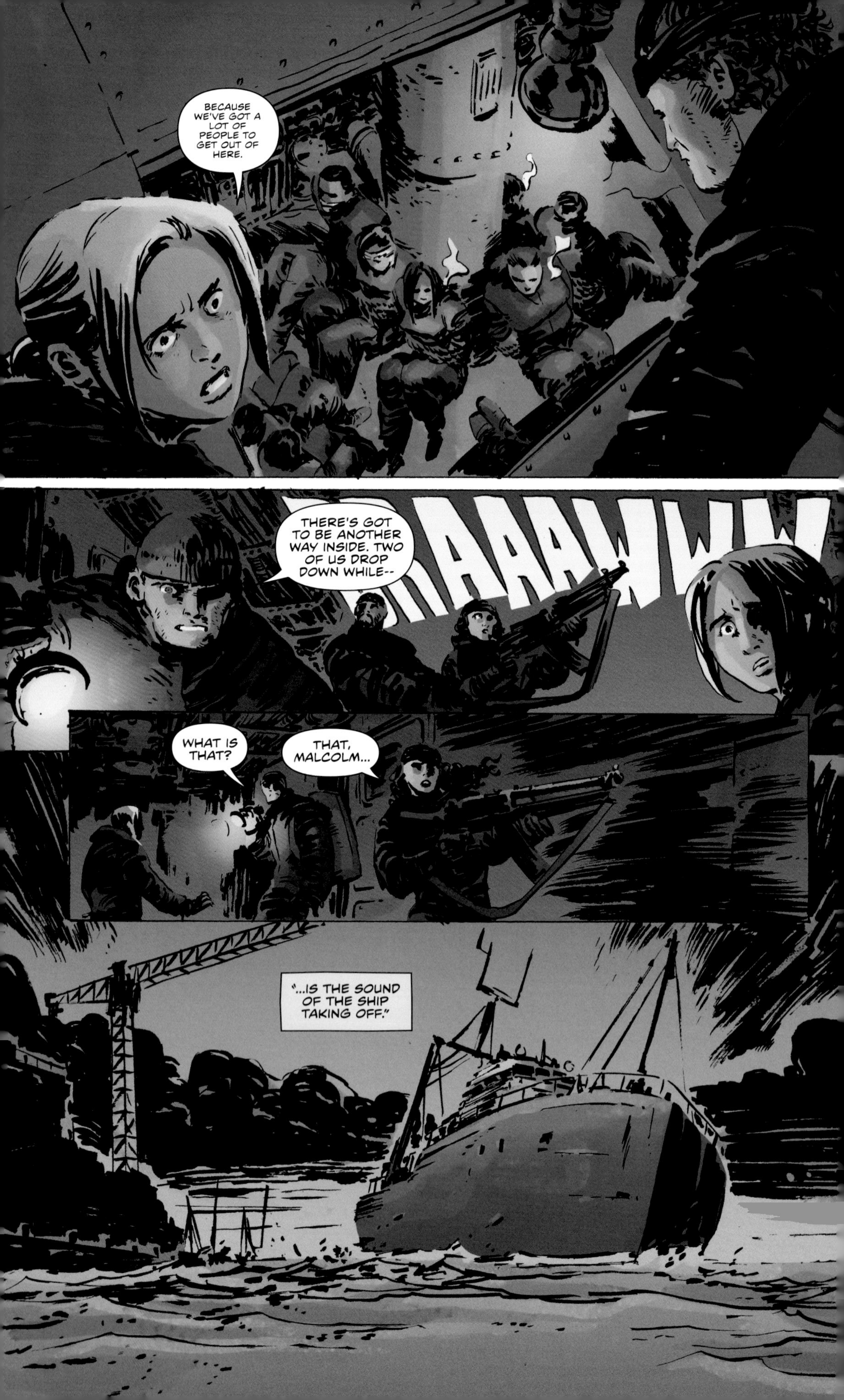

BECAUSE WE'VE GOT A LOT OF PEOPLE TO GET OUT OF HERE.
THERE'S GOT TO BE ANOTHER WAY INSIDE. TWO OF US DROP DOWN WHILE--
BRAAAAWWW
WHAT IS THAT?
THAT, MALCOLM...
"...IS THE SOUND OF THE SHIP TAKING OFF."

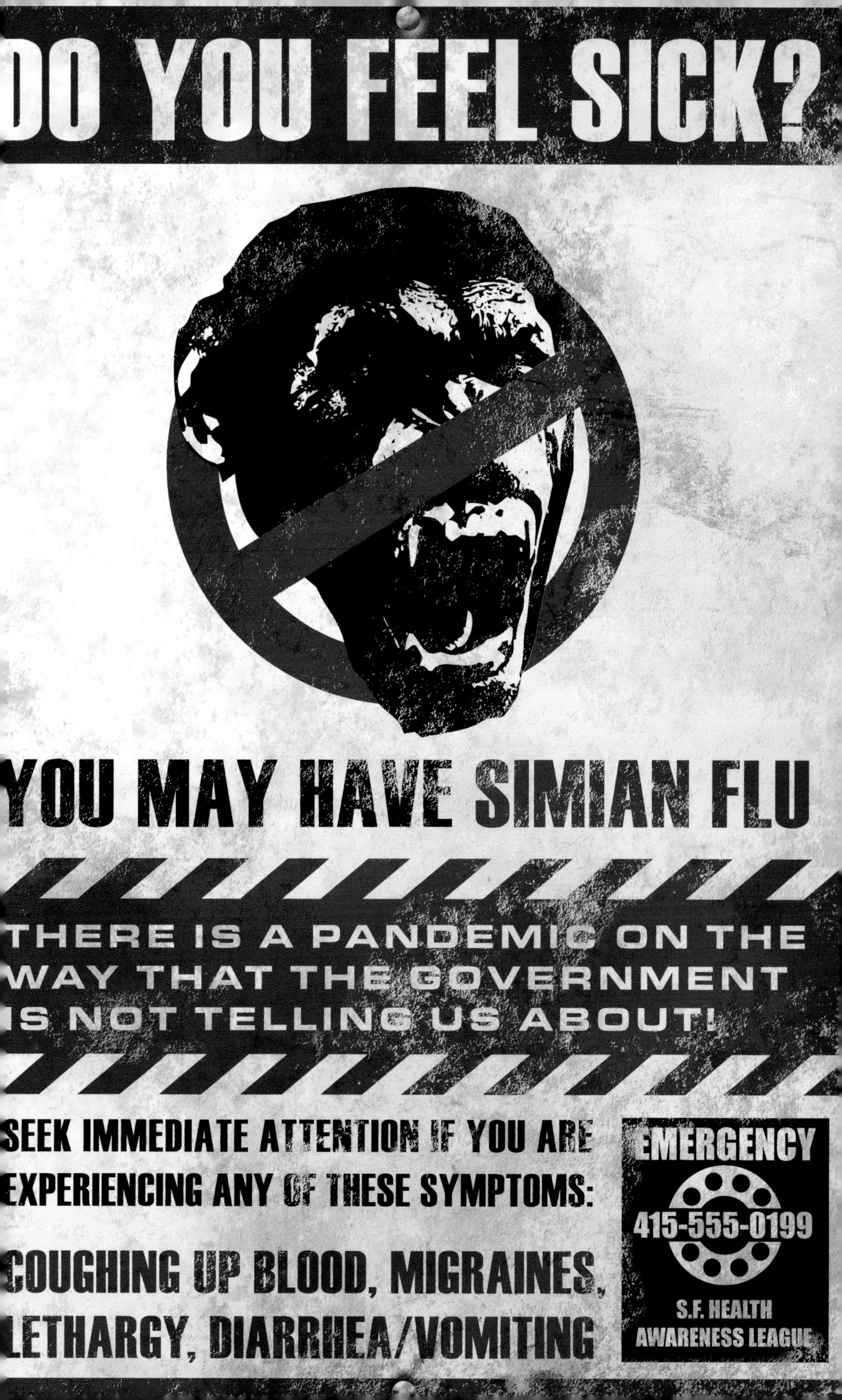
DO YOU FEEL SICK?
YOU MAY HAVE SIMIAN FLU
THERE IS A PANDEMIC ON THE WAY THAT THE GOVERNMENT IS NOT TELLING US ABOUT!
SEEK IMMEDIATE ATTENTION IF YOU ARE EXPERIENCING ANY OF THESE SYMPTOMS:
COUGHING UP BLOOD, MIGRAINES, LETHARGY, DIARRHEA/VOMITING
EMERGENCY
415-555-0199
S.F. HEALTH AWARENESS LEAGUE

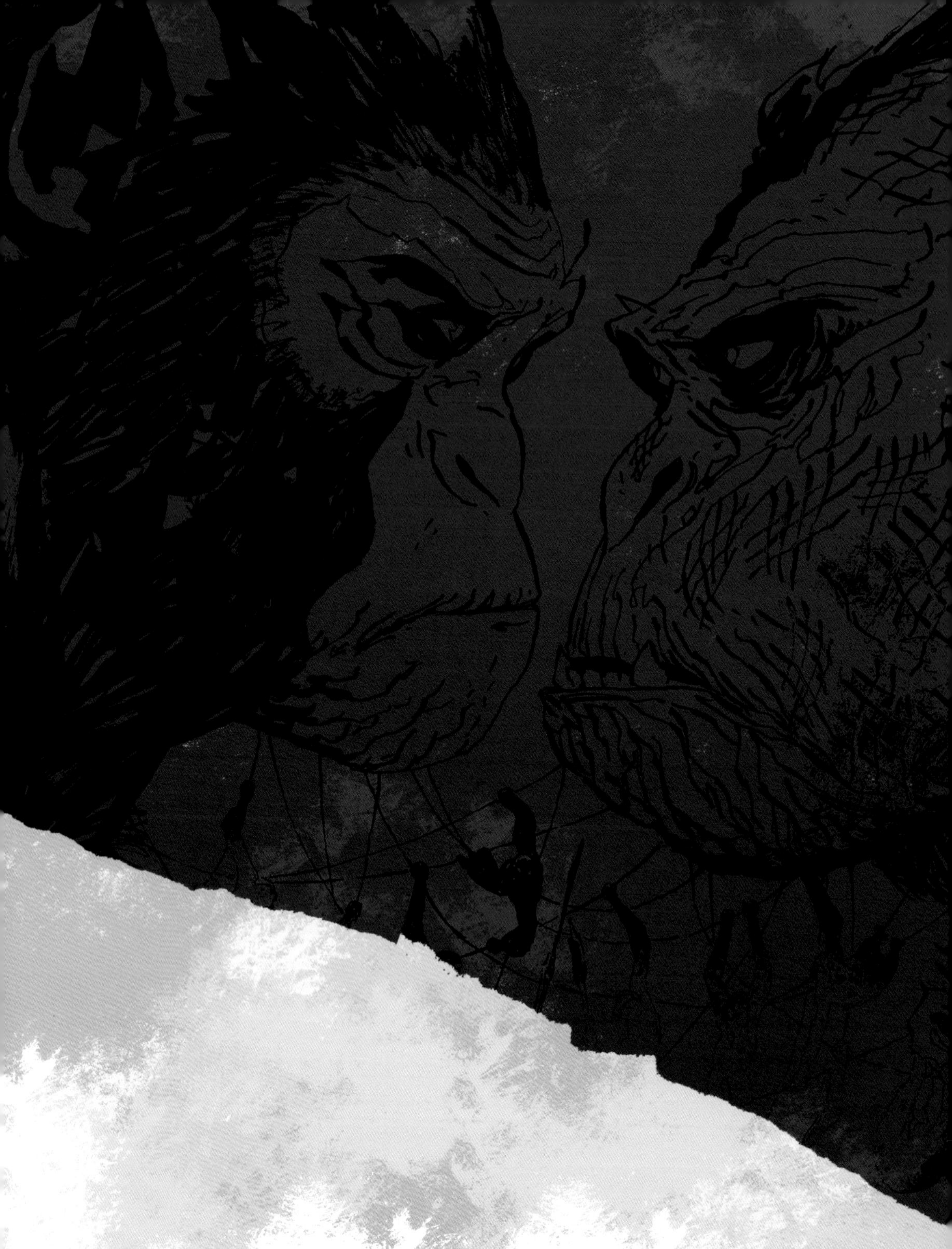

CHAPTER**FIVE**

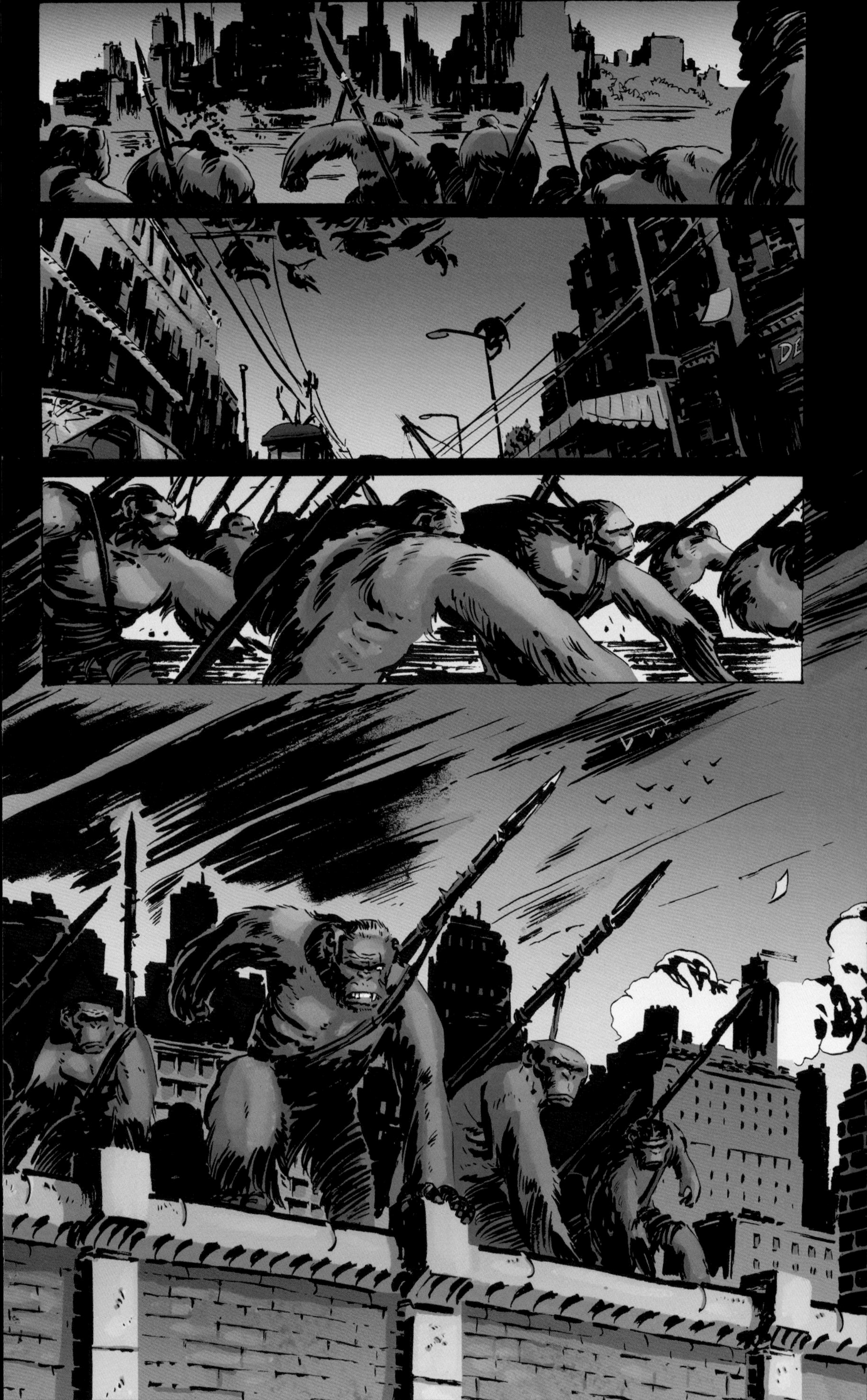

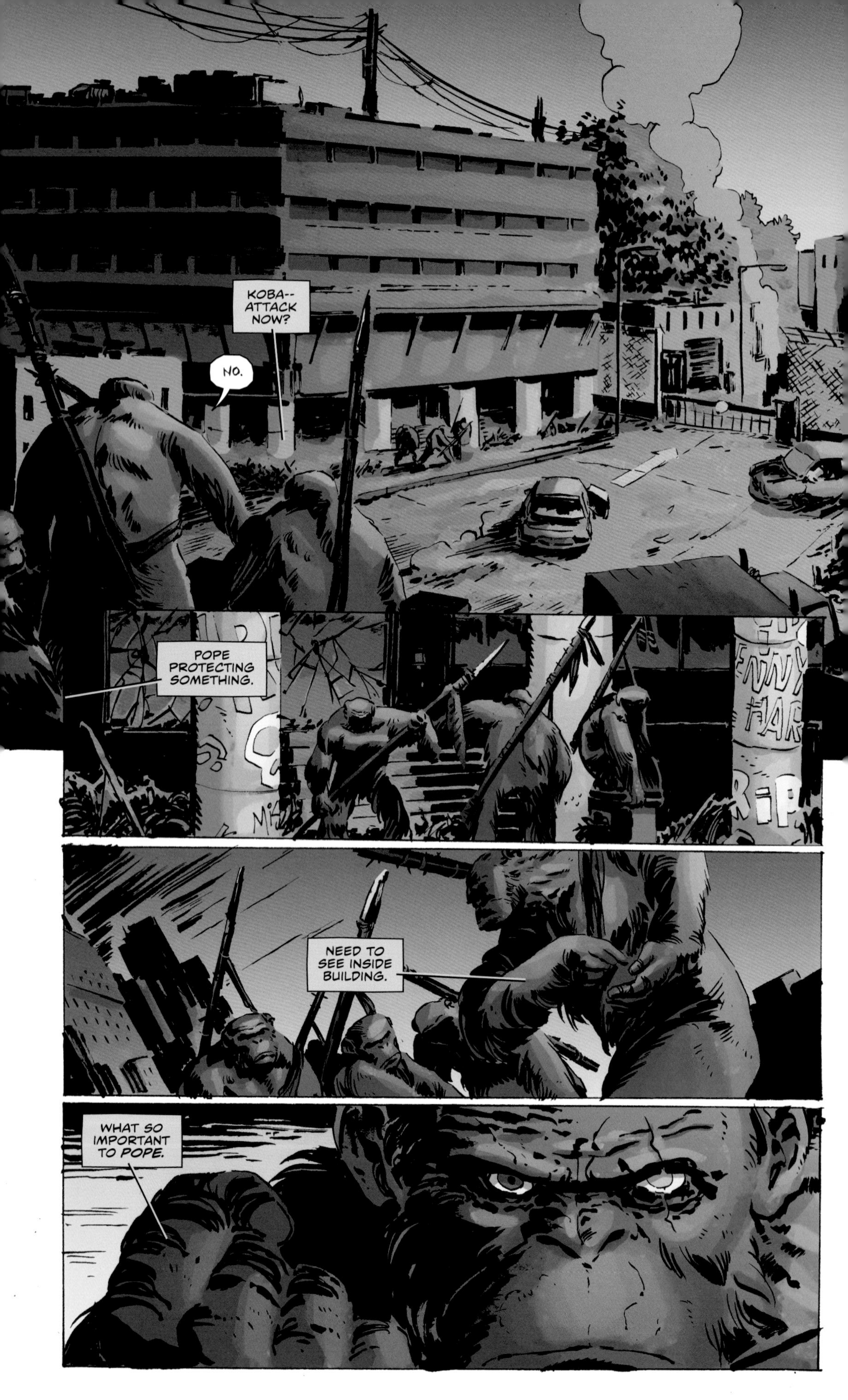

KOBA-- ATTACK NOW?
NO.
POPE PROTECTING SOMETHING.
NEED TO SEE INSIDE BUILDING.
WHAT SO IMPORTANT TO *POPE*.

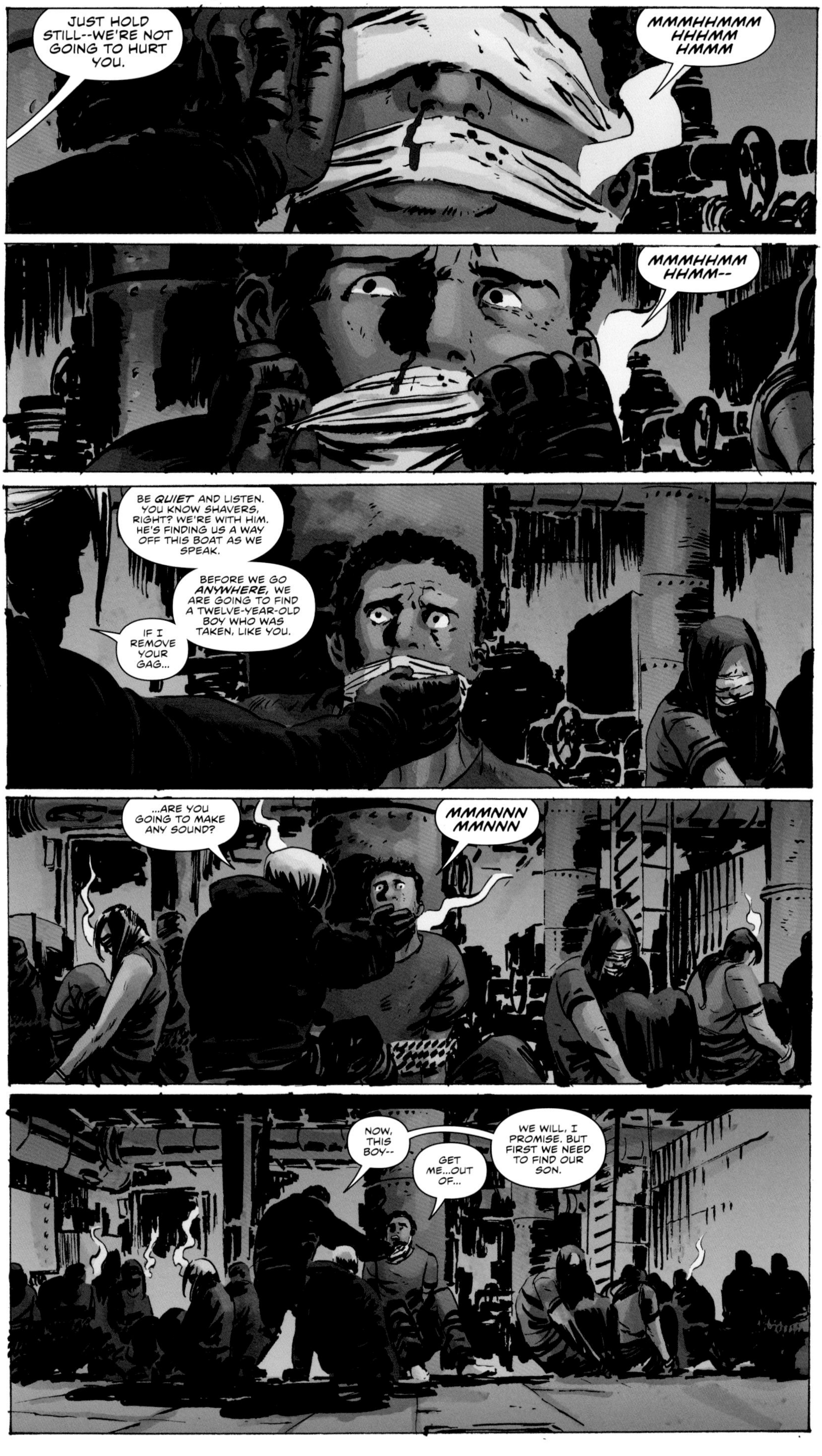

JUST HOLD STILL--WE'RE NOT GOING TO HURT YOU.
MMMHMMM HHMM HMMM
MMMHMM HHMM--
BE *QUIET* AND LISTEN. YOU KNOW SHAVERS, RIGHT? WE'RE WITH HIM. HE'S FINDING US A WAY OFF THIS BOAT AS WE SPEAK.
BEFORE WE GO *ANYWHERE,* WE ARE GOING TO FIND A TWELVE-YEAR-OLD BOY WHO WAS TAKEN, LIKE YOU.
IF I REMOVE YOUR GAG...
...ARE YOU GOING TO MAKE ANY SOUND?
MMMNNN MMNNN
NOW, THIS BOY--
GET ME...OUT OF...
WE WILL, I PROMISE. BUT FIRST WE NEED TO FIND OUR SON.

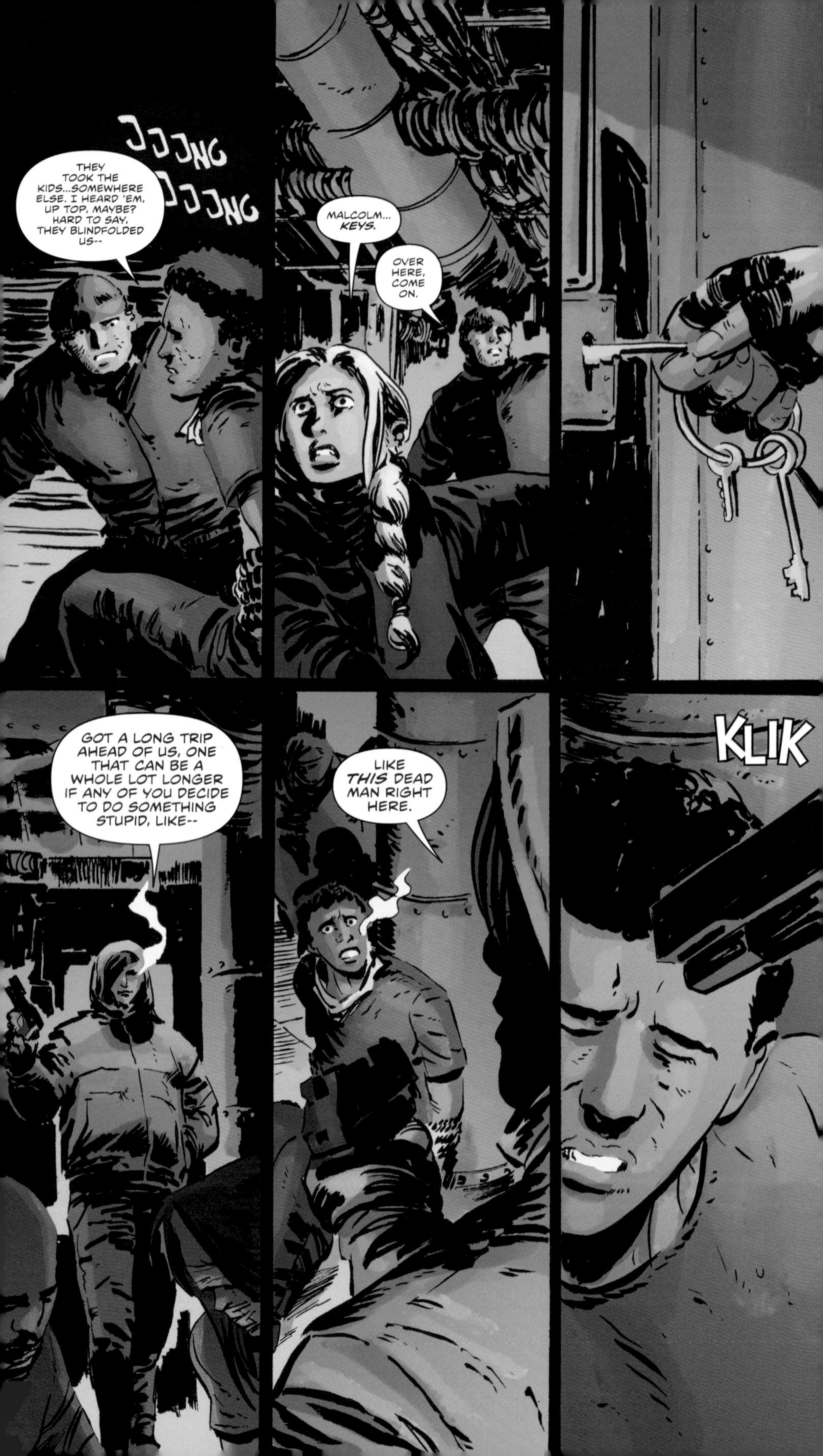
JJJNG
JJJNG
THEY TOOK THE KIDS...SOMEWHERE ELSE. I HEARD 'EM, UP TOP, MAYBE? HARD TO SAY, THEY BLINDFOLDED US--
MALCOLM... KEYS.
OVER HERE, COME ON.
GOT A LONG TRIP AHEAD OF US, ONE THAT CAN BE A WHOLE LOT LONGER IF ANY OF YOU DECIDE TO DO SOMETHING STUPID, LIKE--
LIKE THIS DEAD MAN RIGHT HERE.
KLIK

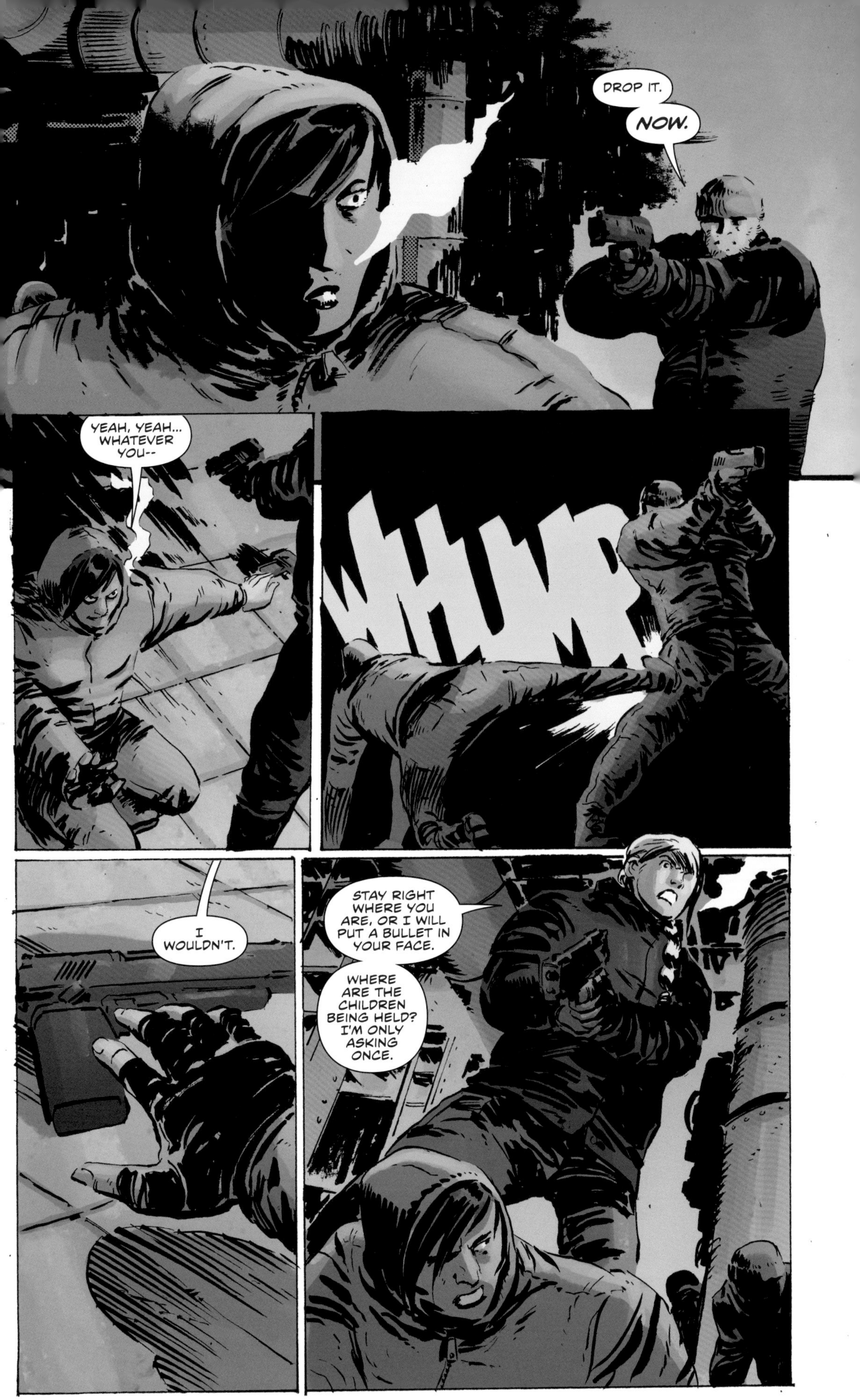
DROP IT.
NOW.
YEAH, YEAH... WHATEVER YOU--
WHUMP
I WOULDN'T.
STAY RIGHT WHERE YOU ARE, OR I WILL PUT A BULLET IN YOUR FACE.
WHERE ARE THE CHILDREN BEING HELD? I'M ONLY ASKING ONCE.

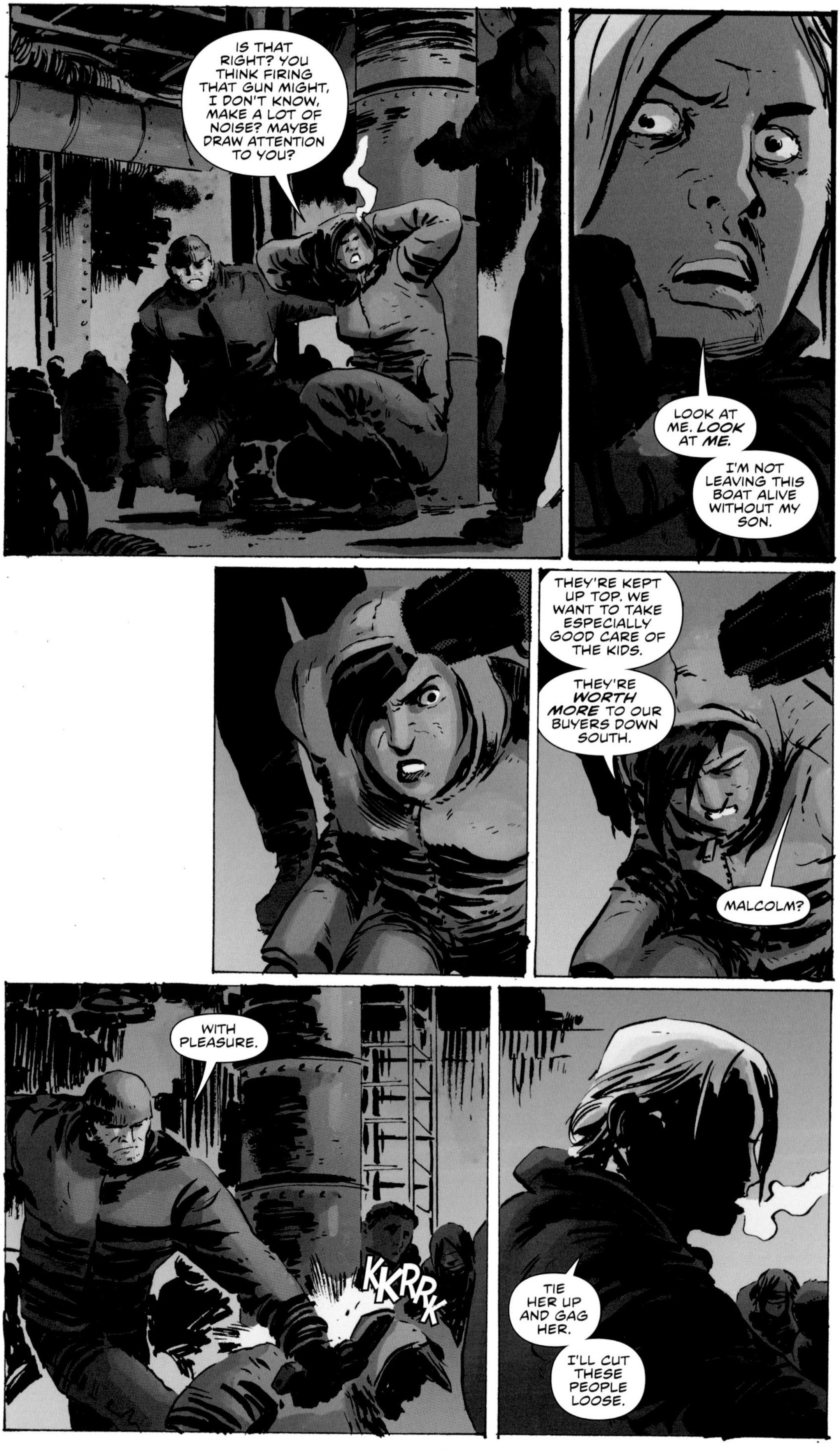
IS THAT RIGHT? YOU THINK FIRING THAT GUN MIGHT, I DON'T KNOW, MAKE A LOT OF NOISE? MAYBE DRAW ATTENTION TO YOU?
LOOK AT ME. LOOK AT ME.
I'M NOT LEAVING THIS BOAT ALIVE WITHOUT MY SON.
THEY'RE KEPT UP TOP. WE WANT TO TAKE ESPECIALLY GOOD CARE OF THE KIDS.
THEY'RE WORTH MORE TO OUR BUYERS DOWN SOUTH.
MALCOLM?
WITH PLEASURE.
KKRRK
TIE HER UP AND GAG HER.
I'LL CUT THESE PEOPLE LOOSE.

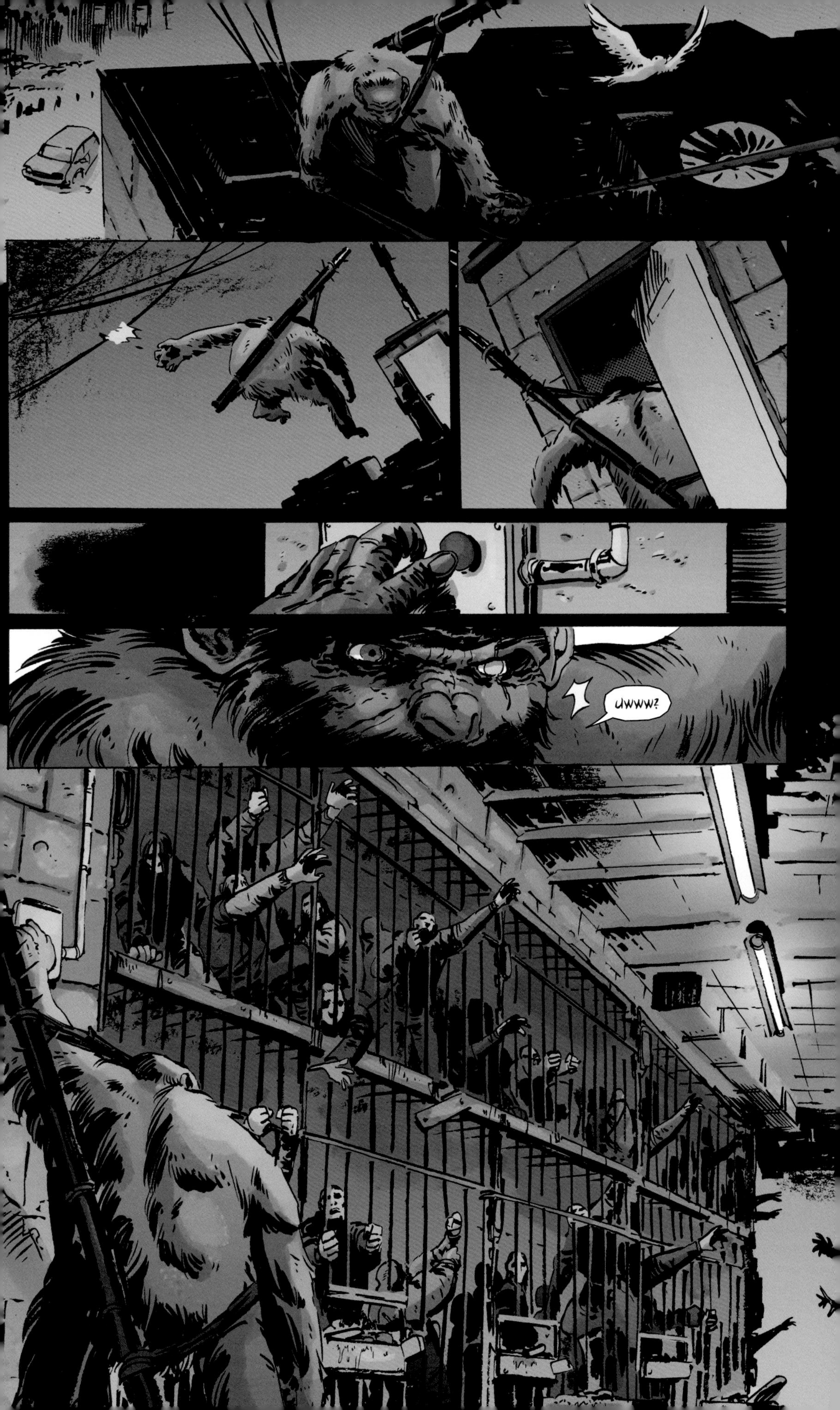
UWWW?

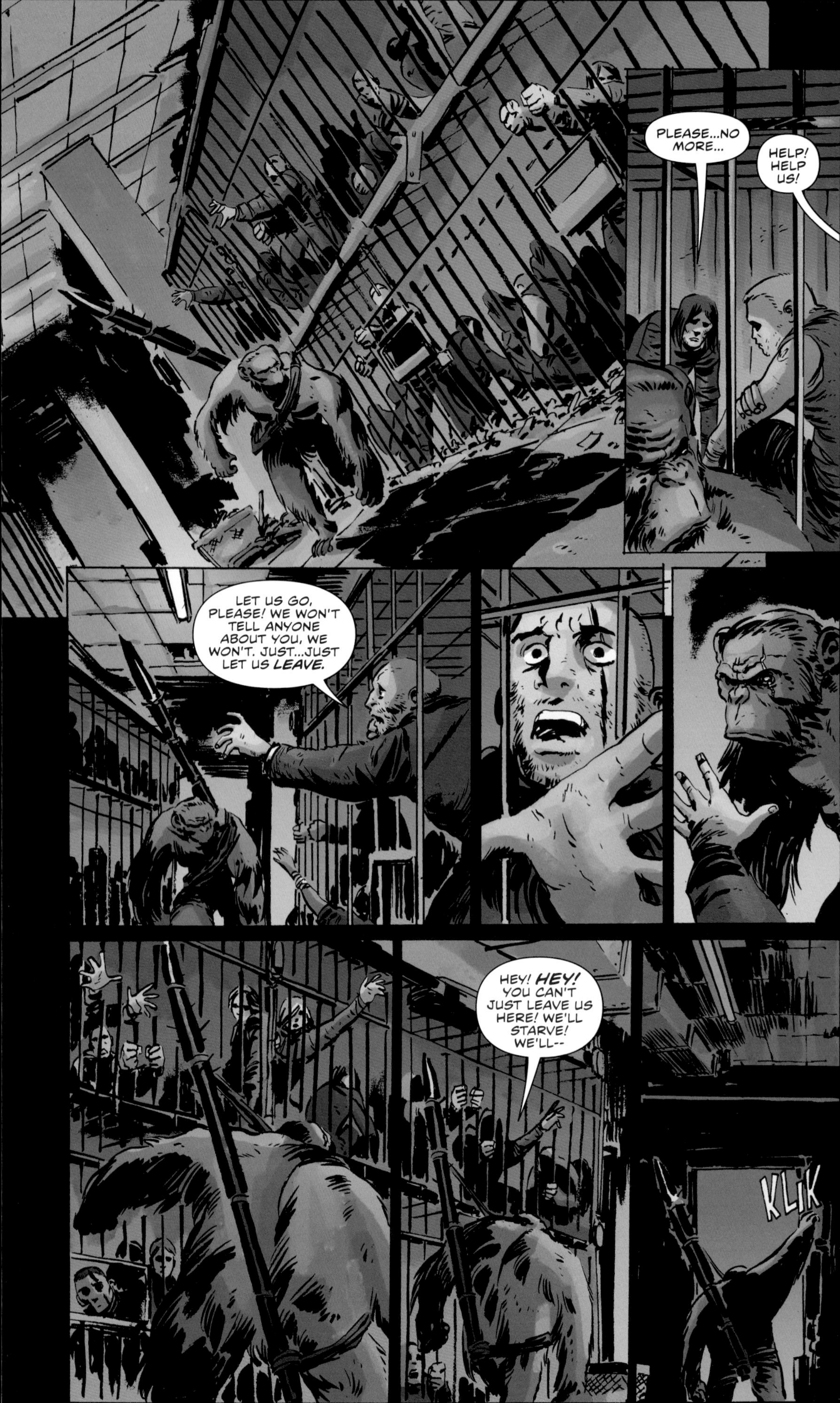
PLEASE...NO MORE...
HELP! HELP US!
LET US GO, PLEASE! WE WON'T TELL ANYONE ABOUT YOU, WE WON'T. JUST...JUST LET US *LEAVE.*
HEY! *HEY!* YOU CAN'T JUST LEAVE US HERE! WE'LL STARVE! WE'LL--
KLIK

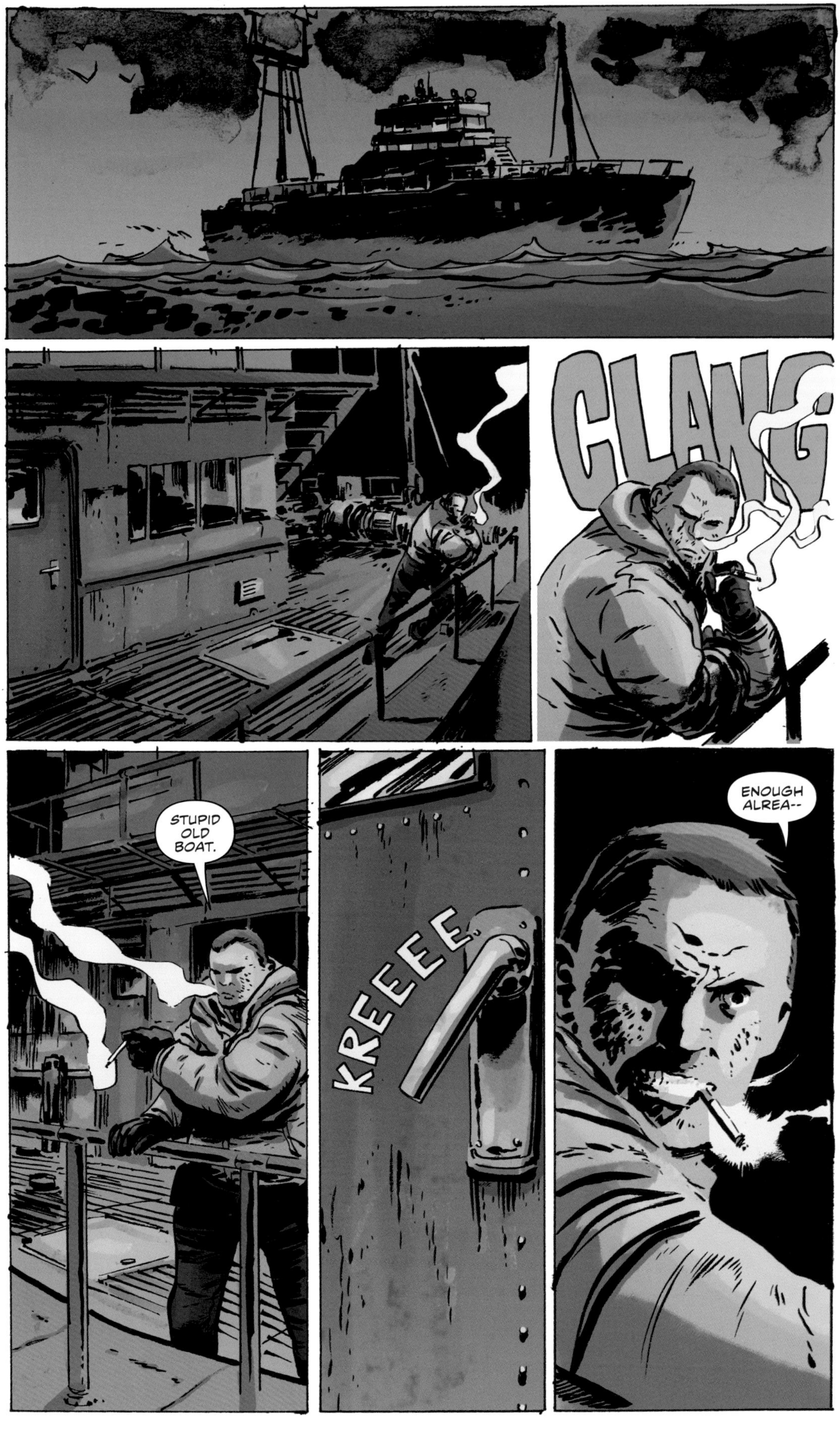
CLANG
STUPID OLD BOAT.
KREEEE
ENOUGH ALREA--

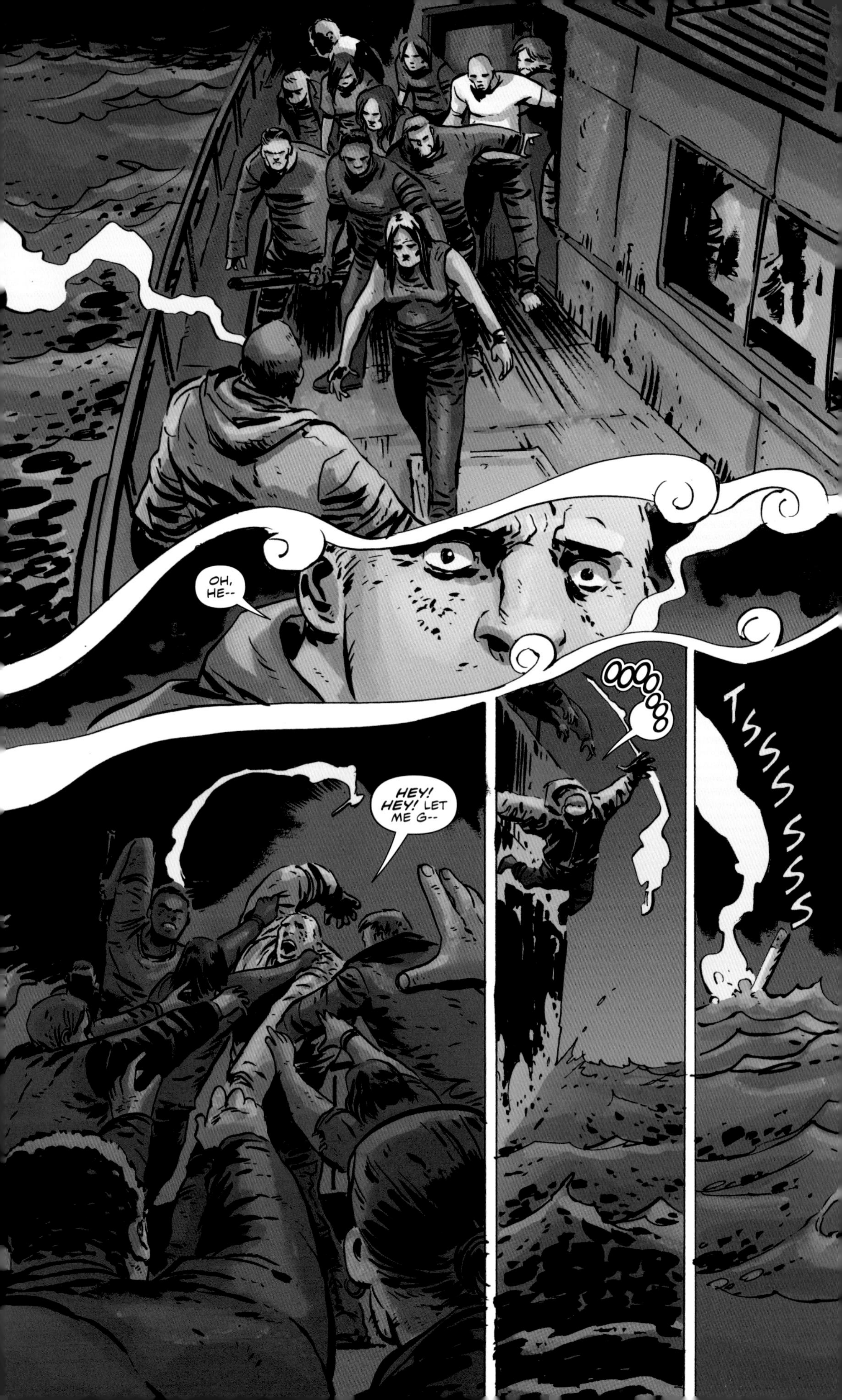

OH, HE--
HEY! HEY! LET ME G--
OOOOOO
TSSSSSSS

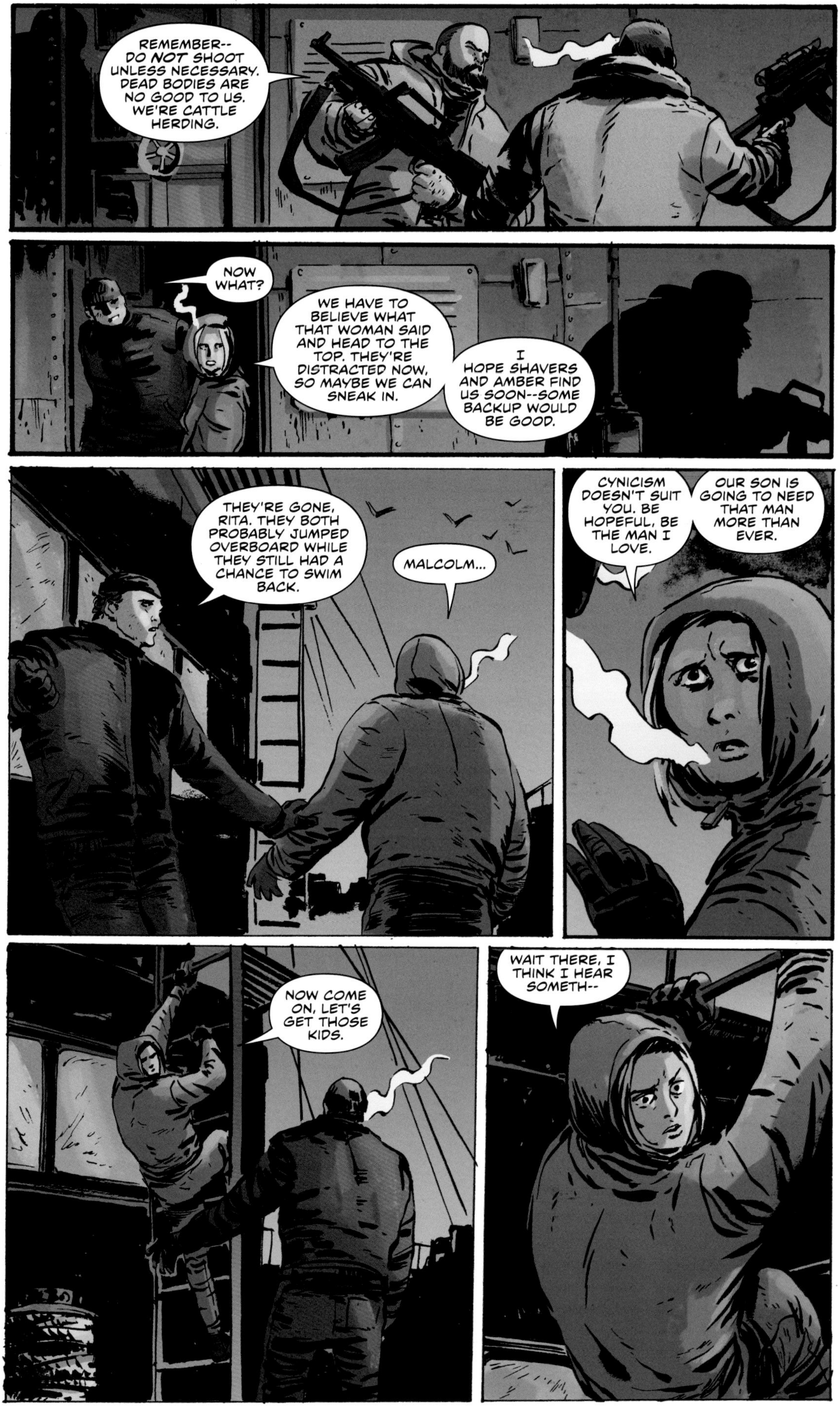
REMEMBER-- DO NOT SHOOT UNLESS NECESSARY. DEAD BODIES ARE NO GOOD TO US. WE'RE CATTLE HERDING.
NOW WHAT?
WE HAVE TO BELIEVE WHAT THAT WOMAN SAID AND HEAD TO THE TOP. THEY'RE DISTRACTED NOW, SO MAYBE WE CAN SNEAK IN.
I HOPE SHAVERS AND AMBER FIND US SOON--SOME BACKUP WOULD BE GOOD.
THEY'RE GONE, RITA. THEY BOTH PROBABLY JUMPED OVERBOARD WHILE THEY STILL HAD A CHANCE TO SWIM BACK.
MALCOLM...
CYNICISM DOESN'T SUIT YOU. BE HOPEFUL, BE THE MAN I LOVE.
OUR SON IS GOING TO NEED THAT MAN MORE THAN EVER.
NOW COME ON, LET'S GET THOSE KIDS.
WAIT THERE, I THINK I HEAR SOMETH--

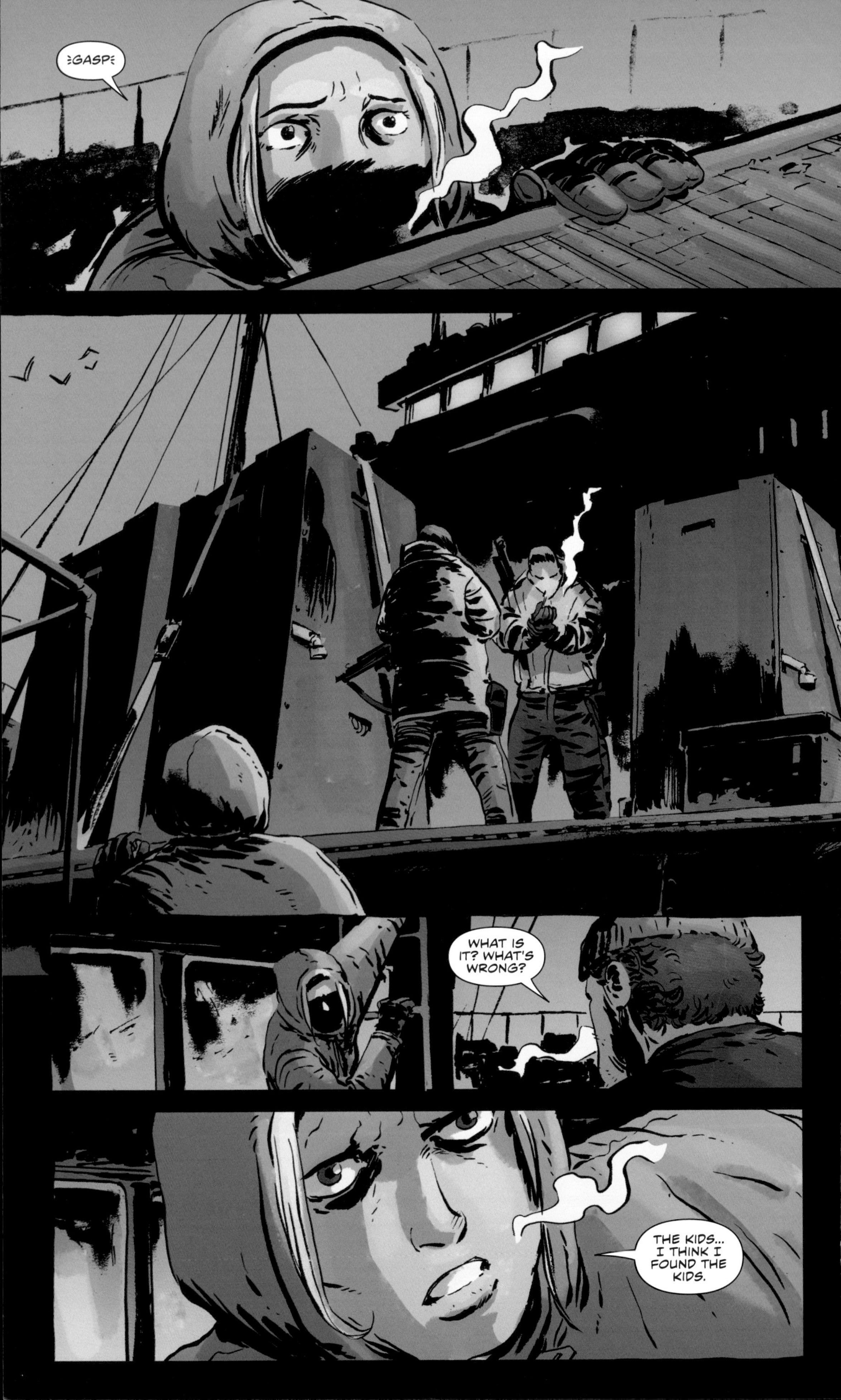
GASP
WHAT IS IT? WHAT'S WRONG?
THE KIDS... I THINK I FOUND THE KIDS.

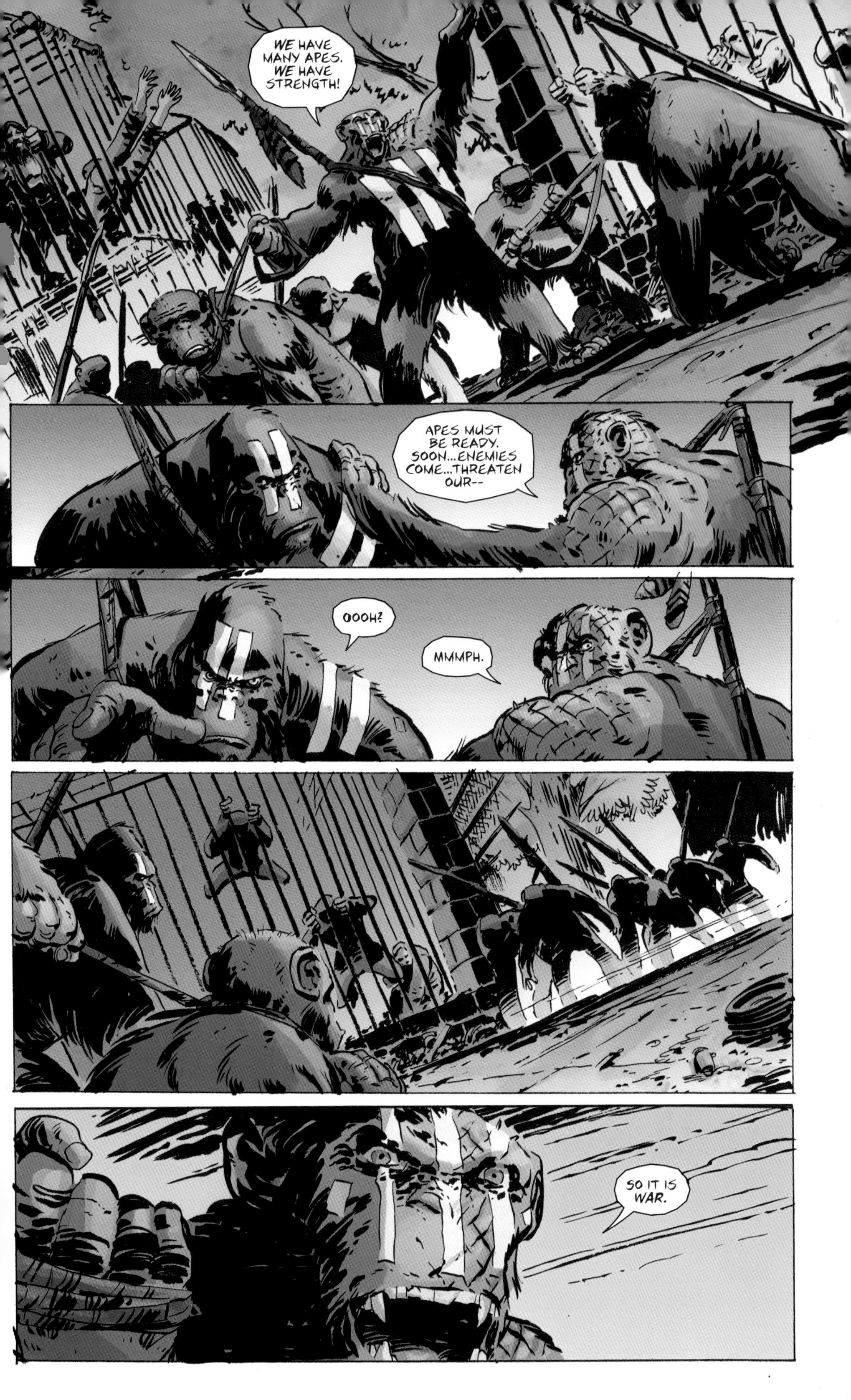
WE HAVE MANY APES. WE HAVE STRENGTH!
APES MUST BE READY. SOON...ENEMIES COME...THREATEN OUR--
OOOH?
MMMPH.
SO IT IS WAR.

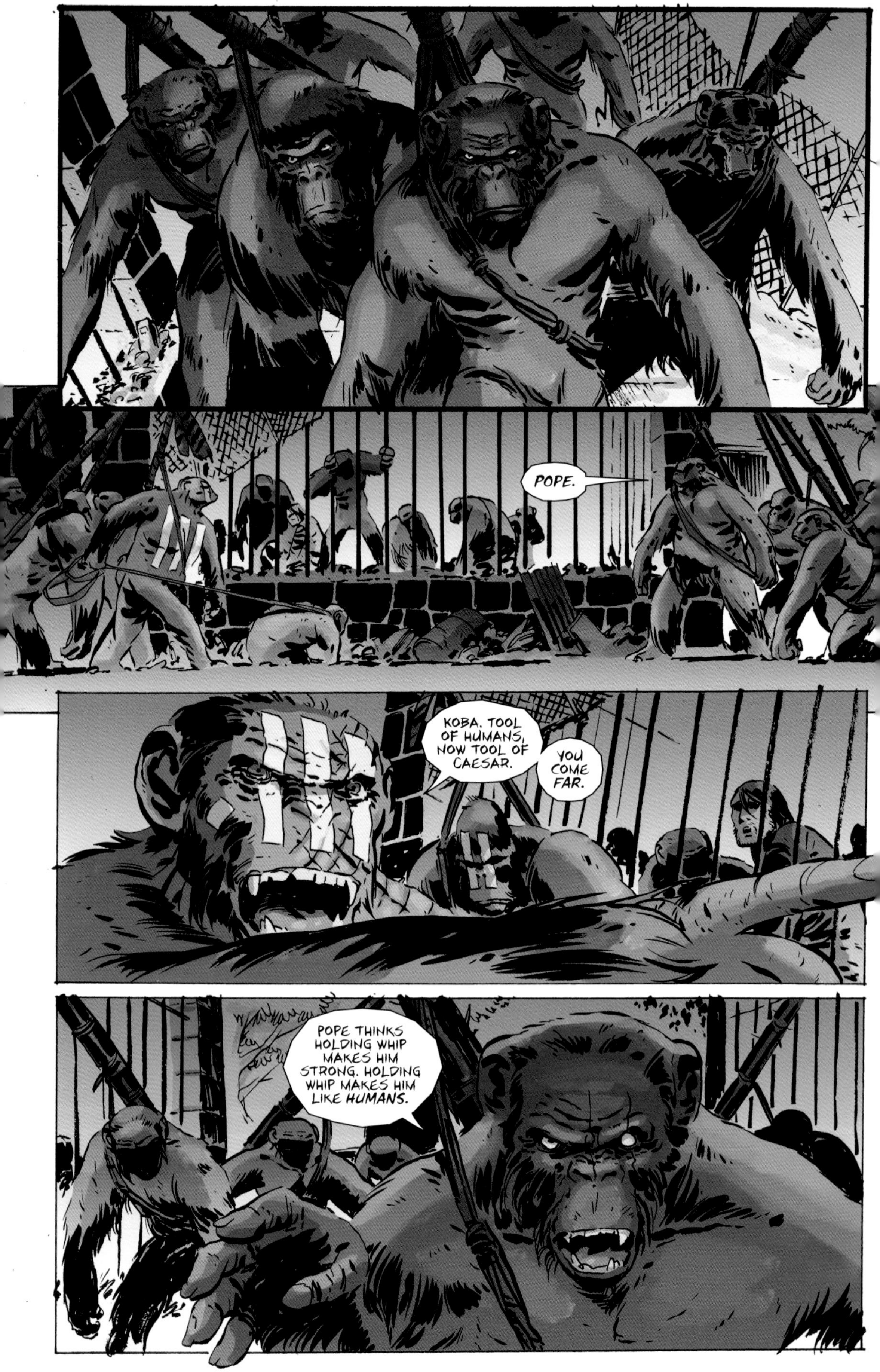
POPE.
KOBA. TOOL OF HUMANS, NOW TOOL OF CAESAR.
YOU COME FAR.
POPE THINKS HOLDING WHIP MAKES HIM STRONG. HOLDING WHIP MAKES HIM LIKE *HUMANS*.

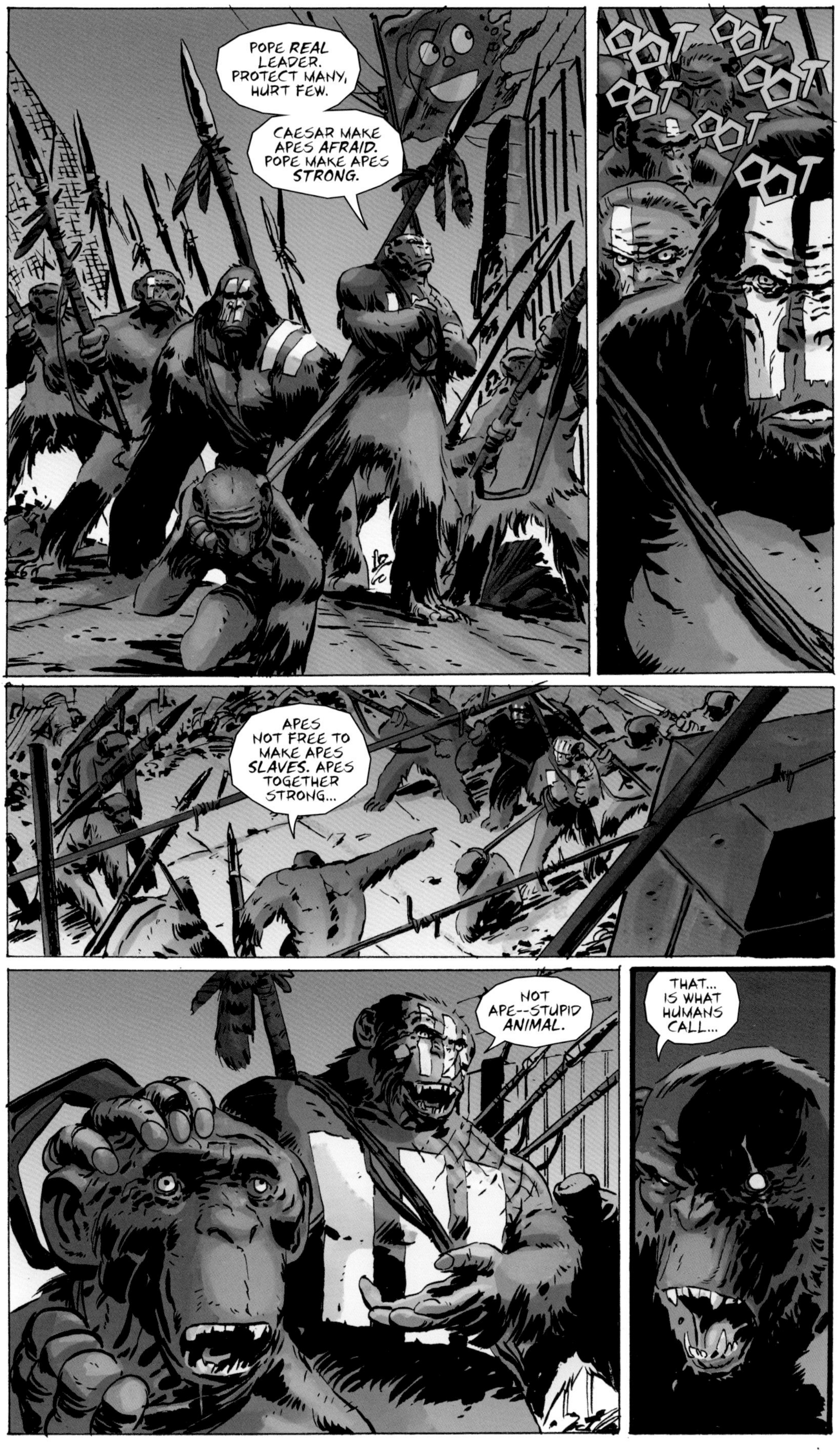
POPE REAL LEADER. PROTECT MANY, HURT FEW.
CAESAR MAKE APES AFRAID. POPE MAKE APES STRONG.
OOT OOT OOT OOT OOT OOT
APES NOT FREE TO MAKE APES SLAVES. APES TOGETHER STRONG...
NOT APE--STUPID ANIMAL.
THAT... IS WHAT HUMANS CALL...

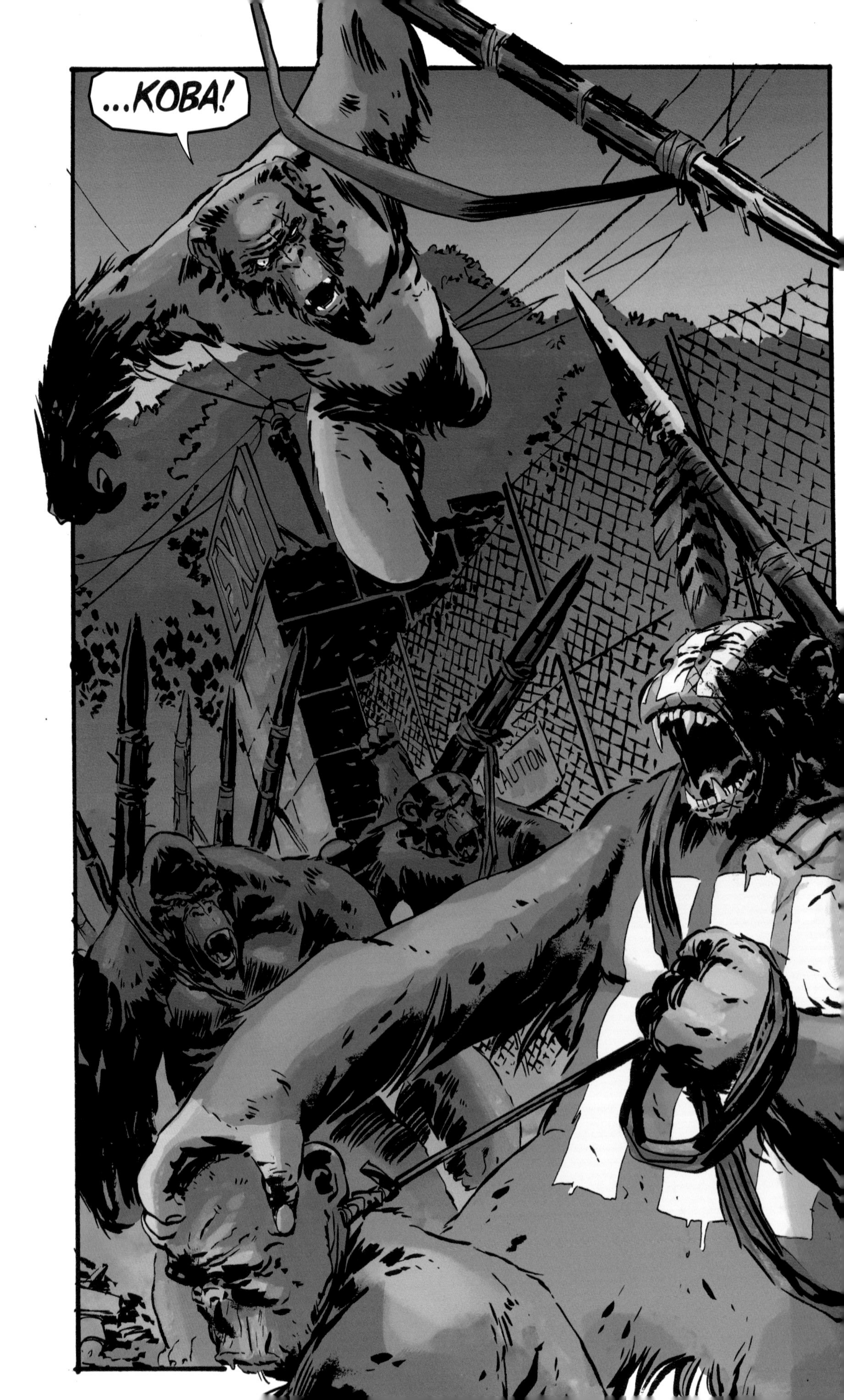
...KOBA!

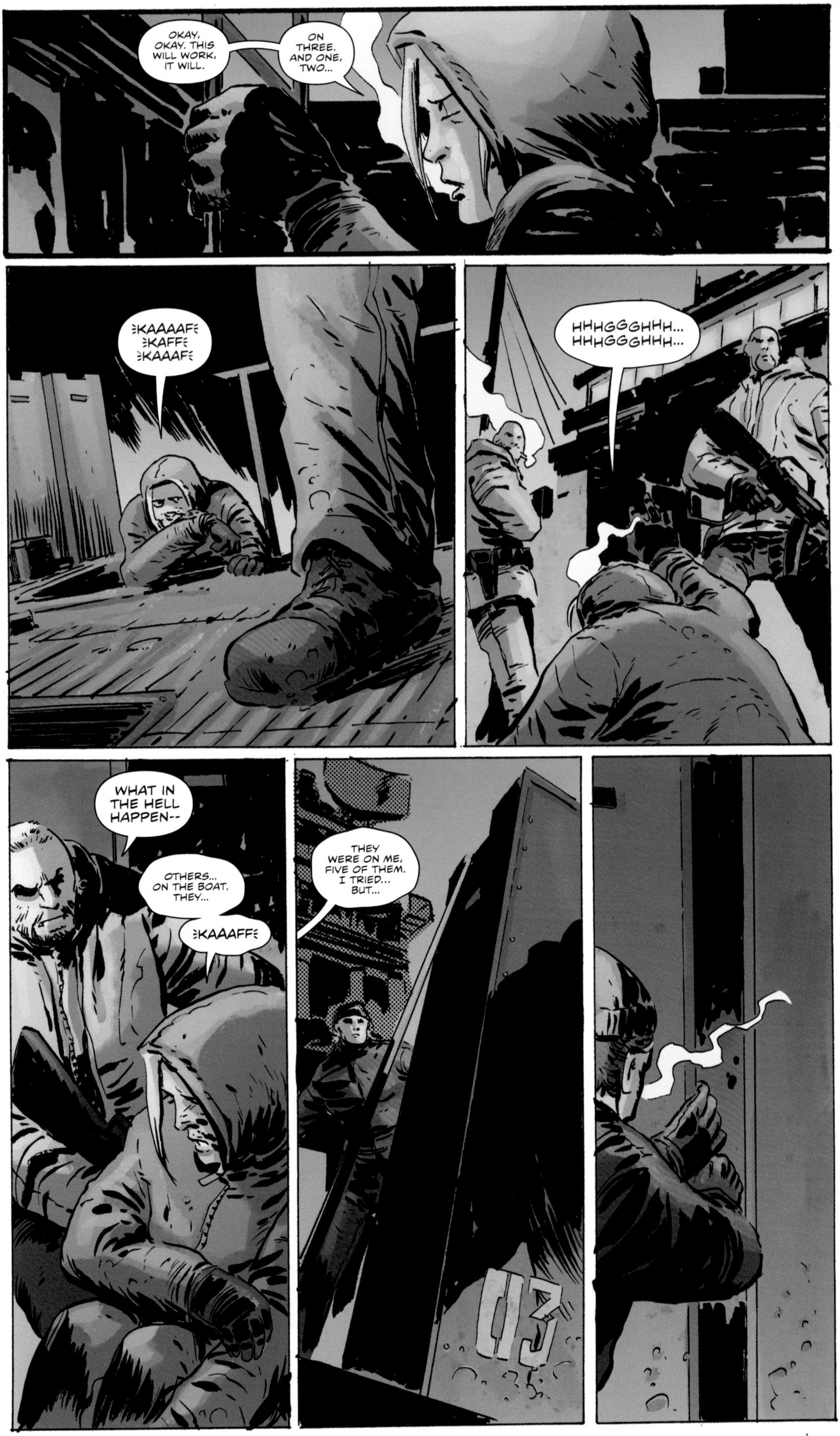
OKAY, OKAY. THIS WILL WORK, IT WILL.
ON THREE. AND ONE, TWO...
KAAAAF KAFF KAAAF
HHHGGGHHH... HHHGGGHHH...
WHAT IN THE HELL HAPPEN--
OTHERS... ON THE BOAT. THEY...
KAAAFF
THEY WERE ON ME, FIVE OF THEM. I TRIED... BUT...
03

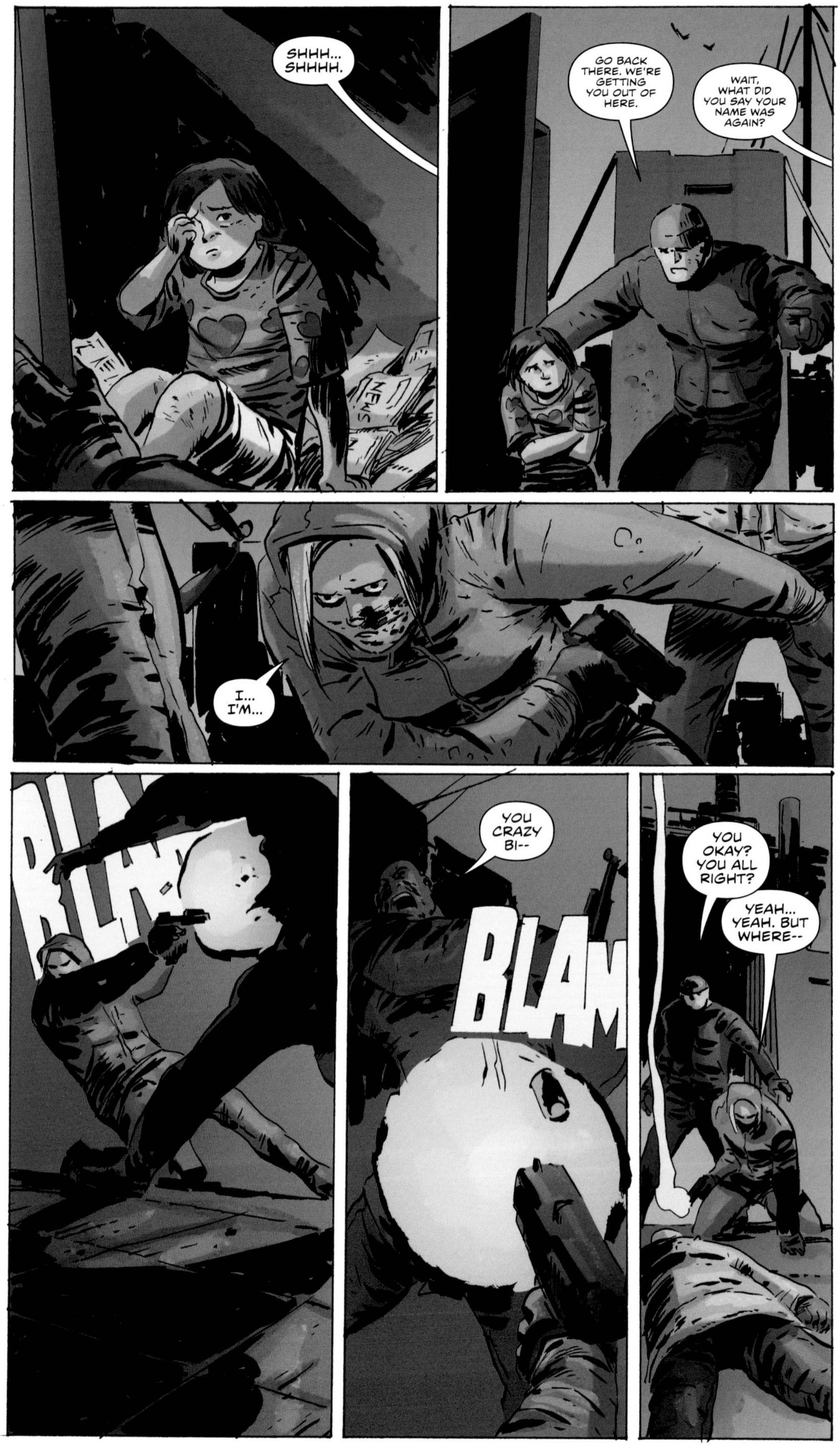
SHHH... SHHHH.
GO BACK THERE. WE'RE GETTING YOU OUT OF HERE.
WAIT, WHAT DID YOU SAY YOUR NAME WAS AGAIN?
I... I'M...
BLAM
YOU CRAZY BI--
BLAM
YOU OKAY? YOU ALL RIGHT?
YEAH... YEAH. BUT WHERE--

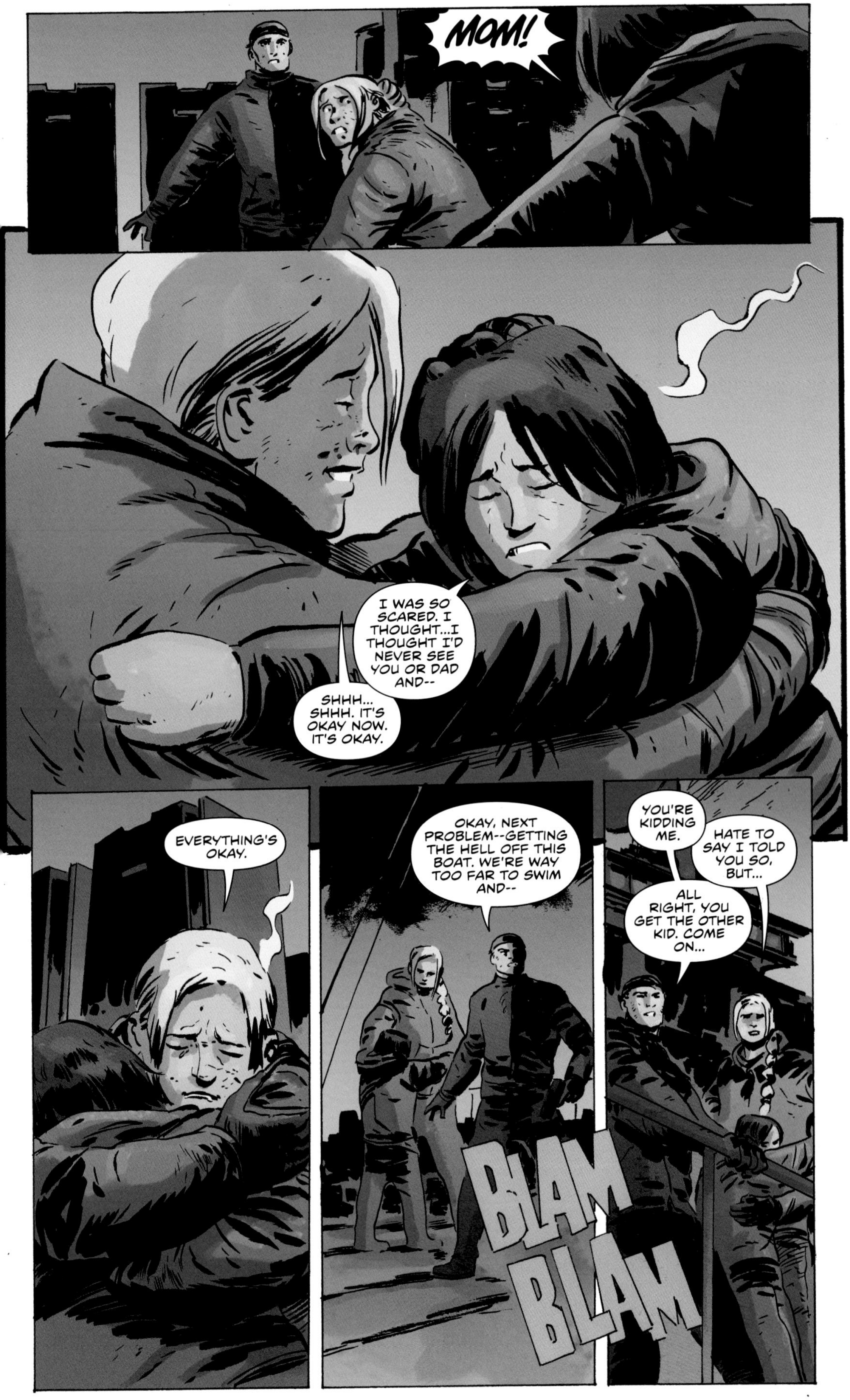
MOM!
I WAS SO SCARED. I THOUGHT...I THOUGHT I'D NEVER SEE YOU OR DAD AND--
SHHH... SHHH. IT'S OKAY NOW. IT'S OKAY.
EVERYTHING'S OKAY.
OKAY, NEXT PROBLEM--GETTING THE HELL OFF THIS BOAT. WE'RE WAY TOO FAR TO SWIM AND--
BLAM
BLAM
YOU'RE KIDDING ME.
HATE TO SAY I TOLD YOU SO, BUT...
ALL RIGHT, YOU GET THE OTHER KID. COME ON...

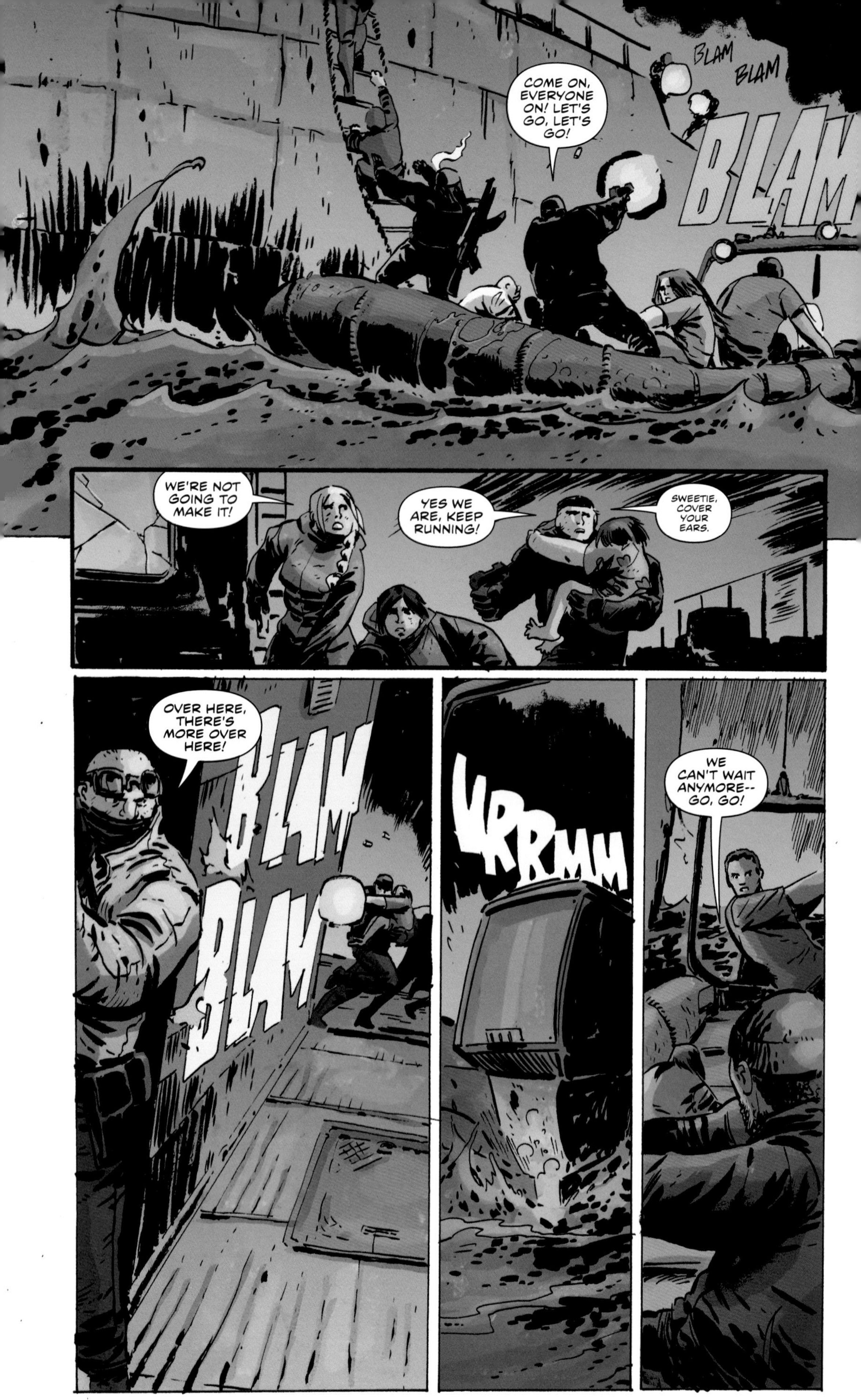
BLAM
BLAM
COME ON, EVERYONE ON! LET'S GO, LET'S GO!
BLAM
WE'RE NOT GOING TO MAKE IT!
YES WE ARE, KEEP RUNNING!
SWEETIE, COVER YOUR EARS.
OVER HERE, THERE'S MORE OVER HERE!
BLAM
BLAM
URRMM
WE CAN'T WAIT ANYMORE-- GO, GO!

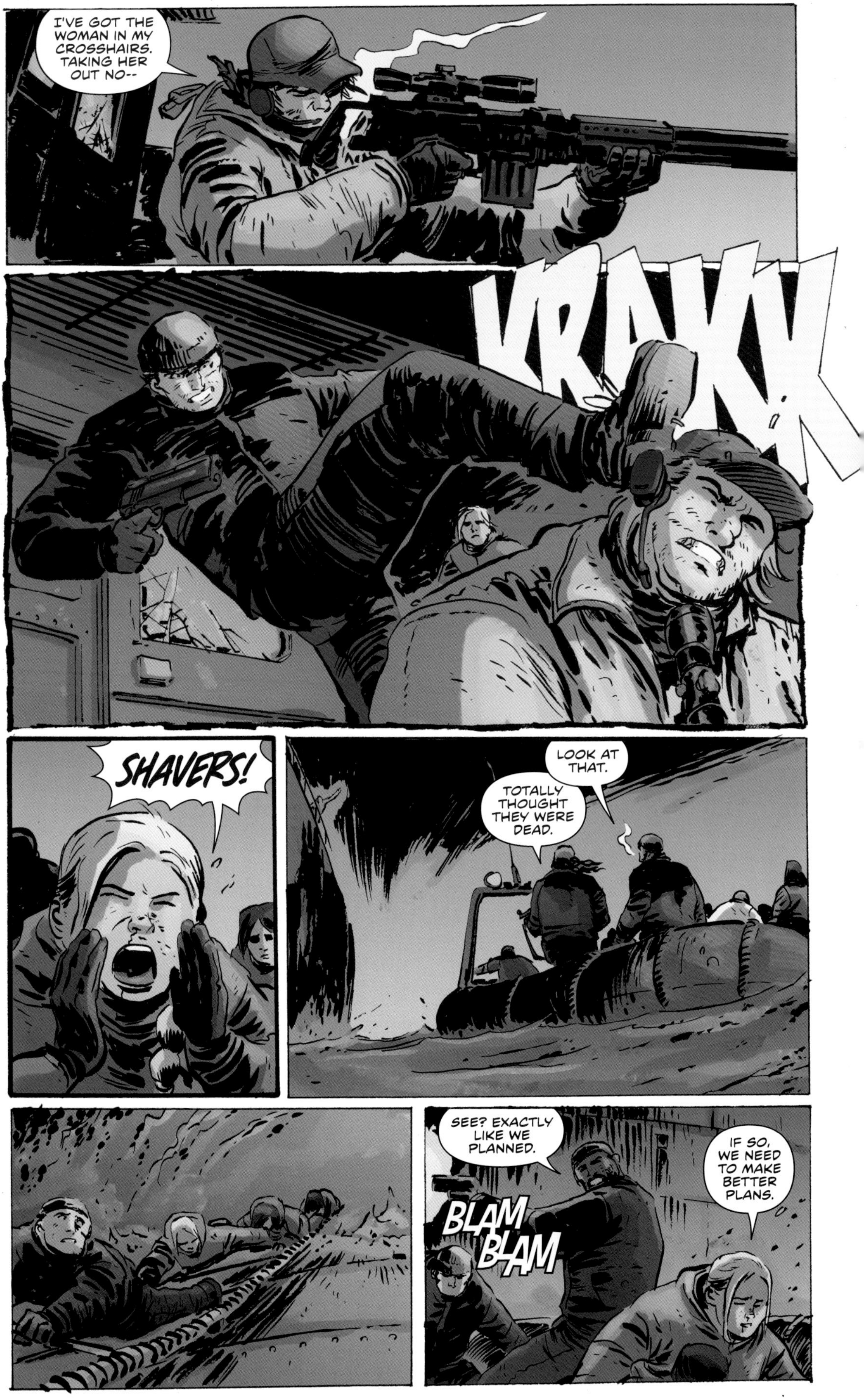
I'VE GOT THE WOMAN IN MY CROSSHAIRS. TAKING HER OUT NO--
KRAKK
SHAVERS!
LOOK AT THAT.
TOTALLY THOUGHT THEY WERE DEAD.
SEE? EXACTLY LIKE WE PLANNED.
BLAM BLAM
IF SO, WE NEED TO MAKE BETTER PLANS.

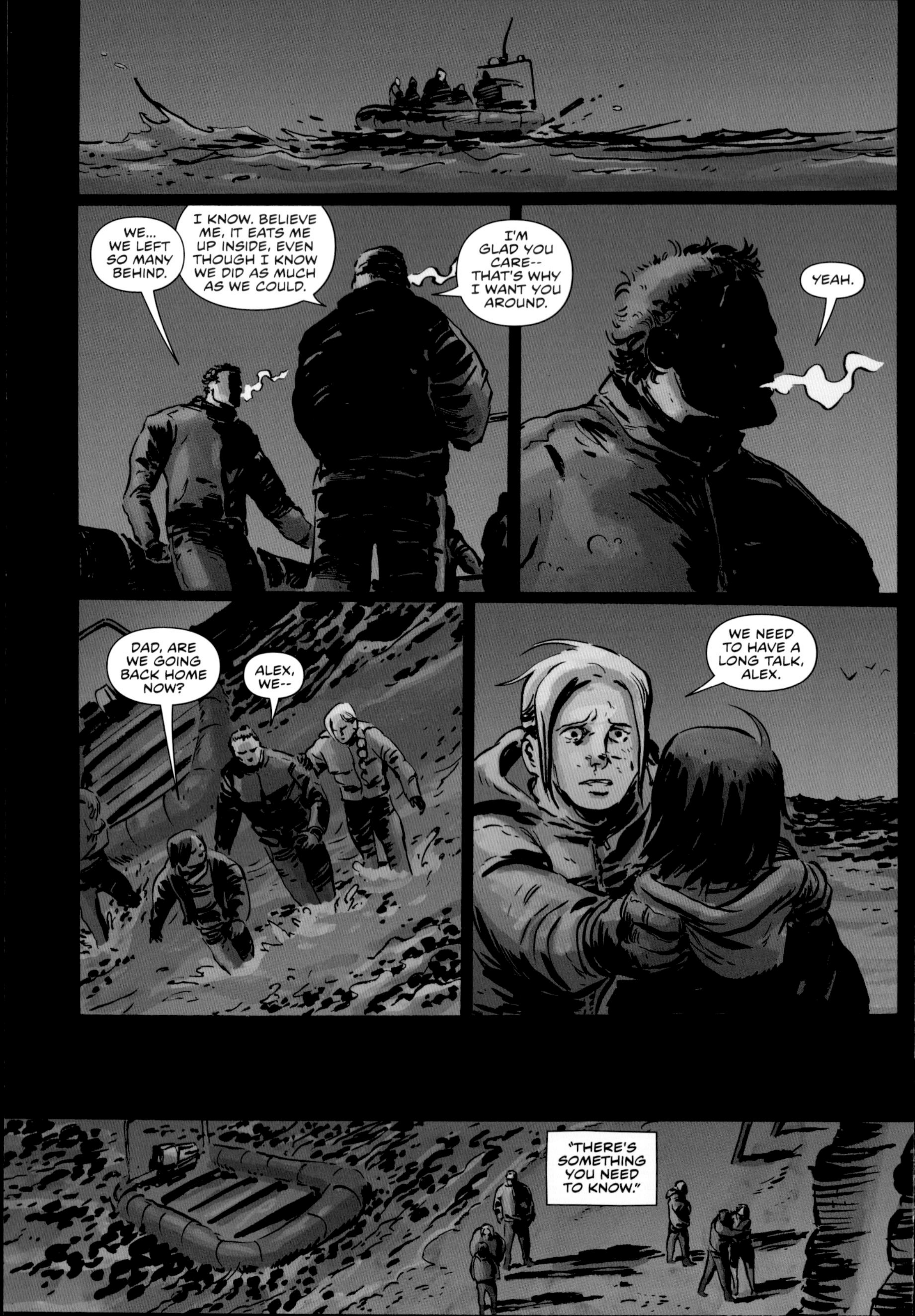

WE... WE LEFT SO MANY BEHIND.
I KNOW. BELIEVE ME, IT EATS ME UP INSIDE, EVEN THOUGH I KNOW WE DID AS MUCH AS WE COULD.
I'M GLAD YOU CARE-- THAT'S WHY I WANT YOU AROUND.
YEAH.
DAD, ARE WE GOING BACK HOME NOW?
ALEX, WE--
WE NEED TO HAVE A LONG TALK, ALEX.
"THERE'S SOMETHING YOU NEED TO KNOW."

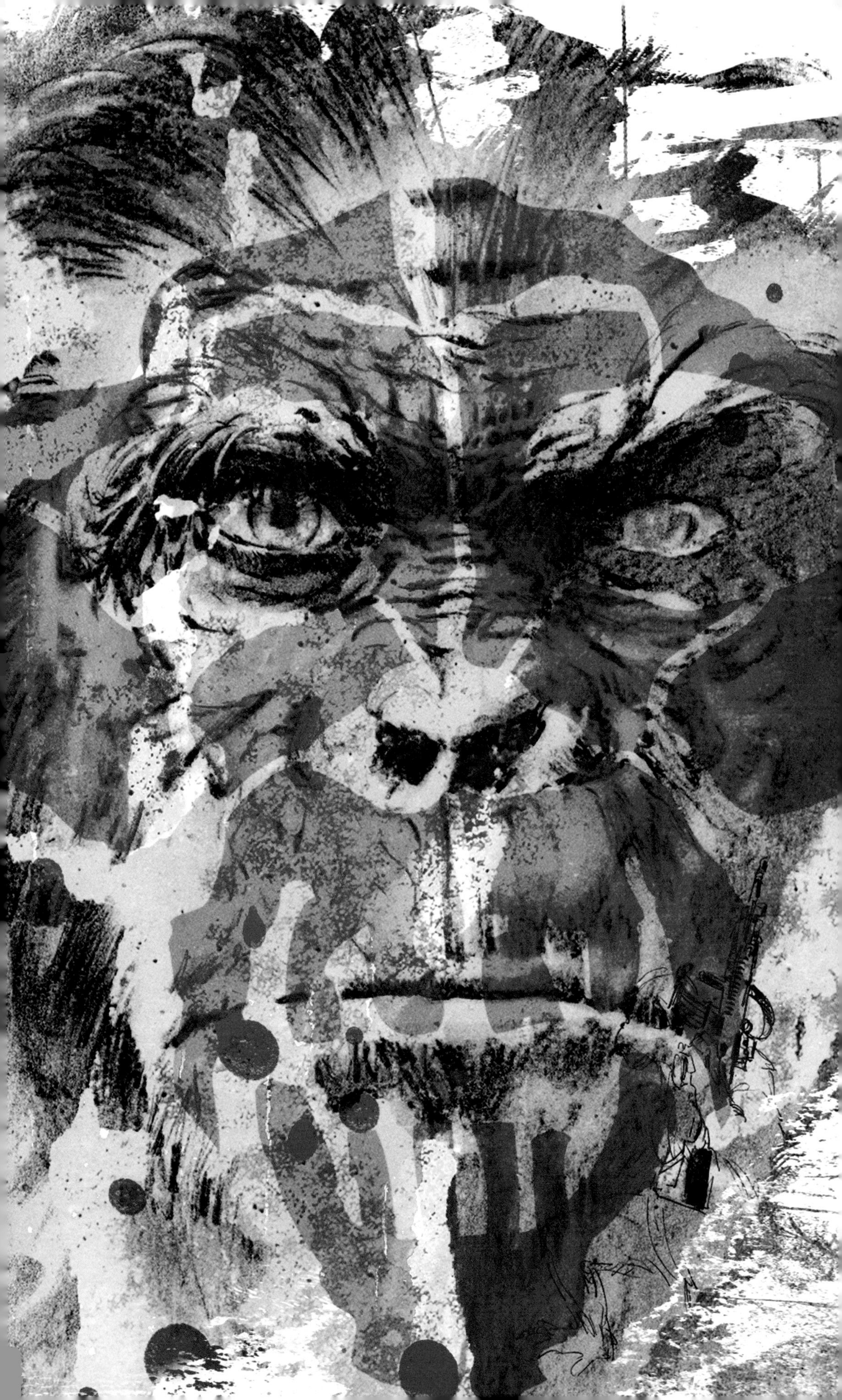

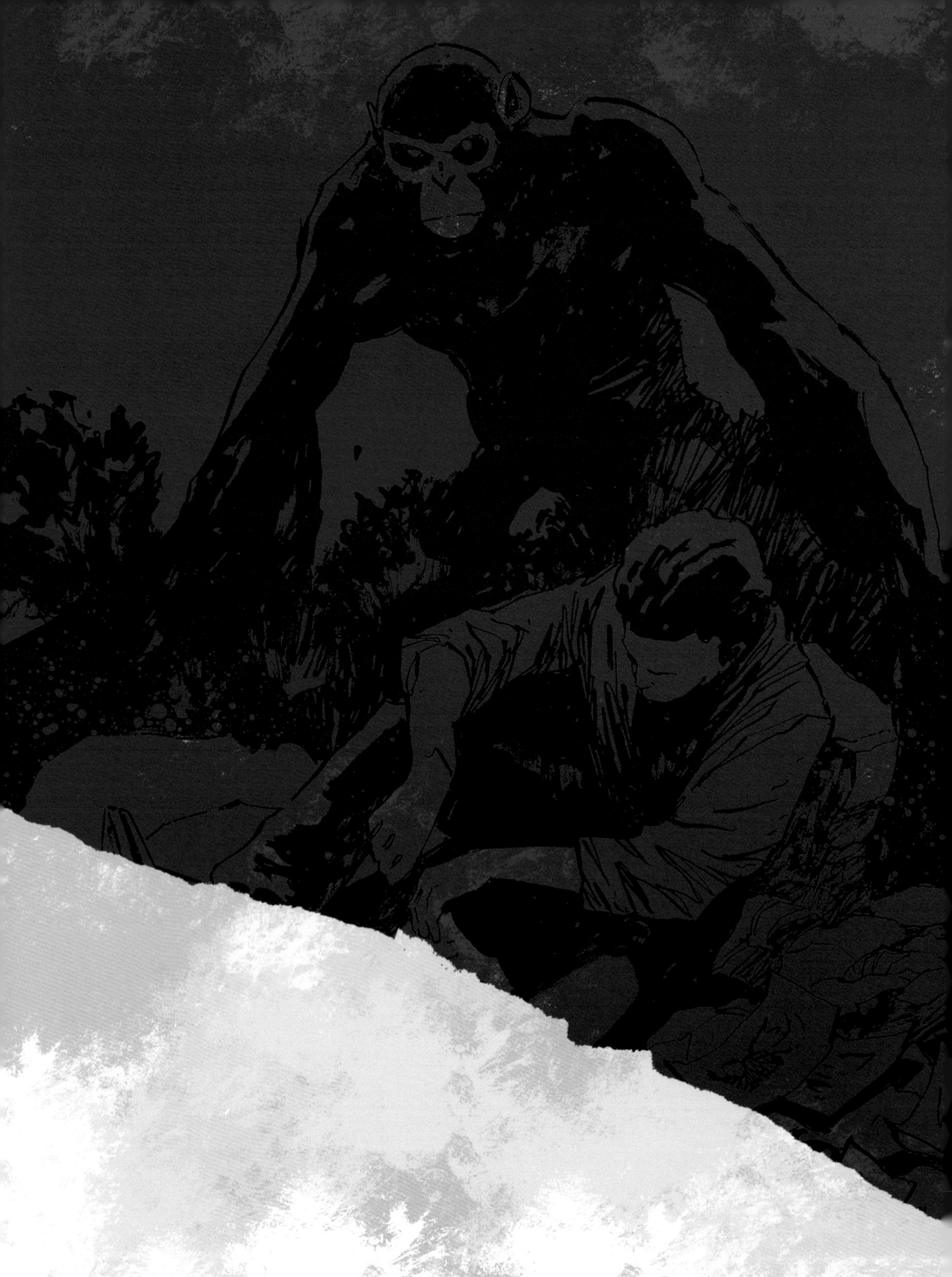

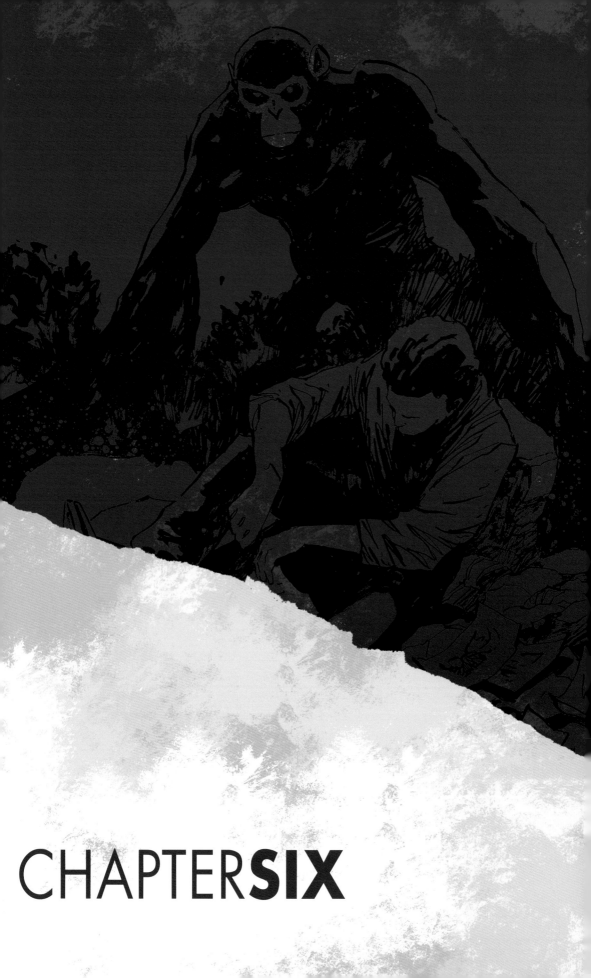

CHAPTER**SIX**

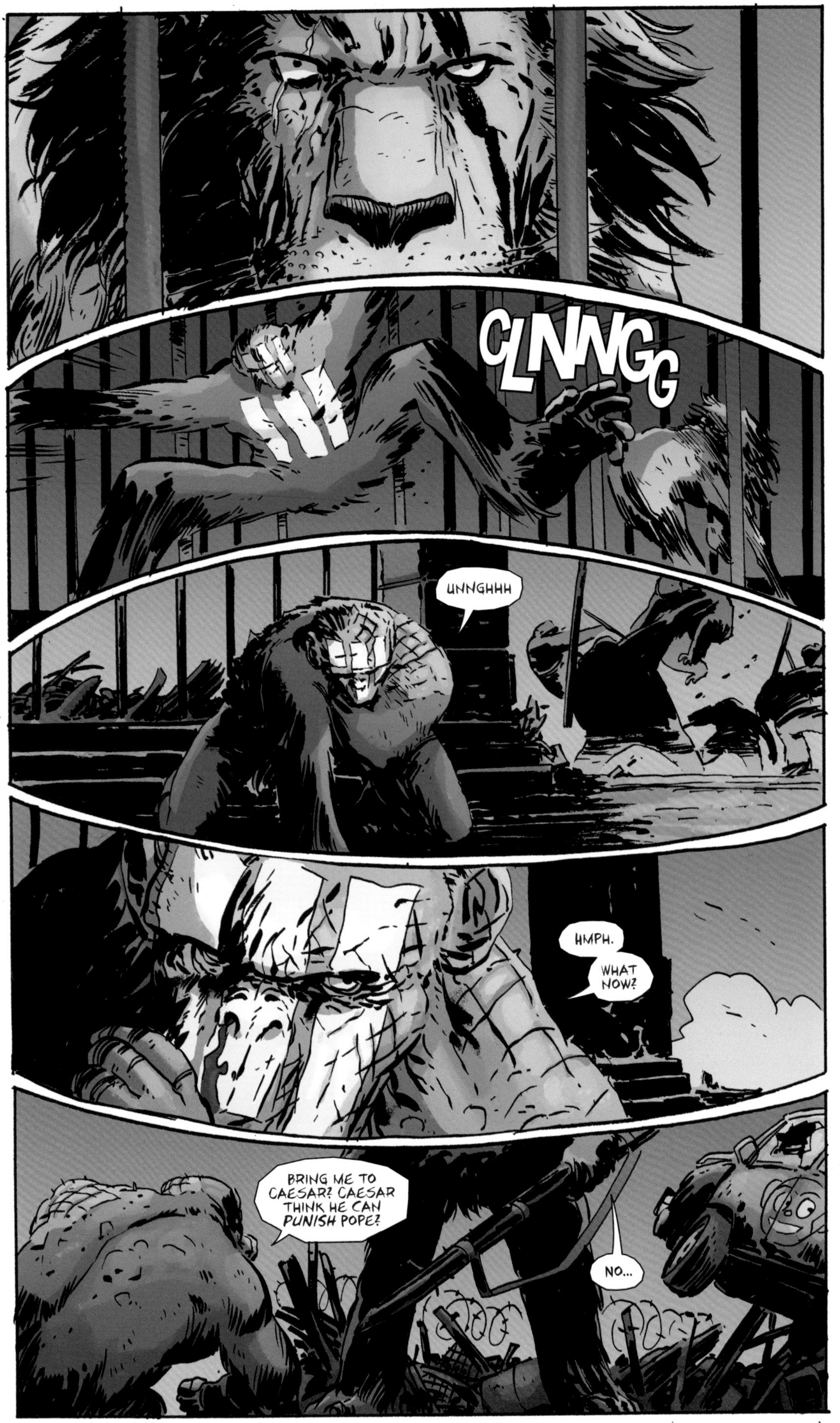
CLNNGG
UNNGHHH
HMPH.
WHAT NOW?
BRING ME TO CAESAR? CAESAR THINK HE CAN PUNISH POPE?
NO...

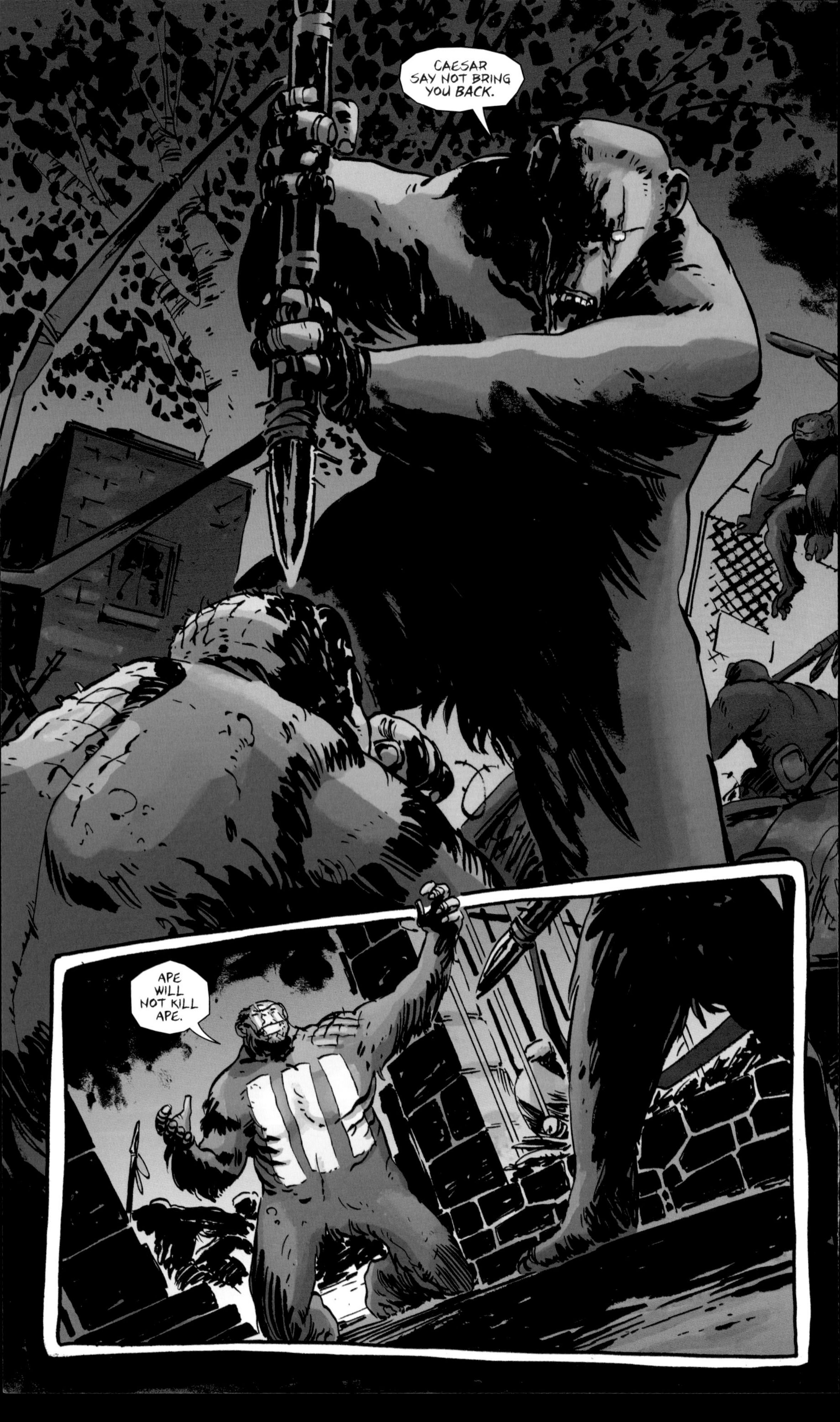
CAESAR SAY NOT BRING YOU BACK.
APE WILL NOT KILL APE.

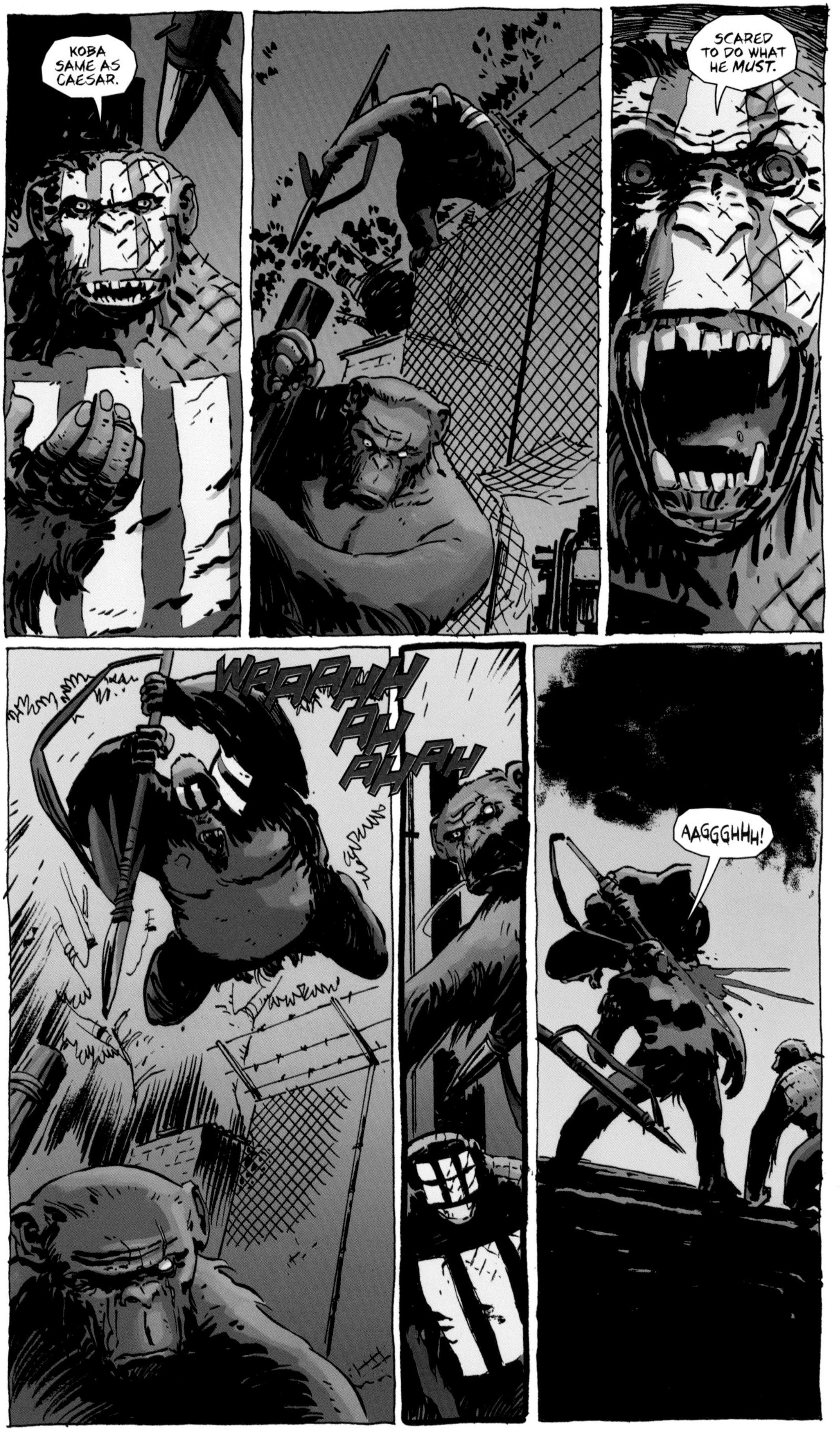

KOBA SAME AS CAESAR.
SCARED TO DO WHAT HE MUST.
WAAAWH AH AWAH
AAGGGHHH!

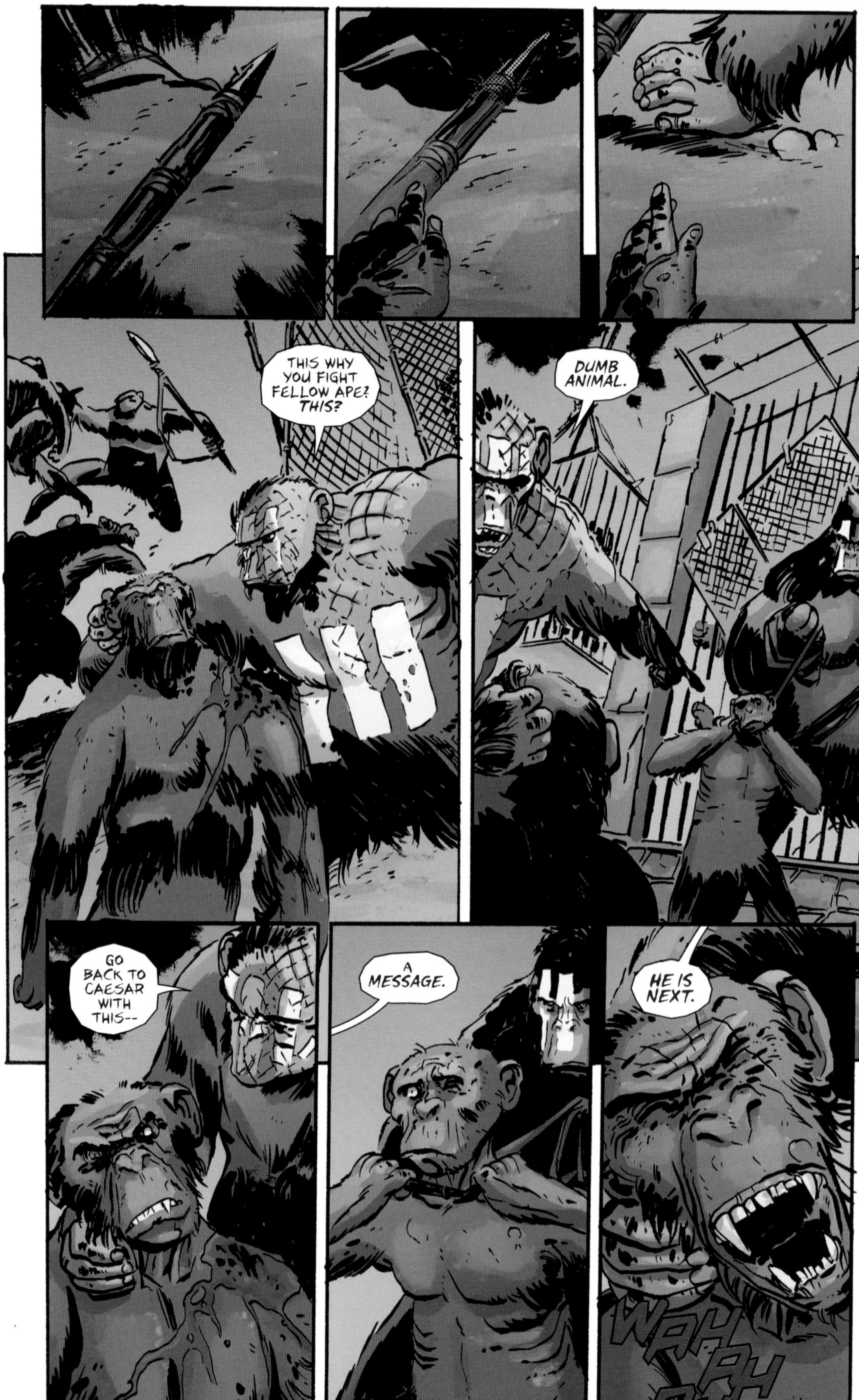
THIS WHY YOU FIGHT FELLOW APE? THIS?
DUMB ANIMAL.
GO BACK TO CAESAR WITH THIS--
A MESSAGE.
HE IS NEXT.
WAH AH AH

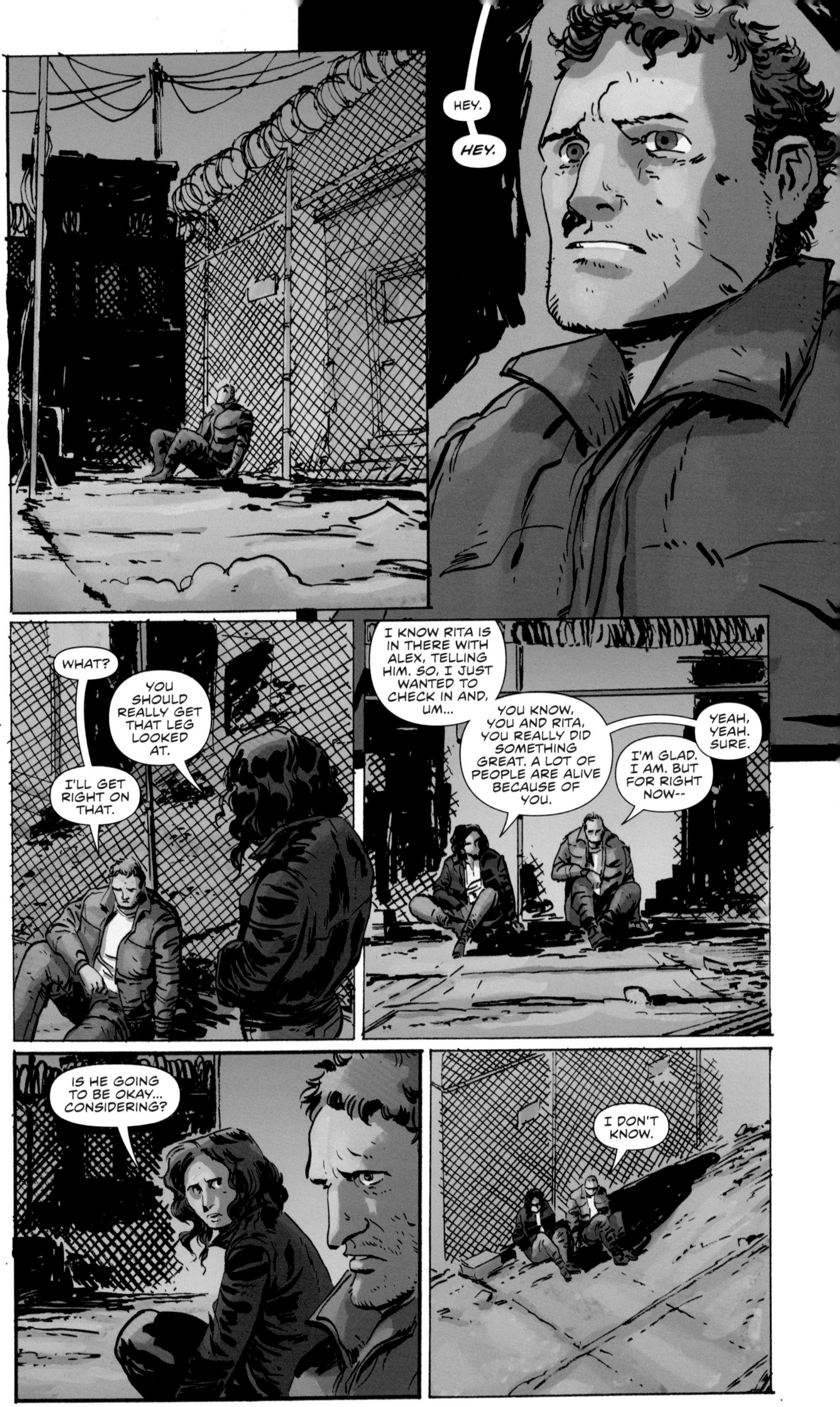
HEY.
HEY.
WHAT?
YOU SHOULD REALLY GET THAT LEG LOOKED AT.
I'LL GET RIGHT ON THAT.
I KNOW RITA IS IN THERE WITH ALEX, TELLING HIM. SO, I JUST WANTED TO CHECK IN AND, UM...
YOU KNOW, YOU AND RITA, YOU REALLY DID SOMETHING GREAT. A LOT OF PEOPLE ARE ALIVE BECAUSE OF YOU.
YEAH, YEAH. SURE.
I'M GLAD. I AM. BUT FOR RIGHT NOW--
IS HE GOING TO BE OKAY... CONSIDERING?
I DON'T KNOW.

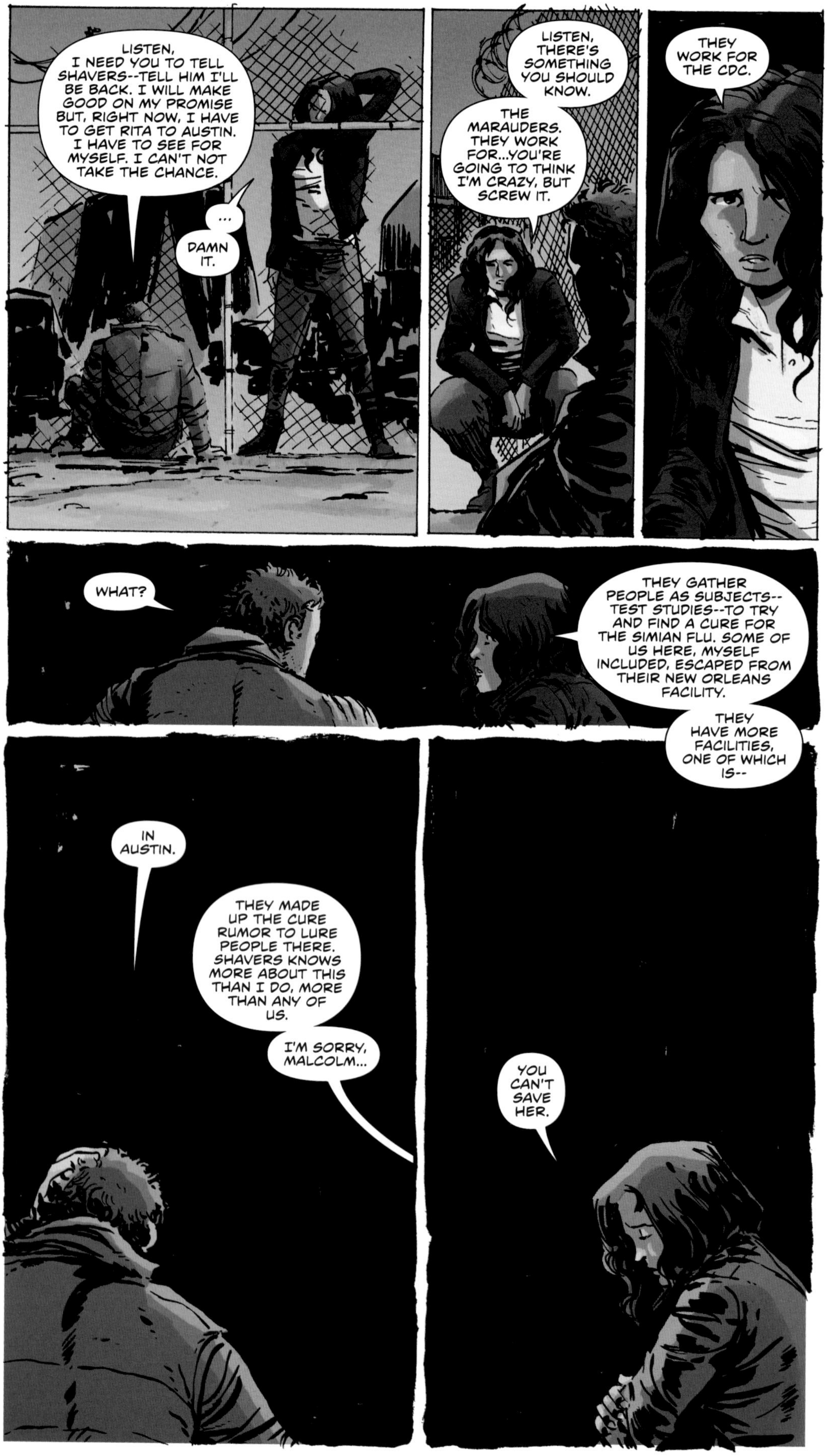
LISTEN, I NEED YOU TO TELL SHAVERS--TELL HIM I'LL BE BACK. I WILL MAKE GOOD ON MY PROMISE BUT, RIGHT NOW, I HAVE TO GET RITA TO AUSTIN. I HAVE TO SEE FOR MYSELF. I CAN'T NOT TAKE THE CHANCE.
...
DAMN IT.
LISTEN, THERE'S SOMETHING YOU SHOULD KNOW.
THE MARAUDERS. THEY WORK FOR...YOU'RE GOING TO THINK I'M CRAZY, BUT SCREW IT.
THEY WORK FOR THE CDC.
WHAT?
THEY GATHER PEOPLE AS SUBJECTS--TEST STUDIES--TO TRY AND FIND A CURE FOR THE SIMIAN FLU. SOME OF US HERE, MYSELF INCLUDED, ESCAPED FROM THEIR NEW ORLEANS FACILITY.
THEY HAVE MORE FACILITIES, ONE OF WHICH IS--
IN AUSTIN.
THEY MADE UP THE CURE RUMOR TO LURE PEOPLE THERE. SHAVERS KNOWS MORE ABOUT THIS THAN I DO, MORE THAN ANY OF US.
I'M SORRY, MALCOLM...
YOU CAN'T SAVE HER.

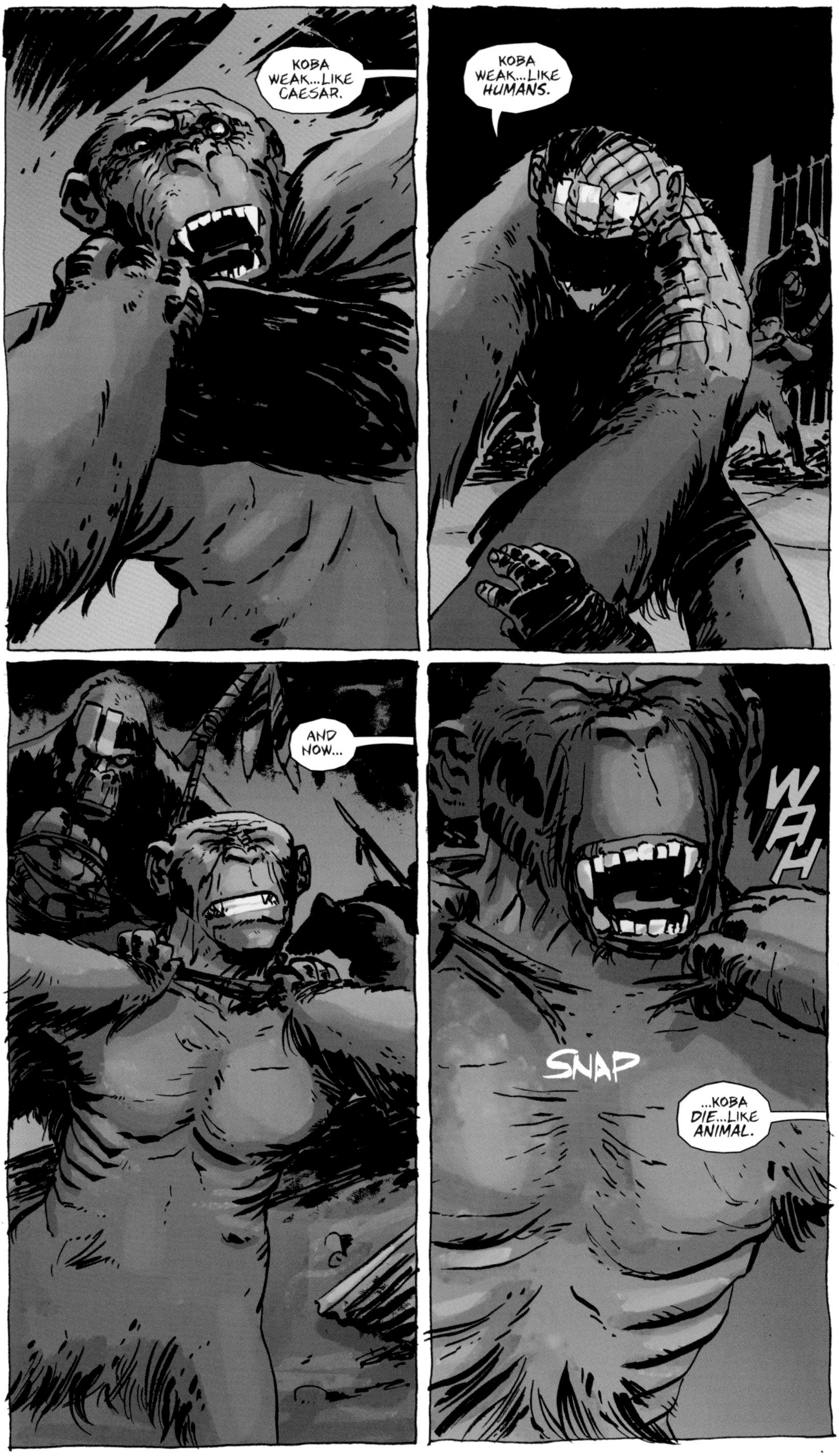
KOBA WEAK...LIKE CAESAR.
KOBA WEAK...LIKE HUMANS.
AND NOW...
WAH
SNAP
...KOBA DIE...LIKE ANIMAL.

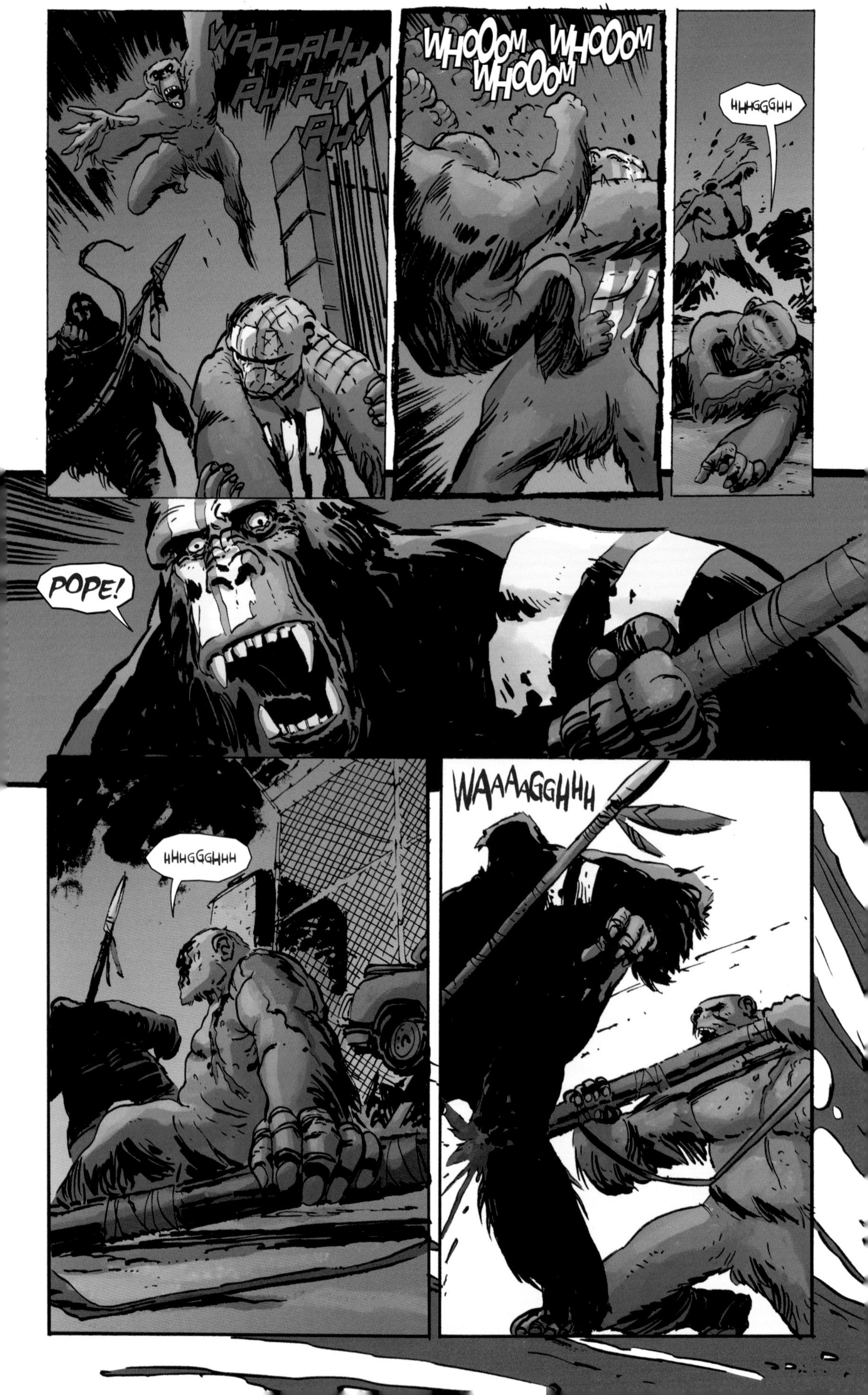
WAAARAHH AH AH AH!
WHOOOM WHOOOM WHOOOM
HHHGGGHH
POPE!
HHHGGGHHH
WAAAAGGHHH

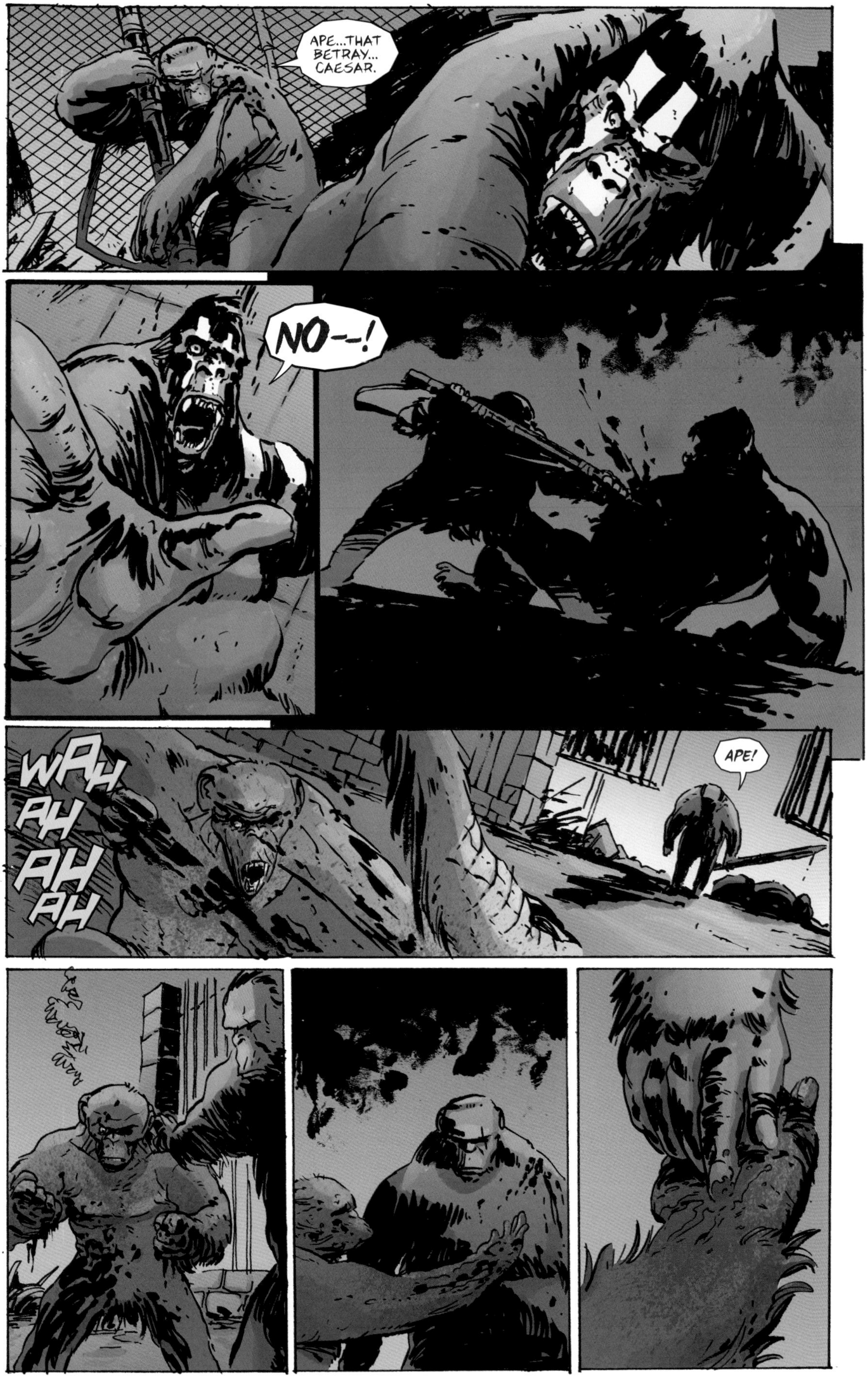
APE...THAT BETRAY... CAESAR.
NO--!
WAH AH AH AH
APE!

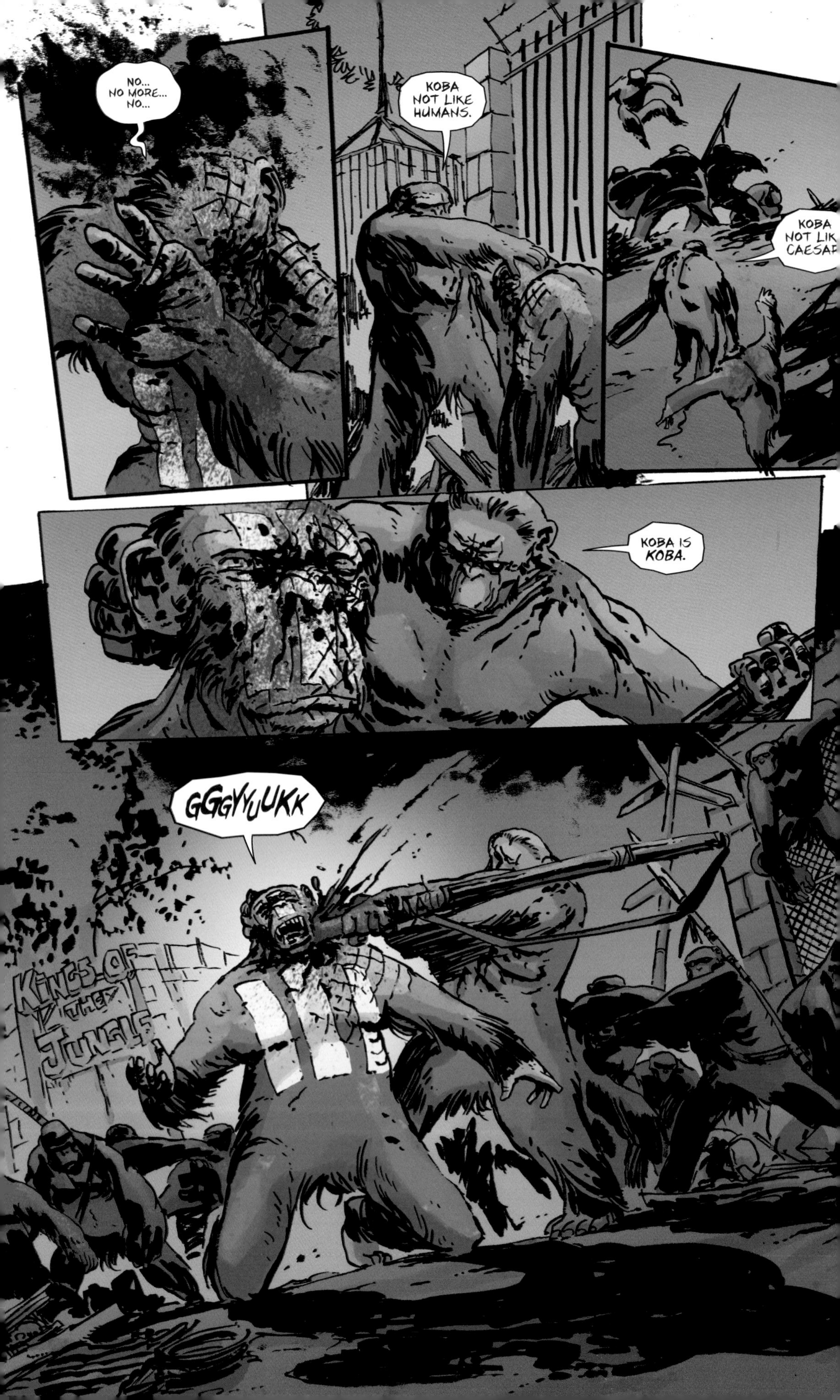
NO... NO MORE... NO...
KOBA NOT LIKE HUMANS.
KOBA NOT LIK CAESA
KOBA IS KOBA.
GGGYYUUKK
KINGS OF THE JUNGLE

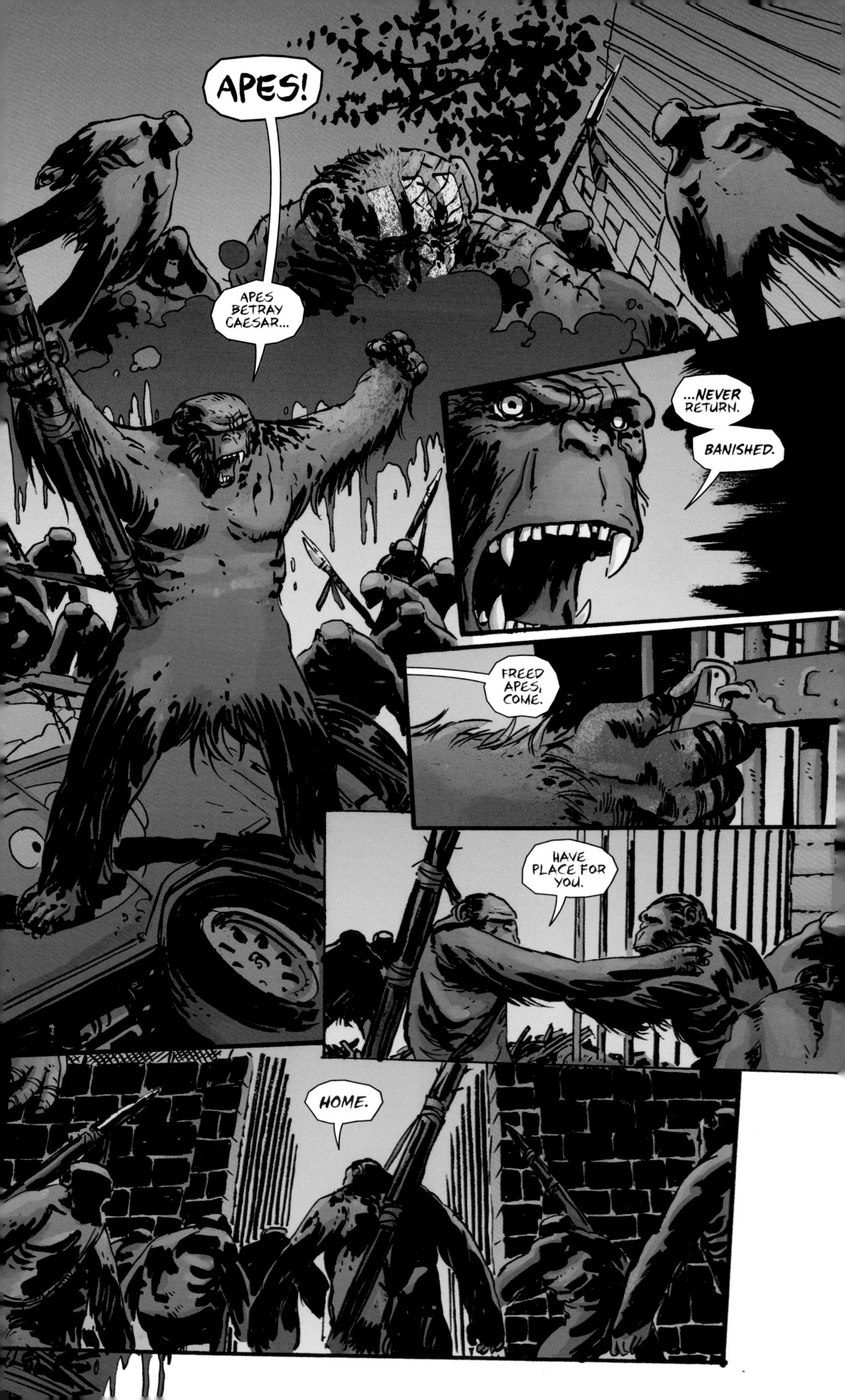
APES!
APES BETRAY CAESAR...
...NEVER RETURN.
BANISHED.
FREED APES, COME.
HAVE PLACE FOR YOU.
HOME.

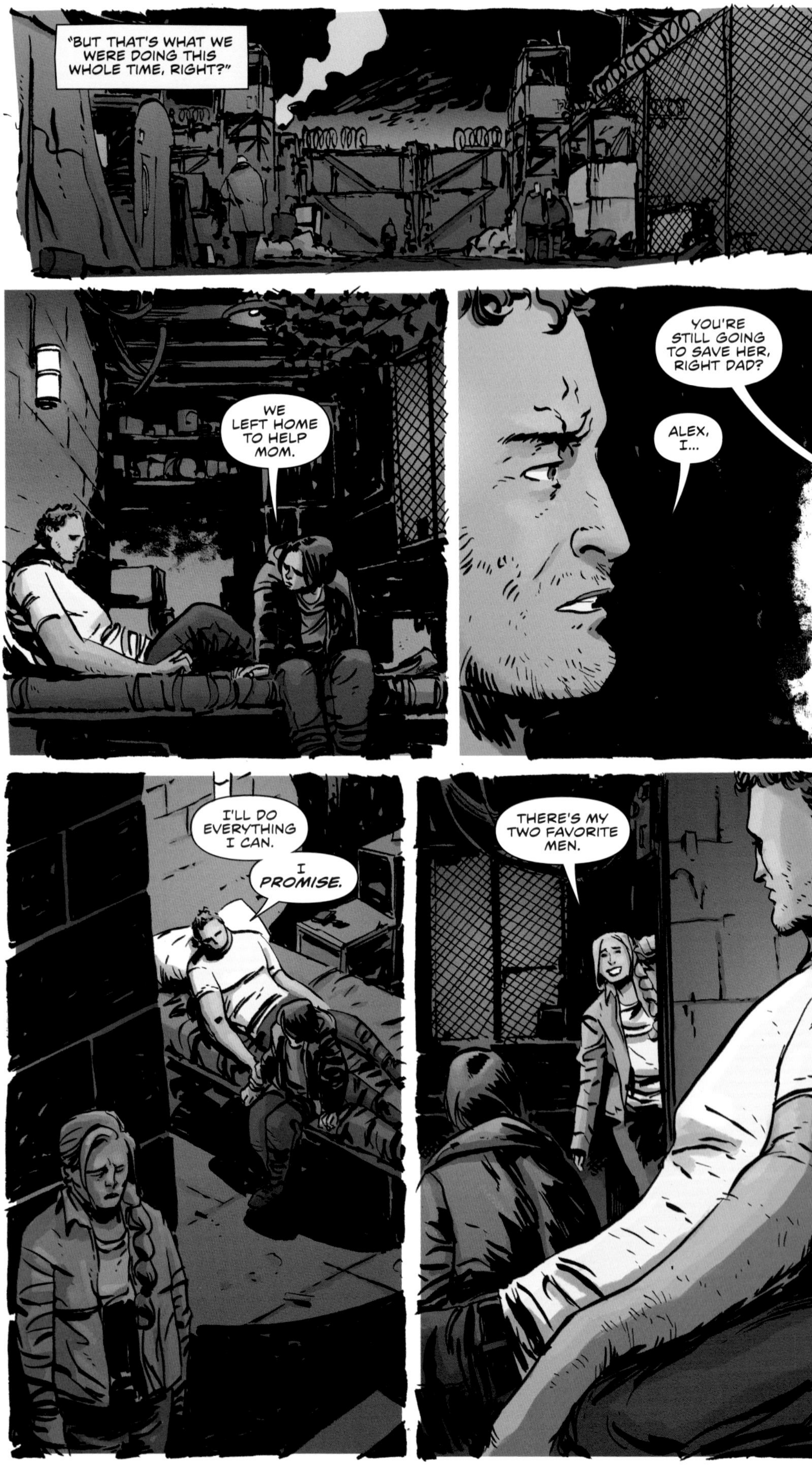
"BUT THAT'S WHAT WE WERE DOING THIS WHOLE TIME, RIGHT?"
WE LEFT HOME TO HELP MOM.
YOU'RE STILL GOING TO SAVE HER, RIGHT DAD?
ALEX, I...
I'LL DO EVERYTHING I CAN.
I *PROMISE.*
THERE'S MY TWO FAVORITE MEN.

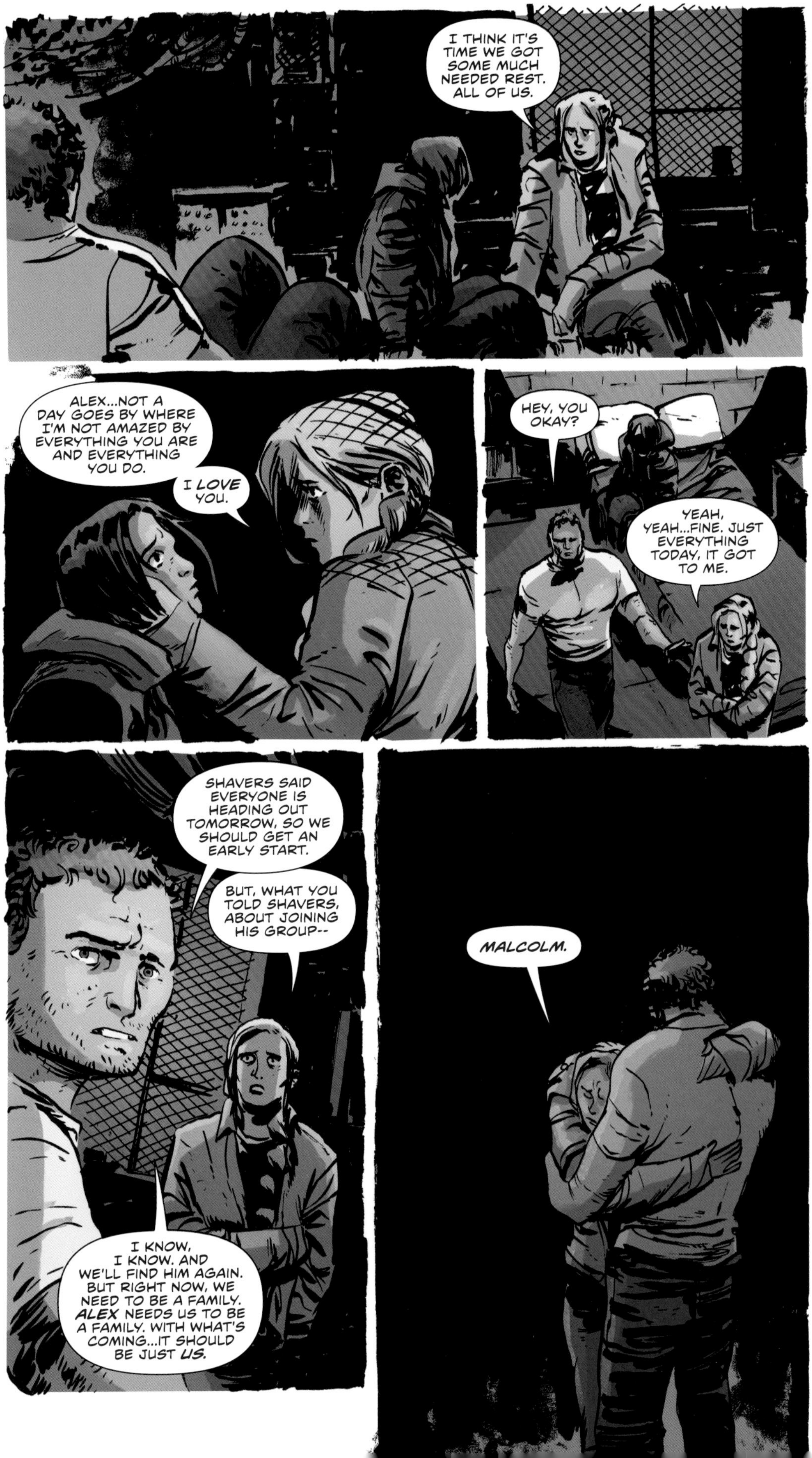
I THINK IT'S TIME WE GOT SOME MUCH NEEDED REST. ALL OF US.
ALEX...NOT A DAY GOES BY WHERE I'M NOT AMAZED BY EVERYTHING YOU ARE AND EVERYTHING YOU DO.
I LOVE YOU.
HEY, YOU OKAY?
YEAH, YEAH...FINE. JUST EVERYTHING TODAY, IT GOT TO ME.
SHAVERS SAID EVERYONE IS HEADING OUT TOMORROW, SO WE SHOULD GET AN EARLY START.
BUT, WHAT YOU TOLD SHAVERS, ABOUT JOINING HIS GROUP--
I KNOW, I KNOW. AND WE'LL FIND HIM AGAIN. BUT RIGHT NOW, WE NEED TO BE A FAMILY. ALEX NEEDS US TO BE A FAMILY. WITH WHAT'S COMING...IT SHOULD BE JUST US.
MALCOLM.

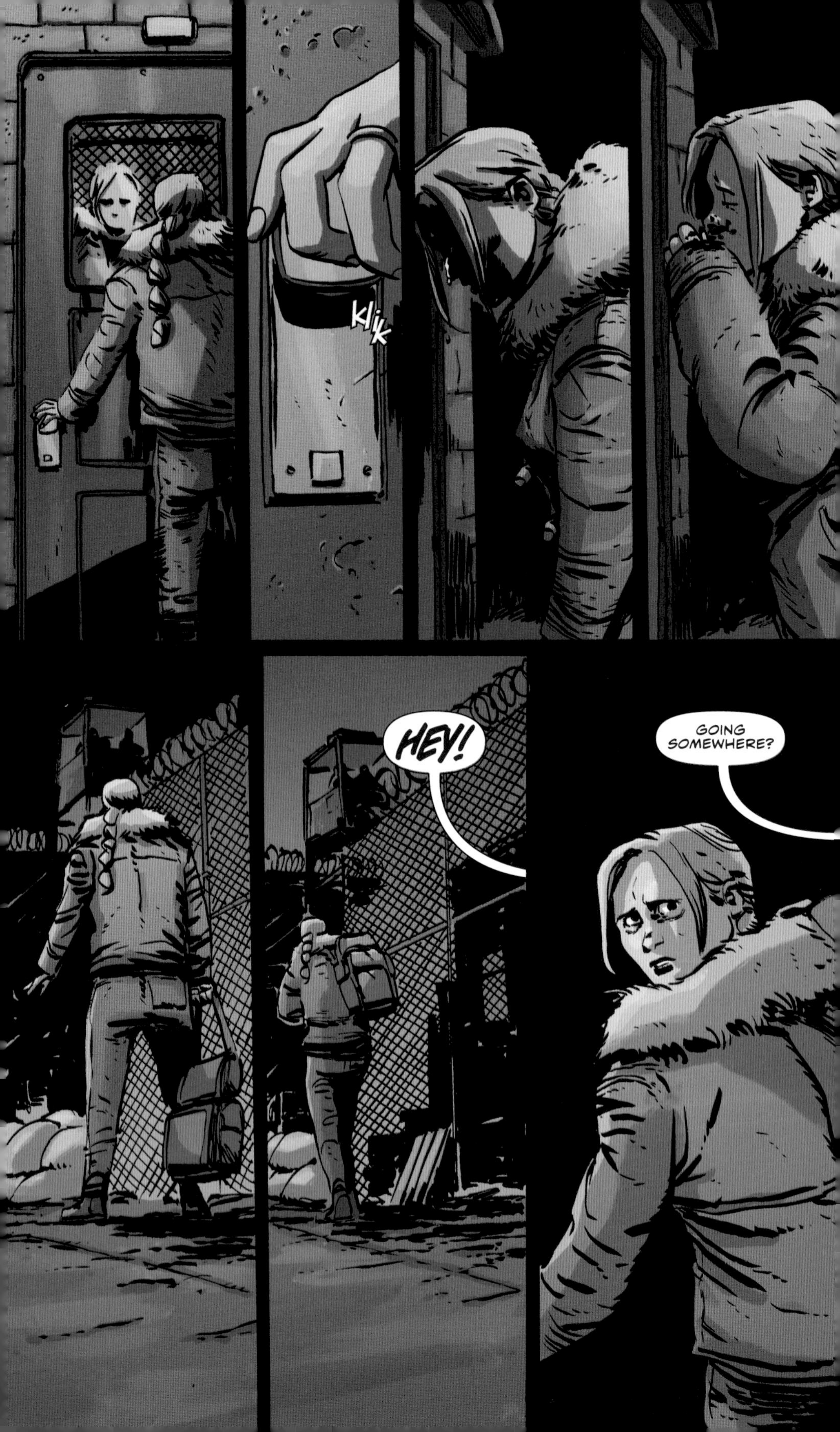
KLIK
HEY!
GOING SOMEWHERE?

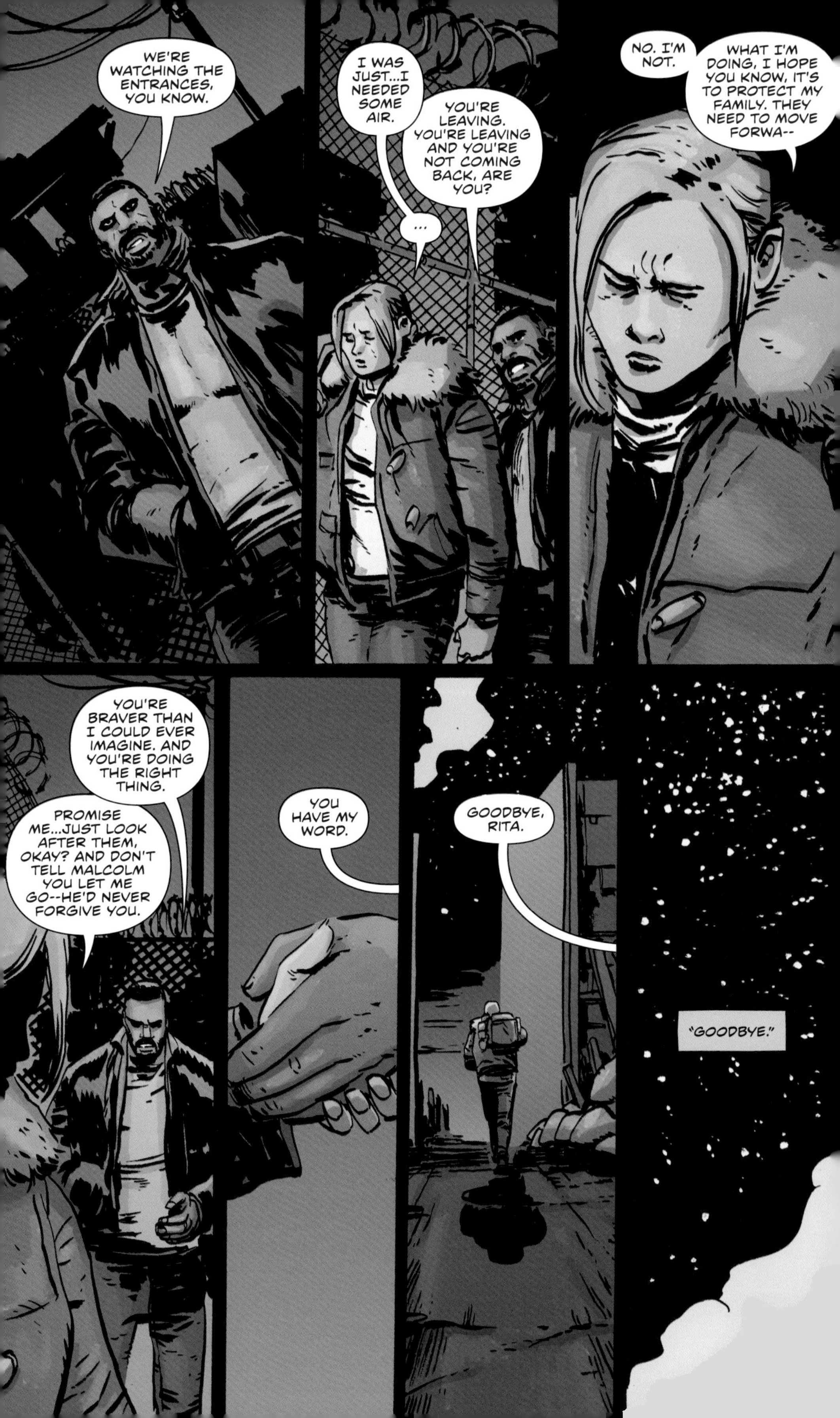
WE'RE WATCHING THE ENTRANCES, YOU KNOW.
I WAS JUST...I NEEDED SOME AIR.
YOU'RE LEAVING. YOU'RE LEAVING AND YOU'RE NOT COMING BACK, ARE YOU?
...
NO. I'M NOT.
WHAT I'M DOING, I HOPE YOU KNOW, IT'S TO PROTECT MY FAMILY. THEY NEED TO MOVE FORWA--
YOU'RE BRAVER THAN I COULD EVER IMAGINE. AND YOU'RE DOING THE RIGHT THING.
PROMISE ME...JUST LOOK AFTER THEM, OKAY? AND DON'T TELL MALCOLM YOU LET ME GO--HE'D NEVER FORGIVE YOU.
YOU HAVE MY WORD.
GOODBYE, RITA.
"GOODBYE."

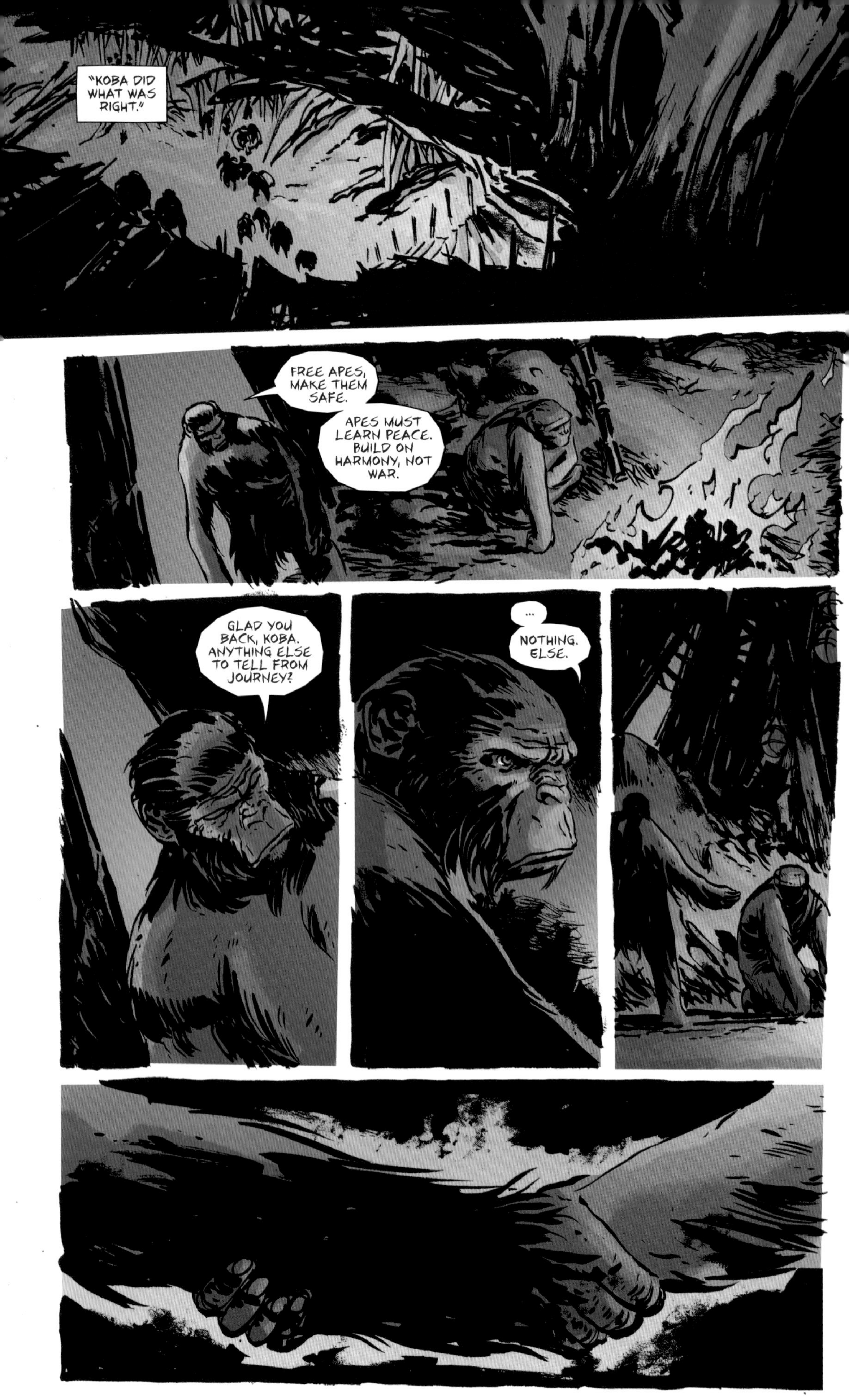
"KOBA DID WHAT WAS RIGHT."
FREE APES, MAKE THEM SAFE.
APES MUST LEARN PEACE. BUILD ON HARMONY, NOT WAR.
GLAD YOU BACK, KOBA. ANYTHING ELSE TO TELL FROM JOURNEY?
...
NOTHING. ELSE.

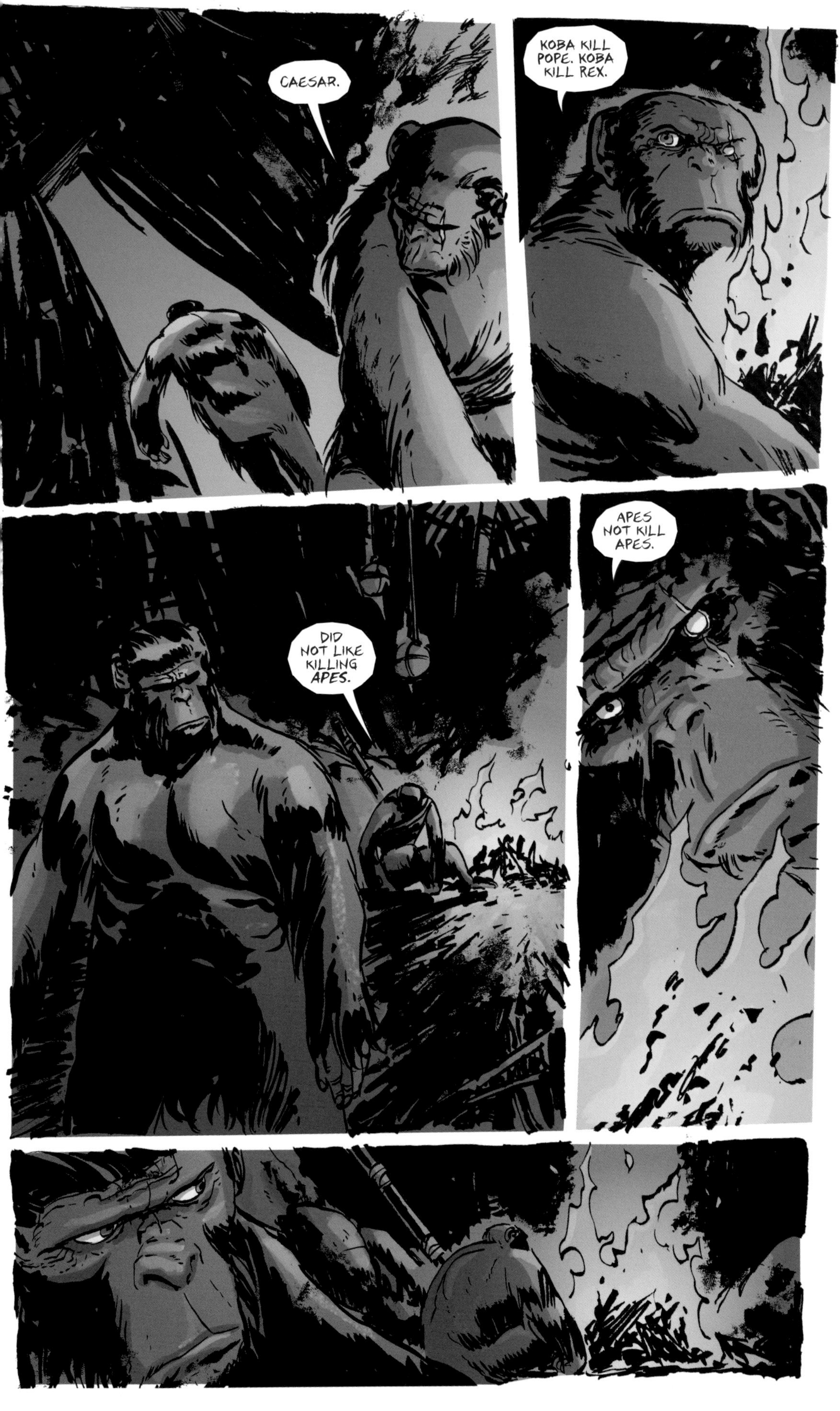
CAESAR.
KOBA KILL POPE. KOBA KILL REX.
DID NOT LIKE KILLING APES.
APES NOT KILL APES.

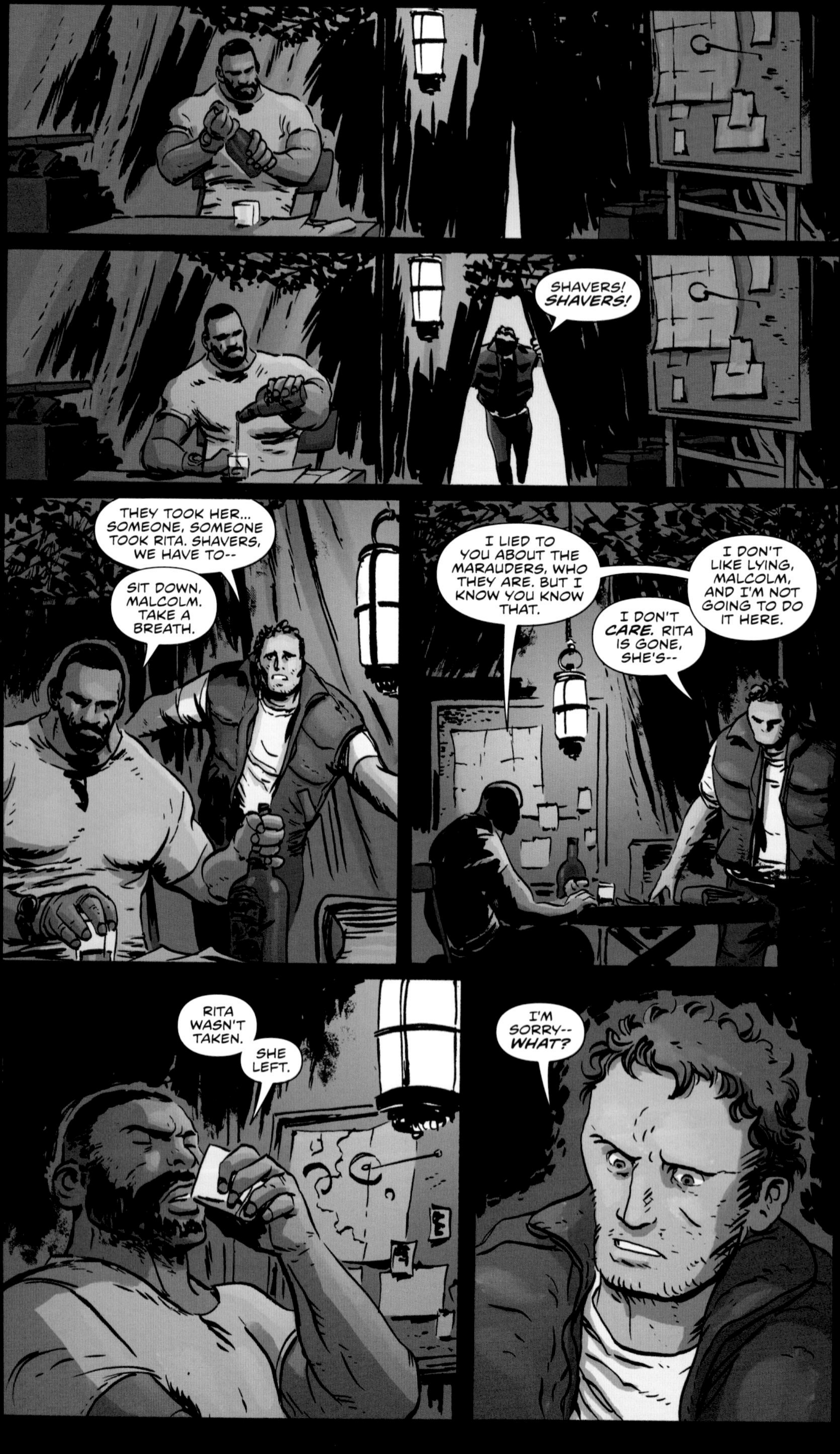
SHAVERS! SHAVERS!
THEY TOOK HER... SOMEONE, SOMEONE TOOK RITA. SHAVERS, WE HAVE TO--
SIT DOWN, MALCOLM. TAKE A BREATH.
I LIED TO YOU ABOUT THE MARAUDERS, WHO THEY ARE. BUT I KNOW YOU KNOW THAT.
I DON'T LIKE LYING, MALCOLM, AND I'M NOT GOING TO DO IT HERE.
I DON'T CARE. RITA IS GONE, SHE'S--
RITA WASN'T TAKEN.
SHE LEFT.
I'M SORRY-- WHAT?

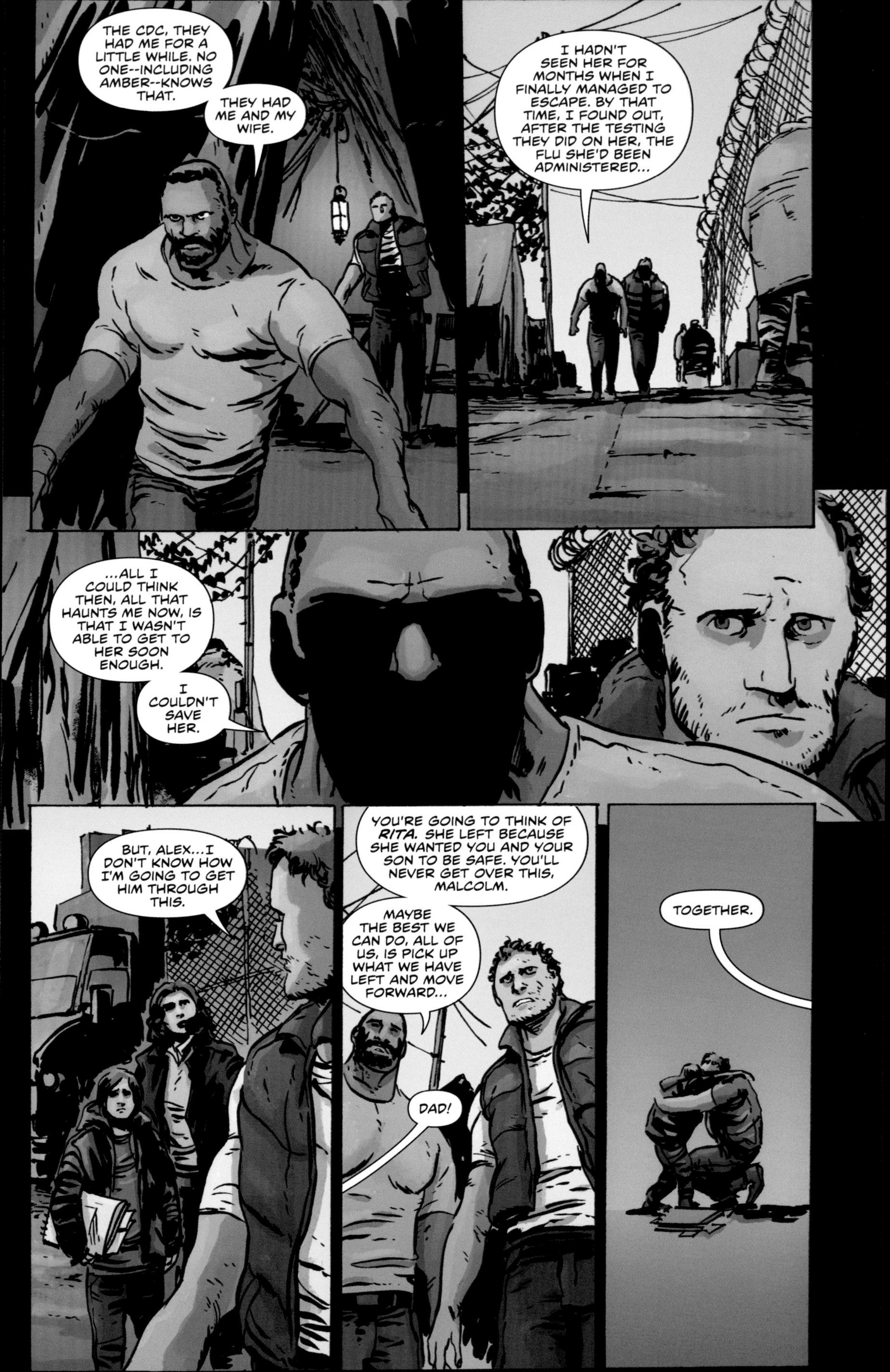
THE CDC, THEY HAD ME FOR A LITTLE WHILE. NO ONE--INCLUDING AMBER--KNOWS THAT.
THEY HAD ME AND MY WIFE.
I HADN'T SEEN HER FOR MONTHS WHEN I FINALLY MANAGED TO ESCAPE. BY THAT TIME, I FOUND OUT, AFTER THE TESTING THEY DID ON HER, THE FLU SHE'D BEEN ADMINISTERED...
...ALL I COULD THINK THEN, ALL THAT HAUNTS ME NOW, IS THAT I WASN'T ABLE TO GET TO HER SOON ENOUGH.
I COULDN'T SAVE HER.
BUT, ALEX...I DON'T KNOW HOW I'M GOING TO GET HIM THROUGH THIS.
YOU'RE GOING TO THINK OF RITA. SHE LEFT BECAUSE SHE WANTED YOU AND YOUR SON TO BE SAFE. YOU'LL NEVER GET OVER THIS, MALCOLM.
MAYBE THE BEST WE CAN DO, ALL OF US, IS PICK UP WHAT WE HAVE LEFT AND MOVE FORWARD...
DAD!
TOGETHER.

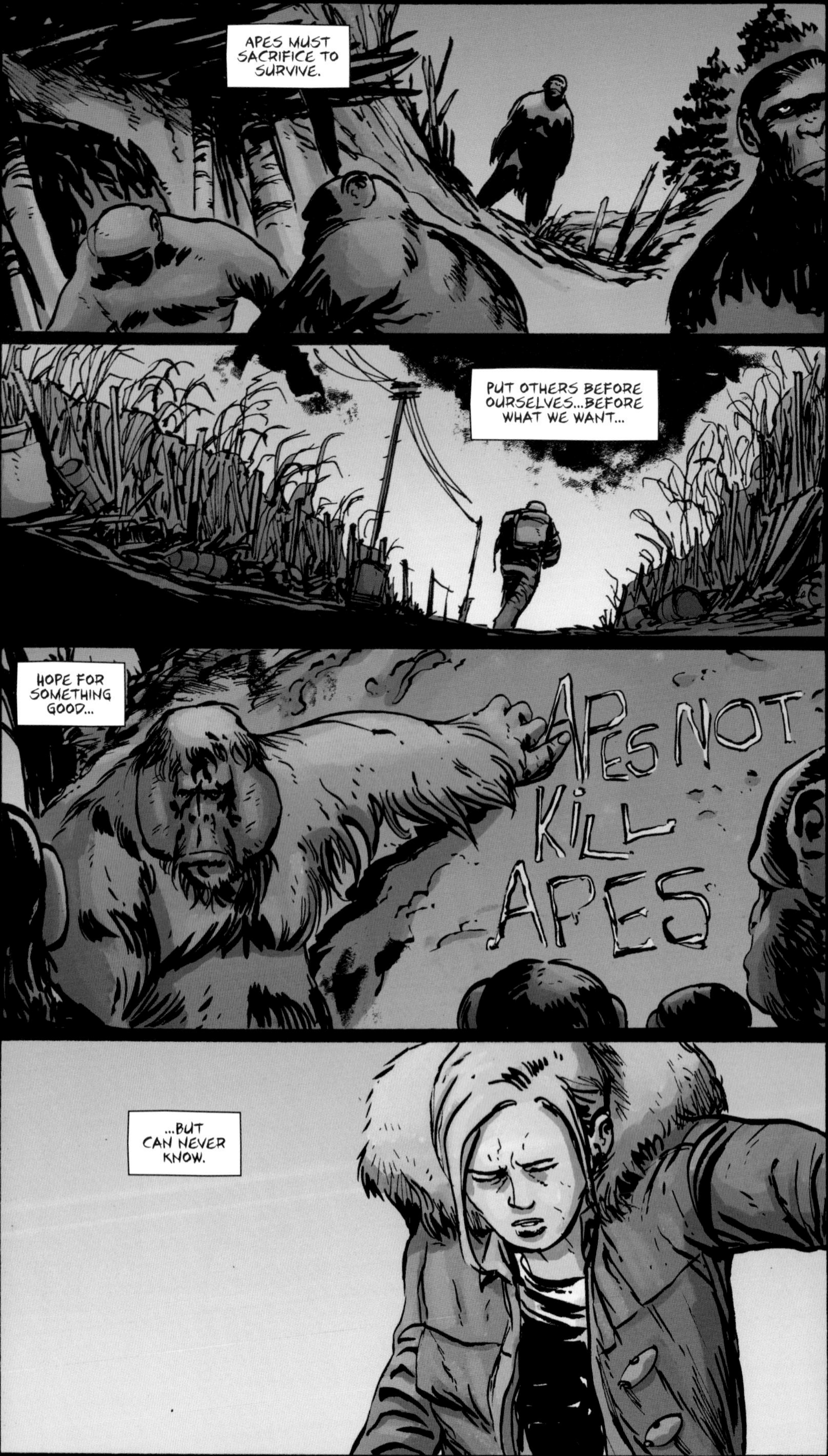
APES MUST SACRIFICE TO SURVIVE.
PUT OTHERS BEFORE OURSELVES...BEFORE WHAT WE WANT...
HOPE FOR SOMETHING GOOD...
APES NOT KILL APES
...BUT CAN NEVER KNOW.

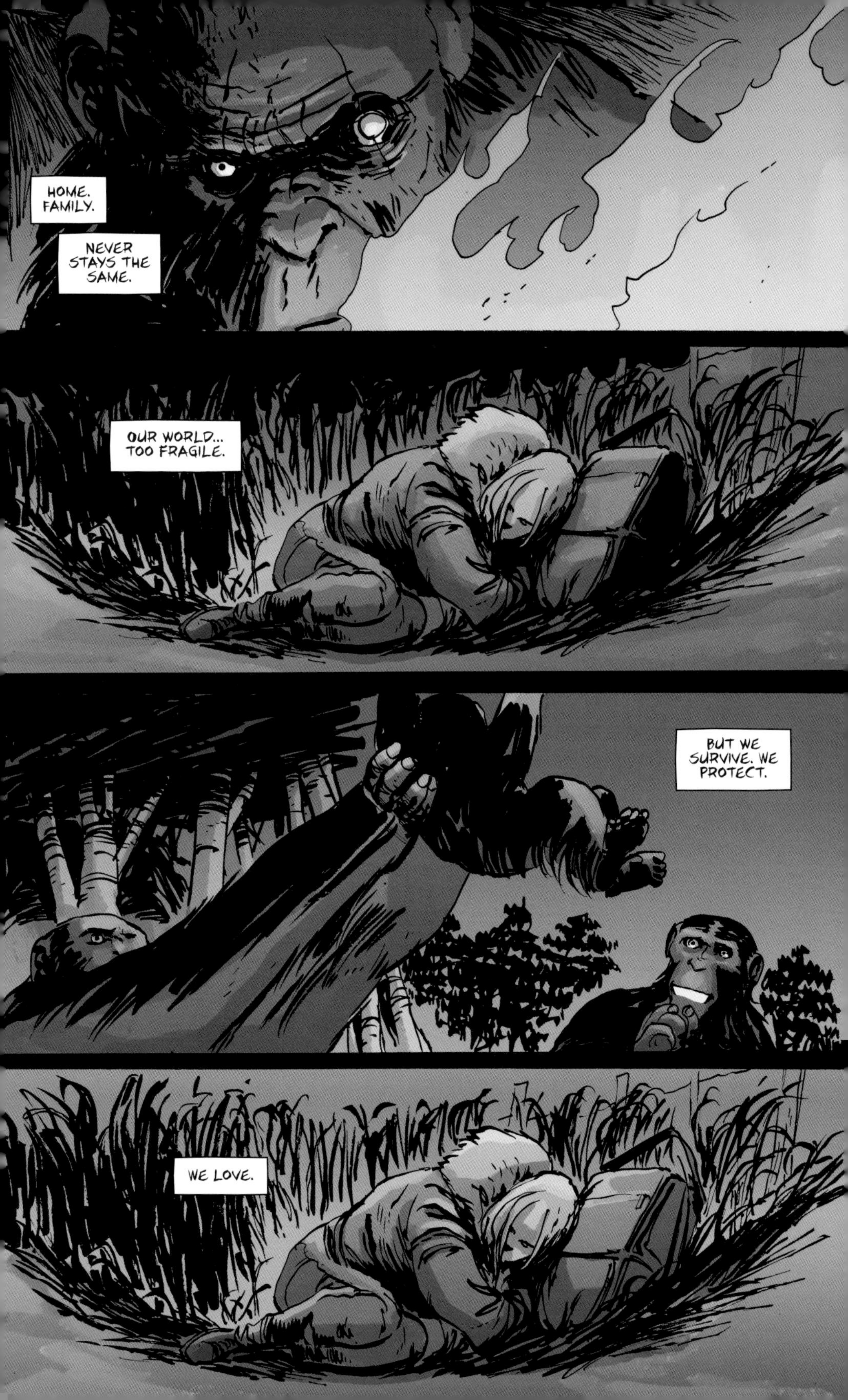
HOME. FAMILY.
NEVER STAYS THE SAME.
OUR WORLD... TOO FRAGILE.
BUT WE SURVIVE. WE PROTECT.
WE LOVE.

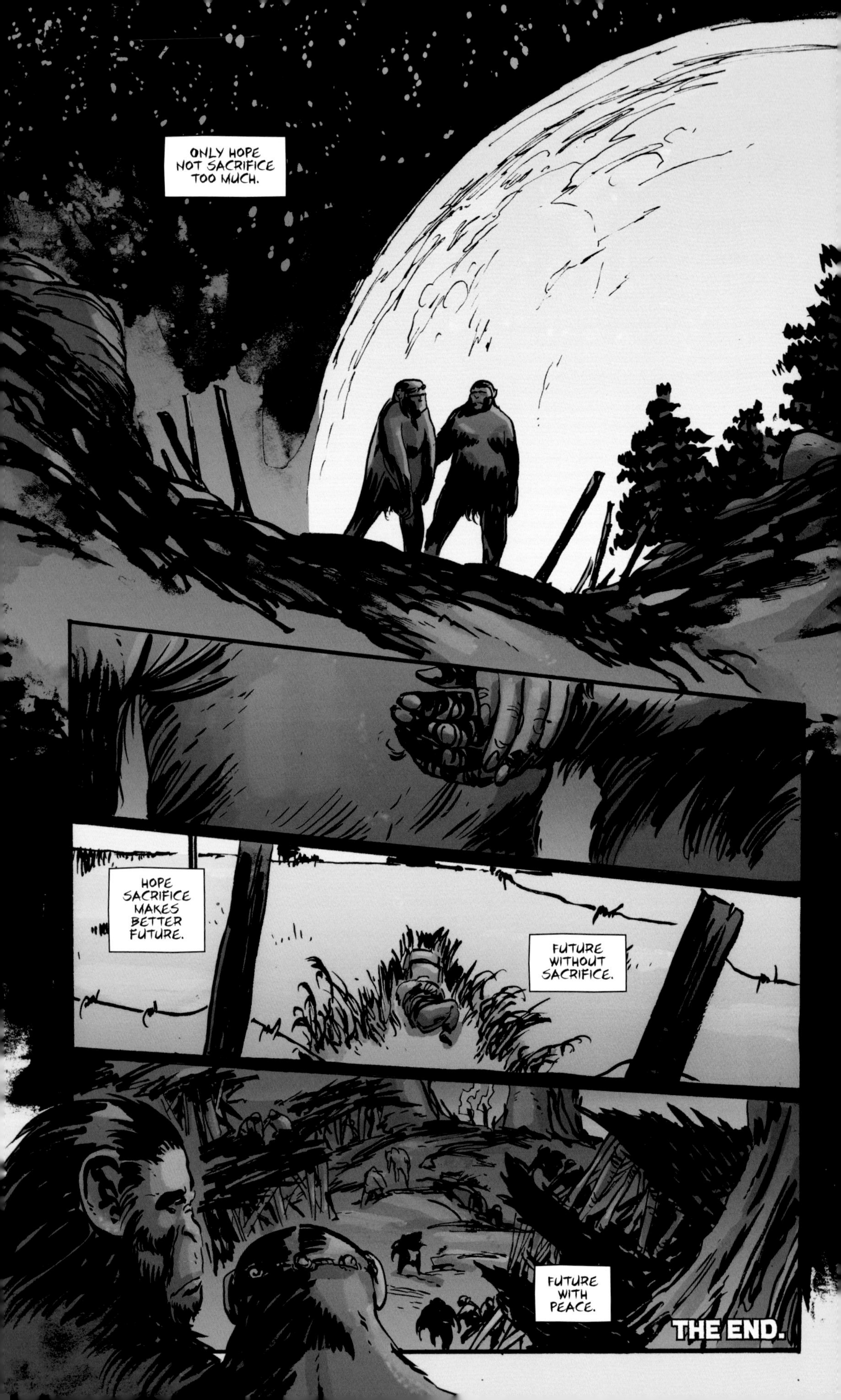
ONLY HOPE NOT SACRIFICE TOO MUCH.
HOPE SACRIFICE MAKES BETTER FUTURE.
FUTURE WITHOUT SACRIFICE.
FUTURE WITH PEACE.
THE END.

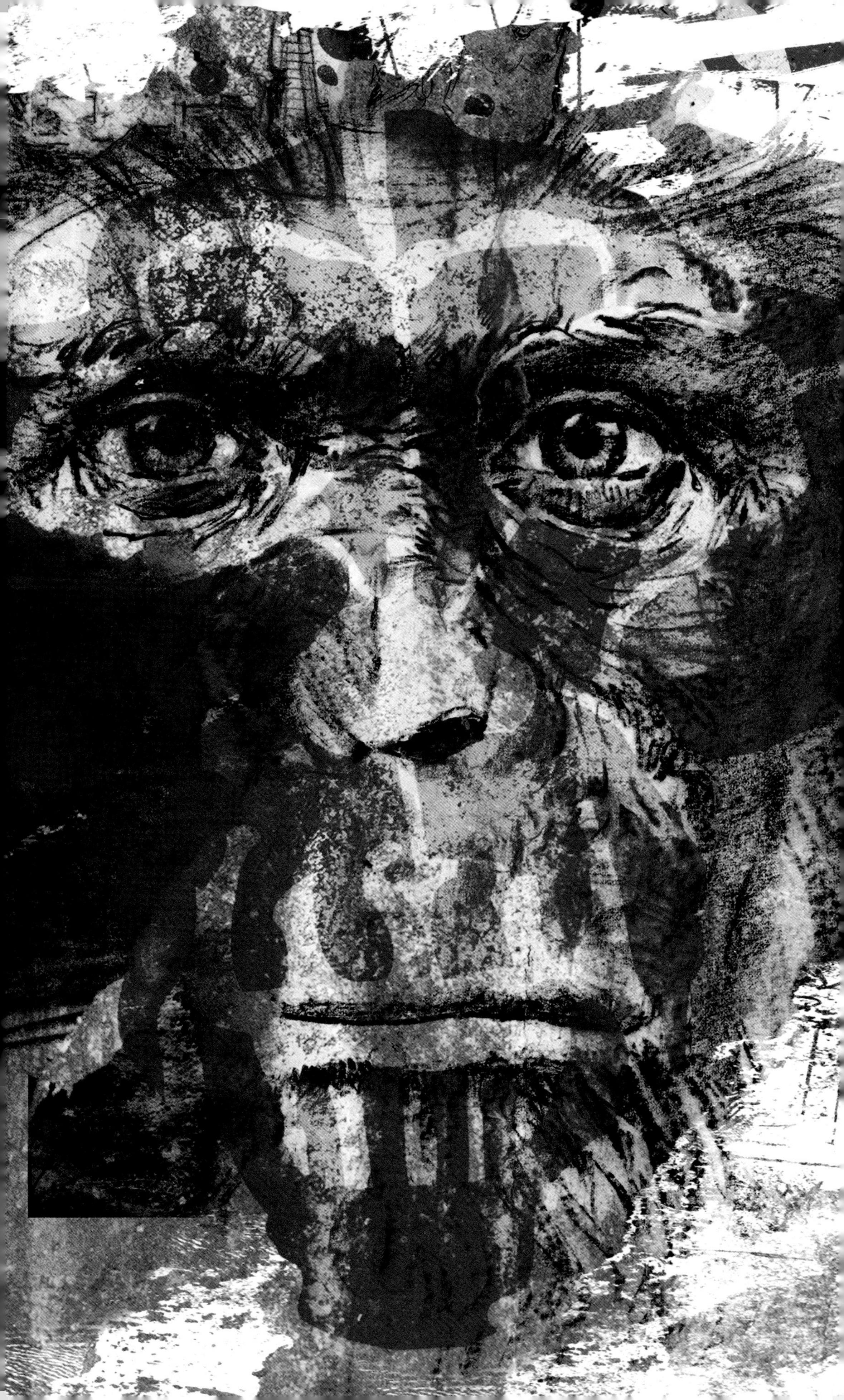

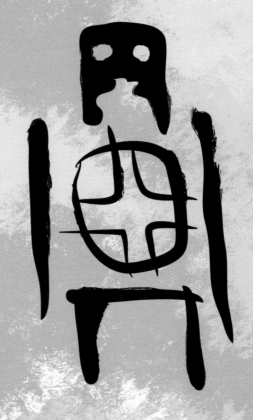

COVERGALLERY

ISSUE #1 COVER **CHRISTOPHER MITTEN**

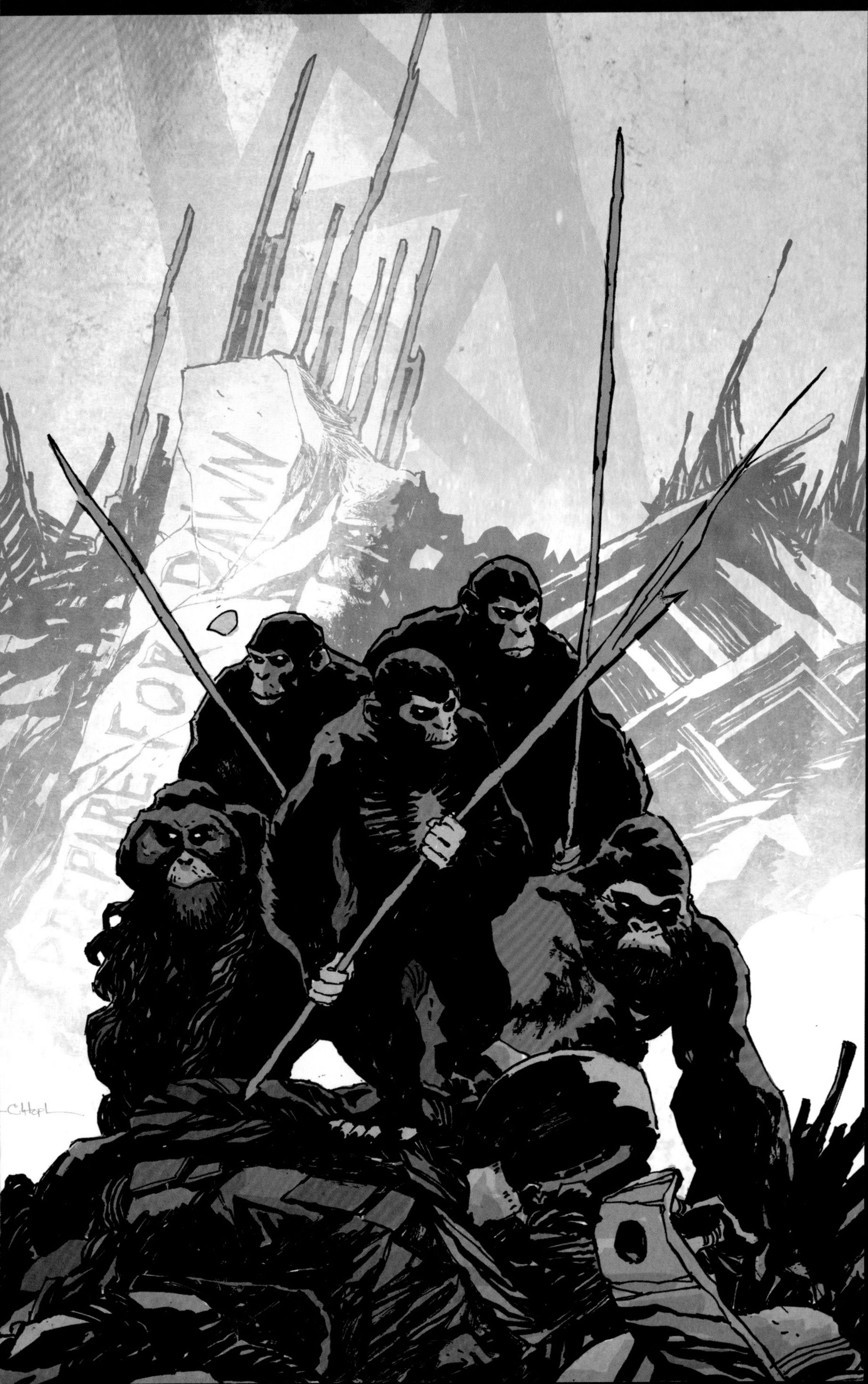

ISSUE #2 COVER **CHRISTOPHER MITTEN**

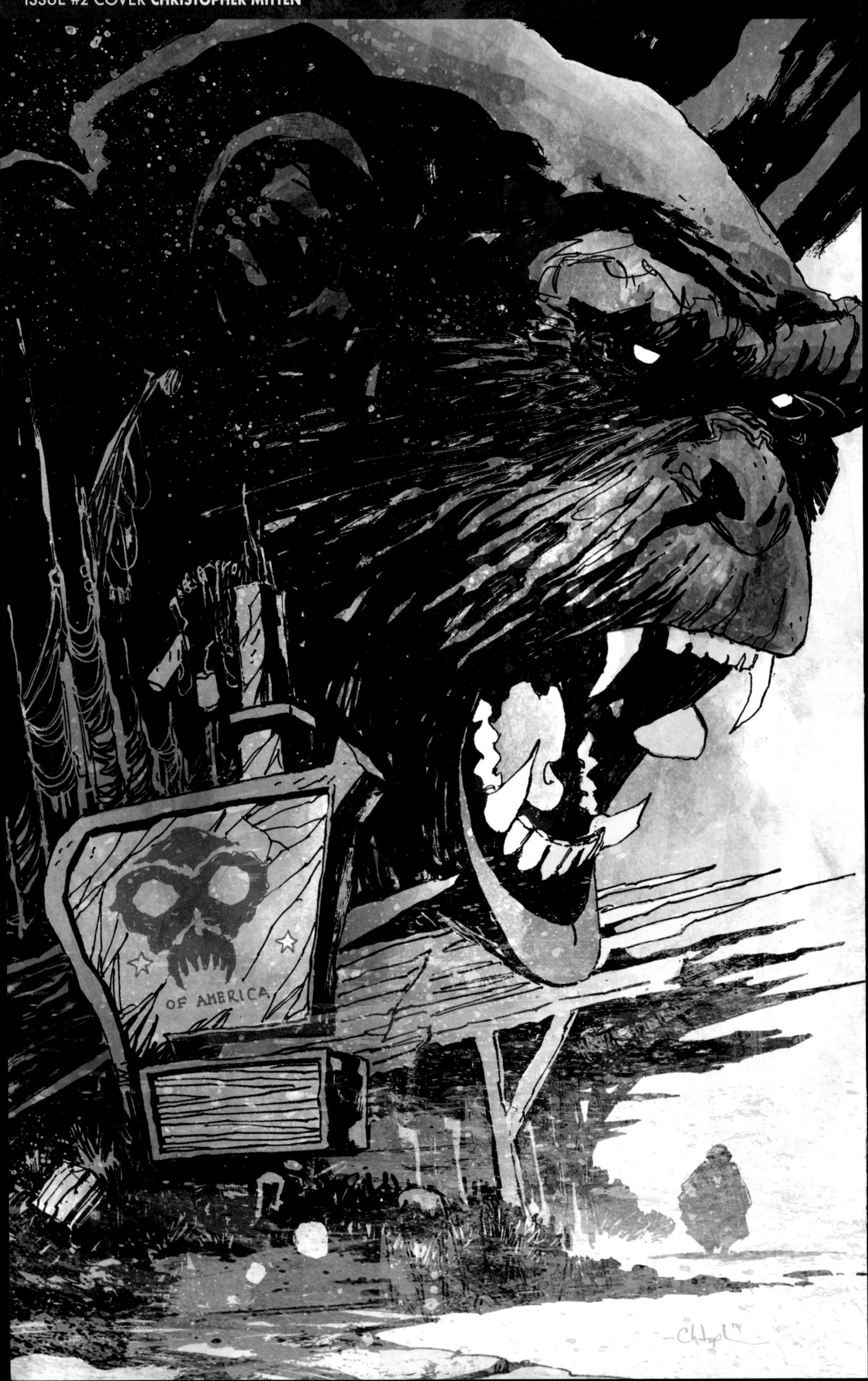
OF AMERICA

ISSUE #3 COVER **CHRISTOPHER MITTEN**

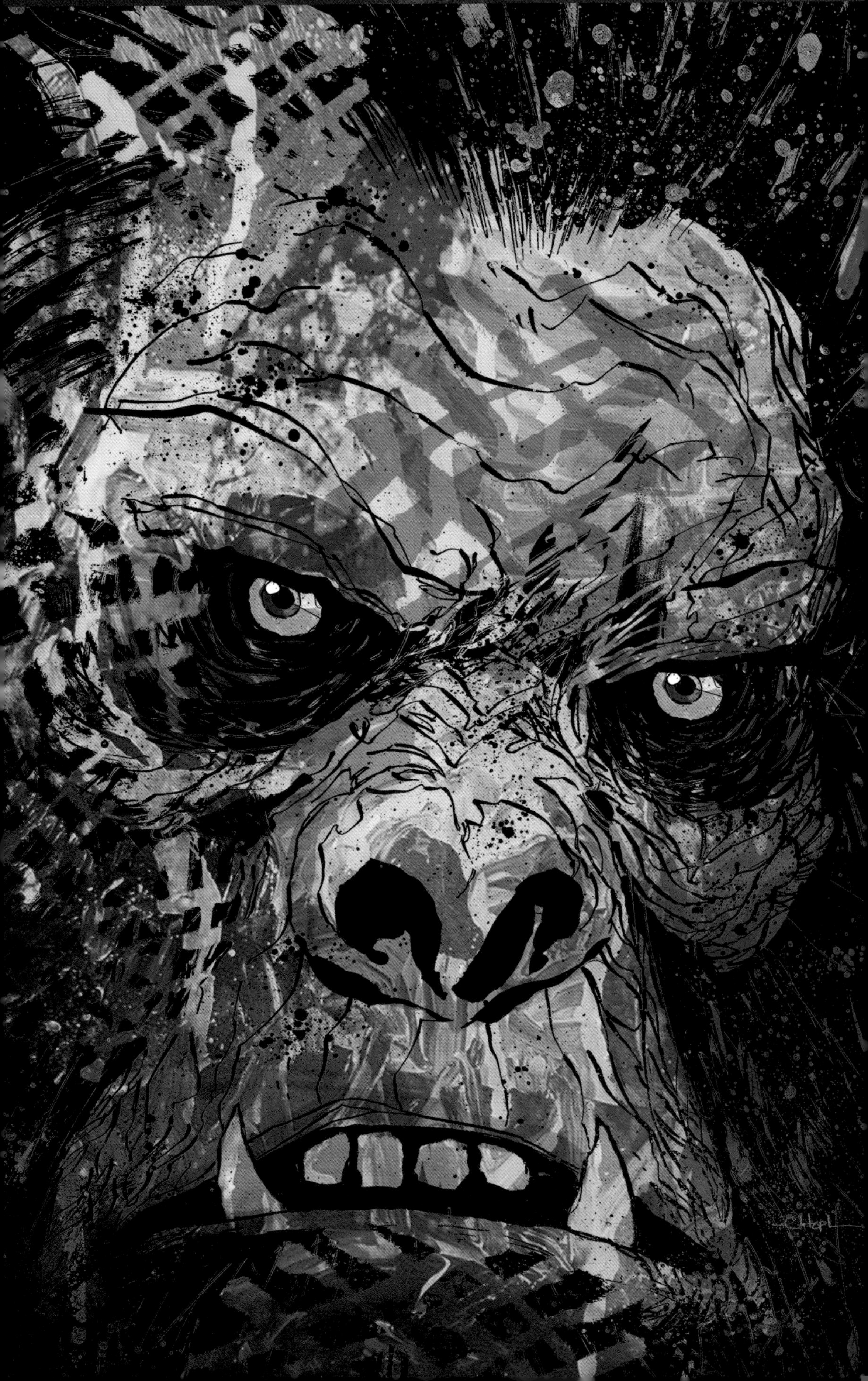

ISSUE #4 COVER **CHRISTOPHER MITTEN**

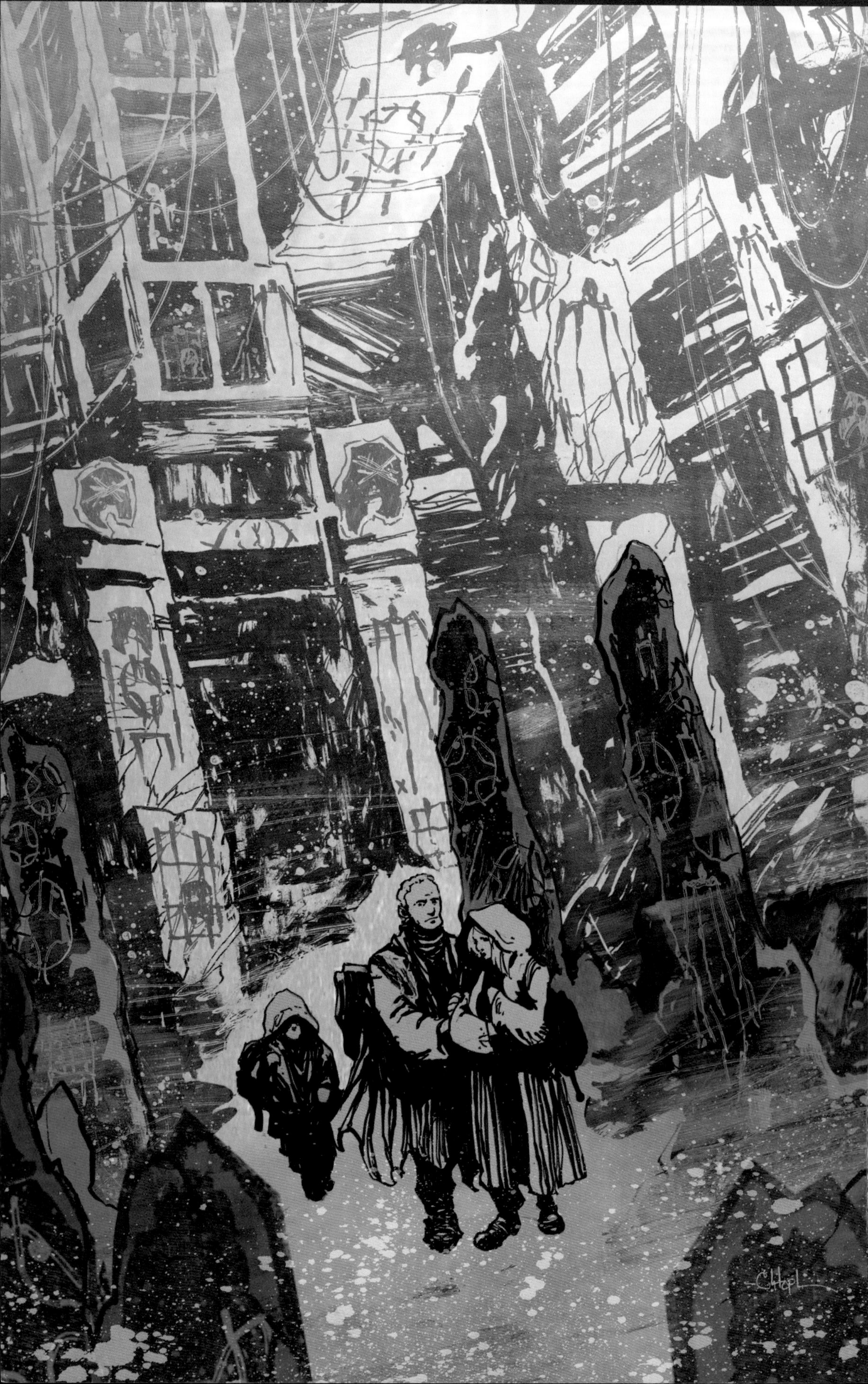

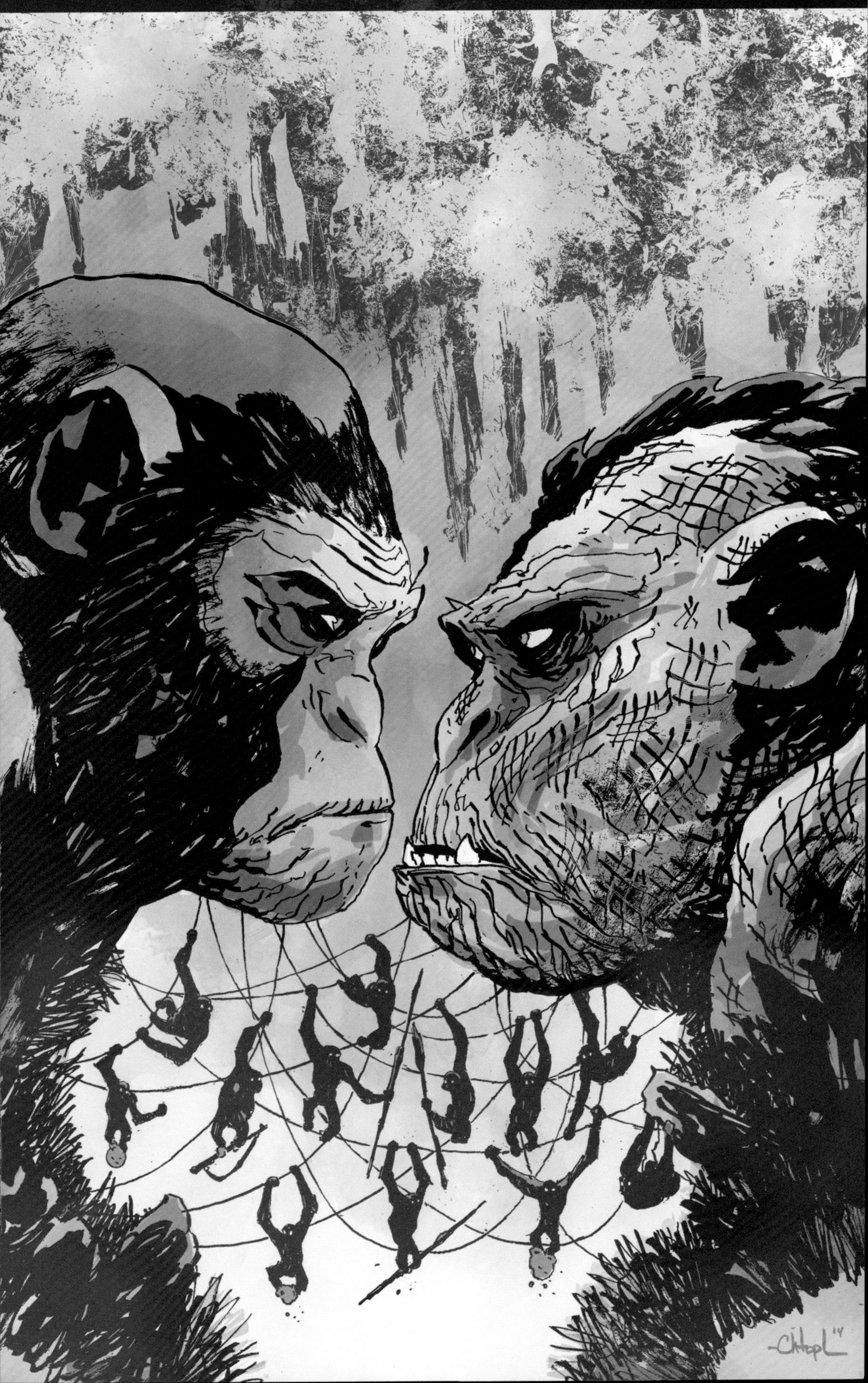

ISSUE #6 COVER **CHRISTOPHER MITTEN**

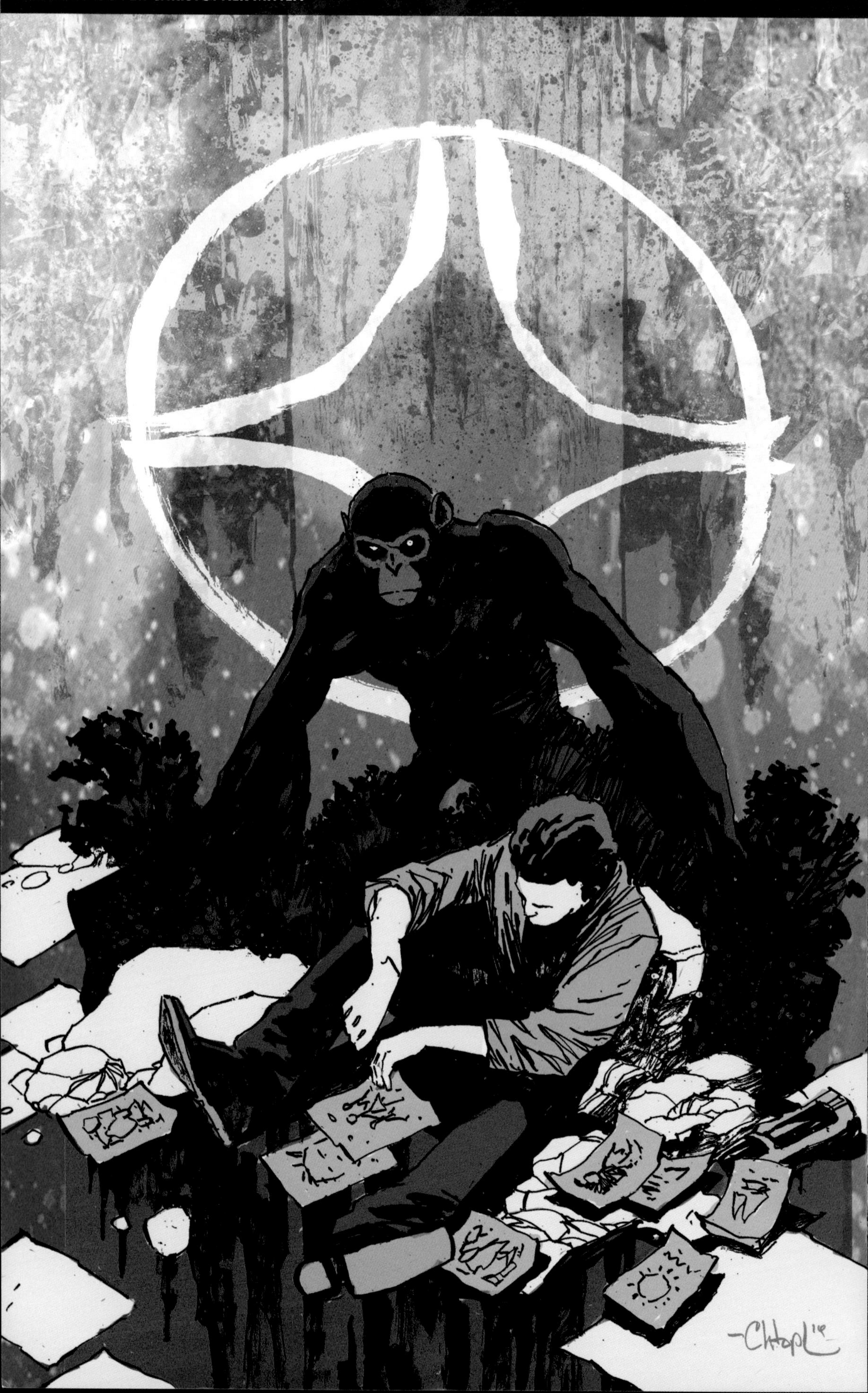

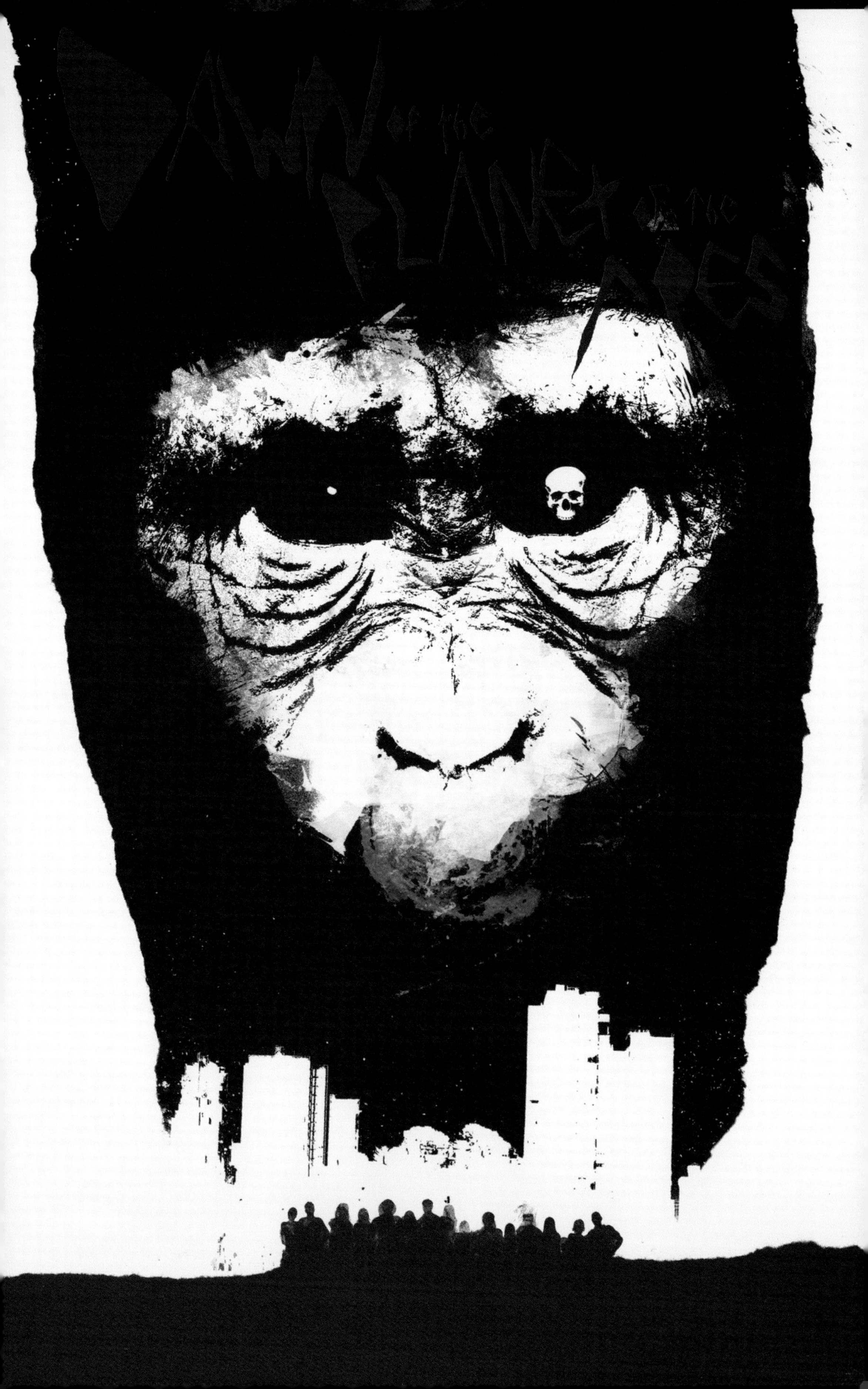
DAWN of the PLANET of the APES

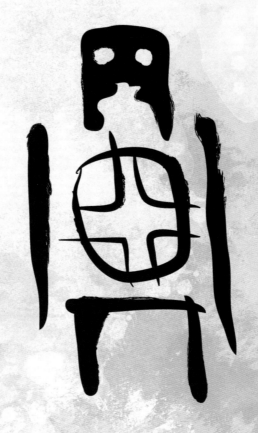

DAN**McDAID**
SKETCH**GALLERY**

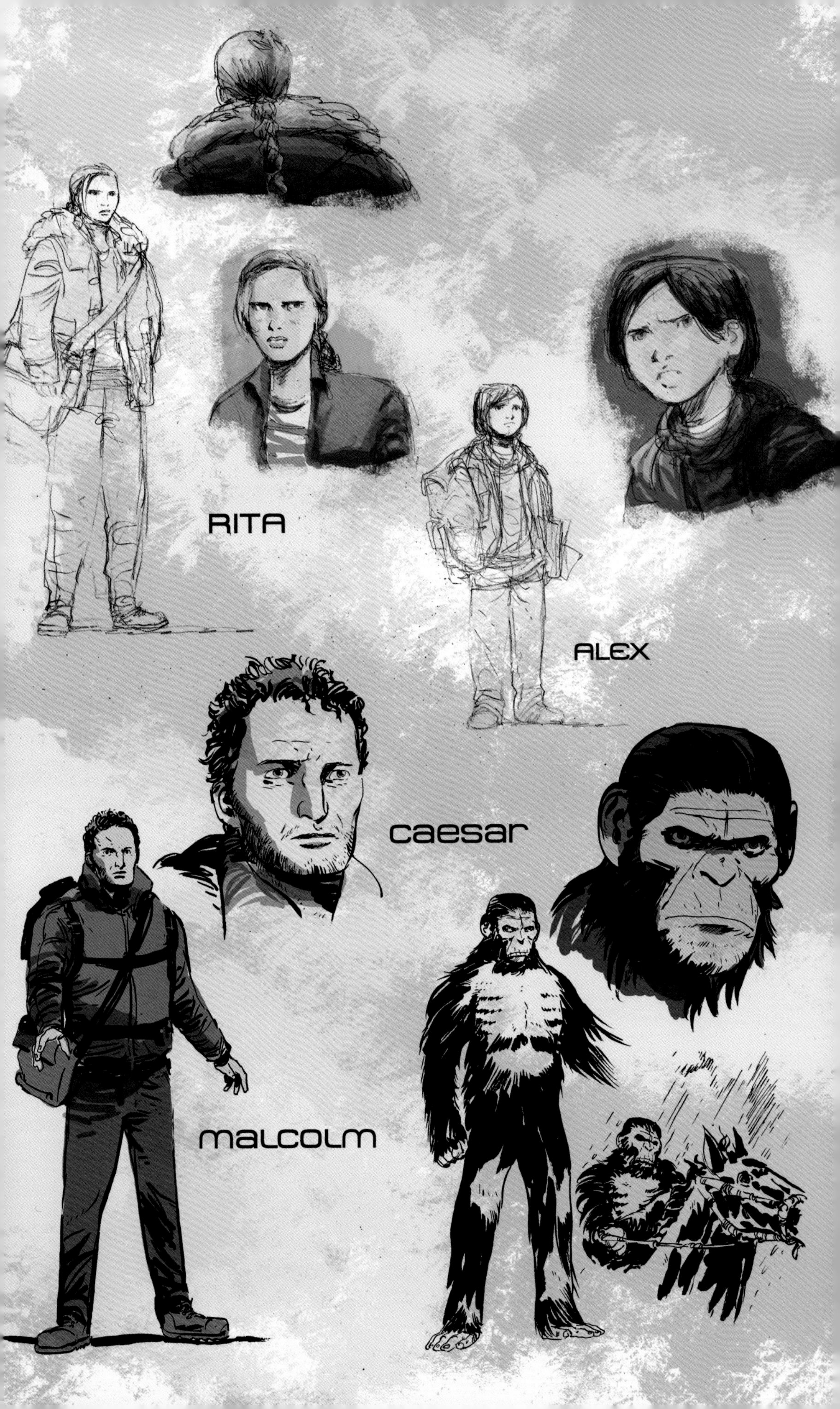
RITA
ALEX
caesar
malcolm

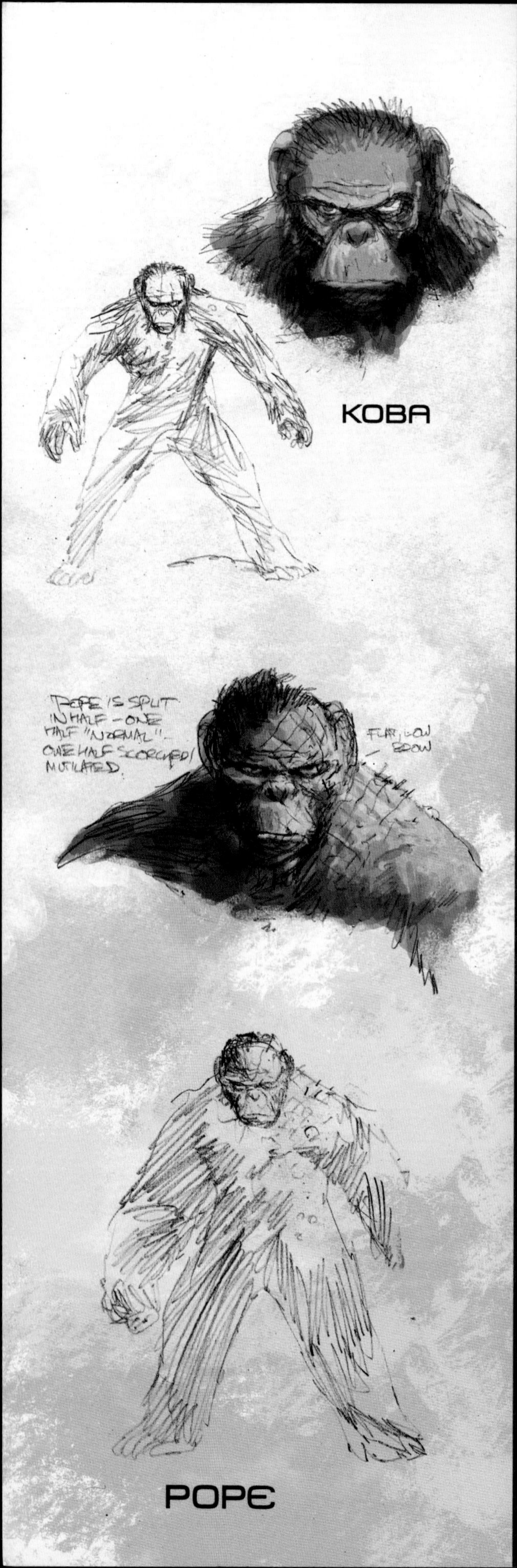
KOBA
POPE IS SPLIT IN HALF - ONE HALF "NORMAL" - ONE HALF SCORCHED/ MUTILATED.
FLAT, LOW BROW
POPE

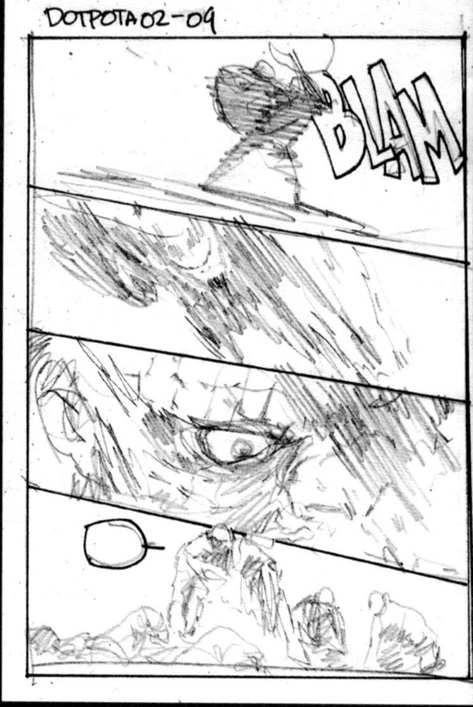
DOTPOTA 02-09
BLAM

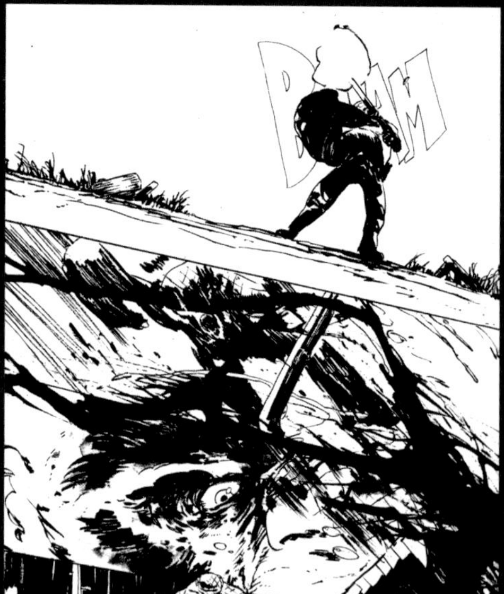

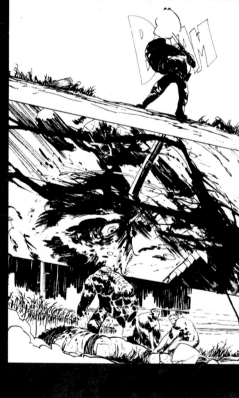

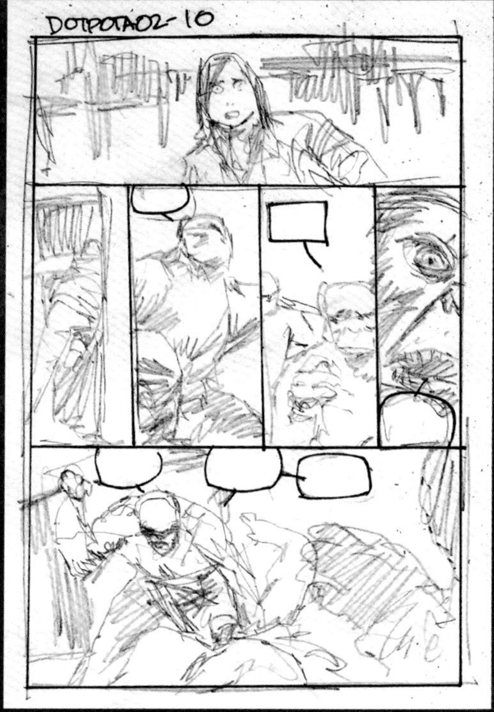
DOTPOTA02-10

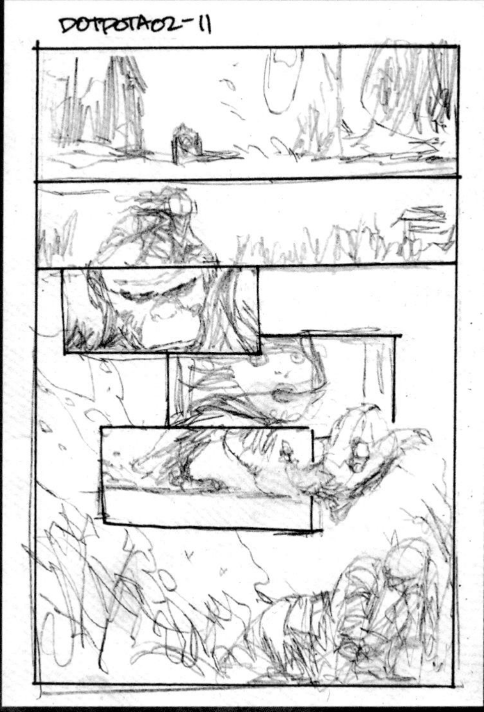
DOTPOTA02-11

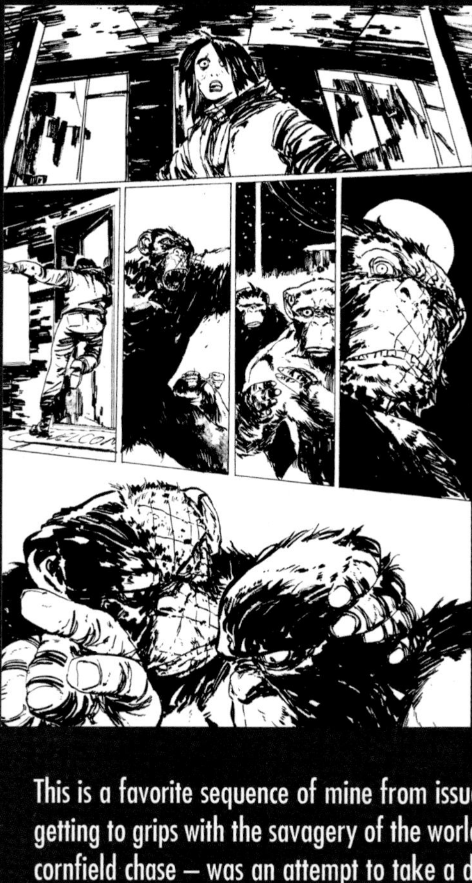

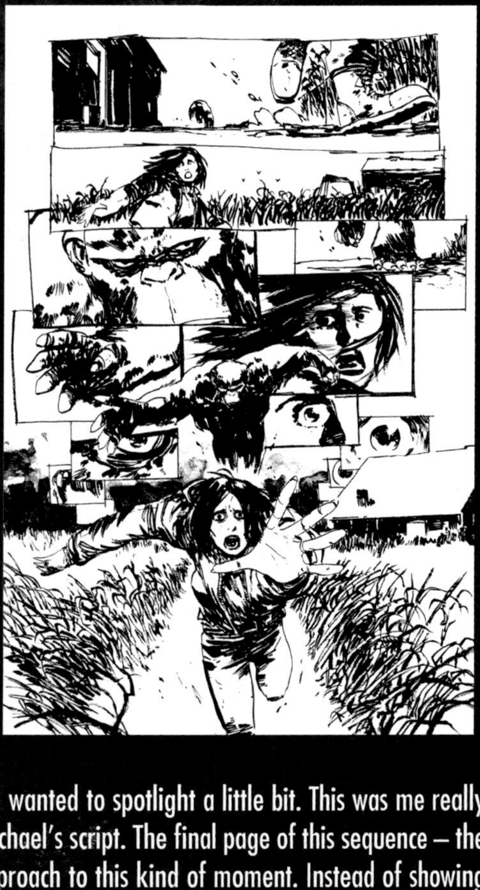

This is a favorite sequence of mine from issue two that I wanted to spotlight a little bit. This was me really getting to grips with the savagery of the world and of Michael's script. The final page of this sequence – the cornfield chase – was an attempt to take a different approach to this kind of moment. Instead of showing the moment sequentially, I thought it might have more punch (and give the reader more to "chew over") if it was presented jigsaw style – a series of fragmented views of the same moment. At the end here, the woman is reaching out to the reader for help – though, of course, none is coming.

-Dan McDaid